Family and
Social Network

Family and Social Network

Roles, Norms, and External Relationships in Ordinary Urban Families

Second Edition

Elizabeth Bott
Preface by Max Gluckman

TAVISTOCK PUBLICATIONS

First published in 1957
by Tavistock Publications Limited
11 New Fetter Lane, London EC4
and printed in Great Britain
in 12pt Bembo type
Photo-litho reproduction by
Lowe & Brydone (Printers) Ltd
London

Second impression 1964
Third impression 1968

Firts published as a Social Science Paperback in 1968
Second edition 1971
Hardback: SBN 422 73490 X
Paperback: SBN 422 75090 5

CONTENTS

TABLES

ACKNOWLEDGEMENTS

The original study of which *Family and Social Network* was a partial report was begun by the Tavistock Institute of Human Relations with the joint sponsorship of the Family Welfare Association. This joint sponsorship continued for a period of three years, during which time the research was financed by the Nuffield Foundation. Subsequently the work was supported out of general funds of the Institute made available by the Rockefeller Foundation. The final (1956) year of preparing material for publication and relating the work to that of other groups was supported by the Grant Foundation of New York.

The original book is here retained intact as it was published in 1957. Several of its chapters had already appeared elsewhere in slightly different forms. A preliminary statement of field techniques was published by Dr J. H. Robb under the title 'Experiences with Ordinary Families' in the *British Journal of Medical Psychology*, 1953, Vol. 26, pp. 215-21. A slightly different version of Chapters III and IV appeared as 'Urban Families: Conjugal Roles and Social Networks' by Elizabeth Bott, in *Human Relations*, 1955, Vol. VIII, pp. 345-84. This paper also appeared as 'A Study of Ordinary Families' in Anderson, N. (Editor) *Studies of the Family*, Tübingen: J. C. B. Mohr (Paul Siebeck). Chapter VI appeared as 'The Concept of Class as a Reference Group', in *Human Relations*, Vol. VII, pp. 259-85, and Chapter VII as 'Urban Families: The Norms of Conjugal Roles', in *Human Relations*, Vol. IX, pp. 325-42.

The aims of the research as a whole required the cooperation of people trained in different disciplines. The core research team consisted of Dr A. T. M. Wilson (medical psycho-analyst), Miss Isabel Menzies (non-medical psycho-analyst), Dr J. H. Robb (social psychologist), and the author (social anthropologist). (I subsequently became a psycho-analyst as well.) Dr Wilson and Miss Menzies were primarily responsible for the psycho-analytic conceptualization of the material. Dr Wilson also supervised the project as a whole and conducted clinical interviews. Miss Menzies discussed and interpreted psychological aspects of the home interviews with the field workers. Dr Robb and the author shared the sociological field work, which consisted of home visits and interviews, although Dr Robb undertook the greater number. Chapter II consists of a joint report on this aspect of the work.

Unfortunately Dr Robb had to leave England to return to New Zealand in 1954, so that he was unable to participate fully in the final stages of conceptual analysis on the research findings.

I am deeply grateful to Dr Robb and to the other members of the research team for many stimulating discussions and for the encouragement they gave me in working out the ideas presented in this book.

Several people assisted the core research team. Mr H. Phillipson and Mr J. Boreham, both psychologists of the Tavistock Clinic, administered and interpreted the Object Relations Tests and took part in case conferences on particular families. Mr Eric Trist of the Tavistock Institute took part in initial methodological discussions and gave much helpful criticism of papers and research reports. Professor Nevitt Sanford (non-medical psycho-analyst) conducted clinical interviews with two couples and took part in case conferences. Mrs Bannister and Mrs Balint, then of the Family Discussion Bureau, conducted clinical interviews with one couple and took part in the case conference on them. We are also indebted to the Family Discussion Bureau as a whole and to Dr Henry Dicks of the Tavistock Clinic for discussions on the possibility of comparing the research families with couples who had sought treatment.

Looking back on the period of working out the ideas that eventuated in *Family and Social Network,* it often seemed touch and go whether any meaningful sociological analysis would come out of it or not. I owe special gratitude to my husband, James Spillius, and to Eric Trist, who in different ways put up with me and encouraged me through months of uncertainty. They shared my pleasure when I thought of the central idea of the book, that conjugal roles were a function of network 'connectedness'. I was somewhat surprised to find that other colleagues too were so generous that they were almost as pleased with the idea as I had been. I remember particularly Max Gluckman and his stimulating and encouraging seminar at Manchester in November 1954, and their collective effort to relate my work to their own, to the enrichment of both. I also treasure a remark by John Bowlby: 'It has the merit of being obvious once one has thought of it. One wonders why one hadn't . . .', a remark often echoed by others later on.

I am also indebted to Professor Raymond Firth who then held Malinowski's chair in anthropology at the London School of Economics; to Dr M. Freedman and Dr H. Himmelweit then of the London School of Economics; to Professor Meyer Fortes and Dr Edmund Leach of Cambridge University; to Professor John Barnes, then of the University of Sydney; to Dr Michael Young and his colleagues then at the Institute of Community Studies; to Dr Rhona Rapoport, then of the Social Rehabilitation Unit, Belmont Hospital; to Dr Yonina Talmon-Garber, then of the Hebrew University, Jerusalem; to Professor Theodore Newcomb, then of the

University of Michigan; to Dr Erving Goffman, then of the National Institute of Mental Health, Bethesda, Maryland—all these and others too numerous to mention helped me with painstaking criticisms of preliminary statements and papers. In writing the new chapter for the second edition, I am particularly grateful for the critical comments of Professor Max Gluckman of Manchester and Professor Daniel Miller of Brunel College. In tracking down the literature I was much assisted by Miss L. Oeser, Miss K. Arnold, and Mrs G. Grayson.

Finally, no person or group is more deserving of thanks than the many people who helped us to contact families, and chiefly the twenty families themselves. They invested a great deal of time and emotional energy in the research, put up with our many questions and our mistakes with tolerance and good humour, and did everything they could to help us understand them. Because of our promise that they should remain anonymous, their identities have been disguised and all names are fictitious.

Preface

I felt very highly honoured when Dr Elizabeth Bott asked me to write a Preface to the new edition of her book on *Family and Social Network*, which was first published in 1957. Around that year, there were published by a number of my pupils books which had a great impact in social anthropology: Professors F. G. Bailey (now at Sussex), *Caste and the Economic Frontier* (1958); I. G. Cunnison (now at Hull), *The Luapula Peoples of Northern Rhodesia* (1959); A. L. Epstein (now at the Australian National University), *Politics in an African Urban Community* (1957); R. J. Frankenberg (now at North Staffordshire), *Village on the Border* (1957); J. C. Mitchell (now at Manchester), *The Yao Village* (1956); V. W. Turner (now at Chicago), *Schism and Continuity in an African Society* (1958); W. Watson (now at Oklahoma), *Tribal Cohesion in a Money Economy* (1958); P. M. Worsley (now at Manchester), *The Trumpet Shall Sound* (1958)—and dare I add my own *The Judicial Process among the Barotse of Northern Rhodesia* (1955) and *Custom and Conflict in Africa* (1955)? Yet greedily I said, when I read Dr Bott's book: 'I wish that book had come out from our group.'

In this new edition Dr Bott gives my colleagues and me some title to claim a part in helping her produce her path-breaking study, for in a new chapter in which she re-considers her analysis in the light of the work it has subsequently 'inspired' (the choice of word is mine), she pays generous acknowledgement to stimulating seminars at Manchester. Presumably what we said in discussing her material and argument was a great help to her— and this is why she invited me to write a preface. I can only remember, somewhat guiltily, that when in 1952 she first presen- ted to us some of the material she had collected on the relationships and conjugal roles of spouses in twenty 'ordinary' London families, and ended by asking us: 'What shall I do with it?' Dr Elizabeth Colson, now at Berkeley, and I said together: 'Write a novel about it.' When recently I reminded Dr Bott of this, she said she now understood why, after her second visit when she presented the new argument of her analysis,[1] I immediately said: 'I was wrong.' And I now am glad publicly to admit how very wrong I was, and to pay tribute to the courage and perseverance with which Dr Bott worked at her material to produce one of the most illuminating analyses ever to emerge from social anthropology. I know of no study in our whole history which I rank as more stimulating than her attempt to relate types of conjugal roles to the shape of the network of relationships around the family, particularly when it is taken with its associated themes of norms, reference groups, and ideologies.

As a Preface is intended to be read first, I set out briefly, and therefore inadequately, one of the main themes. Bott's investigation was part of an attempt sponsored by the Tavistock Institute of Human Relations to assess what a 'normal' English family was like. Together with a medical and a lay psycho-analyst, and a social psychologist, she studied twenty 'chance' families. Twenty families is a very small number—but it was planned as a pilot study, to produce hypotheses. Bott, at least, produced important hypotheses—and these have been followed up by other investigators than the original team, as she shows in her chapter entitled 'Reconsiderations'.

Her own sphere, as a social anthropologist, inevitably included investigation of the roles of husband and wife and relationships with kinsfolk. Anthropologists have concentrated on these problems because in all tribal societies people recognize an extended range of relationships outside the family with kinsmen and kinswomen and relatives-in-law, and a large part of individuals' activities and time is involved in these relationships. Indeed, many of the small and intermediate political groups within a tribe consist of kin and affines, real or putative; and outside these groups men

[1] 'Conjugal roles and social networks', *Human Relations*, Vol. 8, 1955.

and women rely for support, insurance, and protection on other kinds of kin or affines. Thus relationships with relatives control not only domestic, but also the economic, political, and other types of relationship with others. There is a general dependence on a wide range of familial relatives rather than the specialized dependence on various professionals and institutions which marks our own life outside our ring of close relatives. These anthropological studies have examined the two-way process by which relationships in the nuclear family influence the wider 'web of kinship' (to take the title from M. Fortes's classic study of this situation among the Tallensi of Ghana), and by which (to mix a metaphor) that web exerts pressure on relationships within the family. A second significant influence from the anthropological tradition was the fact that within these kinds of relationship, as generally in social life, the tribal peoples have elaborate 'customs', including ritual prescriptions and taboos, to mark the several kinds of relationship; and these customs are linked together with one another in complex patterns.

Bott opens the substantive part of her study of twenty families by describing how there was a considerable variation in the way in which spouses acted in domestic life—how 'husbands and wives performed their conjugal roles'. At one extreme was a family in which the spouses carried out as many tasks as possible separately and independently of each other, with a strict division of labour in the household, to which the husband allocated a set amount of money while he spent the remainder without his wife knowing how he did so. Save for visits to relatives, they spent little leisure together. At the other extreme was a family in which husband and wife shared as many activities as possible and spent as much time as possible together, and in which they stressed that spouses should be equals, helping each other, taking decisions together, and sharing similar interests with common friends. Bott summed up the first family as having 'segregated' roles and the second as having 'joint' roles. Other families fell between these extremes: all conjugal relationships contained some cooperation and exchange of duties (jointness) and some segregation, or independence, but there were marked differences of degree in the extent of segregation and of sharing.

Bott examined whether occupational or class status, or length of marriage (all twenty families were in the early stage of the life-cycle), determined what roles the spouses would adopt, and found that only working-class families fell near the segregation extreme: i.e. membership of the working-class was a necessary but not sufficient condition of more extreme degrees of segregation, since some working-class families had jointish roles. After battling over her data, Bott decided that the variation in conjugal roles seemed to be associated with the immediate social environment of the family. This environment consisted of a network of different relationships with some persons and with social institutions. For some families this network was, as Bott calls it, 'close-knit',[1] in that their relatives, friends, neighbours, and sometimes fellow-workers, knew one another, and often in these various categories were the same people: other families had 'loose-knit' networks in which their relatives, neighbours, friends, and fellow-workers did not know one another. She found that the type of network around the family was associated with the degree of segregation between husband and wife, in that the more closely knit the network of the family, the more were the roles of husband and wife segregated. In the Acknowledgements Bott quotes Dr John Bowlby, so well known for his studies of familial ties, as remarking: 'It has the merit of being obvious once one has thought of it. One wonders why one hadn't . . .' a remark echoed by others in different contexts.

It may be that many a concealed truth, once it is extracted and stated, is a truism. If I may re-state Bott's hypothesis, in the way in which I have always formulated it in writing and teaching (see below)—if we think of a family moving from the country to the town, away from their relatives and long-term neighbours,

---

[1] There is now quite a complex literature on the conception of a 'network', which I leave to Bott's discussion in her new chapter: see also J. C. Mitchell, editor, *Social Networks in Urban Situations*, Manchester University Press, 1969. Bott now says she accepts J. A. Barnes's (see *ibid.*) arguments that speaking of degrees of density in the network is more satisfactory than speaking of 'connectedness'.

husband and wife are likely to be isolated from those who formerly·
helped them and provided friendship from day to day, and they
will be under pressure to depend on each other and to help each
other more and more. But rural life itself is not responsible for
creating segregated conjugal roles, nor urban life joint roles; for
there are urban areas in which families have close-knit networks
and follow Bott's rule. This was shown in a study by M. Young
and P. Willmott of *Family and Kinship in East London*, which
appeared in the same year (1957) as Bott's book, but after publication of her hypothesis in 1955. Here there is a good analysis of the
crisis which struck families moving out of a long-settled London
area to a new housing estate, where the shift entailed the consequences I have outlined above.

Bott took into account this and other studies of conjugal roles
to support her conclusions based on the twenty families she
investigated. The great illumination for me, as an anthropologist,
was that her hypothesis gave us a key to understanding the very
high development of segregation of roles in tribal societies between men and women, husbands and wives, parents and children,
grandparents and grandchildren, in-laws and various other pairs of
relatives. As stated, much anthropological learning has gone into
the description and analysis of the very specific customs, both
prescriptions and taboos, which in tribal society mark the roles of
various kin and affines. A. Van Gennep in his *Les Rites de passage*
(1909) drew attention to these, and to the ceremonies which
marked each change of status. Durkheim, and many sociologists
and anthropologists, had even earlier emphasized this characteristic of tribal and early societies, and tried to explain theoretically
the developments which accompanied the movement from this
situation of 'ritualization of social roles'[1] to the secularization of
modern life, with the development of 'universal' religions in which
membership of a congregation is gained by individuals as individuals, and not in terms of the specific roles of ego *vis-à-vis*
specific others. To emphasize the contrast we have only to read

[1] As I have called it in my essay 'Les rites de passage' in M. Gluckman, editor, *Essays on
the Ritual of Social Relations*, Manchester University Press, 1962.

Leviticus: this brings out how, while among at least large sections of our own population the menstrual period is accepted as the expression of a disappointed uterus (a purely physiological phenomenon), among Ancient Hebrews as in many other societies it was, and is, regarded as ritually defiling, full of occult power, usually dangerous to men and all things virile. In other situations the virile is dangerous to things feminine. The congress of the sexes may be highly ritualized; and either always, or in special circumstances, it may be regarded as containing occult power which can operate for the good or ill of society and its personnel. In short, I saw one significance of custom as residing in its 'exaggeration' of physical and physiological facts, something beyond its clearly serving as a diacritical sign of relationships, a point often made by anthropologists. What the kind of beliefs I have been outlining, with their associated actions, did, was to make the differences between the sexes, and between husband and wife, greater than they were in physiological reality. Other customs, such as taboos and beliefs in occult power, similarly exaggerated the difference between the generations, between old and young, between paternal and maternal relatives, between kin and in-laws, and so forth.

What Bott did was to give us a clue to understanding this all-round segregation of roles. We could assume that families in all tribal societies were the centres of close-knit networks: they lived surrounded by the kin of both spouses, and these kin were therefore neighbours, friends, and workmates. The effect of this was, for example, to pull the spouses apart, and sharply to differentiate their roles. As I put it in an essay from which Bott has quoted at the head of her new chapter, there were created 'estrangements in the family', built-in conflicts of belief, loyalty, allegiance, and value, which prevented the nuclear family from gaining the whole-hearted attachment of its members, as these were compelled to maintain attachments to the larger groups or groupings of kin who constituted the economically and politically functional groups of the society. The Bott hypothesis thus seemed to me to give us a clue to understanding why in Central Africa a man is forbidden to cook in a village, so that he must have a woman to cook for him; why among the Tonga of Zambia a man can only offer to his ancestral spirits beer brewed by his own wife; why among the Tallensi of Ghana a first-born daughter should not look into the granary of her mother or a first-born son use the arrows of his father, and so forth. I thus saw Bott's theory as not merely illuminating for an understanding of family life, but also as going far beyond that—it gave us clues to understanding the process of development of types of social relationships in human history which had been a major concern of many great scholars.

To move from these to my lesser self, shortly after listening to Bott on conjugal roles, I broadcast a series of lectures on *Custom and Conflict in Africa* (1955), in which I set out the general thesis and included reference to Bott. I had started analysis on these lines somewhat earlier; but I can say that Bott's work sharpened greatly my perception of the problems. Hence I affirm that Bott's book should be read with a far wider range of problems in mind than those with which she specifically deals: it leads us deep into all the problems raised as we try to understand how any society, and its constituent groups, are an interweave of loyalties and allegiances, a piling of socio-cultural differences and identities, on top of the coming together of men and men, women and women, men and women, in competitive collaboration. In some ways, for example, I see it as one of the inspirations in the thinking that produced such brilliant analyses as V. W. Turner's social-anthropological inter-pretation of ritual symbols (see his *The Forest of Symbols*, 1967).

It was because I approached Bott's hypothesis from studies of African tribal societies, that I felt—and still feel—that the domi-nant variable in the complex of a close-knit network is the nearby presence of kin of the spouses, separately and together, so that the family's neighbours are its kin, and hence kin form the friends of the spouses, and in certain areas also their workmates. When the hypothesis was first formulated, it appeared to be supported in this amended form not only by the accounts of tribal societies, but also by studies then available on Britain. As one example, I illustrate the way in which Bott was supported by, and illuminated, other data, by detailed citation from the classic study of a rural area in the British Isles which was C. Arensberg's study of farmers in County Clare, Eire, in *The Irish Countryman* (1937) and (with S. T. Kimball) *Family and Community in Ireland* (1948). Arensberg described the division of labour between men and women on the farm, and the rigid segregation of parental and filial generations. He brought out how, as in Africa, the allocation of tasks to women and men was supported by 'occult' beliefs.

'The plough, the harrow, the mower, the scythe, the spade and turf-cutting *slan* are regarded as masculine instruments. The attitudes of the countryside forbid woman's using them. In the same way, they heap ridicule upon the thought of a man's interesting himself in the feminine sphere, in poultry, or in churning.

'Immemorial folklore bolsters this division. The woman is unlucky to masculine enterprises, for instance: it is dangerous to see a woman on the road to the fair. Likewise, man is dangerous to woman's work. If he so much as takes his lighted pipe out of the house while she is churning, he may "take the butter", through fairy magic. . . . The attitudes towards men's and women's work show that their respective skills are regarded also as integral parts of the personalities of all men and women of the countryman's own kind. Here we can see how strongly social dispositions influence both mind and vocabulary. "Natural" is a word frequently on the countryman's lips. Thus, it is "natural" for a woman to be a better milker, her smaller hands are proof. And it is laughably "unnatural" that a man should bother about the sale of eggs. This division is embedded in tradition, too. Luogh still tells a humorous old tale of the spades, men's tools, that used to work themselves in the old days, till a woman forgot to say "God bless the work" to them. This division is bolstered in magic, too, for the "Coulter of a plough", that masculine implement, can bring back the butter the fairies have taken.'

These statements bring out that high segregation of role also means complementarity of roles. And the setting for families is summarized thus: '. . . it very often happens that a comparatively large area will be peopled by individuals standing within near degrees of kinship one to another.' It is perhaps significant that the word for a kinsman here is 'friend'. And 'friends' help one another with economic tasks.

It would be inappropriate in a Preface to discuss all the material then available which seemed to support Bott's hypothesis, both from rural and from urban areas. There was enough to encourage her, and me, in feeling that there was much in it. I have cited Arensberg's study, after my general reference to tribal societies, to bring out why I thought, and still think, that the nearby presence of kin as neighbours, and their association in some way in working together, is the dominant pattern in high segregation of roles. I stress this double element, presence of kin plus at least men working together,[1] for I consider that much of the later work aimed to test Bott's hypothesis has operated on her formulation by testing whether the friends of a family knew one another. She herself cites this work. But H. Fallding, as she quotes, points out that it may be that presence of kin is the significant variable. And in one testing application, of some sophistication, on a Pennine parish, C. Turner found two couples out of 115 whose networks contained a very high proportion of kin: they had the highest degree of marital segregation. But he found that there was no linear relationship between the proportion of kin in the network and the segregation of conjugal roles. The problem requires, perhaps, precise measurement of how and also *what* kin are part of the network, i.e. how far away they live in social terms, and which kin they are. Here it would be interesting to compare, both between and within tribes, whether there is variation in roles,

[1] See e.g. N. Dennis, F. Henriques, and C. Slaughter, *Coal is Our Life* (1956), an account of a Yorkshire coal-mining village, where the high segregation of conjugal roles is brought out and ascribed to the separate working of men in the pits, away from women. But we know of many situations where wives do not enter their husbands' places of work, and there is jointness of roles. What was the position before 1842, when women ceased to work down the pits? It seems that in this mining village many men lived close to, and worked with, their male kin. Was there some variation between families in terms of networks?

given the cultural standardization of roles, in families according to which kin fall in their nearby network.

Turner's analysis has to be set in a' wider perspective. He found that in 115 families in the Pennine parish, 'when kinsfolk are excluded [because husband and wife tend to include the same kinsfolk in their respective social networks], thirty-two couples could be unambiguously identified for whom the husband's friends constituted a close-knit *male* network, and the wife's friends a close-knit *female* network. These thirty-two couples also demonstrated a high degree of conjugal role segregation.'[1] This last finding seems to be part of a wider contention that 'since marital roles are parts of sex roles there is likely to be a fit between mono-sex group membership and role segregation at the logical level. . . .' (to quote C. C. Harris, *The Family*, 1969, p. 174). This is preceded by the statement that 'mono-sex groups are likely to be formed where the sex-roles are themselves rigorously differentiated'. This seems to me to push the problem one stage further back: in which circumstances are mono-sex groups likely to be formed? And here my hunch, inspired by my knowledge of tribal societies illuminated by the Bott hypothesis, is that the close-knit network of nearby kin who also participate together in economic activities produces both segregation in mono-sex groups and in conjugal roles. And I believe also that the tighter the fit between these variables, the more likely is it that segregation of roles (sexual, including marital) will be more than the habits of individual couples—it will contain a high degree of convention, passing into ceremonial and even ritual practices and occult beliefs.[2]

---

[1] C. Turner, 'Conjugal Roles and Social Networks: A Re-examination of an Hypothesis', *Human Relations*, Vol. 20 (1967), pp. 121–30, at p. 125.

[2] See R. O. Blood's 'Kinship Interaction and Marital Solidarity', *Merrill-Palmer Quarterly*, Vol. 15 (1969), pp. 171–84, where marital solidarity is taken to be the satisfaction of the wife with the husband's role performance in the marriage. He concludes that, aside from the fact that in the U.S.A. 'couples with close-knit networks perform more household tasks separately (p. 175), . . . an overdose of kin contact is likely to poison marital health. In proper doses, kin may provide external support for marital solidarity' (p. 183). The reader is referred to Bott's citation from my own 'Estrangements in the Family' for comparison, at the head of her new chapter.

We are here dealing with two distinct and complex sets of variables: first, conjugal roles; and, second, the structure of networks. Conjugal roles need very careful defining, and in my opinion they should be defined not over whole cultural or social spectra, but within particular spectra. In terms of culture, in the West a section of the population that has golf and tennis and bridge as typical of its games, and reading books and attending theatres as other recreations, is more likely to have husband and wife sharing leisure, than is a section with football, cricket, or shove ha'penny as games, and popular newspapers for reading. In terms of income, better-off people are more likely to have domestic servants, and also to be able to afford to entertain together visitors at home and in other ways than are worse-off people. Greater wealth should allow husband and wife to participate more in joint entertainment with kin and friends. Servants exclude many of the questions of sharing tasks; entertainment of visitors regularly may lead to more sharing of leisure. Hence we need to assess jointness and segregation of roles across a 'class' and not between classes. That is, we need to compare families sharing the same 'culture' in terms of social networks, i.e. comparison within the agricultural, working, and middle classes to see if there is differentiation of conjugal roles corresponding with the form of the network, as well as whether there is differentiation across the whole spectrum. In terms of caveats made above, it is notable for example that in African villages, on many British farms, and in Gans's study of Italian workers in the U.S.A. (cited by Bott in her 'Reconsiderations'), even when visitors are entertained at home, there is a segregation in seating, in serving food, in the mode in which persons enter into conversation, by the sexes.

With high mobility, it may be difficult to find a section of the middle and professional classes with close-knit networks, though they may occur in country towns. But what may be significant is what we can draw from novels and biographies: the retirement of the ladies after dinner to the drawing-room while men drank port, and the use of men's clubs as male havens and not only as lunching-points for business. Further back, in ancient Greece, with slaves doing much of the work, the wives of the rich were isolated almost in harem conditions, in general seeing only kin and servants, while the men sought some recreation, such as music, dancing, and the discussion of philosophy and politics, in the company of other men with highly educated 'prostitutes'.

A second set of interconnected problems arises from the study of the networks which surround the family. Several commentators have drawn attention to the importance of investigating the extent to which the networks of the spouses are separated or are interlocked (see Bott on 'Reconsiderations'). Turner, cited by me above, concluded that 'when the networks of husband and wife show considerable overlap, no distinctive pattern of role relationship is associated with them' (op. cit., at p. 6). B. Kapferer cites this finding in an analysis of the networks and the relationships of two African couples in a mining town in Zambia, in terms of the separateness and the overlap of their networks. He restates the Bott hypothesis as follows: 'The conjugal role relationship between spouses varies according to the degree of density [close- or loose-knittedness], clustering in each network, and cross-linkage between the separate networks of the husband and wife and to the degree of cross-linkage between the two networks and the degree of investment [in terms of exchange theory] in these cross-linking relationships. The most important part of this hypothesis concerns the aspect of cross-linking between the husband and wife's networks and the extent of the investment in the cross-links. Thus there will be a tendency towards a joint role-relationship where there are both direct cross-links from the wife to individuals in the husband's network and vice versa, and where these cross-links tend to be high in investment or include individuals who are part of the spouses' intimate networks. The effects of cross-linkage and the extent of investment in these cross-links for the conjugal role relationship of the spouses will be modified by the degree of density, segmentation, and cross-linkage within the individual networks. If there is a high density, but low clustering within a network there will be an increased tendency towards a joint role relationship between the spouses provided there is cross-linkage between the networks. But an absence of cross-linkage between the network factors such as high density and low clustering may increase a tendency towards segregated role relationships.'[1]

Kapferer looks thus at the specific content of relationships in the network and an assessment of his amendment to Bott must wait on publication of his paper. In general, I can only note, in defence of my own hunch, that the pair with most kin in it, has the greater segregation of roles. I feel that 'blood is thicker than water', and that kinship relationships have very intense density.

The problem of how networks are constituted leads, as the citation from Kapferer emphasizes, into consideration of the wider institutional setting of the society. For example, Turner (op. cit.) shows that networks and conjugal roles vary with occupation, extent of social and geographical mobility, and educational level, three factors that are themselves interconnected. Farm work in the Pennines of itself seems to produce some segregation in roles, while educational level is generally associated with some kind of mobility, which in itself must cause links with kin to be dispersed instead of concentrated geographically, even if the total number of kin associated with the family is relatively similar (though as fertility rates in different classes vary this may not in fact be the position). As I have already indicated, I consider that comparisons should be made over cohorts of families in the same class or occupation: and hence Turner's statement (cited above) for all families that there is no linear relationship between proportion of kin and role relationships may need checking in terms of families of similar status and occupation.

The key point may well be what the networks do both in general social life and for individuals. The family produces sons and daughters who are recruited into various groups, relationships, and categories in general society—including other families. In a tribal society, among the most important groups for which it produces recruits, are groups largely composed of kin and in-laws

---

[1] 'Family, Marriage and Work in Urban Zambia: A Discussion of Problems in Network Analysis', to be published in a symposium edited by J. Boissevain and J. C. Mitchell, held at the Afrika Studie-Centrum, Leiden (in press).

(relatives in general); and these groups form the productive, distributive, consuming units of society, political units, religious congregations, etc. In County Clare, Eire, the groups or networks of 'friends' (relatives) were groups with intensive collaboration to solve farming problems and to redress demographic chances. At one time in coal-mining areas men worked underground in groups organized on a kinship basis. And so forth. We need, as Kapferer's study indicates, to specify carefully the content of relationships within the network, and the purposes they serve. Mere friendship is not enough as a means of linking persons in a network. And, I repeat, my own hunch is that the segregating network or networks will be composed of relatives, relationships with whom serve general economic and/or political purposes. I say 'network' or 'networks', because I follow Kapferer and others including Bott herself who argue that the extent of overlap in the separate networks of spouses will be significant. But, I add firmly, these networks have to be seen also in terms of their relation to the total institutional structure—including what Barnes has called the 'total network' (see Bott's 'Reconsiderations').

The research problems here require refined statistical techniques as well as further field investigation. These problems are clearly very complex. Human societies and cultures are so intricate, the product and field of so many interacting variables, that each time an hypothesis is erected it is immediately liable to be amended or even destroyed by some exception. The historians ran into these difficulties long before we did. But Durkhein urged that an illuminating general statement, based on considerable research, should not be abandoned for a few exceptions: the exceptions are illuminating in calling for additional analysis. Bott's is such a statement. It needs to be worked over and over. What is clear, as the later research shows, is that the very search for propositions which can be applied outside particular social contexts, even when the propositions come under question, deepens our understanding of social life.

Such search has very important practical implications. In the first place, spouses who as children have been reared in one type of family, and are then thrown into a situation in which they have to sustain the roles of the other type of family, may find that they are unable to carry out the responsibilities which are pressed upon them by the new network, or miss the support of the old network if it was close-knit. Secondly, and arising from the first point, it may be that welfare workers or clinicians add to these difficulties if they try to help all families through their troubles in terms of the ideal of joint companionship and activity. This is an ideal specific to a particular type of family; and to thrust it on a family with segregated roles may merely increase the strain on the spouses. There is of course no suggestion that spouses whose roles are segregated meet troubles less effectively than others, for the social ties, if not the emotional ties, between them may be strong because of their very complementarity.

I have discussed at length some of the ramifications arising out of Bott's hypothesis, about the systematic structure of social relationships. Let me suggest one other possibility emerging from it. Theoretically, I consider that if the hypothesis is sound in giving us a proposition defining the conditions in which different types of conjugal roles will emerge, it ought also to explain something about the relationships between parents and children. That is, a close-knit network of kin ought also to lead to more segregation of parents and children from one another than a loose-knit network does. This is indeed the situation which we find in tribal societies. As there are taboos differentiating spouses from each other, so too there are taboos and conventions defining much more sharply the distinction between parents and children than we find in our mobile middle-class families. In many tribal societies it is, for example, prohibited for children to discuss their marital affairs with their parents: they must do so through an intermediary, often a grandparent. And so on. In some, the beginning of children's sexuality may require that they move into a separate village from their parents—this is an extreme example of a general tendency. We know that in many middle-class families in Britain children and parents find it difficult to discuss sexual and marital problems: but it is not a social rule, a custom, that this be so. It is partly a personal difficulty, and partly an increasing general difficulty as substantial changes in sexual and other mores occur. I am here interested in the more general implications: for I would expect that in families with close-knit networks young persons would associated with their own age-mates, and it is from these age-mates that they would derive parts of their moral codes, and other parts from their parents or educational establishments. If this is so, the reality in families of this kind conflicts sharply with the general injunction in Britain that parents are responsible for the actions of their younger children, and with exhortations to parents to control criminal delinquents among their children. These problems were touched on in a study (made for other purposes) of young men in a London working-class suburb with close-knit networks, by Dr D. H. Allcorn.[1] He found that those young men who did not become mobile and move out of the local area to attend school and then university, grew up with a small group of friends, what sociologists call a 'peer group' of equals: This group became a powerful influence over the young men during the period between their leaving school and becoming engaged to marry: home became an 'hotel', and all spare time was spent with their 'mates', with whom they went to cinemas, joined clubs, took up and dropped recreational activities.

The peer group encouraged, by boasting and reciprocal teasing, temporary liaisons with young women, but opposed the forming of permanent attachments to them, since these would destroy the group. The strong emotional bonds between the youths must have had a critical effect at this time on the formation of moral codes: and in this background it would be profitable to study how moral codes develop at this stage of the life-cycle. Does each age-stratum of youth develop on its own, or is it influenced by the immediately preceding stratum, so that each society contains layers of codes, set in cultural patterns, for its age-strata? These codes are not, of course, all delinquent.

I have commented on the book's contribution to our understanding of family life in particular and of the structure of socio-cultural

[1] Unpublished Ph.D. thesis, Manchester University: *Young Men with Money* (1954).

systems in general. In conclusion, let me say that I believe it is an invaluable book for teaching. Some time in the 1940s I read, as I remember it in a book on a university course in Communist China when the Communists were confined to Yenan (though I have not been able to trace it again), a saying that is obviously Chinese, but perhaps not obviously Communist. It was to the effect that the first year of a course should give knowledge, the second should give doubt, and the third should give wisdom— which is knowing how little we know. Looking back on how I was taught social anthropology by Mrs A. W. Hoernlé many years ago, I see that she took me along that course. There were then very few books in social anthropology, and for three years we studied largely the same books. At the end of the first year, I had been given knowledge, firmly; soon after the second year started, I realized that there were still fascinating problems left to be solved in the same material; when the third year started, I quickly learnt how very little we knew definitely. We now have very many more books in the social sciences; but I still feel that it would be sound pedagogy in some courses to take students through the same books with decreasing acceptance of what had seemed established in them, and increasing emphasis on doubt and on the problems they raise. I would put Dr Bott's book first on what would be a very select list. Teaching it to first-year students, I found it possible to bring out its immediate illumination and its capacity to order a wide range of facts from many societies.With undergraduates in later years, I found I could use it to draw attention to uncertainty and new problems. With postgraduates, I found it to be an open sesame to riches. C. C. Harris, in a reference to Dr Bott's book in his general account of *The Family: An Introduction* (1969), praises but still underrates the value of *Family and Social Network;* among other comments, he has: 'Now stimulating and seminal as Bott's study is, it is not remarkable for its conceptual clarity.' A trailblazer does not map the whole countryside: but her first glimpses of new vistas of problems may, even in some confusion, continue to point to yet further vistas, while those who map more closely the area she covered as a pioneer sometimes restrict their vision.

Department of Social Anthropology   Max Gluckman
University of Manchester
March 1970

CHAPTER I

Introductory

There is an enormous literature on the family in Western society —a reflection of its importance for the continuation of society and the happiness, and misery, of individuals. The family, we are constantly told, is the backbone of society. But actually not much is known of the relationship between families and society. There are very few studies of the way families interact with external persons and institutions, and there are not even very many studies of families in their natural habitat, the home. Everyone knows a great deal about family structure from personal experience, but it is difficult to extend this personal knowledge to other families, to penetrate the privacy of another home, to absorb its special atmosphere, to observe its unspoken understandings. Considering these difficulties, it is not surprising that there are few field studies of families as social groups, and even fewer attempts to combine such anthropological study with psychological examination of the personalities of husband and wife and of the relationship between them. The research reported in this book was intended to fill this gap.

The research began with a very general aim: to understand the social and psychological organization of some urban families. The core staff consisted of two psycho-analysts working part-time, and a social psychologist and a social anthropologist working full-time. The research was exploratory. We had to develop research techniques as we went along, and it was only after a considerable time that our very general aim took shape and became focused on more limited and concrete problems. Chapter II describes the development of research techniques, including a discussion of the relationships between the research staff and the families, and of the organization of interdisciplinary group research. The succeeding chapters present an analysis of familial roles and external social relationships.

Throughout the book the word 'family' is used to denote the elementary family of husband, wife, and their children. All the families studied formed household units and had young children. Strictly speaking, the research should be called a study of marriage rather than a study of families, for we were chiefly interested in the relationship between husband and wife, and we studied the children and the relationship of parents to their children primarily to improve our understanding of the relationship between husband and wife.

The contribution of this book must lie in its interpretations, not in the facts described. Most readers will be more or less familiar with the facts from their personal experience, and none of the things described here are very novel. Nor can this book claim to make a contribution in the form of a systematic survey of the facts of English family life, for it is clear that the twenty research families cannot be treated as a representative sample of a wider population of families. Indeed, it should be made clear at the beginning that no empirical generalizations are made about a wider population of families. All statements of fact are meant to apply only to the twenty families studied. But an attempt is made to develop interpretations and hypotheses of general relevance. A detailed comparative study of the twenty families has been made, in which each has been considered as a social system. Interpretations and hypotheses have been developed in a form that may be tested on other families, and it is hoped that these hypotheses may lead to further and more systematic comparisons.

In many ways the research families were much alike. These similarities would have been thrown into relief if the research families had been compared, as a class, with radically different families. But since the research families themselves formed the universe of study, attention is focused on variation among them and similarities are dealt with very briefly.

Much of the book is devoted to a sociological analysis of variation in the performance of conjugal roles. The term *role* is defined here more narrowly than it is in much American literature on family sociology. It is *not* used here to mean all behaviour that goes on between people. It means behaviour that is *expected* of any individual occupying a particular social position. A *role-relationship* is defined as those aspects of a relationship that consist of reciprocal role expectations of each person concerning the other. This definition is intended to exclude the great variety of idiosyncratic expectations and private meanings with which all relationships are endowed by the particular individuals who carry them out. But in the case of familial relationships the line between formal institutionalized expectations and individual expectations is often difficult to draw. This problem will be fully discussed in the text. In effect the term role-relationship means those reciprocal role expectations that were thought by husband and wife to be typical in their social circle.

Among the research families there was considerable variation in the role-relationship between husband and wife, particularly in the amount of emphasis placed on shared activities and interchangeable tasks as compared to the emphasis on independent and complementary activities. In some families there was a sharp division of labour between husband and wife in which he had his tasks and she had hers; husband and wife did not share their leisure time and recreation. In other families the husband and wife shared many activities and interests, spent much of their time together, and had a less rigid division of labour in household tasks. In Chapter III these variations are shown to be related to the form of the family's informal social network, that is, to the pattern of social relationships with and among friends, neighbours, and relatives. In brief, these variations in roles are not purely idiosyncratic, but neither are they produced directly by membership in general sociological categories such as social classes, income groups, occupational groups, and so forth. They are associated with the pattern of actual social relationships between the family and their acquaintances and kin, and also with the pattern of relationships among

3

these acquaintances and kin themselves. These patterns depend, in turn, on several factors, some associated with social class, some with physical movement, some with personality. Chapter IV discusses these factors and their effects on the social networks of families.

Until very recently little empirical work was done by anthropologists on kinship in urban areas. Chapter V discusses the kinship system in general, and also analyses variations in its application. Three families are compared in detail with respect to contact with kin and feelings about kinship ties, and an attempt is made to define all the factors necessary to explain the differences between them.

Chapters VI and VII deal with norms, values, and social ideology. The basic thesis here is that individuals and families play an active part in developing their social ideology. Given a chance, they adapt and organize social values and norms so as to make sense of their own first-hand experience. This gives rise to considerable variation in values and norms from one family to another, even though each family may assume, especially in unguarded moments, that their norms are current in the society as a whole or at the very least in their own immediate social circle.

Three things are essential to the method of analysis adopted in this book. First, interpretations have been arrived at by making systematic comparisons in which each family is treated as a social system, that is, as a system of interdependent roles, as an organized group carrying out tasks in a particular social environment. Only those data essential to the comparative analysis are described.

Second, the basic conceptual model is that of field theory (Lewin, 1935 and 1936): Behaviour is a function of a person (or a family) in a situation. Performance of familial roles is a function of the personal needs and preferences of the members of the family in relation to the tasks they must perform, the immediate social environment in which they live and the norms they adhere to. But the form of the immediate social environment and the norms of conjugal roles depend, in turn, partly on the personal needs and preferences of the members of the family and partly on a very complex combination of forces in the total social environment.

Third, familial behaviour is treated as the resultant of multiple factors. No suggestion is made that any one factor is more important than the others in the sense that it will explain more facts. The relative weight of each factor varies according to the particular configuration of the combination.

At several points in this book the data are insufficient for the interpretations suggested. This is regrettable but almost inevitable in an exploratory study. New ways of looking at the material arise only from the interplay of field experience and previous theoretical interests, and by the time a new formulation develops it often happens that not all the facts necessary for precise comparative testing of it have been collected. The achievement of the research consists not so much in finding complete answers as in finding interesting questions to ask.

CHAPTER II

Methodology and Field Techniques

WRITTEN IN COLLABORATION
WITH DR J. H. ROBB

Very few intensive field studies of families are reported in the literature of family sociology. There are studies of families where something is wrong, questionnaire studies of 'normal' families, studies of the familial relationships of students, studies of the socialization of children, and of many related topics, but there are very few intensive empirical studies of ordinary families from a combined sociological and psycho-analytic point of view.

The reasons for the lack of intensive field studies of ordinary families are not hard to find. Family life goes on inside homes, not in the street or in universities, schools, clinics, churches, factories, or any of the other institutions to which research workers might have easy access. Unless one is invited inside a home one cannot learn much about a family as a working group. But ordinary families are not likely to ask a research worker into their homes since they have no particular motivation to come to a research team. They are not likely to know that research is going on, or to take part in it if they do know about it. It is difficult to interest people in a study that probes into their private affairs, especially if the interviews continue for a long period of time. Contacting families by knocking on doors is inappropriate when one is asking for extensive cooperation in the exploration of matters that are felt to be private. It would be more suitable to approach ordinary families through agencies that provide practical services for them. But such agencies usually have contact only with some members of the family, often with a single individual, and only for certain aspects of the family's affairs. Thus the doctor is sometimes concerned with the whole family, but often he treats only some of its members, and in most cases he deals only with health, not with all aspects of family life. Similarly the church, the school, maternity *etc.* and child welfare clinics, birth-control clinics, lawyers, etc., deal only with certain aspects of a family's life. In the course of their normal activities the workers of these agencies may obtain considerable information about various aspects of family life, but almost always within a limited field. Where a good relationship exists between the workers and their clients, additional information may be obtainable, but usually it is difficult to move into fields outside the stated area of interest of the institution, especially if this involves members of the family who do not normally have a direct relationship with the institution and even more so if it requires the introduction of a stranger to the family. The practical difficulties of finding ordinary families to study are therefore considerable.

There are conceptual difficulties too. No comparative study is easy, but in family research the amount of variation from one family to another not only in personality but also in social relationships with external people and groups is so great that it is difficult to decide what to compare and how to set about it. It is hard to combine sociological and psycho-analytic concepts and modes of thought. It is difficult to study families calmly because there is so much emotional concern over what is wrong with them and how they should be made better. It is difficult to be modest and realistic in one's research aspirations since one feels that authoritative statements about families in general are expected at the end of the study.

Because of the nature of the problem and the practical and conceptual difficulties involved, the research team were not able to obtain much direct assistance from their own or other workers' previous research experience. We were engaged in an exploratory study. We started with no well-defined hypotheses or interpretations and no ready-made methodology and field techniques. We could not apply—at any rate not in pure form—the methods and techniques of social anthropology, of surveys, of psychological case studies, or of psycho-analysis. Special techniques had to be developed for getting the two necessary types of data: facts about the organization of the family as a social system, and material for making inferences about the personalities of husband and wife and the unconscious components of their relationship. This chapter describes the end result, a peculiar combination of anthropological and case study techniques.

A. METHODOLOGY

At the beginning we decided to make an intensive study of a small number of families rather than a survey of a large number. This seemed the most appropriate method for an exploratory study.

Our initial aim, that of furthering psychological and sociological understanding of some ordinary urban families, was so general that it could hardly be called a problem. We did not start with well-formed hypotheses that we were trying to test. We had some thought of comparing ordinary families with disturbed families in which the husband or wife had sought treatment, but a few attempts in this direction made it obvious that the problem was so complicated that we did not know where to begin. What should we compare—individual psychopathology, the conjugal relationship—which in any case we did not know how to describe in rigorous conceptual terms—the social environment, some combination of all three? The question seemed premature.

It is hard to decide what to study and how to begin in a very complex situation where there is much variation and any particular piece of behaviour is affected by a multitude of factors. It is also easy to prove what one wants to prove, if one is so inclined. When there are many factors one can choose some particular aspect of the situation and remain blind to the others. One is caught in a dilemma between succumbing in confusion and choosing some simple but false explanation. We decided to succumb in confusion in the hope that it would be temporary. We endured uncertainty for a time in the hope that constant careful comparison would eventually lead to a formulation of specific problems that would do justice to the data without being so complicated as to be meaningless. Our task, in other words, was not to test hypotheses but to develop them, and to be sure that they were appropriate to the field material. Increasing field experience helped us to formulate problems, and the formulation of problems led us to seek new information, although not always soon enough, unfortunately. On many points the data are incomplete.

Intensive comparative study of a small number of groups requires a different method from that of surveys and leads to different results. In the present research no attempt is made to produce general factual statements about a wide population of families by studying a sample. It is impossible to say that because five of the twenty families had a joint role-relationship between husband and wife, 25 per cent of all English urban families will have joint conjugal role-relationships. Throughout the book all descriptive material is intended to refer only to the set of research families.

But an attempt is made to develop hypotheses of general relevance. The research families were studied as examples of urban families, not as a random or representative sample. We have made a comparative study of the relations between several factors for the twenty families, considering each family as a social system. Whether the research families are typical of others is not our concern at this stage. Our aim has been to establish hypotheses that work for the research families, in a form that can be tested on other cases. The other cases might be English families, but some of the hypotheses might be more usefully tested on families in other societies.[1]

[1] Elizabeth Colson makes a very similar statement on the methodology she thinks appropriate to the study of primitive communities (1954, pp. 58-9). 'Whether or not my material for the areas studied is in any way representative of the Tonga people as a whole, I do not know. . . . I do not think that it is a problem which needs to concern the anthropologist who is trying to make a study of the interrelation of social factors in a single social system. . . . I see no reason why information collected on particular small units within a larger area which bears the same tribal name should not be used for comparison

This method may be difficult to accept, since it does not produce factual generalizations about all families, but only hypotheses that may be valid for other families but require further testing. This method is generally accepted in other fields of study, however, such as the comparison of a small number of societies, or local groups, or corporate groups such as factories. The difficulty in applying this method to the study of families seems to lie in conventional selection of units for study. When familial affairs are concerned, the unit that springs to mind is the total society. It must be *the* family, not *some* families. We should therefore like to make it clear that we are discussing only some families, not all families or the family. The interpretations presented in this book may be valid for other families besides the twenty described here; they may not. They have been phrased in general terms so that they can be examined and tested on other material.

Although the research set is not treated as a sample, certain restrictions have been placed on the type of family studied. This was done in order to cut down the number of factors that had to be taken into account in making comparisons. First, all families were 'ordinary'. In practice this meant that the research team went to find them; they did not come to the research team for help. For a time the definition used was 'families whose members have never consulted an outside agency for help with familial problems', but that did not really apply to the research set since two families had sought such help. Moreover, it is obvious that many families who seek help are more 'normal' in the clinical sense than some who do not. As the research went on we became less interested in whether the families were 'ordinary' and more interested in how they worked as systems of social and personal relationships as an end in itself. But even then we needed some way of explaining to the research families why we were doing the study, and 'study of the ordinary family' remained an important com-

---

with information drawn from similar small units within other large areas which bear different tribal names. The result of the intensive study of small units may not make for the best description in the style of a standard ethnography, but it is most likely to provide us with the type of information we need for testing hypotheses and for formulating new research into the relation between various social factors.'

ponent of our explanation throughout the entire investigation.

Second, the families were similar in phase of familial development but different in socio-economic status. Families with children under ten years of age were chosen because this phase is considered to be one of the most crucial in familial development. Socio-economic status was allowed to vary because we wanted to compare the effects of different social environments on the internal organization of the family. All the families had children, one to four in number, the mode being two. The partners had been married from four to eleven years when the interviews began. The incomes of the husbands before deduction of tax ranged from £330 to slightly over £1,800 a year.[1]

Third, the families were English and of mainly Protestant background. One husband was born of a mixed marriage; his father was Protestant, his mother Catholic; he had been brought up a Catholic but had not attended church regularly since his marriage.

Finally, the families lived in various districts of London and did not form an organized group, although there were three pairs of friends among them. At the beginning, we thought of selecting all the families from one local neighbourhood, but the first two or three couples made it clear that anonymity was an essential condition of their participation. This did not mean that they wanted to conceal their part in the research from everyone, but they did want to be able to choose whether to tell their friends or not. They certainly did not want all the neighbours to know. They evidently felt that their neighbours would think there was something wrong with them. Their fears were probably justified.

---

[1] It would also be interesting to study families differing in phase but similar in socio-economic status. It would be difficult to decide on criteria of socio-economic status, however, especially if one wanted to select families of similar 'style of life', because no single criterion is a very good indication of style of life; the Registrar-General's classification and even the Hall-Jones scale (Hall and Caradog Jones, 1950) are too crude for precise comparisons. One might study all the families in a homogeneous local area—if one could find such an area—but if the neighbours knew one another, any sort of intensive interviewing and particularly any clinical interviewing would become very difficult, since people do not like their neighbours to know they are being studied. This technique is possible, however, if the interviews are less intensive and the topics studied less intimate. (*See* Firth, 1956; Young, 1954a and Young and Willmott, 1957; Shaw, 1954; Goldberg, 1953.)

Since few people know anything about sociological or psychological research, the initial assumption of people who were hearing about the study for the first time was that it was some form of social work or treatment. This view was so deeply entrenched that even a careful explanation sometimes failed to dislodge it. Mrs Hartley, one of the research wives, knew several members of a voluntary association with which the field workers held a discussion about the research; she told us with some amusement that after Robb had carefully described the research to the group, stressing that it was a study of ordinary families, one woman commented to another, 'Mr and Mrs Hartley were in it.' 'Oh,' replied the other woman, 'That's funny, I didn't know there was anything wrong with the Hartleys.'

B. FIELD TECHNIQUES

1. *Finding Families*

Great difficulty was experienced in finding suitable families. We were prepared for many families to be unwilling to take part in research such as ours. What we were not prepared for was the extraordinary difficulty of getting in touch with any families, willing or unwilling. The reasons for this difficulty seem obvious enough in retrospect, but at the time we thought we should easily be able to find fifty or even a hundred suitable families through our contacts with general practitioners and a Maternity and Child Welfare Clinic. We had agreed that it would be inappropriate to approach families by knocking on doors, partly because we were asking for such extensive cooperation and partly because we needed to know beforehand whether they fitted our criteria.

The first two families were contacted through a course in social psychology that Robb was teaching; he described the research and two of the students discussed it with friends who agreed to take part. But it was obvious that we should not meet very many families this way. We wanted a single regular channel of contact that would bring us into touch with a large number of families. Wilson therefore approached a Maternity and Child Welfare

Clinic through appropriate medical channels. After obtaining the consent and cooperation of the clinic staff, Robb and Bott attended the clinic, assisting the health visitors with various clerical jobs, the idea being that we could meet the mothers. But a busy queue is not the best place for discussing research. Later on we accompanied the health visitors on many of their home visits, but even here a long discussion about the research with the mother was inappropriate because it interfered with the health visitor's task of inquiring about the child. We therefore explained briefly that we were studying families and asked if we might write to the wife and her husband about it. Altogether we wrote thirteen letters to suitable couples describing the research and asking whether we could visit them for a first interview, which would not commit them in any way, to discuss the study with them. Four couples consented to a first interview. Of these, three were willing but only one fitted our criteria. By this time it had become apparent that no matter how good the relationship between clinic and mother, health visitors were perceived by the mothers and their husbands to be concerned chiefly with child welfare, whereas we were interested in the whole family, particularly in the relationship between husband and wife. We must also have been an embarrassment to the clinic. The staff found it a little difficult to explain to the mothers why we were there. Our research could not easily and naturally be fitted into the work of the clinic.

We had high hopes of general practitioners. We were aware that the family-doctor tradition of the small country town would not be strong in a metropolitan area, but we thought some doctors would be in a close relationship with all members of a family. The research was discussed with six doctors; all were interested in the study but all seemed to have reservations about committing their patients to a long research programme even when they could think of patients whom they knew well and who fitted our criteria. Altogether three doctors provided three referrals. Two of these couples were willing to be studied and became members of the research set. Although none of the doctors said so directly, it seems likely that several of them felt that introducing us might complicate their own relationships with patients. We were really asking the doctor to depart from his professional role. Only those doctors who had close relationships with the Tavistock Clinic were fully prepared to take the risk. But in addition, it appeared that many urban general practitioners were even further removed from the traditional family doctor pattern than had seemed probable at the outset. The doctor was often described as 'a sort of superior plumber'. In nearly every case the family valued the services of their doctor but did not particularly want to know him personally. It was unusual for all the members of a research family to be well known to their doctor. Usually the wife knew him best, and she saw him chiefly when the children were ill. In many cases the husband had never seen the doctor with whom he was registered; in several cases husband and wife were registered with different doctors.

In hunting around for institutions to which all members of the family would belong, we wrote to five clergymen whose names had been given to us by two dignitaries of the Church of England. None replied. A clerical relative of a member of the research team provided an introduction to another clergyman who was a personal friend. This resulted in a single successful contact with a family who were long-standing and very active members of the church. We do not know whether the other clergymen were unresponsive because of what they felt about our inquiry or because of their own relationships with their congregations. But it is evident that many families are not active enough in church affairs to be contacted by this means.

By this time it had become apparent that we would have to cast our net very wide if we were to catch any fish. Altogether we explored forty-two 'contact agencies', as we called them. These fell into sixteen types, which are indicated in *Table 1*. Of the forty-two contact agencies, nineteen provided forty-five referrals to families. Of the forty-five referrals, thirty-one couples received us for a first explanatory interview, and twenty-five of these were willing to be studied. We rejected five who did not fit our criteria, leaving twenty who became research families.

TABLE 1

RESULTS OF ATTEMPTS TO CONTACT FAMILIES FOR RESEARCH

Agencies contacted	No. of agencies providing referrals	Total no. of referrals	No. of families consenting to first interview	No. of families willing to be studied	Research families (i.e. willing and fitting criteria)
6 General practitioners	3	3	3	2	2
1 Hospital almoner	1	2	2	1	1
1 Maternity and child welfare clinic	1	13	4	3	1
7 Schools	2	8	7	6	4
1 Social worker	none	none	none	none	none
1 Settlement	none	none	none	none	none
6 Clergymen	1	1	1	1	1
2 Psychology classes (taught by Robb)	2	3	3	2	2
1 Tenants' Association	1	1	1	1	1
4 Housing officials	none	none	none	none	none
1 Labour Party Branch	1	3	1	1	1
2 Personnel officers	none	none	none	none	none
1 Trades Council	none	none	none	none	none
1 Public Relations Officer of a borough	none	none	none	none	none
5+ Friends and colleagues	5	9	7	6	5
2 Research families	2	2	2	2	2
42+ Contact agencies*	19 agencies† provided referrals	45	31	25	20

* 16 types of contact agency.   † 10 types of agency provided referrals.

We went to officials in these various institutions, usually after an introduction and an exchange of letters, and explained who we were, what we were doing, how the research was financed, and that we wanted help in finding families. The official usually replied that he thought such work interesting but did not think he could introduce us to families in his official capacity. He was more willing to introduce us to a relative, a friend, or some member of his organization with whom he had a personal, friendly relationship in addition to the formal official one. This judgement of the situation was generally correct. If officials tried to introduce us to couples with whom they had a strictly limited professional relationship, the couple usually did not reply to our request for a first interview. Most of the successful introductions were made by friends of the family, or by officials who were friends as well. Introductions were also more likely to be successful if the contact person knew both husband and wife, although this was less important than degree of intimacy between the contact person and family.[1]

After the contact person had discussed the research with couples who might be interested, he sent us their names and addresses and we wrote to them saying we should like to come for a first explanatory interview. We enclosed a stamped postcard, and said that we should come at the suggested time unless the postcard was returned to us suggesting a more convenient time or instructing us not to call. We used this method after finding that many clinic mothers and their husbands did not answer our letters.

At the beginning we regarded all this work with contact agencies as relatively unprofitable as far as finding out facts about families was concerned. Later on we realized that we were learning a good deal about the way families were related to other institutions. From the families themselves we got a picture of their social world as they looked out on it; from the officials we got a picture of families looked at from outside. We began to ask officials about the family life of the members of their organiza-

[1] Full analysis of acceptance and rejection of the research cannot be made since several families may have refused without our knowing about it. We were not in a position to ask the contact persons to keep accurate records of the people they thought of, those they asked, and those that refused. Among the forty-five cases about which we have information, it is clear that both factors mentioned above were significant. Of the twenty-five couples who were willing to be studied, nineteen had friendly relationships with the contact person. Of the twenty families who did not answer our letters or refused to take part, only five had friendly relationships with the contact person (chi-square = 11.61, p < 0.01). In fifteen of the twenty-five cases willing to be studied, the contact person knew both husband and wife, but this was the case in only five of the twenty families who refused to take part in the study or did not answer letters requesting a first interview (chi-square = 5.512, p < 0.02).

tions, and in most cases they knew very little. One thing stood out: in most cases members of a family belonged to formal institutions as individuals, not as members of a family, and these relationships were restricted to one or two aspects of the individual's life. Except for the marginal case of the family doctor and the church (which would have been more important if we had been studying Catholic families), there was no external institution that contained the families in all their aspects. For the research families there was no encapsulating group.

2. *The Home Interviews*

At the first interview, which took place in the evening with husband and wife, the field worker explained who was in the research team, what the Tavistock Institute was, how the research was financed, and what we were trying to find out. We said there had been several studies of families where something was wrong, but few studies of ordinary families. Many people who worked with families where something was wrong tended to think that the ordinary family, by contrast, had no problems and no difficulties, whereas others said they might have just as severe difficulties as overtly disturbed families but could cope with them better. We said we wanted to find out the facts about at least a small number of families. The exact content of this explanation varied from family to family. We were careful to avoid the word 'normal' or 'happy', especially after Mrs Hartley smiled and asked, 'What do you do when you aren't watching us being happy?' With the last few families, especially the more sophisticated, we talked less about the ordinary family in contrast to the disturbed family and said that we wanted to learn how families worked as groups since there was really very little scientific information on the subject.

We also told the couple the content of the home interviews and after we had worked out an interviewing outline we showed it to them. We said that if they decided they wanted to take part, we should like to come about once a week in the evening when we could see both husband and wife, and at least once during the day to meet the children: We said there were usually about eight to twelve interviews. We made it clear that we would not come back unless asked, that they could withdraw at any time, and that we would only come by appointment. We also said that the material would be treated with professional discretion, that we would preserve their anonymity, and that if we wished to publish confidential material that might reveal their identity to readers, we would consult them beforehand. We undertook to pay any expenses they might incur as a result of the investigation.

Although few couples ever mentioned it directly, it was obvious that most of them were thinking about whether they would be called upon to discuss their intimate affairs, especially sexual relations, in front of each other in the presence of the field worker. We said there was a second part of the research that involved individual interviews at the Tavistock Institute with another member of the research team, in which, if they wished, they might discuss more personal matters that might be embarrassing to raise in a three-person situation. We said this was a separate part of the research and they could make up their minds about it later. If they asked about it, they were given full details in the first interview.

The couples were encouraged to ask questions but they usually asked only a few. Sometimes we were asked to explain the organization and financing of the research again. Sometimes there were questions about the other research families; we answered by describing the criteria, but we never talked about other families' personal relationships. Questions about the field worker were common and Robb was often asked about his children and his views on child-rearing. Occasionally we were asked, 'What good will this study do?' To this we replied that it was not intended to be of any direct benefit to the research families themselves, although it might in the long run have some effect on the attitude of the people who were trying to help disturbed families. Robb felt to a greater extent than Bott that the results would be directly useful, but each found it best to reply to this question according to his own feelings. Otherwise the reply was unconvincing.

After these explanations the field worker suggested he should leave, and asked the couple to talk it over and let him know their decision later. Of thirty-one initial interviews, there were only three in which the decision was not given immediately. Twenty-four couples said at once that they were willing to take part, and that in fact they had already made up their minds on the basis of what the contact person had told them. Four refused on the spot. Two others refused after consultation. One agreed after consultation. Of the six families who fitted our criteria but did not want to take part, one refused on grounds of time, which, in the field workers' estimation, was a genuine reason not an excuse. In five cases one partner wanted to take part but the other did not.

With the first four families, the first interview was much less structured because we had not worked out a technique and we had no interviewing outline. We said we wanted to pay an indefinite number of visits, appearing in the role of friend, discussing with the couple any topics they might like to raise. They were told that the aim was to obtain a picture of their family life, partly by observation and partly from the information they supplied. No notes were taken on the spot, but we did not conceal the fact that we took notes later. We adopted this procedure partly because we were not sure what sort of thing couples would be willing to talk about or what sort of thing we wanted to know ourselves. In addition, we were both prejudiced against note-taking and heavily structured interviews, though for rather different reasons. We started our interviews with slightly different experience and aims. Robb had recently been doing clinical work with married couples in the Family Discussion Bureau (Family Discussion Bureau, 1955), and in the research situation he tried at first to use the same techniques for collecting information. But this did not work very well, since one of the main methods of eliciting information in a therapeutic setting is making interpretations or interpretive comments, which is inappropriate in a research setting. Normally such interpretations can only be made when there is a clear understanding that the informant or client is seeking psychological help for acknowledged problems. Bott had

had no clinical experience of this sort, but she had had considerable experience of 'participant observation', or what might more accurately be called 'incognito interviewing', that is, interviewing and observation in which the informants do not know they are being studied. Robb had also done work of this kind. We knew the rich data it could produce, but on the other hand, we had both learned that incognito interviewing makes publication very difficult and gives the field worker acute feelings of guilt about being accepted as a genuine friend when in reality he has a secret concealed purpose. We were trying to keep the advantages of incognito interviewing without the disadvantages.

As time went on it became apparent that this method of casual interviewing and observation was unsatisfactory. First, as we began to formulate problems we wanted comparable data from each family and we could not get these in a free interview situation. Second, the situation was so artificial that it was virtually impossible to maintain it. The field worker was confusing at least three largely incompatible and partly inappropriate roles, those of friend, research worker, and therapist. In spite of the agreement that these were friendly visits, both parties knew that in fact they had a quite different purpose, no matter how friendly they might become. The couple did not talk only about the kind of thing they would have discussed with genuine friends, but also about things they thought should interest a research worker concerned with families. Similarly the field worker was inevitably influenced in his responses and questions (even indirect and open-ended questions) by his theoretical interests and his desire to discover what kind of data could be obtained in this setting. The therapeutic factor entered partly because of the field workers' previous experience, especially Robb's experience as a marital caseworker, which the couples he was interviewing knew about, and partly because the couples seemed tacitly to be seeking some form of reassurance about their family life. But the therapeutic role was incompatible with the research and friend roles.

It was clear that our way of interviewing was making the couples anxious. They did not know what we found significant or what they were revealing about themselves. The field workers were anxious and uncomfortable too. Eventually we decided that the information-collecting aspect of the interviews should be given precedence. On the basis of what the first four families had talked about spontaneously, together with additional questions we thought important, we made out an outline of topics and started asking questions about specific issues. We also began to take notes in the presence of the family. Everyone was relieved. Two couples said that at last they knew what we were getting at and could stop worrying.

There were thirteen home interviews on the average, the range being from eight to nineteen. Each interview began with ten minutes to an hour of casual conversation followed by direct discussion of topics on the interviewing outline for an hour or longer, followed by more casual conversation at the end. The topics were used as a general guide by the field worker; the order of topics and the form of questioning were left to his discretion. Usually he raised a topic and the couple carried on the discussion themselves with occasional additional questions by the field worker. The discussion frequently wandered away from the assigned topic but little attempt was made to restrict such digressions, since all the behaviour of husband and wife towards one another and towards the field worker was held to be significant data.

A copy of the interviewing outline will be found in Appendix A. Questions were asked on five main topics. The first consisted of a social history of each partner and an account of the marriage up until the interviews began. Among the most useful parts of this section were the detailed genealogies collected from both husband and wife. These not only provided useful information for the analysis of kinship, but also gave the field worker an idea of the couple's feelings about their past and their place in society.

The second section of the outline, which was the largest and most complicated, dealt with various aspects of the internal organization of the family. Under this heading the field worker obtained detailed diaries of a day's and a week's activities, and of recurring annual events such as Christmas, birthdays, and holidays. The main work tasks of the family were covered in detail—the husband's job and the wife's too, if she had one, housework, care of children, handling the family finances, and the family's forms of recreation. An attempt was made to establish the nature of the division of labour between the various members of the family, especially between husband and wife. For each activity the field worker tried to discover who did it, who was responsible for seeing that it was done, how decisions about it were made, and what disagreements there were about it and how these were handled. We also tried to find out whether the division of labour between husband and wife had changed in the course of the marriage and how the couple thought their own arrangements differed from those of their parents, other relatives, and friends.

When we first began to use the outline we asked specific questions about particular items, such as 'Who is responsible for the washing-up?' We had a list of such items. Later on we asked more general questions first and then followed these up with specific questions about items the couple had left out. Robb was more careful to inquire about all items than Bott. Both field workers stopped asking direct questions about disagreements, which seemed tactless. We also stopped asking direct questions about how decisions were made, for no one could answer them. We waited until the couple mentioned a decision and then asked how that and other particular decisions had been made.

The third section of the outline covered informal relationships outside the family with relatives, friends, and neighbours. In the case of relatives much of this information had already been obtained under the first section of the outline. In the case of friends the information included a list of individuals (not identified by names or addresses) whom the couple classed as friends, together with details of their sex, age, occupation, the method of meeting, the nature of the relationship, frequency of contact, and whether the relationship was joint or was maintained largely by one or other partner. Similar details were obtained in connection with neighbours, including information on the number of neighbours about whom the couple knew certain facts, such as name, occupation, and number and ages of children. Towards the end of the field work we began to ask specific questions about which friends, neighbours, and relatives saw one another. A good deal of this information had been given spontaneously by earlier families, but it was not systematic.

The fourth section dealt with more formal social relationships such as those with school, church, clubs and neighbourhood associations, health and welfare services (including doctor, dentist, hospital, health visitor, school nurse, social worker, lawyer), political organizations, and trade unions. The reasons for, and method and frequency of, contact and feelings about the relationship and its consequences for the family were investigated in each case.

The final section of the outline dealt with the couple's general views and ideology about family life, social class, money and financial management, and general political, social, and religious questions. Views on these topics had been expressed, or could be inferred, from statements made earlier, but these direct questions at the end of the interviews gave additional information for the analysis of norms and ideology.

The couple's statements about their activities and relationships were recorded in this degree of detail not because the details were considered important in themselves but in order to establish the general pattern with some degree of validity. It proved unwise to rely on an individual's own general assessment of the pattern. One housewife, for example, said in all sincerity that she was particularly free from rigidity in her organization of household duties, but on the basis of a detailed account of her actual behaviour it was clear that she kept to a more inflexible schedule than any other woman in the research set. This rigid pattern and her apparent need to deny its existence were both important factors in her personality and role performance.

It would have been a great help in the research if we could have relied more on observation and less on interviews. In comparison with most anthropological field work, there was very little observation. This came about partly because of our research aims, but also because of the structure of urban society. Of course we observed the couple while we were interviewing them, and the interview when we met the children was particularly instructive. On that occasion family life went on more or less as usual and we observed and took part in it without asking questions or taking notes. But we could not observe the total social life of the family. We could not follow the husband to work, and we could not interview friends, neighbours, and relatives, partly because these people were scattered all over London and did not form a group so that we should have had to get separate agreement to take part from each individual concerned, but also because the families did not want all their acquaintances to know that they were taking part in a research. Occasionally we met relatives and friends when they dropped in to visit the family. By tacit agreement we stopped asking questions and taking notes and joined in the general conversation. We were always introduced as friends. We were frequently asked to dinner and Bott reciprocated by asking some of the first couples she interviewed to have dinner with her. But after we had realized the importance of stressing the information-collecting aspect of our rôle, we postponed such invitations until after the interviews were over. Bott was asked to a wedding which unfortunately she could not attend. On one occasion she went with a wife to the hospital when her youngest child had hurt himself. But for the most part observations of the family's relationships with other people were very sporadic and incomplete.

3. *The Clinical Interviews*

Towards the end of the home interviews the field worker raised the question of clinical interviews. It was pointed out that in the home interviews we had been chiefly concerned with the everyday organization of the family. We said the aim of the clinical interviews was to give people an opportunity to discuss more personal matters that might be difficult to bring up in a three-person situation. We explained that the topics generally covered were health, personal development, and relationships with parents, brothers and sisters, and friends; sexual development, the personal relationship between husband and wife, and the effect of the children on the individual and the family as a whole. We added that this was only a general guide, and that there was a good deal of variation in what people talked about. We said that if possible we should like husband and wife to come together to the first interview where the field worker would introduce them to Wilson, after which, if they were willing, they would be given what we called a 'standardized task'. We explained that this consisted of a set of pictures about which people were asked to tell stories; since the pictures were the same for all couples their answers would give us some idea of how they differed from one another in discussing the same standardized situation. This explanation was worked out as the last and most satisfactory of a series of attempted descriptions of the Object Relations Test (Phillipson, 1955). We found it unwise to use the word 'test', not only because the idea of a personality test is rather frightening, but also because a test means something at which one can pass or fail, which is not at all. the nature of the Object Relations Test.

Fifteen couples attended for clinical interviews. One couple broke off the research contact just before the end of the home interviews; the prospect of clinical interviews probably played a part in their withdrawal. One husband came for one interview and then withdrew. In one of the remaining three cases, the wife was very eager to come but the husband would not have it. In the remaining two cases the decision appeared to be a joint one. We did not press closely for reasons. One couple said politely that they just did not feel they wanted to come. The other said they could not stand doctors. In both cases it seemed likely that they were afraid they might reveal or perhaps also learn things about themselves that they preferred to keep hidden.

The first four or five couples had two clinical interviews each. Later on there were usually three. Wilson took notes almost verbatim as people talked, except when discussing physical sexuality or some topic that seemed particularly embarrassing or disturbing. In one case the clinical interviews were recorded on tape with the prior consent of the couple concerned.

The clinical interviews followed very much the description we gave to the couples. On the first visit the field worker met them at the door of the Tavistock building and took them upstairs. In the first cases the couple were introduced to Wilson and the field worker then left immediately. With the last ten couples the field worker stayed while Wilson described the content of the interviews briefly, answered questions, and made individual appointments with the husband and wife. The field worker then took the couple to meet the two psychologists; all five chatted for a moment or two and then the field worker left and each partner did the Object Relations Test separately with one of the psychologists. The field worker thus provided a link between the familiar and the unfamiliar. After this first joint interview husbands and wives returned separately for individual interviews with Wilson. After the clinical interviews were over, the field worker paid a final home visit to bring the investigation to a close. Frequent supplementary visits have been made with certain families, however, partly to fill in gaps in the information and partly to discuss material with the families prior to publication.

4. Case Conferences

When the interviews with each family had been completed, two or three case conferences were held about them. These were attended by the four members of the core research team and by the two psychologists. The field worker concerned made a summary of the family based on the home interviews. The exact content of these summaries varied as the conceptual scheme was altered and developed. The psychologists summarized the results of the Object Relations Test and the clinical interviewer summarized his impressions of the couple and the relationship between them. In several cases the field worker made a final summary of the family after the case conference on them had been completed. The aim of the case conferences was to achieve a general integrated view of each family in a form that would permit comparison of each family with the others. This aim was not completely achieved during these case conferences although all members learned a good deal from the discussions and altered their analyses of subsequent material.

5. Group Discussions

Before we had fully realized that we should never be able to make empirical generalizations about all English families but only about the twenty we were actually studying, we were worried by the small size of our 'sample' and decided to supplement data obtained from the research families by information collected from a larger number of people. Financial restrictions prohibited a survey. We chose the method of group discussions. The groups were Townswomen's Guilds, Parent-Teacher Associations, Community Centre Groups, and political party branch meetings. We contacted the officials of the organizations, explained our work to them, and suggested that we come as 'speakers' to an ordinary meeting, on the understanding that we would speak very briefly and spend most of the time getting the group's ideas on family life in the past and the present.

Over half the seventeen groups were composed mainly of middle-aged women. Most of the group members were considerably older than the research couples; parents, especially mothers, of young children do not often have enough spare time to attend this sort of voluntary association. The groups varied in size from twelve to fifty, most being between twenty and thirty. The course of the discussion followed more or less the same pattern in all groups. One of the field workers gave a ten- to twenty-minute talk outlining the aims and method of our work, saying that we could only study a very small number of families and should like to know whether the results we were getting were general or not. We suggested several topics they might like to take up—changes in family life, division of labour between husband and wife, financial management, child care, and so forth. After this talk, there were usually three or four rather hostile questions, although the hostility was not usually directed straight at us. Derogatory comments would be made about surveys, Gallup Polls, and so forth. We answered these questions as simply and directly as we could, taking care to agree with the speaker when we really felt he was right, and stressing that in our own research we made a point of studying only people who were genuinely interested in taking part. After this interchange the group usually began to discuss changes in family life. One frequently expressed view was that the family as an institution was less stable and secure than it had been in the nineteenth century and needed moral strengthening and support. This contrasted markedly with the research families, nearly all of whom said they thought the modern family was better than the Victorian family. Issues such as delinquency, divorce, and the irresponsibility of parents towards their children were frequently discussed. It was sometimes assumed that the group members themselves were responsible parents but that other people were not. The younger generation was often criticized. The evils of women working were also mentioned.

In brief, most of the groups expressed firm views in a dogmatic way, although there was considerable variation from one group to another in this respect. It was our impression that the more homogeneous the group in age and sex the more dogmatic were its views, but more experience would be needed to show if this were generally the case. The hostile atmosphere of some of these sessions was very different from the interviews with the families, and the groups seemed to be preoccupied with the feeling that the family was decaying as an institution, whereas the research families were far more hopeful about it. It is possible that this is a generational difference. But certain factors in the group research situation were also important.

First, the group situation seemed to stimulate the expression of what were thought to be the conventional views of the most respectable sections of society. For example, on one occasion one of the field workers had a long conversation with a group member before the meeting, and asked her several of the questions that were later discussed by the group. Her replies were quite similar to those of the research families: divorce might be the only solution in some cases; the modern family had many advantages; women whose children were all at school might work without doing them any damage. But the same woman two hours later agreed with the other group members in flat condemnation of divorce, women who worked, and the modern family. She did not seem to be aware of the discrepancy.

Second, in the group situation the field workers and their research tended to be interpreted as a personal attack on the group. We could not find a way of describing our work and the purpose of the discussion that did not provoke this reaction, at least at the beginning of the discussion. Possibly the group members felt they had been slightly cheated. They had come, as usual, to be given something by a lecturer and instead they were given very little and were asked to give their views instead. They would probably not have minded this if they had felt that they could talk freely in front of one another, but they seemed to feel we were trying to get them to reveal things about themselves and one another in front of us. In the circumstances it is not surprising that they were critical of us. The groups composed of middle-aged women seemed to be especially touchy, perhaps because their children were growing up and leaving home and the group discussion was to some extent a substitute interest replacing their denuded family life. The topic of discussion forced them to talk about the issues they had perhaps come to the group to forget. Discomfort and hostility in the group were most marked on the two occasions when Bott led the discussion while Robb took notes. There was no objection to note-taking as such; we asked permission to take notes beforehand and it was willingly granted. But the combination of woman as leader and man as secretary was too much. On these two occasions most of the discussion was concerned with how inquisitive children were and how they had to be kept under control. When Bott took notes for Robb or when Bott led the discussion and had a female secretary to take notes, the group members were somewhat less anxious and hostile and less time was devoted to discussion of inquisitive children.

The group discussions did not serve their original purpose; the data produced in them were not directly comparable to the data we got in home interviews, for the group members were older and the social situation produced a different type of information. But the discussions did indicate that a comparative study of families in different phases would be extremely rewarding. They also gave another instance of something that was already apparent in the interviews with the research couples—norms and ideology are expressed differently in different contexts. This matter is discussed further in Chapters VI and VII. It would be interesting to make a more systematic study of the expression of familial norms in different situations, especially since many studies of norms and of families by questionnaires assume that what people put on questionnaires is what they think and do in other situations.

C. PHASES IN THE DEVELOPMENT OF THE RESEARCH

In any research, but particularly in an exploratory study, it is obvious that one learns as one goes along. The above account has indicated several points at which we changed our technique and re-defined our method. Looking back, it seems that the work went through several phases.

In the first phase (1950-1), when all but Robb were working part time, we spent most of our time in general discussion of concepts and methods. We were trying to make one another familiar with our ideas and modes of thought. Wilson brought to the research training in medicine and psycho-analysis, experience in psychiatric research, and in Army selection and civil resettlement during the war. Trist, who took part in these initial discussions, brought the basic approach of field theory, together with much experience in social-psychological research, and interest in psycho-analytical concepts. Robb brought training in education and social psychology combined with research experience in sociology, personality psychology, and marital casework. Bott brought training in social anthropology in the United States and England, and research experience with Ojibwa Indians and with a working-class family and their friends in Chicago. While our conceptual and methodological discussions were going on, Robb began interviewing the first two families and we decided we should not try to study all the families in a given local area. We agreed on criteria for choosing families. We began interviewing two more families. Because of other commitments, Trist had to leave the research team at the end of the first phase.

In the second phase (1951-2) we were preoccupied with working out suitable techniques. We were much less concerned with the conceptual analysis of data than with finding suitable families, developing the interviewing technique, learning how to clarify the roles of the field worker and the clinical interviewer, trying to analyse our mistakes in interviewing, and so forth.

The third phase (1952-3) was rather acrimonious. We were beginning to analyse the data, and differences in basic orientation soon became apparent. Bott had a preference for attributing behaviour to social causes rather than to individual personality factors, and a method that consisted of interpreting the internal role structure of a group in terms of its external relationships. At this time she was trying to explain segregation of conjugal roles in terms of differences in occupation and local neighbourhood. Neither attempt had worked and she interpreted almost as a personal affront suggestions that personality factors might provide the answer. To her this meant reducing group behaviour to psychological motives. The analysts—Menzies had joined the team by this time—and psychologists felt that existing psychoanalytic theory did not provide a system of concepts for describing relationships rather than individual personality; they were groping towards developing systematic interpretations of relationships, but the discussion often seemed to get stuck at interpretations of individual personalities. Bott and Wilson were especially concerned about fitting together the psychological and sociological analyses, although they often disagreed on how this should be done. Robb had a more eclectic approach and was less preoccupied with the difficulties of modifying and integrating sociological and psycho-analytic theory.

At this time the 'sociological' contribution to the case

31

conferences on each family was merely a careful description of what husband and wife did. It was hard to see what Robb and Bott were contributing to the research that could not have been provided by any competent interviewer. We were not developing theories or producing hypotheses. As a group, we did not seem to have a clear goal. Faced with our inadequacies in interpreting the field material, we often resorted to heated discussions of concepts in the abstract. At times it seemed that almost the only thing we had in common was the concept of role, but even here there were differences and confusion. Bott tended to use it to mean the standardized expected activities of a social position, whereas the analysts and psychologists sometimes also used it to mean what people actually did—role performance, strictly speaking. Much time was spent in fruitless argument. On one occasion when we were asked the embarrassing question, 'What is the purpose of this research?', we answered, 'To integrate psycho-analytic and sociological concepts.' If we had been asked this question later on we should have replied, 'To understand the families.'

The fourth phase was more productive. Through working together closely on very detailed analyses of three families, Menzies, Robb, Wilson, and Bott began to concentrate on interpreting the facts without bothering about whether the concepts were integrated on some abstract level or not. There was less arguing and more discussion of particular problems such as how a couple were picking and choosing among the various alternatives open to them, how they were using their familial relationships to cope with particular unconscious anxieties, how they were constructing norms and ideology to some extent and projecting them on to other people, and how to interpret statements about the past as an expression of present personality. All this detailed work brought the analysts closer to dealing with relationships systematically, and made it easier for Bott and Robb to provide a useful sociological framework while at the same time collecting and working into it data on personality. Through discussion, reading, and continued interviewing, Robb got a clearer idea of the implications of sociological concepts and of what sort of analysis they could lead to with our data. Bott was able to revise the rather rigid sociological determinism she had propounded earlier. She had been convinced that actual behaviour was somehow a synthesis of personality on the one hand and a fixed, immutable social environment on the other. She moved towards the view that the external social environment permits much choice, and that within broad limits individuals can construct their own environment in accordance with their own conscious and unconscious needs. Norms and ideology, which had previously been interpreted as external rules internalized by the individual, she now began to regard as in part constructed by individuals. Similarly the analysts began to find the sociological analysis something more than mere description or 'structural determinism'; it could be used as a framework for discussing differences in the way people used familial relationships to cope with their problems.

An important change in technique, begun in the third phase, began to bear fruits in the fourth. Menzies held weekly discussions with the field workers about their interviews. The aim of these discussions was to help the field workers with their interviewing problems, particularly their relationship with the families, and to analyse the material, especially though not exclusively from the psychological point of view, while it was being collected. For lack of a better word we call this process 'supervision', although this term is not entirely appropriate because it suggests that Menzies was training people who were beginners in her own discipline, whereas in fact the relationship was one of equality between people in different disciplines. Because of her analytic training and her detachment from the immediate interviewing situation, Menzies could help us to understand why people talked about the things they did, what matters we should probe into further, what we were doing to make the situation awkward (or easy) for the couple and for ourselves; and when the couple were worrying about something, how we could cope with it without adopting a directly therapeutic role. Both Robb and Bott found these discussions extremely helpful. We felt we understood what was going on in the interviews much better. We became more

33

observant and recorded things more carefully. The home interviews became much more useful as a source of information not only for sociological interpretations but also for the analysis of unconscious meanings and attitudes. By the time we got to the case-conference stage we already had a fair understanding of the personalities of husband and wife and of the unconscious components of their relationship. Supervision was so very helpful that we think it should be used more widely in exploratory research. Some general comments on the role of the supervisor are included below in the discussion of the organization of group research.

Another important development during this phase was the decision to publish detailed accounts of two families.[1] Since most of the couples intended to read the book we planned to write about them, and since we had promised that they would be consulted if we published confidential material that would reveal their identity, we decided we must discuss these documents with them in full. This led to still more intensive cooperation, especially between Menzies, Robb, and Bott on the first document and between Menzies, Wilson, and Bott on the second. We learned a good deal about what sort of thing could be put in and what was better left out, what sort of role the field worker should attempt to play when confronting people with interpretations of their own behaviour, and how to help the couple digest the material without disturbing too much their system of defences.

These phases have been described in considerable detail because, from what little is known of the inner workings of other interdisciplinary research projects, they seem to have gone through similar phases. There is a tendency to attribute difficulties of the type described for the third phase to clashes of personality and basic incompatibilities of outlook and orientation, but, although these factors are important, it also seems likely that the third phase is a necessary development in the research process. There is probably an analogous difficult time even in research conducted by one person, but it is less noticeable because it does not take the

---

[1] These accounts are being prepared for publication as part of the book, mentioned in the Acknowledgements, that is being prepared by Dr A. T. M. Wilson.

form of interpersonal conflict. The way out of the third phase lies in continuous attempts to understand the data even if that means having to discard or revise one's favourite concepts.

D. THE ORGANIZATION OF GROUP RESEARCH

From our experience it is possible to make several general comments about group research in exploratory work. First, the smaller the team, the easier the task. In a survey, or in any research where the problem and techniques can be clearly defined at the beginning, no insurmountable problems are created by having a large staff. But in exploratory research new techniques must be worked out, old ideas have to be discarded and new ones tried, so that things are constantly changing. If there is a large staff, all of whom have to agree to each change of plan, too much research time must be spent in meetings.

Exploratory research makes the research staff uncertain and anxious. It is much easier for a small group to contain and bear with these feelings. There is less opportunity for cliques to form and for each to blame the others for failure and delay—although this happened to some extent even in our small group and is something all teams must be prepared to cope with.

A small group also makes interdisciplinary work easier. It is quite difficult enough to learn different modes of thought, to discard favourite theories and concentrate on understanding the facts; it becomes much more difficult to do this in a large group, for one is constantly aroused by the public feeling of group meetings to defend the honour of one's discipline.

Ten years ago interdisciplinary research was very much in vogue. But now its value is often questioned, partly because it has proved difficult to coordinate interdisciplinary group projects, partly too because such projects have not always produced the spectacular integration of results that was expected. In our view too many of the difficulties of interdisciplinary group research are blamed on its interdisciplinary character, and too few on difficulties that are present in any group research. Small interdisciplinary teams with a tradition of working together, such as that of the psychiatrist, the psychologist, and the social worker, do not seem to suffer from the characteristic interdisciplinary difficulties. But no doubt there are special difficulties in interdisciplinary research, especially when the disciplines are very different and the team members have less tradition of working together. In our experience the most serious difficulty arises from expecting too much. We, or at any rate Wilson and Bott, were expecting a complete integration of anthropology and psycho-analysis in the final product of the research, and we were disappointed when it was not forthcoming. In the end integration was achieved, but not in the form we had expected. It happened within the individuals. Through working together, each person modified his own point of view, so that when he or she came to make his contribution, it was considerably influenced by the point of view of the others. We do not assert that this is the only or the best form that integration of different disciplines can take. It was the most appropriate result for our particular configuration of disciplines, personnel, and research problem. We think each person's work gained enormously by exposure to other disciplines, so that the effort of working together was well worth while.

In group research it is essential to have clear definition of roles. There must be consensus on who is responsible for what. In our research it was clear from the beginning that the director, Wilson, was administratively in charge, that he would conduct relations with foundations and other important outside bodies, and that he was generally responsible for the project as a whole. But in the technical aspect of the work—in devising field techniques, working out ideas, and working through material with families—all the staff were treated as colleagues and equals. Each had personal responsibility for making a separate contribution to the final product. This agreement about the allocation of responsibility was maintained at all times, even when we were having sharp differences of opinion on technical matters. Of course this is not the only way a group research could be organized. The director might carry complete responsibility for producing the technical product, in which case the other staff would be assistants, not colleagues. The essential thing is to have consensus and to stick to the agreement in practice. If the director thinks his staff are assistants and they think they are colleagues, there is sure to be trouble.

In exploratory research it is important that the people who do the bulk of the thinking and conceptual analysis should do at least some of the field work, especially if they are not familiar with the type of work required. Growth of new ideas comes from the interaction of old ideas and new data, and the impact of the data is much greater if the field experience is direct.

Group research projects differ greatly in the amount and type of division of labour. Some start off with a division of labour. In our case it was agreed from the start that Wilson would do clinical interviewing, that Bott and Robb would do home interviews, and that the psychologists would administer and interpret the Object Relations Test. Sometimes a division of labour develops in the course of the work: Bott began to specialize in conceptual analysis and Robb in field work. Or a new person or a new role may be added, as when Menzies became supervisor-consultant to Bott and Robb. The ideal situation is for each person to feel that he is doing what he is best at, and that his individual specialization dovetails nicely with the others so as to contribute a necessary part of the solution to the common group task.

Achievement of this idyllic state of affairs depends on many factors. It is easier if the group is small. It is easier if there is consensus on responsibility, for dissension on responsibility and status is likely to take the form of intractable differences of opinion on goals, techniques, and personal specializations. It is easier if the group goal is flexible. It is easier if care is taken in the initial selection of staff. But no amount of care can ensure success in this matter, especially if the staff are colleagues rather than assistants. Assistants can be told what to do, but colleagues must be allowed a considerable measure of autonomy if they are to make the emotional investment in their work that is necessary for original thought. If they should insist on going their separate ways it may

37

become necessary to split the project into a number of smaller studies.

The role of supervisor-consultant requires special comment. In our view, three conditions must be fulfilled if this role is to be performed satisfactorily. First, it works best if the supervisor-consultant does not do any of the interviewing himself. This is shown by the fact that Bott and Robb were never willing to supervise each other's interviews. We often discussed our difficulties and asked each other for bits of advice, but we would not make systematic criticisms. This was partly because we were too close to the interviewing situation to give a disinterested opinion, but it was also because we were potential competitors and rivals. In order that we might continue to work together harmoniously, neither of us could afford to suggest that he was more expert than the other. For similar reasons we should not have liked supervision by Wilson. He was doing some of the interviewing, and even though it was a different sort from ours, we should have not welcomed the implied comparison of our skills with his.

Second, there must be genuine consensus between the field worker and the supervisor-consultant on the type and degree of authority the supervisor-consultant is to have. The relative balance of authority and responsibility between supervisor and trainee is likely to be a delicate issue in any supervisory situation. Even in conventional supervision, in which an expert trains a beginner in his own discipline, there is a potential conflict between the trainee's recognition of the supervisor's superior skill and right to tell him what to do, and his growing feeling that he should be allowed to make decisions for himself. This conflict comes into the open if trainee and supervisor disagree on what should be done. An even more difficult conflict is implicit in a situation such as ours, in which the field workers and supervisor-consultant belong to different disciplines and are colleagues. In this case responsibility for interviewing and conceptual analysis rests with the field workers.

In our research satisfactory performance of the supervisory role was made possible by fulfilment of three conditions. First,

Menzies stood a little outside the project; she was not the project director and she had no official authority over the field workers. Indeed, in our view it would be a mistake for a project director to act as supervisor if the field workers were defined as colleagues with independent responsibility to produce a personal contri-bution to the research. It would be possible for the director to act as supervisor if it was agreed that the other members of the team were trainee or research assistants; in this case supervision would simply be part of his direction and control of the work.

Second, Menzies always treated the field workers as colleagues. She read our interviews with great care. She recognized that we were in charge of the interviewing and that we should decide whether or not to probe on touchy issues. She never suggested that there was something personally wrong with us if we did not want to follow her suggestions about how and what to tackle in the next interview. She never tried to make therapeutic inter-pretations to us. In any case she realized that we could not predict exactly how our informants would behave in the next interview and that we could not raise topics that were out of keeping with the immediate social situation. In brief, she interpreted her role of super-visor-consultant as one of helping us to understand the families' feelings towards us and ours towards them. She was not directing research, and she was not psycho-analysing the field workers.

A third condition for successful supervision is that it should be done in private. Robb and Bott were supervised together, but this worked satisfactorily because we were not afraid to admit our mistakes to each other, and the situation did not feel like one of public exposure.

A final point about supervision. In our view it is useful for any field worker, however experienced and responsible, to discuss new or unfamiliar work with a colleague while the work is going on. A disinterested opinion helps him to see things more clearly, and in the course of explaining what is happening he usually gets new ideas about it himself. Such help is much more useful when the work is in progress than it is when the field work is over and one cannot check up on points one has missed.

E. THE RELATIONSHIP BETWEEN FAMILY
AND FIELD WORKER

We are often asked why the families took part in the research. We cannot answer this question fully because we have so little information on why families who might have taken part decided not to, but on the basis of the research families themselves it is possible to hazard some guesses. Ostensibly, they gained nothing. But it is unlikely that any couple would take part unless they expected, however vaguely, to get something out of it. When we asked them what they felt about it in the last interview, they usually said they were interested in research, or that they wanted to be of assistance to the research team or, more often, to the community at large, even though they realized the service was very indirect. One man said he thought taking part in a research gave people a bit of extra kudos. A need to help people was characteristic of many of the research couples in a wide range of activities. But in addition to the appeal of the research to their reparative drives, it seems likely that there were other factors of which they were not very much aware.

It has often been suggested to us that they were making a disguised bid for therapy. In a sense this may be true, but it was very much disguised; in those cases where the couple began to feel that they could not conceal their difficulties from one another or from the field worker, they tended to withdraw from the research rather than to ask directly for treatment. The reasons for participation probably varied considerably from one couple to another, but the most general factor seemed to be a wish to evaluate themselves in comparison with other families or with families in general. One husband expressed this directly. He said his main reason for taking part was wondering about himself. He said that considering his background and the fact that he was now having children of his own, he really wanted to find out from Mr Robb how he was doing. Such direct expression of this aim was unusual. More commonly the questions, 'How good are we? How bad are we? Can we stand examination?' were left unsaid. But most couples seemed to be putting themselves to a test. At the same time, the research was arranged so that they could withdraw if they began to feel that they were not finding it as easy and as comfortable as they had hoped. The somewhat ambiguous meaning of 'ordinary' was a help; if they wanted to continue, they could feel that they were ordinary in the sense of being 'all right'; if they wanted to withdraw, they could feel they were ordinary in the sense that no right-minded couple would engage in such a peculiar activity anyway.

It is obvious that neither the research couples nor the field workers were 'objective' about the research in the sense of not being emotionally involved in it and with each other. The research relationship could not have been maintained over a period of months and even years in some cases without serious emotional involvement on both sides. As outsiders—Robb was from New Zealand and Bott from Canada—we seemed slightly strange, especially at the beginning, and it was convenient not to have accents that placed us socially, but our stranger-value soon wore off. We were treated more or less as friends and we in turn developed friendly feelings for our informants. But we were more anxious about the relationship than friends usually are. We were worried that we were exploiting the couples. We were always slightly worried, especially with the earlier families, that they might break off the relationship or that we might do them some harm without meaning to. We were easily upset by signs of antagonism or emotional disturbance and we sometimes felt depressed after an interview without knowing why. Perhaps the impression that our emotional involvement was high is partly the result of self-consciousness. Our aim was not to eliminate emotional involvement but to understand it and to find out how it affected the data.

At the beginning of the investigation the field workers acted as if their role were a combination of fact-collector, friend, and therapist. With the first four families, as has been described above, we were muddled about these three aspects; the development of the interview outline and note-taking was a major step in role clarification, and from then on we stressed the collection of facts as our central activity. We stopped trying to adopt a directly therapeutic role, although we continued to keep up an informal friendly relationship, which implied a reciprocal exchange of information instead of the question-and-answer pattern of fact-collecting. Robb was often asked about his family, his house, about New Zealand, what he would do when he went home, and so forth. Bott was asked similar questions, except that in her case people were curious about her private life but did not like to ask directly; only one wife asked whether she went out on dates and suggested that she might come down to their neighbourhood if she wanted to meet someone.

We found it necessary to try to understand the feelings the research couples had about the field worker, partly so as to continue the research relationship as smoothly as possible, and partly because such feelings and reactions were an important source of data on personality. We were working on the assumption, which is generally accepted in psycho-analysis, that a person's feelings towards other people will be determined not only by what the other person is really like, but also by patterns of perception and feeling built up through past experiences with people who were emotionally important, especially parents and siblings. Such transference is held to be an important aspect of all human relationships. We tried to keep track of manifestations of possible transference, especially after supervision of interviews had begun, and we went carefully over the interviews to work out how the couple's feelings about the interviewer might be affecting the things they talked about. But we did not make use of the transference situation in the way a psychotherapist would. We tried to deal with it in a manner more appropriate to the research setting. Thus, for example, when Mr Redfern spoke deferentially about a teacher in a way that suggested he felt this about Robb too—he knew that Robb had been a teacher—Robb did not suggest, as he would have done in a therapeutic interview, that Mr Redfern might also be feeling this about Robb himself. Instead Robb related a comparable story about himself and a university lecturer. By doing this he dissociated himself from the transference component of the situation and made it clear that he was more like Mr Redfern than the teacher. Bott used a similar method when a wife said how much she envied a friend who had gone to a university and was very clever. When couples made critical remarks about intellectuals, or snoopers, or prying neighbours, we usually said nothing about it directly, but in case this might be a reference to us as well as to the other people mentioned, we slowed down the process of questioning and tried to see if there was some topic about which the couple were particularly troubled.

On occasion people tried to put us more obviously into a therapeutic role. Our advice or opinion was directly sought, particularly on child care. Robb had many requests of this sort, partly because he had children of his own and partly because some of the couples he interviewed knew that he had done therapeutic work. We tried to avoid giving advice as experts on families, but expressed sympathy with the problem and said what we felt about it and, if pressed, what we should do or had done in similar situations. We tried to avoid assuming a directly therapeutic or advice-giving role. Implicitly we kept stressing the fact-finding aspects of our work, although by making Wilson's position as a psycho-analyst clear and by indicating that he had connections with the Tavistock Clinic, it was suggested by implication that if a couple wanted direct therapy it could easily be arranged.

There was counter-transference as well as transference. It was here that the discussions with Menzies were particularly helpful; before they began we were less aware of our own reactions to the couples. Menzies tried to elucidate our feelings towards the couples and the changes that took place as the relationship developed, partly in order to see how such feelings and reactions were affecting the situation, and partly because they were a valuable source of information about the people being studied, particularly about their personalities.

Thus when Bott noted down after a first interview, 'They remind me of people at the University of Chicago', the aim in supervision was to find out what they had done that had produced this feeling. In this case they had talked easily and brightly about their emotional 'problems' in a clever intellectual way. This did not mean that Bott's judgement of them was correct; her feeling was one datum among many others. No attempt was made to rid the field worker of her attitudes towards the University of Chicago. That was for her to worry about if she wanted to. The point was to use her feelings as a source of information. And no attempt was made to rid her of her feelings towards the couple; that too was her concern. But it was hoped that if the field workers understood what they felt they could avoid some of the pitfalls that can arise from acting on feelings without knowing what one is doing.

Discussing a problem with Menzies usually helped the field workers considerably, even though they sometimes did not understand why. For example, Robb always had difficulty in talking to working-class families about rent and housing. He felt they must think him a fraud and a snob because he felt he was as hard up as they and yet he was prepared to spend four or five times as much on rent. After discussing this with Menzies and Bott and trying to see why one couple pointedly raised this question with him, his attitude changed, although he was never clear how or why.

Looking back, it seems that we got into the most awkward entanglements with the families we liked most. Two of the couples Robb interviewed had had important emotional experiences similar to one he had himself gone through. In one case he felt particularly friendly with the family and discussed his experience with them; he became rather identified with them and with their problem and unwittingly encouraged the clinical interviewer to make these interviews more therapeutic than usual, which the couple found upsetting since they had not come to the interviews with a conscious desire for treatment. Again, Bott was particularly fond of one wife and felt, without knowing it, that this wife should react to everything in the same way as herself. Bott disliked taking psychological tests, and by the time she had finished describing the Object Relations Test, the wife was extremely anxious and upset about it and had the greatest difficulty in getting through the test at all. After a colleague pointed out how and why Bott had produced this effect on the wife, she managed to avoid communicating her dislike of tests so vividly to subsequent couples. On another occasion she was so much upset by a wife's decision to return to work when her baby was very young that she did little more in the interview than attempt to conceal her own feelings about it. A discussion afterwards with Menzies and Robb helped her to sort out what was her concern and what was the wife's, so that in the next interview she was able to elicit the necessary information about what the wife thought about it herself.

We had more difficulties of this sort with the earlier families, partly because we were less experienced and partly because systematic discussions between Bott, Robb, and Menzies had not been begun. The most disturbing experience was the withdrawal of a family, the Newbolts, just before the last two interviews on ideology. There were various reasons for this in their own social situation—their feeling that they must conceal the research from their friends, neighbours, and relatives and the difficulty of doing so, their feeling of awkwardness at having joint interviews, and their fear of doctors and reluctance to travel outside their own neighbourhood for clinical interviews. But their withdrawal might have been avoided, or might have aroused less disturbance in the field worker if she had been aware of what she and they were feeling at the time. Bott's feeling of depression after the withdrawal of this family made it even more clear than it had been before that this sort of interviewing led to very great emotional involvement and that it would be essential to understand its nature in order to deal with the work task as realistically as possible.

With two families a special type of relationship was developed because material was discussed with them for publication. Publication presents serious problems when one is studying groups in one's own society. Should one publish what one likes and take the risk of wrecking the reputation of research workers in general? Should one trust to a disguise? What are the rights, legal and moral, of people and groups who let themselves be studied? What are the professional responsibilities of research workers?[1] In our case the choice was clear. There were only twenty families. All of them knew that a book was to be written about them, and most of them intended to read it. In order to make the method of combined sociological and psycho-analytic interpretation clear, it seemed necessary to publish detailed case material. This material has been disguised so that even people who knew the families would have difficulty in recognizing them; but in these very detailed exhaustive accounts it was impossible to work out a disguise so complete that the couple would not recognize themselves. Many of the things that would have had to be altered for such a disguise were essential to the analysis. Furthermore, we had told the families that if we wanted to publish any confidential material that would reveal their identity we should discuss it with them beforehand.

We chose families that we thought could stand this additional stress with comparative ease. We wrote many drafts before reaching one that was accurate enough psycho-analytically without appearing to be too fantastic and frightening. Once the drafts were prepared, small sections were taken along to be discussed with the husband and wife. This required twelve additional interviews by Robb with the first family, and some twenty-six interviews by Bott and five with each partner by Wilson with the second. All in all, the process took the equivalent of one person's working-time for more than a year. These interviews faced the couples with an additional task that at times they found upsetting, but they said it was much more acceptable than finding themselves laid bare in print without any prior consultation. Perhaps they were also a little flattered by having been chosen. We took it for granted that the process of digesting an analysis of themselves in sociological and psychological terms would be disturbing, and

[1] *See* A. T. M. Wilson, 'A Note on the Social Sanctions of Social Research' (Wilson, A. T. M., 1955).

we accepted the responsibility of helping them with it in so far as they felt the need of assistance. We did not try to force 'therapy' on them. It is very difficult to describe exactly what role we played in these 'working-through' interviews. Our activities were much more like therapy than they had been in the earlier interviews, for we were trying to help the couples to accept things emotionally. But the psycho-analytic inferences did not have the effect of clinical interpretations because they were made in such a different way and in such a different context. We were not interested in changing the couple's anxieties and defences, or even in getting them to agree with our inferences. The real task was to help them over the feeling of indignation that outsiders could see or imply the existence of things in them that they thought were concealed or, even more difficult, things they were not consciously aware of at all. When things were difficult to accept they could to some extent dismiss them as the views of crazy psychologists, but they could not do this with much conviction because they had built up a relationship with the research team over a considerable period of time and had committed themselves to the belief that we were sincerely trying to understand them.

On the whole we feel these discussions have been productive in that much confidential material can be published, the couples' reactions to our interpretations have helped us to revise our analysis at several points, and all four individuals seem to have come through the experience without harm. Their personalities do not seem to have been much changed, certainly not in any very profound way. Their basic anxieties, defence systems, and modes of adaptation probably remain much the same. In their own view, the experience has been unusual, a little disturbing at times, but rewarding on the whole. One couple said, 'It brings back your nappy days,' and that it helped them to understand their own children. When their baby got very angry with his mother the husband would say, 'You've become a cruel giant to him now,' and after the baby had got over the worst of his rage she would smile and rub her cheek on his and play with him a bit to show she still loved him and knew he loved her too. The husband of the second couple summed up the experience by saying, 'Well, it's enlightening in a way about one's own behaviour and that of others but I shouldn't say that it's had any actual effect on the way we behave.'

It would be impractical to go through this lengthy procedure for all the material one wishes to publish. We have had briefer discussions with other families on more limited subjects, and some material that was neutral or could be well disguised or described in general terms equally applicable to several families has not been discussed with the couples. In general, our future policy for work of this kind will be that it is permissible to publish material that may reveal a family's identity if one is sure the material is innocuous; it is permissible to publish bits of more confidential material if it can be so disguised that the people will not recognize themselves; but if the material is confidential and cannot be disguised, it should be worked out with them beforehand, especially when they or their friends may read it. These are the usual precautions of professional work and are based on a detailed consideration of what might conceivably harm the persons concerned.

F. COMPARISON WITH OTHER METHODS
AND TECHNIQUES

We have worked out a technique that is not entirely anthropological or psycho-analytical; neither is it the method of the survey or the case-history, although it has some aspects of each.

It resembles anthropology in that we studied groups as working wholes. But it differs from ordinary anthropological field method in that there was comparatively little direct observation and proportionately more interviewing. In home interviews we observed the family while we were there, but we saw them chiefly as they would behave when entertaining a visitor—although a visitor of a special kind. One could observe a more varied range of behaviour if one lived with a family, but few families would permit such constant observation. Because there was relatively little direct observation of behaviour, we often had to take the couples' descriptions of their behaviour as actual fact. There is no reason to suppose that they were not telling the truth as they saw it, but it is well known that people sometimes distort things without knowing it. We considered it reasonably safe to take their behaviour at face value if four conditions were met: first, if the events described were simple and concrete rather than complex and abstract; second, if the events described took place in the present or the recent past rather than the distant past; third, if both husband and wife agreed on the description and neither seemed emotionally upset about it; and fourth, if the description seemed consistent with the behaviour we had observed.

The technique of this research also differed from anthropological field method in that the unit of study was not a total society or a local group. But it is doubtful if anthropological methods could be used in studying urban neighbourhoods without serious modification of the basic approach, because most urban neighbourhoods are not organized groups. Among many of the research families, the greater number of important social relationships were conducted not with neighbours but with friends and relatives who lived at some distance from the family being interviewed. It would be instructive to study all the members of a network of friends and relatives as a social system, but even this would be a difficult task because acceptance by one member of a network does not mean that one will be accepted by the others. In the following chapters the immediate social environments of the research families are discussed in detail. The argument is that the families, as social wholes, were not contained within organized groups, only within networks. In an organized group one need not study every member to understand the group as a whole. In a network one can get a general picture of the structure of the network from a small number of informants, but one cannot find out the exact content of the relationships and activities of all the members.

49

Our technique bears little resemblance to that of a survey except that we tried to collect roughly the same information from all families so that we could compare them. But our interviews were more intensive than those of a survey, and the basic method was quite different because we did not treat the twenty families as a sample and we were not trying to make empirical generalizations about a wider population of families.

The technique resembles the case-study method, but attention is focused not on the individual but on the marital couple and the family as a group.

The technique resembles psycho-analysis only in that much of the material was interpreted in terms of psycho-analytic personality theory and we tried to take the effects of transference and counter-transference into account both as data in themselves and in the evaluation of data. But research interviewing differs from psycho-analysis in aim and in technique, and we made very few attempts at therapeutic interpretations.

The technique served our purposes fairly well. If we were extending the study we might make certain alterations. Certain families might be easier to study if two field workers interviewed them. It might be wise to interview clinically only a few families since these interviews make some couples apprehensive, and the technique of supervision of field workers by an analyst can make the home interviews a useful source of information on personality factors. We might use the Rorschach Test in addition to or instead of the Object Relations Test. We should attempt to study the personalities of the children.

Besides experimenting further with the technique as such, we should ask different questions and make different observations even if we were studying the same problems again. There are many gaps in the data, chiefly because we did not work out certain hypotheses and interpretations until the field work was nearly over. We should ask more detailed questions about the relationships of friends, relatives, and neighbours with one another. We should work out more precise criteria of the division of labour between husband and wife. We should ask different questions about norms. These additional data would help to prove or disprove the hypotheses set forth in the following chapters. But, as stated above, the task of the research was primarily to develop hypotheses in a testable form. Some progress has been made in this task in that we now know what questions we want to ask and how to analyse the answers.

CHAPTER III

Conjugal Roles and Social Networks

A. INTRODUCTION

There was considerable variation in the way husbands and wives performed their conjugal roles. At one extreme was a family in which the husband and wife carried out as many tasks as possible separately and independently of each other. There was a strict division of labour in the household, in which she had her tasks and he had his. He gave her a set amount of housekeeping money, and she had little idea of how much he earned or how he spent the money he kept for himself. In their leisure time, he went to cricket matches with his friends, whereas she visited her relatives or went to a cinema with a neighbour. With the exception of festivities with relatives, this husband and wife spent very little of their leisure time together. They did not consider that they were unusual in this respect. On the contrary, they felt their behaviour was typical of their social circle. At the other extreme was a family in which husband and wife shared as many activities and spent as much time together as possible. They stressed that husband and wife should be equals: all major decisions should be made together, and even in minor household matters they should help one another as much as possible. This norm was carried out in practice. In their division of labour, many tasks were shared or interchangeable. The husband often did the cooking and sometimes the washing and ironing. The wife did the gardening and often the household repairs as well. Much of their leisure time was spent together, and they shared similar interests in politics, music, literature, and in entertaining friends. Like the first couple, this husband and wife felt their behaviour was typical of their social circle, except that they felt they carried the interchange-ability of household tasks a little further than most people. One may sum up the differences between these two extremes by saying that the first family showed more segregation between husband and wife in their role-relationship than the second family. In between these two extremes there were many degrees of variation. This chapter attempts to interpret these differences in degree of segregation of conjugal roles.

The organization of familial activities can be classified in many ways. For the purposes of this research I find it useful to speak of 'complementary', 'independent', and 'joint' organization.[1] In *complementary organization* the activities of husband and wife are different and separate but fitted together to form a whole. In *independent organization* activities are carried out separately by husband and wife without reference to each other, in so far as this is possible. In *joint organization* activities are carried out by husband and wife together, or the same activity is carried out by either partner at different times.

All three types of organization were found in all families. In fact, familial tasks could not be carried out if this were not so. But the relative amounts of each type of organization varied from one family to another. The phrase *segregated conjugal role-relationship* is here used for a relationship in which complementary and inde-pendent types of organization predominate. Husband and wife have a clear differentiation of tasks and a considerable number of separate interests and activities. They have a clearly defined divi-sion of labour into male tasks and female tasks. They expect to have different leisure pursuits, and the husband has his friends out-side the home and the wife has hers. The phrase *joint conjugal role-relationship* is here used for a relationship in which joint organiza-tion is relatively predominant. Husband and wife expect to carry

---

[1] At the beginning of the research a very much more complicated classification was used; it has gradually been simplified into the present form. Changes in mode of classification are described in Appendix B.

out many activities together with a minimum of task differentiation and separation of interests. They not only plan the affairs of the family together but also exchange many household tasks and spend much of their leisure time together.

Among the research couples there were some general resemblances in the type of organization characteristically followed in a particular type of activity but, within these broad limits, there was a great deal of variation. Thus in all families there was a basic division of labour, by which the husband was primarily responsible for supporting the family financially and the wife was primarily responsible for housework and child care; each partner made his own differentiated but complementary contribution to the welfare of the family as a whole. But within this general division of labour, there was considerable variation of detail. Some wives worked, others did not. Some families had a very flexible division of labour in housework and child care by which many tasks were shared or interchangeable, whereas other families had a much stricter division into the wife's tasks and the husband's tasks.

Similarly, there were some activities, such as making important decisions that would affect the whole family, that tended to be carried out jointly by husband and wife. But here too there was considerable variation. Some husbands and wives placed great emphasis on joint decision, whereas others hardly mentioned it. Couples who stressed the importance of joint decisions also had many shared and interchangeable tasks in housework and child care.

In activities such as recreation, including here entertaining and visiting people as well as hobbies, reading, going to the cinema, concerts, and so forth, there was so much variation that it is impossible to say that one form of organization was consistently dominant in all families.

Thus, although all three modes of organizing activities—complementary, independent, and joint—were found in all families, there were marked differences in the relative amounts of each, particularly in the amounts of joint and independent organization.

I use the phrase *degree of segregation of conjugal roles* to compare the combination of the three modes of organization in different families. By degree of segregation of conjugal roles I mean the relative balance between complementary and independent activities on the one hand, and joint activities on the other. And, as noted above, a highly segregated conjugal role-relationship is defined as one in which husband and wife have a relatively large proportion of complementary and independent activities and a relatively small proportion of joint activities. In a joint conjugal role-relationship the proportion of complementary and independent activities is relatively small and the proportion of joint activities is relatively large. These are differences of degree. Strictly speaking, it would be more correct to say that a conjugal relationship was 'highly segregated relative to the other research couples' or less segregated relative to the other research couples' or 'intermediate in degree of segregation relative to the other research couples'; but in order to simplify the language I shall refer to them as 'highly segregated', 'joint', and 'intermediate'. If the hypothesis to be discussed in this chapter were to be tested quantitatively, it would be necessary to arrange the families on a scale according to degree of conjugal segregation. But the data on modes of organization, although detailed, were not collected with quantification in mind so that we did not make exactly the same observations or ask exactly the same questions of each couple. Rather than attempt a shaky quantitative analysis, I have left the definition in qualitative terms.

The research couples made it clear that there had been important changes in their degree of conjugal segregation during their married life. In the first phase, before they had children, all couples had had far more joint activities, especially in the form of shared recreation outside the home. After their children were born the activities of all couples had become more sharply differentiated and they had had to cut down on joint external recreation. Data from the group discussions with wives in the third phase, when the children were adolescent and leaving home, suggest that most husbands and wives do not return to the extensive joint organization of the first phase even when the necessity for differentiation produced by the presence of young children is no longer so great.

But the differences in degree of segregation of conjugal roles among the research families cannot be attributed to differences in phase of development, because all the families were in more or less the same phase. Early in the research, it seemed likely that these differences were related in some way or another to forces in the social environment of the families. In first attempts to explore these forces an effort was made to explain conjugal segregation in terms of social class. This attempt was not very successful. The results are set out in *Table 2*. From this table it will be seen that the husbands who had the most segregated role-relationships with their wives had manual occupations, and the husbands who had the most joint role-relationships with their wives were professional or semi-professional people, but there were several working-class families that had relatively little segregation and there were professional families in which segregation was considerable. Having a working-class occupation is a necessary but not a sufficient cause of the most marked degree of conjugal segregation. An attempt was also made to relate degree of segregation to the type of local area in which the family lived, since the data suggested that the families with most segregation lived in homogeneous areas of low population turnover, whereas the families with predominantly joint role-relationships lived in heterogeneous areas of high population turnover. Once again, however, there were several exceptions.

But there was a more important difficulty. These attempts at rudimentary statistical correlation did not make clear how one factor affected another; it seemed impossible to explain exactly how the criteria for class position or the criteria for different types of local area were actually producing an effect on the internal role structure of the family. It therefore appeared that attempts to correlate segregation of conjugal roles with factors selected from the generalized social environment of the families would not yield a meaningful interpretation. This does not mean that social class

TABLE 2

RELATION BETWEEN CONJUGAL SEGREGATION, OCCUPATION, AND OCCUPATIONAL GRADING

Families in descending order of conjugal segregation	Occupation of husband	Type of occupation (rated by research staff)	Rating of occupation by Hall-Jones scale*
Newbolt	Finisher in large boot and shoe firm	semi-skilled manual	7
Mudge	Police constable	semi-skilled manual	5
Dodgson	Owner-operator of small tobacco and sweet shop	semi-skilled manual	4
Barkway	Accounts clerk in department store	clerical	3
Redfern	Draughtsman in firm of architects	semi-professional	3
Baldock	Self-employed in radio repairs	skilled manual	4
Apsley	General commercial manager in light engineering firm	professional	1
Wraith	W.E.A. lecturer	professional	1
Appleby	Painter and decorator	skilled manual	7
Fawcett	Clerk in insurance firm	clerical	5
Butler	Plumber	skilled manual	6
Thornton	Manager of health food shop	semi-professional	4
Hartley	Sundry supplies buyer for medium-sized industrial firm	semi-professional	3
Salmon	Establishments officer in public health department of local authority	semi-professional	3
Jarrold	Repairer of optical instruments in large optical instrument firm	skilled manual	6
Bruce	Temporary clerk in Gas Board	clerical	5
Denton	Accounts executive in advertising agency	professional	3
Bullock	Statistician in welfare agency	professional	1
Woodman	Pottery designer, working as occupational therapist in hospital	semi-professional	2
Daniels	Deputy manager of fire department in insurance firm	semi-professional	2

*I am indebted to Dr. Hilde Himmelweit and her colleagues at the London School of Economics for rating the husbands' occupations according to the Hall-Jones Scale (Hall and Caradog Jones, 1950). This scale has eight divisions: 1. Professionally qualified and high administrative; 2. Managerial and executive; 3. Inspectional, supervisory, and other non-manual (higher grade); 4. Inspectional supervisory, and other non-manual (lower grade); 5. Routine grade of non-manual work; 6. Skilled manual; 7. Semi-skilled manual; 8. Manual, routine.

The Hall-Jones ratings and the research staff's ratings were both based on the actual occupations, which are here disguised. It will be noted that certain discrepancies exist between the two sets of ratings, especially in the cases of Mudge, Dodgson, Appleby, and Denton. These discrepancies exist because of differences in rating criteria used in the scales.

is unimportant. But it does mean that mere correlation of social class with other factors is not very illuminating in itself. It is necessary to explain the correlation, to examine negative cases, to uncover the mechanisms by which social class and conjugal segregation are related to each other. I shall return to this topic in the next chapter.

Because I could not understand the relationship between conjugal segregation, social class, and neighbourhood composition, I put social class and neighbourhood composition to one side for the time being and turned to look more closely at the immediate environment of the families, that is, at their actual external relationships with friends, neighbours, relatives, clubs, shops, places of work, and so forth. This approach proved more fruitful.

First, it appeared that the external social relationships of all families assumed the form of a *network* rather than the form of an organized group.[1] In an organized group, the component individuals make up a larger social whole with common aims, interdependent roles, and a distinctive sub-culture. In network formation, on the other hand, only some, not all, of the component individuals have social relationships with one another. For example, supposing that a family, X, maintains relationships with friends, neighbours, and relatives who may be designated as A, B, C, D, E, F . . . N, one will find that some but not all of these external persons know one another. They do not form an organized group in the sense defined above. B might know A and C but none of the others; D might know F without knowing A, B, or E. Furthermore, all of these persons will have friends, neighbours, and relatives of their own who are not known by family X. In a network the component external units do not make up a larger

[1] In sociological and anthropological literature, the term 'group' is commonly used in at least two senses. In the first sense it is a very broad term used to describe any collectivity whose members are alike in some way; this definition would include categories, logical classes, and aggregates as well as more cohesive social units. The second usage is much more restricted. In this sense, the units must have some distinctive interdependent social relationships with one another; categories, logical classes, and aggregates are excluded. To avoid confusion, I use the term 'organized group' when it becomes necessary to distinguish the second usage from the first.

social whole; they are not surrounded by a common boundary.[1]

Second, although all the research families belonged to networks rather than to groups, there was considerable variation in the *'connectedness'* of their networks. By connectedness I mean the extent to which the people known by a family know and meet one another independently of the family. I use the word *'close-knit'* to describe a network in which there are many relationships among the component units, and the word *'loose-knit'* to describe a network in which there are few such relationships. Strictly speaking, 'close-knit' should read 'close-knit relative to the networks of the other research families', and 'loose-knit' should read 'loose-knit relative to the networks of the other research families'. The shorter terms are used to simplify the language, but it should be remembered that they are shorthand expressions of relative degrees of connectedness and that they are not intended to be conceived as polar opposites.

A qualitative examination of the research data suggests that the degree of segregation of conjugal roles is related to the degree of connectedness in the total network of the family. Those families that had a high degree of segregation in the role-relationship of husband and wife had a close-knit network; many of their friends, neighbours, and relatives knew one another. Families that had a relatively joint role-relationship between husband and wife had a loose-knit network; few of their relatives, neighbours, and friends knew one another. There were many degrees of variation between

---

[1] The idea of network is often met in anthropological, sociological, and psychological literature, although it does not always bear this name: e.g. Rivers' concept of the 'kindred' (Rivers, 1924), Fortes' 'web of kinship' (Fortes, 1949), Armstrong's 'grouping' (Armstrong, 1928). See also Merton (1949), Moreno (1934), and Loomis and others (1953). Most of these authors are more concerned with the fact that a person has relationships with a number of people than with the pattern of relationships among these other people themselves. Radcliffe-Brown used the term network metaphorically, as in his definition of social structure as 'a complex network of social relations' (Radcliffe-Brown, 1940).

In finding it convenient to use the term 'network' to describe a set of social relationships for which there is no common boundary, I follow the recent usage of John Barnes: 'Each person is, as it were, in touch with a number of people, some of whom are directly in touch with each other and some of whom are not. . . . I find it convenient to talk of a social field of this kind as a *network*. The image I have is of a set of points some of which are joined by lines. The points of the image are people, or sometimes groups, and the lines indicate which people interact with each other.' (Barnes, 1954, p. 43.)

these two extremes. On the basis of our data, I should therefore like to put forward the following hypothesis: *The degree of segregation in the role-relationship of husband and wife varies directly with the connectedness of the family's social network.* The more connected the network, the greater the degree of segregation between the roles of husband and wife. The less connected the network, the smaller the degree of segregation between the roles of husband and wife.

At first sight this seems to be an odd relationship, for it is hard to see why the social relationship of other people with one another should affect the relationship of husband and wife. What seems to happen is this. When many of the people a person knows interact with one another, that is when the person's network is close-knit, the members of his network tend to reach consensus on norms and they exert consistent informal pressure on one another to conform to the norms, to keep in touch with one another, and, if need be, to help one another. If both husband and wife come to marriage with such close-knit networks, and if conditions are such that the previous pattern of relationships is continued, the marriage will be superimposed on these pre-existing relationships, and both spouses will continue to be drawn into activities with people outside their own elementary family (family of procreation). Each will get some emotional satisfaction from these external relationships and will be likely to demand correspondingly less of the spouse. Rigid segregation of conjugal roles will be possible because each spouse can get help from people outside.

But when most of the people a person knows do not interact with one another, that is, when his network is loose-knit, more variation on norms is likely to develop in the network, and social control and mutual assistance will be more fragmented and less consistent. If husband and wife come to marriage with such loose-knit networks or if conditions are such that their networks become loose-knit after marriage, they must seek in each other some of the emotional satisfactions and help with familial tasks that couples in close-knit networks can get from outsiders. Joint organization becomes more necessary for the success of the family as an enterprise.

No claim is made here that connectedness of the family's network is the only factor affecting segregation of conjugal roles. Among the other variables affecting the way conjugal roles are performed, the personalities of husband and wife are of crucial importance. Most of this chapter will be devoted to a discussion of the effect of connectedness, however, because the importance of this variable has been insufficiently stressed in previous studies of family role structure. What I am trying to do is to make a comparative study of the relationship between conjugal role segregation and network-connectedness for each of the twenty families considered as a social system. In so doing I have developed a hypothesis that, with further refinement of definition, preferably in quantifiable terms, might be tested on other families and might facilitate further and more systematic comparisons.

The analysis of social networks presented in this and the following chapter is only a first step. Before the analysis can become at all precise it will be necessary to define degrees of intimacy and obligation of the various relationships. A first attempt in this direction is made in the analysis of relationships with kin in Chapter V. If possible it would be advisable to interview several members of a network, following the links of interaction from one person to another, instead of relying on what each couple say about their network, as I have done. Precise definition of connectedness would require quantitative analysis of the total network, of the independent networks of husband and wife, of their joint network (the people with whom they have joint relationships), and of that part of the total network composed of kin, that composed of friends, and that composed of neighbours. But the data of the present research are not consistent or detailed enough to permit such quantitative analysis.

B. DESCRIPTION OF THE DATA

If the families are classified according to the extremes of the two dimensions of conjugal segregation and network-connectedness, four patterns are logically possible: (a) segregated conjugal role-relationship associated with a close-knit network, (b) joint conjugal role-relationship associated with a loose-knit network, (c) segregated conjugal role-relationship associated with a loose-knit network, and (d) joint conjugal role-relationship associated with a close-knit network. Empirically, two of these patterns, (c) and (d), did not occur. There were no families in which a highly segregated conjugal role-relationship was associated with a loose-knit network; there were no families in which a joint conjugal role-relationship was associated with a close-knit network.

Six of the research families were clustered in the first and second patterns. One family conformed to the first pattern, a high degree of conjugal segregation being combined with a close-knit network. Five families conformed to the second pattern, a joint conjugal role-relationship being associated with a loose-knit network. These six families represent the extremes of the research set. Nine families were intermediate in degree of conjugal segregation and similarly intermediate in degree of network-connectedness, and five families appeared to be in a state of transition with respect both to their network formation and their conjugal role-relationship.

Table 3 lists the families according to degree of conjugal segregation, type of network, and type of occupation. This table shows that degree of conjugal segregation is more closely associated with type of network than with type of occupation. It also shows that there is some clustering at certain points along a continuum from a highly segregated to a very joint conjugal relationship, and along a second continuum from a close-knit to a loose-knit network. The families did not fall sharply into separate types, and divisions are somewhat arbitrary. But for convenience of description I divide the families into four sets: 1. highly segregated conjugal role-relationship associated with close-knit network; 2. joint conjugal role-relationship associated with loose-knit network; 3. intermediate degrees of conjugal role-segregation and network-connectedness; and 4. transitional families. No claim is made here that these are the only patterns that can occur; further research would probably reveal others. The following discussion will be chiefly concerned with the fact that the order according to degree

TABLE 3

RELATION BETWEEN CONJUGAL SEGREGATION, TYPE OF NETWORK,
AND TYPE OF OCCUPATION

Families in descending order of conjugal segregation	Type of network	Type of occupation
Newbolt	close-knit	semi-skilled manual
Mudge	medium-knit	semi-skilled manual
Dodgson (changing reluctantly from highly segregated to more joint)	transitional (move already made)	semi-skilled manual
Barkway	transitional (contemplating move)	clerical
Redfern	transitional (about to move)	semi-professional
Baldock	medium-knit	skilled manual
Apsley	medium-knit	professional
Wraith (becoming more joint)	transitional (several moves already made)	professional
Appleby	medium-knit	skilled manual clerical
Fawcett	medium-knit	clerical
Butler (changing eagerly from highly segregated to more joint)	transitional (move already made)	skilled manual
Thornton	medium-knit	semi-professional
Hartley	medium-knit	semi-professional
Salmon	medium-knit	semi-professional
Jarrold	medium-knit	skilled manual
Bruce	loose-knit	clerical
Denton	loose-knit	professional
Bullock	loose-knit	professional
Woodman	loose-knit	semi-professional
Daniels	loose-knit	semi-professional

of conjugal segregation follows the order according to degree of connectedness of networks, and with the mechanisms by which this relationship operates.

1. Highly Segregated Conjugal Role-Relationship associated with Close-Knit Network

The research set contained only one family of this type, the Newbolts. They had been married six years when the interviewing began and had three small boys. In the following discussion, I describe their actual behaviour, indicating the points at which they depart from their norms.

Although I am not primarily concerned here with whether the research families are typical of others, the literature suggests that there are many such families, chiefly in certain sections of the urban working class. (See Hopkinson, 1954; Jephcott and Carter, 1955; Kerr, 1955; Mays, 1954; Mogey, 1956; Packer, 1947; Shaw 1954; Slater and Woodside, 1951.) There is some evidence of similar conjugal segregation in 'lower-class' American families (Davis, 1941, 1943, and 1944; Davis and Havighurst, 1946 and 1947; Dollard, 1937; Frazier 1940; Maas, 1951).

The role of the husband-father in such families is often described as 'authoritarian', implying that he has clear authority over his wife and children in most or all of their activities. Although I agree that the husband has the right to control the actions of his wife in certain activities, I think the characterization of his role as 'authoritarian' is too sweeping. Male authoritarianism is often confused with segregation of conjugal roles; this comes about because authors assign to the financial and sexual arrangements of these families the same psychological meaning as they would have to families where husband and wife expected to have a joint relationship. This view is supported by the fact that authors also describe these families as 'mother-centred', although this description is not usually put side by side with that of male authoritarianism because the two characterizations sound contradictory. But both are valid, for each partner has authority and responsibility in his own sphere.

Many authors attribute this pattern of family life to working-class status. But several studies show that not all working-class families have pronounced segregation of conjugal roles (Jephcott and Carter, 1955; Young and Willmott, 1957; Mogey, 1956; Hammond, 1954). This is discussed further in the following chapter.

Although I have found no studies analysing conjugal segregation in terms of external relationships and network-connectedness,

CONJUGAL ROLES AND SOCIAL NETWORKS

there are some suggestions in the literature that families like the Newbolts have many important relationships outside the family, especially with kin, and it is sometimes implied or can be inferred that these external people are well known to one another. (See Dotson, 1951; Gorer, 1955; Jephcott and Carter, 1955; Kerr, 1955; Mays, 1954; Shaw, 1954; Sheldon, 1948; Townsend, 1957; Young, 1954a, 1954b; Young and Willmott, 1957; Zweig, 1952.)

a. External social relationships. Mr Newbolt had a semi-skilled manual job at a factory in Bermondsey. He and his wife lived in a nearby area of the same borough. He said that several other men in the local area had jobs at the same place as himself, and that others were doing similar jobs at other factories and workshops nearby. Mrs Newbolt did not work, but she felt that she was unusual in this respect. Most of the neighbouring women and many of her female relatives had jobs; she did not think there was anything morally wrong with such work, but she said that she had never liked working and preferred to stay at home with the children. Mr Newbolt expressed the same view, and added that it was a bit of a reflection on a man if his wife had to go out to work.

The Newbolts used the services of a local hospital and a maternity and child welfare clinic. They expected to send their children to the local primary school. They were also in touch with the local housing authority because they were trying to find a new flat. These various service institutions were not felt to have any particular relationship to one another, except in the sense that they were all felt to be foreign bodies, not really part of the local life. Mrs Newbolt was a little afraid of them. On one occasion, while waiting with her baby and myself in an otherwise empty hospital room for a doctor to attend to the baby, she said in a whisper, 'My husband says that we pay for it (the hospital services, through National Health subscriptions) and we should use it, but I don't like coming here. I don't like hospitals and doctors, do you?'

To the Newbolts the local area was definitely a community, a place with an identity of its own and a distinctive way of life.

65

They spoke of it with pride and contrasted it favourably with other areas. 'It has a bad name, they say we are rough, but I think it's the best place there is. Everyone is friendly . . . there is no life over the water up West. They drink champagne and we drink beer. When things are la-di-da you feel out of place.' They took it for granted that the other inhabitants had similar feelings of local pride and loyalty. Trips outside the area were like ventures into a foreign land, especially for Mrs Newbolt. Few informal social relationships were kept up with people outside the area, and physical distance was felt to be an almost insuperable barrier to social contact.

Physically, the area was far from ideal as a place to live in, for the houses were old-fashioned, inconvenient and crowded. The Newbolts were faced with a difficult choice of moving out of London to a modern flat on a new housing estate or remaining in cramped quarters in the old familiar local area with friends and relatives. They knew of other young couples faced with a similar dilemma. Group discussions at a local community centre and the research of the Institute of Community Studies indicate that many residents of such areas feel this to be an important social and personal problem (Young, 1954b, 1956; Young and Willmott, 1957).

The Newbolts felt their neighbours were socially similar to themselves, having the same sort of jobs, the same sort of background, the same sort of outlook on life. Because the Newbolts had grown up in the area, as had many of their relatives and neighbours, they knew a considerable number of local people, and many of these people were acquainted with one another. In other words, their social network was close-knit. There was overlapping of social roles; instead of there being people in separate categories—friend, neighbour, relative, and colleague—the same person frequently filled two or more of these roles simultaneously.

The Newbolts took it for granted that Mr Newbolt, like other husbands in their social circle, would have some recreation with men away from home. In his case it was cycle-racing and cricket, although the most common form of recreation was felt to be drinking and visiting friends in the local pub where many husbands spent an evening or two a week; frequently some of these men were friends of long standing who had belonged to the same childhood gang; others were colleagues at work. Mr Newbolt had kept in touch with one or two childhood friends; he also played cricket and went to matches with some of his work colleagues; several of his friends knew one another. Mrs Newbolt knew a little about these men, but she did not expect to join in their activities with her husband. She had a nodding acquaintance with two or three of the wives, and occasionally talked to them when she was shopping.

Mrs Newbolt had separate relationships in which her husband did not expect to join. She knew many female neighbours, just as they knew one another. She took it for granted that a friendly relationship with a neighbour would end if the woman moved away. Neighbours saw one another on the landings, in the street, in shops; they hardly ever asked each other inside the flat or house. They talked over their affairs and those of other neighbours. Neighbours frequently accused one another of something—betraying a confidence, taking the wrong side in a children's quarrel, failing to return borrowed articles, or gossip. One has little privacy in such a situation. But if one wants to reap the rewards of companionship and small acts of mutual aid, one must conform to local standards and one must expect to be included in the gossip. Being gossiped about is as much a sign of belonging to the neighbourly network as being gossiped with. If one refuses contact with neighbours one is thought odd and eventually one will be left alone; no gossip, no companionship.

With the exception of visiting relatives and an occasional Sunday outing with the children, the Newbolts spent little of their leisure in joint recreation. Even though they could have asked relatives to mind the children for them, they rarely went out together. In particular, there was no joint entertaining of friends at home. From time to time Mr Newbolt brought a friend home and Mrs Newbolt made tea and talked a little. Female neighbours often dropped in during the evening to borrow something, but they did not stay long if Mr Newbolt was there. There was no planned joint entertaining in which Mr and Mrs Newbolt asked another husband and wife to spend an evening with them. Such joint entertaining as existed was carried on with relatives, not with friends. Poverty does not explain the absence of joint entertaining, for the Newbolts considered themselves relatively well-off. It did not seem to occur to them that they might spend money on entertaining friends; they felt surplus money should be spent on furniture, new things for the children, or gatherings of relatives at weddings, funerals, and christenings.[1]

There was much visiting and mutual aid between relatives, particularly the women. The Newbolts had far more active social relationships with relatives than any other research family, and there was also a great deal of independent contact by their relatives with one another in addition to their contacts with the Newbolts themselves. Thus the network of kin was close-knit, probably more so than those of neighbours or friends. The women were more active than the men in keeping up contacts with relatives, with the result that the networks of wives were more close-knit than the networks of their husbands. Although husbands were recognized to be less active in kinship affairs than their wives, Mr Newbolt paid occasional visits to his mother, both by himself and with his wife. Furthermore, there were some activities in which joint participation by husband and wife was felt to be desirable. At weddings, funerals, and christenings, there were large gatherings of relatives and it was felt to be important that both husband and wife should attend. Such basic kinship ceremonies formed an important topic of discussion throughout the interviews with the Newbolts.

In a group discussion, a man living in the same local area as the Newbolts and having a similar sort of family life and kinship network summed up the situation by saying, 'Men have friends. Women have relatives,' succinctly describing the difference be-

[1] The absence of joint entertainment of friends made our technique of joint interviewing somewhat inappropriate for this family.

tween men and women in external relationships, and implying segregation between husband and wife. Wives, through their close relationships with their children and with their parents, are deeply involved in activities with kin. Husbands are more concerned with jobs and friends. This man's epigram also suggests the overlapping of roles mentioned above. Mrs Newbolt had no independent category of 'friend'; friends were either neighbours or relatives. She had had a succession of girl-friends in her adolescence, but she said that she did not see so much of them since they were all married with children. She always described them as 'girl-friends' not as 'friends'. Both Mr and Mrs Newbolt used the term 'friend' as if it applied only to men. The term 'neighbour', on the other hand, seemed to refer only to women. Mr Newbolt looked rather shocked when I asked him if he saw much of the neighbours.

Later in the group discussion the same man observed, 'Women don't have friends. They have Mum.' In Mrs Newbolt's case the relationship between herself and her mother was very close. Her mother lived nearby in the same local area, and Mrs Newbolt visited her nearly every day, taking her children with her. She and her mother and her mother's sisters also visited Mrs Newbolt's maternal grandmother. These women and their children formed an important group, helping one another in household tasks and child care, and providing aid in crises. (See also Chapter V and Young, 1954a and 1956; Young and Willmott, 1957.) Within the network of relatives, there was thus a nucleus composed of the grandmother, her daughters, and her daughters' daughters; the relationships of these women were sufficiently intense and distinctive to warrant the term 'organized group' in the sense defined above. Mrs Newbolt's female relatives provided some of the domestic help and emotional support that the wives of other research families expected to get from their husbands. Mrs Newbolt was tremendously attached to her mother emotionally. She felt that a bad relationship between mother and daughter was unnatural, a complete catastrophe. She would have been shocked by the seemingly cold and objective terms in which some of the wives in other research families analysed their mothers' characters. The close tie with the mother is not only a source of help in families like the Newbolts, but may also be a potential source of friction, for if her husband and her mother do not get along well, a young wife is likely to feel torn by conflicting loyalties. Mrs Newbolt felt she was fortunate in that her husband and her mother liked each other.

In brief, there was considerable segregation between Mr and Mrs Newbolt in their external relationships. In effect Mrs Newbolt had her network and Mr Newbolt had his. The number of joint external relationships was comparatively small. At the same time, there were many links between their networks. The husbands of some of Mrs Newbolt's neighbours worked at the same place as her husband, some of her relatives also worked there, some of her male relatives were Mr Newbolt's friends, and in a general way his family had been known to hers before their marriage. In other words, the connectedness of their combined networks was high compared with that of the families to be discussed below. But the Newbolts' total network was sharply divided into the husband's network and the wife's. Furthermore, her network was more close-knit than his; many of the relatives and neighbours with whom she was in contact saw one another independently of her, whereas there appeared to be fewer independent links between Mr Newbolt's colleagues, his cricketing and cycle-racing associates, and his friends from childhood, although quantitative analysis would be necessary to establish this.

b. Conjugal segregation. The previous description reveals considerable segregation between Mr and Mrs Newbolt in their external relationships. There was a similar segregation in the way they carried out their internal domestic tasks. They believed there should be a clear-cut division of labour between them, and that all husbands and wives in their social circle organized their households in a similar way. One man said in a group discussion, 'A lot of men wouldn't mind helping their wives if the curtains were drawn so people couldn't see,' and this was how the Newbolts felt about it too.

Although the Newbolts felt that major decisions should be made jointly, in the day-to-day running of the household he had his jobs and she hers. He had control of the money and gave her a housekeeping allowance of £5 a week. Mrs Newbolt did not know how much money he earned, and it did not seem to occur to her that a wife would want or need to know this. Although the Newbolts said £5 was the amount given to most wives for housekeeping, Mrs Newbolt had difficulty in making it cover the cost of food, rent, utilities, and five shillings' saving for Christmas. She told her husband whenever she ran short, and he left a pound or two under the clock when he went out next morning. She said he was very generous with his money and she felt she was unusually fortunate in being spared financial quarrels.

Mrs Newbolt was responsible for most of the housework although Mr Newbolt did household repairs and she expected him to do some of the housework if she became ill. This was usually unnecessary because her mother or sister or one of her cousins came to her aid. These female relatives helped her greatly even with the everyday tasks of housework and child care.

Like all the research couples, the Newbolts took it for granted that husband and wife should be jointly responsible for the welfare of their children. In practice, Mrs Newbolt carried out most of the actual tasks of caring for the three boys, though Mr Newbolt helped to entertain them in the evenings and on Sundays. Occasionally he put them to bed and sometimes he got up when they cried in the night. He bought them many presents. Mrs Newbolt felt that he was a very good father. She said fathers took more of an interest in children nowadays than they used to, but that even allowing for this, Mr Newbolt was exceptional.

The children were not put to bed until they fell asleep. The Newbolts seemed to feel, although they never said so directly, that it was unkind to put children in a dark room to sleep, away from the light and company around the fire. Except when they were tired, both Mr and Mrs Newbolt seemed to take pleasure in the children's company and liked to hold them and talk to them. At the same time, Mrs Newbolt made no bones about the fact that she got fed up with them sometimes—'They don't half get on my nerves, round my feet all day, especially Billy' (the youngest). But the youngest was also her favourite and she made no bones about that either.

Mrs Newbolt got considerable help in looking after the boys. Her husband did a good deal but her mother helped even more. Her mother even 'borrowed' the eldest child for a fortnight because she was lonely. Mrs Newbolt also took the children to visit their father's mother, but these visits were less frequent and the relationship was less intense. But it was not only relatives who helped with the children. The two older children (aged five and three) played on the street with a group of children under the general supervision of several mothers who kept an eye on them from the doorways. Mrs Newbolt was soon told if something went wrong.

The Newbolts said they did not believe in punishing children. Mrs Newbolt said she would slap them when they made her angry but she would never beat them. Mr Newbolt used to threaten not to get them something they wanted if they were very disobedient. But Mrs Newbolt said he never carried out his threats.

Mrs Newbolt said the most important thing about children was getting them to eat enough. The eldest had been bottle-fed, although she had breast-fed the two younger ones until they were a year old. Until the eldest child was three or more he used to suck at a bottle as long as no one was watching him. Mrs Newbolt urged the children to eat all they wanted, but she did not force them to finish their food if they were disinclined.

Neither parent was ambitious for the children to do well at school. Mrs Newbolt had a vague dream that the youngest might go to a 'nice' school, but Mr Newbolt was not keen on educational advancement. They both wanted the children to live the same sort of life as themselves. Neither had any plans for the children's future although Mr Newbolt thought that one of them might go into business if he were inclined to it, because if a man had his own little business he would be secure. Mrs Newbolt summed up this talk of the future by saying, 'I wouldn't try to change them. I don't think you can when they're old. Or when they're young. I can't do much with Billy when he doesn't want to. I just wait.'

c. Attitudes toward the role-relationship of husband and wife. Mr and Mrs Newbolt took it for granted that men had male interests and women had female interests and that there were few leisure activities they would naturally share. In their view, a good husband was generous with the housekeeping allowance, did not waste money selfishly on himself, helped his wife with the housework if she got ill, and took an interest in the children. A good wife was a good manager, an affectionate mother, a woman who kept out of serious rows with neighbours and got along well with her own and her husband's relatives. A good conjugal relationship was one with a harmonious division of labour, but the Newbolts placed little stress on the importance of joint activities and shared interests. It is difficult to make any definite statement on their attitudes towards sexual relations, for they did not come to the Tavistock Institute for clinical interviews. Judging from Mrs Newbolt's references to such matters when her husband was absent, it seems likely that she felt physical sexuality was an intrusion on a peaceful domestic relationship rather than an expression of such a relationship. It was as if sexuality were felt to be basically violent and disruptive. The findings of clinical workers and of other research workers suggest that among families like the Newbolts there is little stress on the importance of physical sexuality for a happy marriage (Slater and Woodside, 1951).

2. Families Having a Joint Conjugal Role-Relationship associated with a Loose-Knit Network

There were five families of this type. The husbands had professional, semi-professional, and clerical occupations. Two of the husbands considered their occupations to be of higher social status than the occupations of their fathers. One husband had an occupation of lower social status. All five families, however, had a well-established pattern of external relationships; they might

73

make new relationships, but the basic pattern was likely to remain the same. Similarly, all had worked out a fairly stable division of labour in domestic tasks.

a. External social relationships. The husbands' occupations had little intrinsic connection with the local areas in which they lived. All five husbands carried on their work at some distance from their areas of residence, although two did some additional work at home. In no case was there any feeling that the occupation was locally rooted.

Whether or not wives should work was considered to be a very controversial question by these couples. Unless they were very well-off financially—and none of them really considered themselves to be so—both husband and wife welcomed the idea of a double income, even though much of the additional money had to be spent on caring for the children. But money was not the only consideration; women also wanted to work for the sake of the work itself. It was felt that if she desired it, a woman should have a career or some special interest and skill comparable in seriousness to her husband's occupation; on the other hand, it was felt that young children needed their mother's care and that ideally she should drop her career at least until the youngest child was old enough to go to school. But most careers cannot easily be dropped and picked up again several years later. Two of the wives had solved the problem by continuing to work; they had made careful (and expensive) provision for the care of their children. One wife worked at home. The fourth had a special interest (shared by her husband) that took up almost as much time as a job, and the fifth wife was planning to take up her special interest again as soon as her youngest child went to school.

These husbands and wives maintained contact with schools, general practitioners, hospitals, and in some cases local maternity and child welfare clinics. Most of them also used the services of a solicitor, an insurance agent, and other similar professional people as required. Unlike the Newbolts, they did not feel that service institutions were strange and alien; it did not bother them when they had to go out of their local area to find such services. They were usually well informed about service institutions and could exploit them efficiently. They were not afraid of doctors. There was no strict division of labour between husband and wife in dealing with service institutions. The wife usually dealt with those institutions that catered for children, and the husband dealt with the legal and financial ones, but either could take over the other's duties if necessary.

These husbands and wives did not regard the neighbourhood as a source of friends. In most cases the husband and wife had moved several times both before and after marriage, and none of them were living in the neighbourhood in which they had grown up. Four were living in areas of such a kind that few of the neighbours were felt to be socially similar to the family themselves. The fifth family was living in a suburb which the husband and wife felt to be composed of people socially similar to one another, but quite different from themselves. In all cases these husbands and wives were polite but somewhat distant to most neighbours. One couple had found two friends in the neighbourhood through their children. Another couple had friendly though rather formal and gingerly relations with three or four neighbours. In order to become proper friends, neighbours had not only to be socially similar to the family themselves, but also had to share a large number of tastes and interests. Establishing such a relationship requires exploratory testing, and it seems to be considered dangerous to approach neighbours since one risks being pestered by friendly attentions one may not wish to return. Since many neighbours probably had similar feelings, it is not surprising that intimate social relationships were not rapidly established. Since these families had so little social intercourse with their neighbours, they were less worried than the Newbolts about gossip and conformity to local norms. In the circumstances one can hardly say that there were any specifically local norms; certainly there was not a body of shared attitudes and values built up through personal interaction since childhood as was characteristic of the area inhabited by the Newbolts.

The children showed less of this discriminating outlook. Unless restricted by their parents, they played with anyone in the street. This caused some of the parents to be anxious because of the social heterogeneity of the area. Others thought mixing with children of other social classes was a good thing. In any case, all relied on their own influence and on the education of the children to erase any possibly bad effects of such contact.

It seemed very difficult for these families to find the sort of house and local area in which they wanted to live. They wanted to own a reasonably cheap house with a garden in central London, a house within easy reach of their friends, of theatres, concert halls, galleries and so forth. Ideally they wanted a cheap, reliable char-cum-baby-sitter to live nearby, possibly even with the family if they could afford it. Only one family had achieved something approaching this aim. The others were making do with various compromises, impeded by lack of money as well as by the scarcity of suitable houses.

For these families, friends were felt to provide the most important type of external relationship. It was not usual for a large number of a family's friends to be in intimate contact with one another independently of their contact with the family. In brief, the network of friends was typically loose-knit. Husband and wife had usually established friendships over a period of years in many different social contexts—at school, during the course of their occupational training, in the services, in various jobs, and, very occasionally, through living in the same neighbourhood. Their friends were scattered all over London, sometimes even all over Britain. Because the network of friends was so loose-knit, their social control over the family was dispersed and fragmented. The husband and wife were very sensitive about what their friends thought of them, but since these people had relatively little contact with one another, they were not likely to present a unified body of public opinion. Taking into account all the different pieces of advice they might receive, husband and wife nevertheless had to make up their own minds about what they should do. They were less persecuted by gossip than the first type of family but also less sustained by it. Their friends did not form a solid body of helpers.

In marked contrast to the Newbolts' situation, nearly all of the husband's and wife's friends were joint friends. It was felt to be important that both husband and wife should like a family friend, and if he or she was married, then it was hoped that all four people involved would like one another. Exceptions were tolerated, especially in the case of very old friends, but both husband and wife were uncomfortable if there was real disagreement between them over a friend. Friendship, like marriage, required shared interests and similar tastes, although there was some specialization of interests in this respect. For example, one couple might be golfing friends whereas others might be pub and drinking friends; still others were all-round friends, and it was these who were felt to be the most intimate.

Joint entertainment of friends was a major form of recreation. Even when couples did not have enough money to arrange dinners or parties, friends were still asked over jointly even if only for coffee or tea in the evening. It was considered 'provincial' for husbands to cluster at one end of the room and wives at the other; everyone should be able to talk to everyone else. These husbands and wives usually had enough shared interests to make this possible.

After these couples had children, it became increasingly difficult for them to visit their friends, who often lived at a considerable distance. Since most friends were also tied down by young children, mutual visiting became more and more difficult to arrange. Considerable expense and trouble were taken to make such visiting possible. It was obvious that friends were of primary importance to these families.

There were usually other forms of joint recreation, such as eating in foreign restaurants, going to plays, films, concerts, and so forth. After children were born, there had been a marked drop in external joint recreation in favour of things that could be done at home. Going out became a special event with all the paraphernalia of a baby-sitter and arrangements made in advance. All these

77

couples felt that it was not quite right for one partner to go out alone. It happened occasionally, but joint recreation was much preferred.

These five families had far less contact with their relatives than the Newbolts. Their relatives were not concentrated in the same local area as themselves. In most cases they were scattered all over the country and did not keep in close touch with one another, thus forming a loose-knit network. It was felt that friendly relations should be kept up with parents, and in several cases the birth of the children had led to a sort of reunion with parents. Becoming a parent seems to facilitate a resolution of some of the emotional tensions between adult children and their own parents, particularly between women and their mothers. Possibly the arrival of children may exacerbate such tensions in some cases, but none of these five families had had such an experience. There are obvious practical advantages in increased contact with parents; they are usually fond of their grandchildren so that they make affectionate and reliable baby-sitters and if they live close enough to take on this task their services are appreciated.

Among the families with loose-knit networks, there was not the very strong stress on the mother-daughter relationship that was described for Mrs Newbolt, although women were usually more active than men in keeping up kinship ties. There were fewer conflicts of loyalty; it was felt that if conflicts arose between one's parents and one's spouse, one owed one's first loyalty to one's spouse. Unless special interests, particularly financial ties, were operating among relatives, there was no very strong obligation towards relatives outside the parental families of husband and wife. Even towards siblings there was often very little feeling of social obligation. These couples were very much less subject to social control by their relatives than the Newbolts, partly because they saw less of them, but also because the network of kin was dispersed and loose-knit so that its various members were less likely to share the same opinions and values.

In brief, the networks of these families were more loose-knit than that of the Newbolts; many of their friends did not know one another, it was unusual for friends to know relatives, only a few relatives kept in touch with one another, and husband and wife had very little contact with neighbours. Furthermore, there was no sharp segregation between the wife's network and the husband's network. With the exception of a few old friends and some colleagues, husband and wife maintained joint external relationships.

b. Conjugal role-segregation. As described above, these families had as little segregation as possible in their external relationships. There was a similar tendency towards joint organization in their carrying out of domestic tasks and child care. It was felt that efficient management demanded some division of labour, particularly after the children came. There had to be a basic differentiation between the husband's role as primary breadwinner and the wife's as mother of young children. In other respects such division of labour as existed was felt to be more a matter of convenience than of inherent differences between the sexes. The division of labour was flexible and there was considerable sharing and interchange of tasks. Husbands were expected to take a very active part in child care. Financial affairs were managed jointly, and joint consultation was taken for granted on all major decisions.

Husbands were expected to provide much of the help that Mrs Newbolt was able to get from her female relatives. The wives of the families with loose-knit networks were carrying a very heavy load of housework and child care, but they expected to carry it for a shorter time than Mrs Newbolt. Relatives helped them only very occasionally; they usually lived at some distance so that it was difficult for them to provide continuous assistance. Cleaning women were employed by four couples and a children's nurse by one; all couples wanted to have more domestic help but could not afford it. In spite of their affection for their children, all five couples were looking forward to the time when they would be older and less of a burden. In so far as they could look ahead, they did not expect to provide continuous assistance to their own married children.

79

It seems that in the case of Mrs Newbolt and other wives with close-knit networks, the burden of housework and child care is more evenly distributed throughout the lifetime of the wife. When she is a girl she helps her mother with the younger children; when she herself has children her mother and other female relatives help her; when she is a grandmother she helps her daughters.

Like all the research couples, those with loose-knit networks took it for granted that husband and wife should be jointly responsible for the welfare of the children. But the husbands were expected to help more than Mr Newbolt. Mrs Newbolt thought her husband was a very good father because he took an interest in the children; the wives of families with loose-knit networks took it for granted that husbands would take an interest in the children. Husbands had to help their wives because the wives got less help from relatives and neighbours. But it was more than that. Co-parenthood was considered to be a most vital part of the joint conjugal relationship. Even so, the wives carried most of the burden of child care because, with the exception of those who had full-time jobs, they were at home most of the day.

In spite of the great number of child-care activities that were shared by husband and wife, it was taken for granted that the relationship between mother and child was different from that between father and child. The difference was greatest when the children were infants. It was felt, although never explained in so many words, that the relationship between mother and infant was a special very close relationship, almost one of bodily union, that a father could never achieve. At most he could be an auxiliary mother, and if he tried to be more the wife felt he was poaching on her territory. When the children were older the gap between the mother-child relationship and the father-child relationship was less marked. As far as I could tell, these couples did not feel that fathers should be the final authorities and disciplinarians and that mothers should be more warm-hearted. They thought husband and wife should be more or less equal both in authority and in warm-heartedness.[1] But there was a recognized tendency for fathers to specialize in entertaining the children. Two of the five fathers also had closer relationships with the oldest child than with the others, although it was felt that favouritism by either parent was bad for the children and attempts were made to conceal it from the children.

It is difficult to describe the child-rearing practices of these couples because there was considerable variation. But in one respect they contrasted strongly with the Newbolts: they were more self-conscious about themselves as parents. At first I attributed this to their higher level of education, but later I decided that direct experience of differences in child-rearing theories and practices among friends was extremely important too. There were several intermediate couples that were equally well educated but much less self-conscious about themselves as parents. There appeared to be more agreement among the friends, neighbours, and relatives of these intermediate families on how children should be brought up.

On the whole the children in the families with loose-knit networks were more strictly and more consistently disciplined than the Newbolts' children, even by those parents who felt they should be permissive. All five couples disapproved of beatings and delayed punishments, but children were sent to their rooms and were sometimes denied something they wanted.

There seemed to be a gulf between parents and children that the Newbolts did not feel. It was generally assumed that children's talk would not interest adults and that adult conversation would not or should not interest children. At the same time, all five couples were making concerted efforts to talk and play with their

[1] This finding contradicts Parsons' ideal type of the elementary family, in which the father, the 'instrumental leader', is feared and respected whereas the mother, the 'expressive leader', is loved more warmly (Parsons and Bales, 1955). This discrepancy may be due to the fact that Parsons looks at the situation chiefly from the point of view of the child and I am looking at it from the point of view of the parents. But in general I think Parsons overestimates the difference in the roles of husband and wife in this respect, particularly for families with loose-knit networks. I agree that the basic division of labour between husband and wife, in which the husband supports the family financially while the wife cares for the house and children, is of fundamental importance, but I think Parsons underestimates the amount of variation in conjugal segregation.

children and to enjoy their company. Like Mrs Newbolt, the mothers got fed up with their children occasionally, but they phrased it differently. One (a highly educated woman) said, 'You must excuse me if I sound half-witted. I've been talking to the children all day.'.

Both partners seemed to feel more burdened by the children than the Newbolts, partly because they had less help in caring for them, partly because they had stricter standards of good behaviour and partly because they were continually wrestling with the problem of whether it was better to allow children to behave as they liked or to stop them from being obstreperous and ill-mannered.

All five couples thought it was bad for parents to be ambitious for their children. Their idea was that parents should help children to realize their potentialities but that children should not be forced to become something they were not capable of or did not want to be. None of the children were openly urged to do well at school, but at the same time, all parents hoped that their children would do well of their own accord.

c. *Attitudes towards the role-relationship of husband and wife.* Among the families with loose-knit networks, there were frequent discussions as to whether there really were any psychological or temperamental differences between the sexes. These differences were not simply taken for granted as they were by the Newbolts. In some cases so much stress was placed on shared interests and sexual equality (which was sometimes confused with identity, the notion of equality of complementary opposites being apparently a difficult idea to maintain consistently) that one sometimes felt that the possibility of the existence of social and temperamental differences between the sexes was being denied. In other cases, temperamental differences between the sexes were exaggerated to a point that belied the couple's actual joint activities and the whole pattern of shared interests felt to be so fundamental to their way of life. Quite frequently the same couple would minimize differences between the sexes on one occasion and exaggerate them on another. Sometimes these discussions about sexual differences were very serious; sometimes they were witty and facetious; but they were never neutral—they were felt to be an important problem. Such discussions may be interpreted as an attempt to air and resolve the contradiction between the necessity for joint organization with its ethic of equality, on the one hand, and the necessity for differentiation and recognition of sexual differences on the other. 'After all,' one husband said to conclude the discussion, '*vive la différence*, or where would we all be?'

It was felt that in a good marriage, husband and wife should achieve a high degree of compatibility, based on their own particular combination of shared interests and complementary differences. Their relationship with each other should be more important than any separate relationship with outsiders. The conjugal relationship should be kept private and revelations to outsiders or letting down one's spouse in public were felt to be serious offences. A successful sexual relationship was felt by those couples to be very important for a happy marriage. It was as if successful sexual relations were felt to prove that all was well with the joint relationship, whereas unsatisfactory relations were indicative of a failure in the total relationship. In some cases one almost got the feeling that these husbands and wives felt a moral obligation to enjoy sexual relations, a feeling not expressed or suggested by the Newbolts.

The wives in these families seemed to feel that their position was rather difficult. They had certainly wanted children, and in all five cases they were getting a great deal of satisfaction from their maternal role. But at the same time, they felt tied down by their children and they did not like the inevitable drudgery associated with child care. Some were more affected than others, but most complained of isolation, boredom, and fatigue. They wanted a career or some special interest that would make them feel they were something more than children's nurses and housemaids. They wanted more joint entertainment with their husbands and more contact with friends. These complaints were not levelled specifically at their husbands—in most cases they felt their husbands were trying to make the situation easier—but against the social situation and the conflict in which they found themselves. One wife summed it up by saying, 'Society seems to be against married women. I don't know, it's all very difficult.'

It may be felt that the problem could be solved if such a family moved to an area that was felt to be homogeneous and composed of people similar to themselves, for then the wife might be able to find friends among her neighbours and would feel less isolated and bored. It is difficult to imagine, however, that these families could feel that any local area, however homogeneous by objective criteria, could be full of potential friends, for their experience of moving about in the past and their varied social contacts make them very discriminating in their choice of friends. Further, their dislike of having their privacy broken into by neighbours was deeply rooted; it diminished after the children started playing with children in the neighbourhood but it never disappeared entirely.

3. Intermediate Degree of Conjugal Segregation Associated with Medium-Knit Network

There were nine families of this type in the research set. There was considerable variety of occupation among them. Four husbands had professional or semi-professional occupations very similar to the occupations of the second type of family described above. It was in recognition of the fact that these four families were similar to the second set of families in occupation but different in degree of conjugal segregation that I concluded that conjugal segregation could not be attributed to occupational level alone. Of the five remaining husbands, one was a clerical worker, three were skilled workers and one was semi-skilled. One of the skilled workers changed to an office job after the interviewing was completed.

There was considerable variation among the nine families in conjugal segregation. Some tended to have a fairly marked degree of segregation, approaching that of the Newbolts, whereas others were closer to the second set of families in having a relatively joint role-relationship. These variations in degree of segregation of conjugal roles within the nine intermediate families did not follow exactly the order according to occupational level. If the occupations of the husbands are arranged in order from the most joint to the most segregated conjugal role-relationship, the order is as follows: Skilled worker, semi-professional, semi-professional, semi-professional, clerical worker, skilled worker, professional, skilled worker, semi-skilled worker. The variations in degree of segregation follow more closely the variations in degree of network-connectedness. The families with the most loose-knit networks had the most joint conjugal relationships, and the families with the most close-knit networks had the most segregated conjugal relationships. The families with the most loose-knit networks were those who had moved a great deal so that they had established relationships with many people who did not know one another.

For brevity of description, I shall treat the nine intermediate families collectively, but it should be remembered that there were variations in degree among them, and that both network-connectedness and conjugal role-segregation form continua so that it is arbitrary to divide families into separate types.

a. *External social relationships.* The data suggest two possible reasons for the intermediate degree of connectedness in the networks of these families. First, most of the husbands and wives came from families whose networks had been less connected than that of the Newbolts, but more connected than those of the second set of families. Furthermore, with one exception these couples had moved around less than the second type of family both before and after marriage, so that more of their friends knew one another. Several of these families had had considerable continuity of relationships since childhood, and they had not developed the pattern of ignoring neighbours and relying chiefly on friends and colleagues that was described as typical of families with loose-knit networks.

Second, these families felt that many of the neighbours were socially similar to themselves. In four cases these were 'suburban' areas; in five cases they were mixed working-class areas in which the inhabitants were felt to be similar to one another in general occupational level although they worked at different jobs. Of the nine families, five were living in or near the area where one or both of the partners had lived since childhood. In two of the remaining four cases, the area was similar to the one in which husband and wife had been brought up. In two cases, the present area differed considerably from the childhood area of one or other partner, but the couple had acclimatized themselves to the new situation.

If the husband and wife were living in the area in which they had been brought up, each was able to keep up some of the relationships that had been formed before marriage. This was also true of the Newbolts. The intermediate families differed from the Newbolts chiefly in that their jobs or education had led them to make relationships with people who were not neighbours. Many neighbours were friends, but not all friends were neighbours. Even in the case of families in which one or both partners had moved to the area after marriage, each partner was able to form friendly relationships with at least some of the neighbours, who were in most cases felt to be socially similar to the couple themselves. Husband and wife were able to form independent, segregated relationships with neighbours. Many of the wives spent a good deal of their leisure time during the day with neighbouring women. Husband and wife joined local clubs, most of these clubs being uni-sexual. (Voluntary associations appear to thrive best in areas where people are similar in social status but do not know one another well; the common activity gives people an opportunity to get to know one another better.)

In local areas inhabited by the intermediate families, many of the neighbours knew one another. There was not the very great familiarity built up through continuous residence as in the area inhabited by the Newbolts, but there was not the standoffishness typical of the families with very loose-knit networks. The intermediate families had networks of neighbours that were midway in degree of connectedness, and the husbands and wives were

86

midway in sensitivity to the opinions of neighbours—more susceptible than the second set of families, but better able to maintain their privacy than the Newbolts.

Husbands and wives had some segregated relationships with neighbours, but they could also make joint relationships if all four partners to the relationship liked one another. Some relationships were usually kept up with friends who had been made outside the area. Couples usually tried to arrange joint visits with these friends. These friends usually did not become intimate with the neighbours, however, so that the network remained fairly loose-knit.

Relations with relatives were much like those described above for the second set of families. But if relatives were living in the same local area as the family, there was considerable visiting and exchange of services, and if relatives lived close to one another, the kinship network was fairly close-knit.

The networks of these families were thus less close-knit than that of the Newbolts, but more close-knit than that of the second set of families. There was some overlapping of roles. Neighbours were sometimes friends; some relatives were both neighbours and friends. The overlapping was not as complete as with the Newbolts, but there was not the complete division into separate categories characteristic of the second set of families. The networks of husband and wife were less segregated from each other than those of the Newbolts, but more segregated than those of the second set of families.

b. Conjugal role-segregation. In external relationships husband and wife thus had some joint relationships, particularly with relatives and friends, and some segregated relationships, particularly with neighbours and local clubs.

In carrying out household tasks and child care, there was a fairly well-defined division of labour, a little more clearly marked than in the second type of family, more flexible than in the case of the Newbolts. Husbands helped, but there was a greater expectation of help from neighbours and relatives (if they lived nearby) than among the second set of families. Mrs Hartley summed up the division of labour between herself and her husband as follows:

'We knew we would fall somewhere between the two extremes of doing everything together and doing nothing together, but we didn't know just where, and we thought we would be able to work it out without any trouble.'

The division of labour in child care was similar to that of families with loose-knit networks. But on the whole, parents were less self-conscious about themselves as parents and there was not so wide a gulf between parents and children. Women complained less of being cooped up with their children, partly because they got more help from neighbours and relatives, but partly also because their children spent a lot of time playing outside with the neighbouring children. On the whole, they were less uneasy about such play than the second set of families because most of them lived in areas where they felt the neighbours were socially similar to themselves.

c. Attitudes towards the role-relationship of husband and wife. Although there were variations of degree, considerable stress was placed on the importance of shared interests and joint activities for a happy marriage. In general, the greater the stress placed on joint organization and shared interests, the greater the importance attached to sexual relations. Like the families with loose-knit networks, the intermediate families stressed the necessity for conjugal privacy and the precedence of the conjugal relationship over external relationships, but there was a greater tolerance of social and temperamental differences between the sexes and an easier acceptance of segregation in the activities of husband and wife. Wives often wanted some special interest of their own other than housework and children, but they were able to find activities such as attending evening classes or local clubs that could be carried on without interfering with their housework and child care. And because most of them felt that some of the neighbouring women were similar to themselves, they found it relatively easy to make friends among them. They complained less frequently of isolation and boredom than the wives in families with very loose-knit networks.

4. Transitional Families

There were five families in varying states of transition from one type of network to another. Two phases of transition can be distinguished among these five families: (a) families in the process of deciding to move from one local area to another, a decision that was requiring considerable restructuring of their networks, and (b) families who had radically changed their pattern of external relationships and had not yet adapted themselves fully to their new situation. Other families had gone through the process of transition and had more or less settled down to the pattern typical of families with loose-knit or medium-knit networks.

a. Families in process of deciding to move. There were two such families. Both had relatively close-knit networks, and both had been socially mobile and were contemplating moving to suburban areas more compatible with their new social status. In both cases this meant cutting off old social ties with relatives and neighbours and building up new ones. One couple, not quite ready to break with the old network, said they did not want to lower their current standard of living by spending a lot of money on a house. The second family moved after the interviewing was completed and a brief return visit suggested that they would in time build up the intermediate type of network and conjugal role-segregation.

b. Families in process of radical transition. There were three such families. All three had been brought up in close-knit networks similar to that of the Newbolts and all had moved away from their old areas and from the people of their networks. For such a family, any move outside the area is a drastic step. This contrasts with the intermediate families who were not too much upset by moving provided they moved to an area inhabited by people felt to be socially similar to themselves.

One family had been very mobile occupationally, although they had moved primarily because of the requirements of the husband's occupation rather than to find a neighbourhood compatible with their achieved status. They were living in relative isolation, with very few friends, almost no contacts with neighbours, and very little contact with relatives, most of whom lived at a considerable distance. They seemed to be rather stunned by the change. They had some segregated interests, but they felt joint organization and shared interests were the best basis of a conjugal relationship.

The other two families, the Dodgsons and the Butlers, were working-class and had not been occupationally mobile. These two families were particularly important to the conceptual analysis of conjugal role-segregation, for although they were similar to the Newbolts in occupational level and in general cultural background, their conjugal relationships were more joint. It was their relatively loose-knit networks that distinguished them from the Newbolts. Their networks had become loose-knit when they moved away from their old neighbourhoods.[1]

These two families had moved because they could not find suitable accommodation in their old neighbourhoods. They also wanted the amenities of a modern flat, and since their parents had died and many of their relatives had moved away, they felt their main ties with the old area were gone. Both couples seemed to feel they were strangers in a land full of people who were all strangers to one another, and at first they did not know how to cope with the situation. They did not react to their new situation in exactly the same way. In both cases, husband and wife had turned to one another for help, especially at first, but for various personal reasons, one couple continued to make a concerted effort

[1] Several other studies confirm this finding. Young and Willmott (1957) report that Bethnal Green families who moved to a housing estate at Debden had less contact with relatives and developed a more joint relationship between husband and wife, even when the husband's occupation remained unchanged. Mogey (1955 and 1956) similarly reports that families who moved to a new housing estate in Oxford developed a less rigid division of labour and less contact with relatives. Kuper, Mitchell, and Lupton, and Smith and Hodges all report an increased desire for privacy on housing estates, although they do not make so detailed an analysis of changes in external relationships and in the conjugal relationship as Young and Mogey (Kuper, 1953; Mitchell and Lupton, 1954; Hodges and Smith, 1954).

to develop joint activities and shared interests, whereas the second couple, especially the husband, did not take to the idea of a joint role-relationship with any enthusiasm.

The first couple tried to develop more joint relationships with friends, but this was difficult for them because they had had so little practice. They did not know the culture of a joint role-relationship, and their new acquaintances were in a similar predicament so that they got little external support for their efforts. The husband tried to persuade his wife to join in his club activities, but the structure of the club was such that her activities remained segregated from his. He helped his wife extensively with household tasks and child care, although he continued to control the family finances. In the second case, the husband busied himself with his work and friends and various committees. His wife was becoming isolated and withdrawn into the home. They had more joint organization of domestic tasks than before; she urged him to help her because her female relatives lived too far away to be of much assistance.

In both cases, however, nothing could really take the place of the old network built up from childhood, and both couples felt a good deal of personal dissatisfaction. The husbands were less drastically affected since they continued to work at their old jobs and their relationships with colleagues gave them considerable continuity. Both husbands and wives often blamed their physical surroundings for their malaise, and they idealized their old areas. They remembered only the friendliness and forgot the physical inconvenience and the unpleasant part of the gossip. Although one family had carried the process further than the other, both seemed to be developing a more joint division of labour than they had had before, and it seemed they would eventually settle down in some intermediate form of network-connectedness and conjugal role-segregation.

The research set did not contain any families who had moved from a loose-knit to a more close-knit network. But personal knowledge of families undergoing such change suggests that this type of change is also felt to be somewhat unpleasant. The privacy of husband and wife is encroached upon, and each is expected to take part in segregated activities, a state of affairs they regard as provincial. Such couples can refuse to enter the local network of social relationships, but in most cases they feel the husband's career requires it.

C. THE NATURE OF THE RELATIONSHIP
BETWEEN SEGREGATION OF CONJUGAL ROLES
AND CONNECTEDNESS OF NETWORKS

The data having been described, the nature of the relationship between conjugal segregation and network-connectedness may now be re-examined in general terms.

Close-knit networks are most likely to develop when husband and wife, together with their friends, neighbours, and relatives, have grown up in the same local area and have continued to live there after marriage. Many people know one another and have known one another since childhood. Women tend to associate with women and men with men. The only legitimate forms of heterosexual relationship are those between kin and between husband and wife. Friendship between a man and woman who are not kin is suspect.

In such a setting, husband and wife come to marriage each with his own close-knit network. Each partner makes a considerable emotional investment in relationships with the people in his network. Each is engaged in reciprocal exchanges of material and emotional support with them. Each is very sensitive to their opinions and values, not only because the relationships are intimate, but also because the people in the network know one another and share the same norms so that they are able to apply consistent informal sanctions to one another. The marriage is superimposed on these pre-existing relationships.

Although the networks of husband and wife are distinct, it is very likely, even at the time of marriage, that there will be overlapping between them. Judging by the Newbolts' account of their genealogy, one of the common ways for husband and wife

to meet is through introduction by a person who is simultaneously a friend of one and a relative of the other. Male relatives of
the wife are likely to be friends or colleagues of the husband, and,
after a marriage has continued for some time, the husbands of a
set of sisters are likely to become friends.

As long as the couple continue to live in the same area, and as
long as their friends, neighbours, and relatives also continue to
live within easy reach of the family and of one another, so long
will the segregated networks of husband and wife continue, with
minor changes. The husband is likely to stop seeing some friends
of his youth, particularly those who work at a different place or
go to different pubs and clubs. After children are born, the wife
will see less of her former girl-friends and more of her mother
and other female relatives. The wife becomes deeply embedded
in activities with kin. Her children bring her into a new and even
closer relationship with her own mother, who now becomes the
children's grandmother. The husband is to some extent drawn
into his wife's kinship circle, although he keeps in touch at least
with his own mother. But more of his time is spent with colleagues and friends than with relatives. His life is centred on work
and some form of recreation away from home; his wife's life is
centred on her home, her children, and her relatives.

The data suggest that the woman's network of kin is likely to
be more close-knit than the husband's network of friends, partly
because relationships with kin are harder to break off, but also
because kin have more mutual aid and material assistance to offer
one another. Friends cannot use their resources, particularly their
slender financial resources, to help one another when their first
obligation is to look after their own wives and children and then
their parents and more distant relatives. But this difference in
degree of connectedness within the total network needs further
and more precise study. It would be necessary to compare the
type and degree of intimacy and obligation toward friends,
neighbours, and relatives. It would also be necessary to quantify
the connectedness not only of the total network, but also of that
part of the network composed of kin, that composed of friends,

and that composed of neighbours, and it would be advisable to compare the connectedness of the total network with that of the independent networks of husband and wife and with that of their joint network.

Apart from minor readjustments, then, husband and wife can carry on their old external relationships after marriage, and they continue to be influenced by them. In spite of the conjugal segregation in external relationships the overlapping of the networks of husband and wife tends to ensure that each partner learns about the other's activities. Although a wife may not know directly what a husband does when with his friends, one of the other men is likely to tell his wife or some female relative and the information is passed on. Similarly any important activity of the wife is likely to be made known to her husband.

Because old relationships can be continued after marriage, both husband and wife can satisfy some personal needs outside the marriage, so that their emotional investment in the conjugal relationship need not be as intense as it is in other types of family. The wife, particularly, can get outside help with domestic tasks and with child care. A rigid division of labour between husband and wife is therefore possible. The segregation in external relationships can be carried over to activities within the family.

But although external people may help the elementary family, close-knit networks may also interfere with conjugal solidarity. A wife's loyalty to her mother may interfere with her relationship with her husband. Similarly her relationship with her husband may interfere with her relationship with her mother. A man's loyalty to his friends may interfere with his obligations to his wife and vice versa.

Networks become loose-knit when people move from one place to another or when they make new relationships not connected with their old ones. If both husband and wife have moved considerably before marriage, each will bring an already loose-knit network to the marriage. Many of the husband's friends will not know one another; many of the wife's friends will not know one another. Although they will continue to see some old friends after marriage, they will meet new people too, who will not necessarily know the old friends or one another. In other words, their external relationships are relatively discontinuous both in space and in time. Such continuity as they possess lies in their relationship with each other rather than in their external relationships. In facing the external world they draw on each other, for their strongest emotional investment is made where there is continuity. Hence their high standards of conjugal compatibility, their stress on shared interests, on joint organization, on equality between husband and wife. They must get along well together, they must help one another in carrying out familial tasks, for there is no sure external source of material and emotional help. Since their friends and relatives are physically scattered and few of them know one another, the husband and wife are not stringently controlled by a solid body of public opinion. They are also unable to rely on consistent external support. Through their joint external relationships they present a united front to the world and they reaffirm their joint relationship with each other. Joint relationships with friends give both husband and wife a source of emotional satisfaction outside the family without threatening their relationship with each other. Heterosexual relationships with non-kin are allowed, but they are controlled by being made into joint relationships.

Between these two extremes are the families with medium-knit and transitional networks. In the medium-knit type, husband and wife have moved a certain amount so that they seek continuity with each other and make their strongest emotional investment in the conjugal relationship. At the same time, they are able to have some segregated relationships outside the family and to rely on considerable casual help from people outside the family, so that a fairly clearly defined division of labour into male tasks and female tasks can be made.

The transitional families illustrate some of the factors involved in changing from one type of network to another. Husbands and wives who change from a close-knit to a loose-knit network find themselves suddenly thrust into a more joint relationship without the experience or the attitudes appropriate to it. The eventual out-come depends partly on the family and partly on the extent to which their new neighbours build up relationships with one another. An intermediate form of network-connectedness seems to be the most likely outcome. Similarly, in the case of families who change from a loose-knit to a more close-knit network, the first reaction is one of defensiveness over their privacy, but in time they tend to develop an intermediate degree of network-con-nectedness and conjugal segregation.

CHAPTER IV

Factors Affecting Social Networks

Having discussed the relationship between segregation of conjugal roles and connectedness of social networks, I should like now to consider the factors affecting connectedness itself. In the next chapter an attempt is made to show how these various factors work out in the particular case of kinship, but here the aim is to point out in general terms what the factors are.

On the basis of the facts collected from the research families, it is impossible to analyse the pattern of forces affecting their networks. In order to consider these factors at all, it is necessary to go beyond the field data to draw on general knowledge of urban industrialized society. In the following discussion I consider the general features characteristic of all familial networks in an urban industrialized society and then some of the factors affecting variations from one network to another.

This is no simple matter. In part, network-connectedness depends on the family themselves. One family may choose to introduce their friends, neighbours, and relatives to one another, whereas another may not. One family may move a great deal so that its network becomes loose-knit, whereas another family may stay put. The personalities of husband and wife are one very important factor affecting such choices, but choice is also limited and shaped by a number of forces over which the family does not have direct control. It is at this point that the total social environment becomes relevant. The economic and occupational system, the structure of formal institutions, the ecology of cities, and many

97

other factors affect the connectedness of networks by limiting and shaping the decisions that families make. These factors do not operate singly, but rather in most complex combinations. Among others, factors associated with social class and neighbourhood composition affect segregation of conjugal roles, not solely and not primarily through direct action on the internal structure of the family, but indirectly through their effect on its network. Conceptually, the network stands between the family and the total social environment. The variability in the total environment permits choice in the field of external social relationships; choice is affected both by situational factors and by the personalities of the members of the family.

A. FACTORS AFFECTING THE GENERAL FEATURES
OF URBAN FAMILIAL NETWORKS

As described above, all the research families maintained relationships with external people and institutions—with a place of work, with service institutions such as school, church, doctor, clinic, shops, with voluntary associations such as clubs, evening classes, and recreational institutions. They also maintained more informal relationships with colleagues, friends, neighbours, and relatives. It is therefore incorrect to describe these families as 'isolated'; indeed no urban family could survive without its network of external relationships.

However, although urban families have many external relationships, they are not contained within organized groups. The institutions and persons with which they are related are not linked up with one another to form an organized group. Although individual members of a family frequently belong to groups, the family as a whole does not. There are marginal cases, as when all the members of the family belong to the same church or consult the same general practitioner, but in these cases the external institution or person controls only one aspect of the family's life and can hardly be said to 'contain' the family in all its aspects.

In the literature on family sociology, there are frequent references to 'the family in the community', with the implication that the community is an organized group within which the family is contained. Our data suggest that this usage is misleading. Of course every family must live in some sort of local area, but few urban local areas can be called communities in the sense that they form cohesive social groups. The immediate social environment of urban families is best considered not as the local area in which they live, but rather as the network of actual social relationships they maintain, regardless of whether these are confined to the local area or run beyond its boundaries. ·

Small-scale, more isolated, relatively 'closed', local groups provide a marked contrast. This type of community is frequently encountered in primitive societies, and in certain rural areas of industrialized societies. A family in such a local group knows no privacy; everyone knows everyone else. The situation of the urban family with a close-knit network is carried one step further in the relatively closed local group. In many cases the networks of the component families are so closely connected and the relationships within the local group are so clearly marked off from external relationships that the local population can properly be called an organized group. Families are encapsulated within this group. Their activities are known to all and they cannot escape from the informal sanctions of gossip and public opinion. Their external affairs are governed by the group to which they belong.

In many small-scale primitive societies, the elementary family is encapsulated not only within a local group but also, particularly in the sphere of domestic affairs, within a corporate kin group. But when there are exogamous corporate kin groups, the conjugal partner who marries into the corporate kin group is always in a special position. Politically, jurally, and ritually, she (or he, in the case of matrilineal systems) remains affiliated with the corporate kin group she was born into. When there are corporate local groups and kin groups, segregation of conjugal roles is likely to become even more marked than that described above for urban families with close-knit networks. Marriage becomes a linking of kin groups rather than preponderantly a union between individuals acting on their own initiative.

These differences between the immediate social environment of families in urban industrialized societies and that of families in some small-scale primitive and rural communities exist, ultimately, because of differences in the total economic and social structure. The division of labour in a small-scale society is relatively simple; the division of labour in an industrial society is exceedingly complex. In a small-scale, relatively closed society, most of the services required by a family can be provided by the other families in the local group and in the kin group. In an urban industrialized society, such tasks and services are divided up and assigned to specialized institutions. Whereas a family in a small-scale, relatively closed society belongs to a small number of groups each with many functions, an urban family exists in a network of many separate, unconnected institutions each with a specialized function. In a small-scale relatively closed society the local group and the kin group mediate between the family and the total society; in an urban industrialized society there is no single encapsulating group or institution that mediates between the family and the total society.

One of the results of this difference in the form of external relationships is that urban families have more freedom to govern their own affairs. In a small-scale society the encapsulating groups have a great deal of control over the family. In an urban industrialized society the doctor looks after the health of individual members of the family, the clinic looks after the health of the mother and child, the school educates children, the boss cares about the individual as an employee rather than as a husband, and even friends, neighbours, and relatives may disagree among themselves as to how the affairs of the family should be conducted. In brief, social control of the family is split up among so many agencies that no one of them has continuous, complete, governing power, and within broad limits, a family can make its own decisions and regulate its own affairs.

The situation may be summed up by saying that urban families are more highly *individuated* than families in relatively closed\ communities. I think this term describes the situation of urban families more accurately than the more commonly used term 'isolated'. By 'individuation' I mean that the elementary family is separated off, differentiated out as a distinct, and to some extent autonomous, social group. Of course in most societies the elementary family is individuated to some extent; one could not say it existed as a distinct group if it were not. The difference in individuation between an urban family and a family in a relatively closed community is one of degree. It should be remembered, however, that urban families differ among themselves in degree of individuation; families with close-knit networks are less individuated than those with loose-knit networks.

The individuation of urban families provides one source of variation in role performance. Because families are not encapsulated within governing and controlling groups, other than the nation as a whole, husband and wife are able, within broad limits, to perform their roles in accordance with their own personal needs. These broad limits are laid down by the norms of the nation as a whole, many of which exist as laws and are enforced by the courts. But informal social control by relatives and neighbours is much less stringent and less consistent than in many small-scale societies, and much variation is possible.

B. FACTORS AFFECTING VARIATIONS IN CONNECTEDNESS

Although the immediate social environments of all urban families resemble one another in assuming network form, there are important differences from one urban family's network to another. As has been demonstrated in the preceding chapter, one important type of difference is the degree of connectedness of the network. Such differences are most clearly marked in the area of informal relationships, that is, in relationships with friends, neighbours, and relatives. These relationships are felt to be of much greater personal and emotional importance than the more specialized and formal relationships that are maintained with doctors, clinics, schools, and so forth, and they are usually maintained with people who are felt to be socially similar to the family themselves.

The highly developed division of labour in an industrial society produces not only complexity but also variability. Sometimes conditions are created that favour the development of relatively close-knit networks, sometimes conditions are created that favour relatively loose-knit networks. To examine these conditions in detail would take the discussion far away from families and their networks into a study of the ecology of cities and the economic structure of industries and occupations, a task obviously beyond the scope of this chapter. I should like, however, to suggest tentatively several factors that appear likely to affect connectedness. The situation is very complicated, for these factors are partly dependent on one another and they operate not singly but in complex combinations.

1. *Economic Ties among the Members of the Network*

Economic ties operate more forcibly between relatives than between friends and neighbours, but there is a wide range of variation in the operation of such cohesive forces even among relatives. The connectedness of the kinship network is enhanced if relatives hold property rights in common enterprises, or if they expect to inherit property from one another.

Connectedness of kinship networks is also increased if relatives can help one another to get jobs. Only certain types of occupation allow such help; in occupations requiring examinations or other objective selection procedures—and most professional and semi-professional occupations fall into this category—relatives cannot give one another much help in this respect, whereas in some less skilled occupations and in certain businesses, particularly family businesses, relatives are able to help one another more directly.[1] (This will be discussed further in Chapter V.)

---

[1] Cf. Talcott Parsons (1943 and 1949). But where Parsons stresses the uniform action of the economic and occupational systems in making the elementary family individuated, I emphasize the varied effects produced by different types of job and occupational structure.

The important point here is that neither the occupational system nor the distribution of property is uniform. Different families are affected in different ways. This means that although families' networks in general and their kinship networks in particular do not play a very large part in the economic and occupational structure, there is a great deal of variation in the way in which economic forces affect families' networks.

2. Type of Neighbourhood

Type of neighbourhood is important not so much in and of itself, but because it is one of the factors affecting the 'localization' of networks. If a family's network is localized, that is, if most of the members live in the same local area so that they are accessible to one another, they are more likely to know one another than if they are scattered all over the country.

Since the members of the informal network are usually felt by the family to have the same social status as themselves, localized networks are most likely to develop in areas where the inhabitants feel that they are socially similar to one another, that they belong to the same social class, whatever their definition of class may be. Such feelings of social similarity appear to be strongest in long-established working-class areas in which there is a dominant local industry or a relatively small number of traditional occupations. As described above, the Newbolts, the family with the most close-knit network, were living in such an area. It was also an area of low population turnover, at least until the recent war. Formerly the same people lived there all their lives. Close-knit networks could develop not only because the local area was homogeneous but also because there was continuity. Now, as some of the inhabitants move away, the networks of even those people who remain in the area are becoming less connected.

In the research set there were no comparable homogeneous neighbourhoods of people belonging to one of the full professions. Neighbourhoods were found, however, in which the inhabitants were relatively homogeneous with regard to income, although they had different occupations. The type and cost of the dwelling were probably an important factor contributing to this type of homogeneity. Such neighbourhoods were found in suburbs; they were also found in certain mixed working-class areas in which there was no dominant local industry. Most of the families with intermediate and transitional networks were living in such areas. One family with a loose-knit network was living in an area of this kind, but they ignored their neighbours, who they felt were socially similar to one another but not to themselves. Finally, there were some areas that were extremely heterogeneous with regard to occupational level, income, educational background of the inhabitants and so forth; four of the families with very loose-knit networks were living in such areas.

In a very complex way, neighbourhood composition is related to occupation and social class. It is possible to have fairly homogeneous areas of, say, dockworkers, or furniture workers, although not all manual occupations are heavily localized. But the structure of the professions is such that it would be most unusual to find a homogeneous area of, say, doctors or lawyers or chartered accountants. On the basis of our data on families, no attempt can be made to analyse the many factors contributing to the formation of local neighbourhoods. The most one can say is that the industrial and occupational system is so complex that it gives rise to many different types of urban neighbourhood. Some are more homogeneous and stable than others. If one were making a detailed study of network-connectedness in relation to neighbourhood composition, it would be necessary to work out criteria of homogeneity so that neighbourhoods could be systematically compared. One could then study the relation of different degrees and types of objective homogeneity to the attitudes of local inhabitants towards one another. One could also compare the formation of the networks of families in different types of area. My guess would be that one would not find families with close-knit networks in heterogeneous areas of high population turnover, but that one might find both families with close-knit networks and families with loose-knit networks in relatively homogeneous, stable areas.

It is most unlikely that one would be able to predict degree of connectedness from knowledge of the local area alone. Too many other factors are involved—type of occupation, where the husband works, how long the family has lived in the area, perception of the area, and so forth. The family's perception of the people in the area is particularly important. Objective measures of social homogeneity give only a rough indication of how families will feel about their neighbours. Furthermore, it is always necessary to remember that a neighbourhood does not simply impose itself *Some are* on a family. Within certain limits families can choose where they *more limited* will live, and even if they feel that their neighbours are similar to *than others* themselves they are not compelled to be friendly with them; other criteria besides felt social similarity enter into the selection of friends.

3. *Opportunities to Make Relationships outside the Existing Network*

Networks are more likely to be close-knit if members do not have many opportunities to form new relationships with persons unknown to the other members of the network. Thus, in the case of the Newbolts, the husband's work, the relatives of husband and wife, and their friends were all concentrated in the local area. There are no strong sanctions preventing such families from making relationships with outsiders, but there is no unavoidable circumstance that forces them to do so. In the case of the professional families, on the other hand, their education and professional training had led them to make many relationships with colleagues and friends who did not know one another. Even if such families keep on living in the same area throughout their lives, which is unusual though possible, the husband's pursuit of an occupational career leads him to make relationships with people who do not belong to the family's neighbourhood network, so that the network tends to become loose-knit.

In brief, connectedness does depend, in part, on the husband's occupation. If he is engaged in an occupation in which his colleagues are also his neighbours, his network will tend to be localized and its connectedness will tend to be high. If he is engaged in an occupation in which his colleagues are not his neighbours, his network will tend to become loose-knit. One cannot predict this solely from knowledge of occupational level. Most professional occupations require a man to get his training and do his work in different areas from the one he lives in. Some manual occupations require or permit this too; others do not.

4. Physical and Social Mobility

Network-connectedness depends on the stability and continuity of the relationships. A family's network will become more loose-knit if either the family or the other members of the network move away physically or socially so that contact is decreased and new relationships are established.[1]

Table 4 gives some indication of the relationship between connectedness and physical mobility among the research families. (No systematic information is available on the physical mobility of the members of their networks.) The numbers are too small to be taken very seriously, but it is evident that on the average, the families with loose-knit networks had lived in far more places than those with medium-knit, transitional, and close-knit networks.

Many factors affect physical mobility. Here again the occupational system is a relevant factor. Some occupations permit or encourage social and physical mobility so that networks become loose-knit; other occupations encourage stability of residence and social relationships. Physical mobility is often associated with occupational and social mobility. In the research set, eight husbands had been occupationally mobile. Three of these families had moved or were contemplating moving to an area appropriate to their achieved status. The other five had moved too, but not primarily for status reasons. In general, the networks of socially mobile families tend to become less connected not only because they move physically but also because they are likely to drop old

---

[1] Some effects of physical mobility on families' external relationships are clearly shown in the work of Young and Willmott (1957) and Mogey (1955 and 1956). Contact with kin and friends in the old area is gradually reduced.

TABLE 4

TOTAL NUMBER OF LOCAL AREAS LIVED IN BY HUSBAND AND WIFE BOTH BEFORE AND AFTER MARRIAGE*

Type of network	Family	Total number of areas lived in by each husband and wife	Average number of areas lived in by husband and wife for each type of network formation
Close-knit	Newbolt	2	2
Loose-knit	Daniels	19	19
	Woodman	19	
	Bullock	9	
	Denton	26	
	Bruce	22	
Medium-knit	Jarrold	25	8.2
	Salmon	6	
	Hartley	7	
	Thornton	10	
	Fawcett	5	
	Appleby	9	
	Apsley	6	
	Baldock	3	
	Mudge	3	
Transitional	Redfern	7	9.6
	Barkway	6	
	Wraith	10	
	Butler	11	
	Dodgson	14	

*If husband and wife were brought up in the same area, it is counted only once. In all cases service career is counted as one 'area'.

social ties and form new ones. Among the mobile families of the research set, most of the rearranging had been done in adolescence and in the early years of the marriage, and it involved chiefly friends and distant relatives. However mobile the family, husband and wife felt an obligation to maintain contact with their parents; occupational and social achievements were usually felt to be a positive accomplishment for parents as well as for the husband and wife themselves.

Occupation may affect physical mobility even when there is no social mobility. Among the research families many of the professional couples had moved frequently from one local area to another and even from one city to another, and they tended to treat the requirements of the husband's career as the most important factor in deciding whether to move or not. This applied as much to families who were not socially mobile as to those who were. The manual and clerical workers were less likely to give the demands of the husband's career as a chief reason for moving, and only one such family had moved very frequently. The relations between occupation and physical and social mobility are obviously very complex. The important fact is that the occupational system is not uniform; it permits much variation in physical and social mobility and hence much variation in connectedness of networks.

But decisions to move depend not only on occupational considerations but also on the housing shortage, the type and cost of the house or flat, the family's views on the welfare of their children, relations with relatives, neighbours and friends in the old area and potential relations in the new area, and doubtless many other factors as well. All these considerations must be weighed together when the decision to move is made, although one or other factor may be dominant. Sometimes all considerations point in the same direction; more frequently they have to be balanced against one another. But whatever the reasons, once the move has been made the family's network becomes less connected. Even if the family itself does not move, its network will become less connected if friends and relatives move away.

Connectedness thus depends on a very complex combination of economic and social forces. Instead of the relatively homogeneous environment of a small-scale, relatively closed society, the total environment of an urban family is exceedingly complex and variable. Many forces affect a family's network, and there is considerable latitude for the family to choose among several courses of action; a wide range of variation is possible.

5. Personality Characteristics as a Factor Affecting Connectedness

The connectedness of a family's network depends not only on external social forces, but also on the family itself. Although the members of a family cannot control the forces of the total environment, they can select from among the various courses of action to which these forces give rise. It is the variability of the total environment that makes choice possible, but it is the family that makes the actual decisions. Decisions are shaped by situational factors, but they also depend on the personalities of the members of the family, on the way they react to the situational factors.

Because of particular combinations of situational factors and personal needs, husband and wife may affect the connectedness of their network, often without any deliberate intention of doing so. By changing the connectedness of their network they affect in turn their conjugal segregation. Thus, if a family with a close-knit network move out of their old area to a new housing estate, their network will rapidly become less connected and for a time at least husband and wife will develop a more joint relationship with each other. If a professional couple with a loose-knit network move to a university town because of the husband's career, their network is likely to become slightly more connected even though they may not plan to make it so. If a couple with a loose-knit network decides to move to a distant suburb because that is the only place where they can find a house they can afford to buy, they may find themselves extremely isolated—cut off from their friends, unable to make relationships easily with their neighbours, and even more dependent on each other than usual.

Among the research set there were several couples who, for various personal reasons, had almost no informal network at all. Two families were living in a state of voluntary isolation or near-isolation. They kept up necessary contacts with service institutions, paid a few duty visits to relatives, and had superficial contacts with neighbours, but that was all. In so far as they had informal networks they were loose-knit, but there were far fewer members in them than usual.

One of the intermediate families could, if they had wished, have had a network almost as close-knit as that of the Newbolts, for they were living in an area where many of their relatives lived and worked, and at least by objective criteria, their neighbours were socially similar to themselves. But their personal needs were such that they had cut themselves off from this close-knit network. The husband was completely absorbed in his work and his home; the wife kept up the most important external relationship, that with her mother, but she had relatively little contact with other kin, and she had substituted work in a voluntary association for contacts with neighbours. This couple had a more joint division of labour than the Newbolts. They also had more shared interests and joint recreation. I suspect this family had had to withstand a certain amount of disapproval by relatives and neighbours, but they had reached the point where they felt impervious to their criticism. They liked their own way of doing things. Families of this type, aware that their behaviour does not coincide exactly with their own norms, feel slightly deviant, although they usually do not like to discuss the matter unless they feel they are above the norm rather than below it. (Deviance will be more fully discussed in Chapter VII, which deals with norms.)

Voluntary isolation of this sort produces the same effect as a loose-knit network. Husband and wife must depend on each other for help and companionship and they tend to adhere to the norms of a joint relationship.

Personality characteristics may thus indirectly affect segregation of conjugal roles because they are a factor in shaping choices that affect the form of the family's network. But personal needs and attitudes, both conscious and unconscious, also directly affect performance of conjugal roles. Two families may have similar networks but slightly different degrees of conjugal segregation. Thus, two of the transitional families discussed in Chapter III were living in approximately the same social situation, but one couple were trying to develop as joint a conjugal relationship as possible, whereas the other couple were not. Personality factors are of necessity involved in performance of familial roles—or of any role for that matter—but it is only where there is a lack of fit between the personal needs of husband and wife, the social situation in which they find themselves, and the expectations of the members of their networks that such needs stand out clearly as a separate factor.

C. THE RELATION OF CONNECTEDNESS
TO SOCIAL CLASS

Because of the complexity of the situation it is not surprising that we could not find a simple correlation between class position and segregation of conjugal roles. On this point the literature is incomplete and self-contradictory. I have not found any studies in which both conjugal segregation and external social relationships are systematically compared according to class. Most of the studies reporting marked conjugal segregation concern working-class families (Hopkinson, 1954; Jephcott and Carter, 1955; Kerr, 1955; Mays, 1954; Packer, 1947; Shaw, 1954; Slater and Woodside, 1951). But Young and Mogey report considerable variation in external social relationships and in the conjugal relationship among families of the same, working-class, status. In these cases physical movement was the important factor in reducing connectedness and segregation (Young and Willmott, 1957, and Mogey, 1955 and 1956). Considerable variation in these respects among working-class families can also be inferred from the work of Jephcott and Carter (Jephcott and Carter, 1955). Wilson reports a rigid division of labour between husband and wife at all social levels in a mining town (Wilson, C. S., 1953). Several American studies, chiefly by students and colleagues of Warner, report marked differences in family life according to class, but they are concerned with general patterns and do not deal with variations within each class. There is little precise information on conjugal segregation or network-connectedness. (See Davis, 1941, 1943 and 1944; Davis and Havighurst, 1946 and 1947; Dollard, 1937; Maas, 1951; McGuire, 1951 and 1952.) The work of Herbst and Hammond in Australia contradicts the usual finding of greater conjugal segregation in the working class (Herbst, 1954, and

Hammond, 1954). Eighty-two per cent of husbands in the 'self-employed and employer class' had predominantly 'autonomic' (segregated) relationships with their wives, whereas 64 per cent of skilled workers had predominantly 'syncratic' (joint) relationships with their wives. Data are not given on external social relationships so that it is impossible to tell whether the families with 'autonomic' conjugal relationships had highly connected networks.

In my view segregation of conjugal roles is more directly related to connectedness of networks than to class status as such, although there are probably some aspects of class position that affect segregation of conjugal roles directly. For example, if both husband and wife are highly educated, they are likely to have a common background of shared interests and tastes, which makes a joint relationship easy to conduct. Although it is unlikely that teachers deliberately plan to teach children about joint conjugal relationships, higher education is probably a chief means of passing on the ethic appropriate to a joint relationship from one generation to another, and of teaching it to socially mobile individuals whose parents have had a more segregated relationship. But it is doubtful whether such education alone could produce joint conjugal relationships; it works in conjunction with other factors.

But for the most part factors associated with class—however one defines that complex construct—affect segregation of conjugal roles indirectly through having an effect on the connectedness of the family's network. To sum up the empirical resultant: families with close-knit networks are likely to be working class. But not all working-class families will have close-knit networks.

It is only in the working class that one is likely to find a combination of factors all operating together to produce a high degree of connectedness: concentration of people of the same or similar occupations in the same local area; jobs and homes in the same local area; low population turnover and continuity of relationships; at least occasional opportunities for relatives and friends to help one another to get jobs; little demand for physical mobility; little opportunity for social mobility.

In contrast, the structure of professions is such that this pattern of forces almost never occurs. Homogeneous local areas of a single profession are very rare; a man's place of work and his home are usually in different local areas; professional training leads him to make relationships with people who do not know his family, school friends, and neighbours; in most cases getting a job depends on skill and training rather than on the influence of friends and relatives; many professional careers require physical mobility. Almost the only factor associated with high class status that tends to increase connectedness is ownership of shares in common enterprises by relatives—and this is less likely to occur among professional people than among wealthy industrialists and commercial families.

But because a man has a manual occupation he will not automatically have a close-knit network. He may be living in a relatively heterogeneous area, for not all manual occupations are localized. He may live in one place and work in another. He may move from one area to another. Similarly his friends and relatives may move or make new relationships with people he does not know. A high degree of connectedness may be found in association with manual occupations, but the association is not necessary and inevitable.

In brief, one cannot explain connectedness as the result of the husband's occupational or class status considered as single determinants. Connectedness depends on a whole complex of forces—economic ties among members of the network, type of local area, opportunities to make new social contacts, physical and social mobility, etc.—generated by the occupational and economic systems, but these forces do not always work in the same direction and they may affect different families in different ways.

Finally, connectedness cannot be predicted from a knowledge of situational factors alone. It also depends on the family's personal response to the situations with which they are confronted, and this response depends in turn on their conscious and unconscious needs and attitudes.

CHAPTER V

Relationships With Kin

The last chapter was devoted to general discussion of the factors affecting the connectedness of families' networks. This chapter discusses the particular factors affecting one part of the network, that composed of kin. I am interested not only in the general structure of the kinship system, but also in the way it is handled in particular cases. The relationships of three families with their kin are compared and analysed in detail in an attempt to interpret variations in patterns of contact.

Genealogies were collected from all couples, usually in the first three or four interviews. The field worker asked about the age, occupation, residence, and marital status of all known relatives. Couples were also asked about their contacts with kin in the past and at the time of interviewing. No attempt was made to collect precise information on kinship terminology. Comments about kin that were made in the course of general discussions or interviews on other topics were noted, and a record was kept of all contacts with kin mentioned throughout the interviews. Occasionally the field workers met relatives when they came to call on the family, but for reasons discussed in Chapter II, no attempt was made to interview either these relatives or others. Couples were encouraged to talk about their relatives in detail if they wished to do so, and no attempt was made to restrict them to a precise list of questions. Some couples talked spontaneously about relatives much more than others, partly because they were interested in the topic and partly because they could sense whether the field worker was particularly interested. Because of these variations, and because interviews with the first four or five families were less systematic than those with subsequent families, more material on kinship was collected from some families than from others. Relatively complete data are available for the three cases selected for detailed comparison.

A. THE GENERAL CHARACTERISTICS OF WESTERN EUROPEAN KINSHIP SYSTEMS

It is a commonplace of sociology and anthropology that kinship does not play a very important part in industrialized societies. The elementary family of father, mother, and dependent children is said to stand alone. Relations with other kin are not considered important, except in certain rural areas (Arensberg and Kimball, 1948; Rees, 1950; Brown, 1952; Curle, 1952). But very few field studies have been made of kinship in urban areas. Talcott Parsons has presented an analysis that is of primary importance as an interpretation of the effect of the occupational system on the kinship system, but it is not based on field research and it is confined to the kinship system of the middle class (Parsons, 1943 and 1949). In one of the few empirical studies of non-rural kinship, Bossard and Boll report considerable variation in relationships with kin as described by sixty-eight students (Bossard and Boll, 1946). Codere, on the other hand, reports that the genealogies of 200 Vassar girls were uniformly meagre and impoverished (Codere, 1955). Schneider and Homans present a suggestive analysis of American kinship terminology, but they make little attempt to study behaviour towards kin or to analyse the kinship system as such (Schneider and Homans, 1955). Several American studies give a certain amount of information on relationships with kin, but none presents a systematic analysis of the kinship system. Thus Dotson reports that fifty working-class families in New Haven had many relationships with kin but few with voluntary associations (Dotson, 1951); Albrecht reports a survey of contact between old people and their children (Albrecht, 1953 and 1954); von Hentig and Sussman report that parents help their married children with gifts and services and by acting as baby-sitters (von Hentig, 1946;

Sussman, 1953); according to Sussman, parents and married children are most likely to keep in touch with each other if the children marry people of similar cultural background (Sussman, 1954).

Firth appears to have made the first empirical study of urban kinship using a method of observation and interviews similar to that employed by social anthropologists in small-scale societies (Firth, 1956). He reports that English working-class and Italianate families in London have extensive and important relationships with their relatives. He also points out that, in a Western urban setting, kinship provides a field for personal choice and selectivity. Following these studies by Firth and his students, the Institute of Community Studies has made a detailed study of the relationships of working-class families with their relatives in Bethnal Green (Young, 1954a, 1954b, 1954c, 1956; Young and Willmott, 1957; Townsend, 1955a, 1955b and 1957).

In general these recent studies indicate that certain working-class families, at least, have a great deal of contact with their relatives. The elementary family does not stand alone; its members keep up frequent and intimate relationships with parents and with at least some of the siblings, uncles and aunts, and cousins of the husband and wife. But, at the same time, it is quite clear that kinship does not provide the basic framework of the total social structure as it does in so many small-scale primitive societies, even those with a bilateral kinship system of the same basic type as that found in Western Europe.

In bilateral kinship systems, persons are affiliated in the same way, actually or potentially, with both their mother's and their father's relatives and they may transmit rights and obligations, including rights to land and other property, to their sons, to their daughters, or to both (Rivers, 1924, p. 12; Murdock, 1949, pp. 44–5; Radcliffe-Brown, 1950, p. 13; Firth, 1955, p. 864; Barnes, 1955). In the English system the patrilineal inheritance of surnames and certain titles and the inheritance of certain landed estates by the eldest son give the system a slight patrilineal stress, although since the Administration of Estates Act of 1925 the law of intestacy has been completely bilateral and there are no formally prescribed differences in relationships with relatives on the paternal side and those on the maternal side.

In bilateral systems the characteristic social configurations that are defined purely in kinship terms are the 'unrestricted descent group' and the 'kindred' (Goodenough, 1955). The unrestricted descent group consists of all the descendants through men or women of a common ancestor. The kindred consists of a set of persons who have a relative in common, regardless of whether kinship is traced through men or women (Rivers, 1924, p. 16; Murdock, 1949, pp. 56–7; Goodenough, 1955, pp. 71–2). Each individual in the society, or rather each set of full siblings, will have a different kindred. With the exception of his full siblings, the various members of a person's kindred will have kindreds of their own that overlap but never coincide with one another. The kindred, therefore, is not a corporate group.

As Radcliffe-Brown has pointed out, all kinship systems are bilateral in the sense that individuals have personal networks of relationships with both paternal and maternal kin (Radcliffe-Brown, 1929, p. 50). But bilateral systems proper are distinguished by the absence of exclusive corporate kin groups recruited on the basis of descent. Of itself, bilateral descent cannot give rise to enduring corporate kin groups. Only unilineal descent can give rise to corporate groups defined purely in kinship terms. If exclusive, enduring corporate groups of kin are formed in a bilateral system, some additional non-kinship principle must be used as the basis of group formation. Corporate groups of kin may be formed on the basis of residence, according to land use as distinct from potential rights to use the land, or according to choice of affiliation with the kin-residence group of one parent rather than the other (Firth, 1929, p. 98; Goodenough, 1955). As Goodenough points out, all these principles may be considered as structural alternatives to the use of unilineal descent as a basis for the formation of corporate groups of kin.

In the bilateral systems of small-scale primitive societies, kinship is all-important in determining rights to land and other productive resources (Firth, 1929; Barton, 1919 and 1949; Gluckman,

1950; Morris, 1953; and Geddes, 1954). Here lies the chief difference from bilateral systems in urban industrialized societies. In England and other Western European industrialized societies, work groups are seldom recruited on the basis of kinship, individuals may earn a living without depending on relatives for their means of livelihood, productive resources may be owned by individuals who are not related to one another, and, although kinship obligations may play an important part in the disposal of property, many individuals do not own any productive resources and have indeed little property of any kind to bequeath to their descendants. Furthermore, the industrial and occupational system is so constituted that individuals may be mobile physically and occupationally so that relatives may be separated from one another both geographically and socially. This reduced importance of kinship in economic affairs is associated with a narrower range of kin recognition, with absence of corporate groups of kin recruited according to residence or some other non-kinship principle, with less frequent and intense contact among relatives and correspondingly greater individuation of elementary families, and with a much greater degree of variability in kinship and behaviour and norms.

In contrast with a small-scale primitive society, the articulation of the kinship system and the economic system in an industrialized society is exceedingly variable and complex. Within broad limits, the operation of the economic system permits a wide variation of kinship norms and behaviour. It creates variable conditions and permits a wide range of choice. Variability is a characteristic of the system. But, as I shall attempt to show, choice is not entirely random and unpredictable. By comparing the contacts of three families with their kin, I shall attempt to analyse several factors that limit and shape the choices families make in the field of relationships with kin.

B. FACTORS AFFECTING THE RELATIONSHIPS OF THREE FAMILIES WITH THEIR KIN

The three families are the Newbolts, the Hartleys, and the Daniels. The Newbolts have been described in Chapter III.

The Hartleys lived in a suburban neighbourhood and felt that their neighbours were broadly similar to themselves in occupational status and income. Mr Hartley was a sundry supplies buyer for a medium-sized industrial firm. Mrs Hartley did not have a job; she was fully occupied caring for their three small girls. The Hartleys described themselves as 'middle middle-class', adding that Mr Hartley's parents were 'working-class'. His father was dead; his mother lived in another neighbourhood in the same borough as the Hartleys themselves. Mrs Hartley's parents were both dead; her father had been an office manager in the north of England and the Hartleys described him as 'middle middle-class' like themselves.

The Daniels lived in a heterogeneous neighbourhood and had only a little contact with their neighbours. Mr Daniels was the deputy manager of the fire department of an insurance firm. Mrs Daniels was confidential secretary to the general manager of another insurance firm. They had two small children, a boy and a girl. The Daniels described themselves, with a slight smile, as 'upper working-class'. His father had been the manager of a small canning factory; her father used to own a shop, selling marine equipment. Both fathers were dead and both their mothers were alive.

Briefly, the contact of these three families with their kin may be summed up by saying that the Newbolts had a great deal of contact with their kin, the Hartleys had much less, and the Daniels still less. Similarly, the Newbolts' relatives had a great deal of contact with one another, the Hartleys' relatives had less, and the Daniels' relatives had still less.

A more precise indication of the three families' relationships with kin is given in *Table 5*.[1]

It will be observed that relationships with relatives have been classified into four degrees of social distance—'intimate', 'effective', 'non-effective', and 'unfamiliar'. This classification has been made on the basis of two related and overlapping criteria; inti-

[1] All tables in this chapter are presented as a form of condensed description; statistical procedures are not used analytically.

TABLE 5

RECOGNITION OF KIN AND RELATIONSHIPS WITH KIN OF THREE FAMILIES

Kin	Newbolt		Hartley		Daniels	
	No.	%	No.	%	No.	%
Intimate kin	40	29	1	2	3	3
Effective kin	29	21	21	40	18	20
Non-effective kin	63	45	21	40	51	57
Unfamiliar kin	7	5	9	18	18	20
Total recognized living kin	139	100	52	100	90	100
Recognized kin now dead	17		27		34	
Total recognized kin	156		79		124	

macy of contact with relatives, and degree of knowledge of them.[1] In reality there is a continuum from the most intimate kin to the least familiar, so that this typology is arbitrary and does some violence to each couple's own concepts of social distance, but some first approach to standardization was necessary for making comparisons.

'Intimate' relatives are those with whom there was frequent visiting, and mutual aid when necessary. But one important exception to this criterion was allowed: many couples had parents living at some distance so that they could not visit them frequently, but if they visited their parents when possible, wrote to them frequently, and spoke of them at length, their parents were included as intimate kin. 'Effective' relatives are those with whom the relationship was not close enough to be called intimate, although some contact was maintained. Informants had considerable knowledge about these relatives; they knew not only gross facts such as name, age, occupation, and so forth, but also the relative's general interests, pursuits, and tastes. If the relative lived nearby and could be easily visited the relationship was classed as effective if there was contact about once in two months; if the

[1]These criteria are similar to those used by Firth in his study of working-class families' contacts with their extra-familial kin (see Firth, 1956).

relative lived at some distance, the relationship was classed as effective if there was contact when the relative came to London or when the family went to the relative's part of the country. Effective kin usually sent Christmas presents or cards, although data were not collected on this point for all families. Effective kin were usually asked to the couple's wedding and to children's christenings. Separating intimate from effective kin was not an easy matter, particularly when the kin lived at some distance, but the crucial criterion used was the amount of contact combined with the amount of effort people put into making special visits to the relative. 'Non-effective' relatives are those with whom there was no contact but about whom informants had some knowledge, although this knowledge was restricted to gross facts such as name and occupation. 'Unfamiliar' relatives are those about whom informants knew virtually nothing beyond the fact that the relative existed.

If one compares the figures given in *Table 5*, certain differences are immediately obvious. The Newbolts had a much larger proportion of intimate kin than the Hartleys and the Daniels, 29 per cent as contrasted with 2 per cent and 3 per cent respectively. The Newbolts and the Daniels had about the same proportion of effective kin (20 per cent) whereas the Hartleys had a much larger proportion of kin in this category (40 per cent). The Daniels had proportionately more non-effective and unfamiliar kin than the Newbolts and the Hartleys.

Although the present discussion is restricted to a detailed analysis of these three families as examples, the fact that other families showed a similar range of variation should be noted. Two transitional families resembled the Newbolts in having a great many intimate and effective relatives; they were contemplating moving to new local areas, however, and they expected that their contacts with kin would be drastically reduced. Ten families resembled the Hartleys, more or less, although there was a good deal of variation among them. Six of these ten families had had extensive contact with kin at some time in the past, but they had moved to new local areas and their contacts with relatives had been greatly decreased. There were five families that resembled the Daniels in amount of contact with kin.

In first attempts to explain variations in contacts with kin I tried to correlate them with class status. The association was not very close. Families who had the most contact with kin were or had been working-class, and the husbands of the families who had least contact with kin had professional or semi-professional occupations, but the association was far from complete. There were several working-class families who did not have much contact with their relatives, and there were marked variations among the professional families in the amount and type of contact with relatives. In any case it was impossible to see exactly how class position was actually producing an effect on the families and their relationships with their kin.

For a time I adopted the view that relationships with kin were entirely a matter of free personal choice, that is, that the only really important factors affecting relationships with kin were the personalities of the various people concerned and the personality-fit between them. But this interpretation was obviously too simple. Clearly there were other factors. People tended to be less intimate with relatives who lived far away even if they liked them; people tended to be less intimate with genealogically distant relatives than with close ones, and so forth. After several attempts to explain all the data in terms of single factors, I came to the conclusion that behaviour towards kin must be regarded as a complex resultant of several factors operating in combination with one another. Chief among these are:

1. Economic ties among kin.
2. Residence and physical accessibility of kin.
3. Type of genealogical relationship.
4. The connectedness of the kinship network.
5. The presence and preferences of 'connecting relatives'.
6. Perceived similarities and differences in social status among relatives.
7. Idiosyncratic combinations of conscious and unconscious needs and attitudes.

Only those factors necessary to the comparative analysis of the three families are included. No claim is made that this list of factors is exhaustive. Certain other relevant factors that have been controlled, incorporated by implication, or ignored, will be taken up separately below.

These various factors represent forces of different kinds. Economic ties and physical accessibility of kin are 'ecological' factors in the field-theory sense of setting the boundary conditions of kinship relationships (Lewin, 1952, p. 170). Factors concerning genealogical relationship and network formation are 'sociological'. Likes and dislikes based on perceived similarities and differences of social status would probably be considered 'socio-psychological' factors by most social scientists. And conscious and unconscious needs and attitudes would be termed 'psychological' factors.

In order to do justice to the empirical facts of relationships with kin it is therefore necessary to use the concepts of several disciplines. In empirical reality all these factors operate simultaneously and any particular instance of kinship behaviour may be affected by several factors, sometimes operating to the same end, sometimes in conflict with one another. Moreover, the factors are not independent of each other. Kin may visit each other frequently because, among other factors, they live near one another; but they may continue to live near one another because, among other factors, they are able to use their relationships with one another for economic ends. But for simplicity of presentation I shall discuss the factors consecutively, starting with the ecological ones and working towards the psychological. No suggestion is made that any one of these factors is more important than any of the others in the sense that it will explain more facts. The relative weight of each factor will vary according to the particular configuration of the combination. Further, no claim is made that a knowledge of these factors will enable one to predict *exactly* how they will be combined in particular individual cases. But I do claim that this type of analysis illuminates some of the properties of the kinship system and gives some idea of what to expect in individual instances of its operation.

1. *The Effect of Economic Relations among Kin*

In urban industrial society kinship does not play much part in the economic and occupational structure. In most cases people do not have to depend on their relatives for access to some means of earning a living. Each family-household is supposed to be economically self-supporting and, compared to most small-scale non-industrialized societies, there are few economic ties and obligations among extra-familial kin.[1] But the effects of the occupational and economic systems are not uniform; there is considerable variation in the extent to which relatives are linked to one another by economic ties.

The greater the degree to which relatives hold property rights in common enterprises and the greater their expectancy of inheriting property from one another, the closer will be the ties among them. The three families considered here, the Newbolts, the Hartleys, and the Daniels, and indeed the entire set of research families, did not show much contrast along this dimension. There were no research families in which many relatives held property rights in common enterprises. There were two individuals who had inherited small amounts when their parents died, Mrs Hartley being one of these. Three others had expectations of inheritance but in all cases the inheritance was to come from parents with whom, as will be discussed below, all couples had close relationships in any case.

Ties among kin are likely to be stronger if the kin are able to help one another occupationally. Although kin groups do not form the basic units of the economic and occupational structure, and although kinship status does not automatically entitle one to a livelihood, there are variations in the extent to which relatives can help one another to find jobs. They cannot help one another directly if occupational training and selection are based on examinations and objectively determined skill. In less skilled occupations, and in certain business and professional occupations,

---

[1] Following Firth, I use the term 'extra-familial kin' to mean kin outside the family of procreation if the speaker is married or outside the family of orientation if he is single (Firth, 1956).

particularly family businesses, relatives may be able to help one another more directly. It seems likely that the presence of economic ties among relatives will not be closely correlated with class status and prestige, for some occupations of high status enable relatives to help one another whereas others do not, and some manual occupations permit relatives to help one another whereas others do not.

The research families provided considerable contrast along this dimension. None of the husbands with professional, semi-professional, or clerical occupations, such as Mr Hartley and Mr Daniels, had found their jobs through the direct influence of relatives. Objective principles of selection had been strictly applied and their parents had helped them only by encouraging them and by trying to provide them with the appropriate sort of education. Of the seven working-class families, however, three husbands had at one time or another found jobs through their relatives, and at the time of interviewing, two of the three had settled down permanently in such jobs. Mr Newbolt said that when he got married his father-in-law put in a word for him with the employment officer of the firm where he worked and Mr Newbolt was taken on. Several other relatives in the Newbolts' network of kin had helped one another to find jobs and it was evident that similar activities had gone on among the relatives of the other research husbands who had found jobs through relatives. In some areas of London where there is a dominant local occupation, such as working at the docks, employers evidently give first preference to relatives of reliable employees.

In a similar way relatives are sometimes able to help one another to find places to live. Among the research set two families were living in the same house as the parents of one of the partners and two others had found a flat through the influence of relatives. In the block of flats studied by Firth and his students the owners had a policy of giving vacant flats to relatives of good tenants (Firth, 1956). Young and Willmott report a similar practice in the privately owned blocks of flats in Bethnal Green. The London County Council and borough councils, however, allocate the flats strictly according to need (Young, 1954b, Young and Willmott, 1957). Mogey reports a similar situation in Oxford (Mogey, 1956).

If possible, then, people use their existing contacts with relatives to find jobs and houses, and the possibility of using their kin in this way helps to maintain and possibly even to develop the existing relationships. But the action of the occupational system is not uniform. Sometimes it leads to the establishment of economic ties among relatives or permits them to use their relationships with one another for economic ends; sometimes it does not. Among the research set such opportunities were greater among the working-class families. But even when it was possible for relatives to help one another economically they did not feel compelled to do so. Among the research families four of the seven working-class husbands had found jobs and five had found places to live independently of their relatives. Contacts with relatives were only one among several possible channels of access to economic ends.

2. Physical Accessibility of Kin

The facts of residence in relation to type of relationship with kin are set out in *Table 6*. The differences among the three families are striking. Two-thirds of the Newbolts' kin lived in the same or adjoining boroughs, whereas only about one-seventh of the Hartleys' relatives and none of the Daniels' were so readily accessible.

All forty intimate kin mentioned by the Newbolts lived in the same or neighbouring boroughs. It would seem that geographical accessibility of relatives accounts for the fact that the Newbolts had so many more intimate kin than the Hartleys and the Daniels. But residence does not explain everything. The Newbolts had as many non-effective as intimate kin living nearby, so that it is obvious that they were not compelled to see relatives simply because they lived near them. Furthermore, they had four effective relatives outside London even though they considered physical distance to be an almost insuperable barrier to social relationships.

TABLE 6

TYPE OF RELATIONSHIP MAINTAINED WITH KIN IN RELATION TO PHYSICAL ACCESSIBILITY OF THE KIN

	Newbolt	Hartley	Daniels
Kin living in same or adjoining boroughs of London			
Intimate	40	1	0
Effective	16	6	0
Non-effective	41	0	0
Unfamiliar	0	0	0
	97	7	0
Kin living in more distant boroughs of London			
Intimate	0	0	2
Effective	9	3	3
Non-effective	10	0	7
Unfamiliar	6	0	0
	25	3	12
Kin living in Great Britain but outside London			
Intimate	0	0	1
Effective	4	12	11
Non-effective	6	16	41
Unfamiliar	0	0	13
	10	28	66
Kin living abroad			
Intimate	0	0	0
Effective	0	0	4
Non-effective	6	5	3
Unfamiliar	1	4	0
	7	9	7
Residence of kin not known			
Intimate	0	0	0
Effective	0	0	0
Non-effective	0	0	0
Unfamiliar	0	5	5
	0	5	5
Total living recognized kin	139	52	90

The Hartleys and the Daniels had far fewer accessible kin and a much smaller proportion of intimate kin than the Newbolts. There was a tendency for the Hartleys and the Daniels to maintain at least effective relationships with their relatives in London, although the Daniels had some non-effective relatives in this area. Within the category of relatives living in Great Britain but outside London, comparative physical distance did not have much effect on the type of relationship. Variations in physical distance between the family and these relatives does not explain why the Hartleys had a much larger proportion of effective relatives outside London than the Daniels, nor does it explain either family's selection of some relatives as effective, others as non-effective or unfamiliar. Similar reservations apply to kin living abroad.

In brief, physical accessibility of relatives to a family facilitates but does not necessitate intimacy. It is very difficult for a family, especially a family with young children, to maintain intimate relationships with geographically distant relatives. But if relatives live nearby the family may keep in close contact with them but are not compelled to do so.

3. Type of Genealogical Connection

All three families, and indeed all families of the research set, were alike in range of recognition of kin. The range was very narrow, extending vertically to grandparents, although not to the siblings of grandparents, and laterally to first cousins. Mogey reports a similar narrow range in Oxford (Mogey, 1956). Within this range informants had systematic knowledge of kin. Beyond it their knowledge was sporadic and unsystematic and they felt no obligation to know very much. Over half the couples knew something about an odd relative or two outside the normal range, usually a great-grandparent, a great-aunt, or 'some sort of cousin', but they felt such knowledge was unusual and they explained that it was caused by special encounters with relatives in childhood or by such factors as family legends of illustrious ancestry in a particular line. Even when informants knew something about their great-grandparents or great-great-grandparents their knowledge did not extend correspondingly to third or fourth cousins. Although some couples knew of 'distant cousins', they often did not know exactly how they were related to them. There was no agreement on the terminology for cousins and the field workers were frequently asked what the terminology for cousins should be. Informants expected that as they grew older they would know about and maintain relationships with their own grandchildren but not with the children of nieces and nephews. The system grows at the bottom and is cut off at the top but the vertical range and the corresponding lateral range are much narrower than those of bilateral systems in many small-scale societies, and indeed of bilateral systems in some rural areas of Western European society, where knowledge and contact may extend to third cousins and sometimes further.[1]

The Newbolts, the Hartleys, and the Daniels were alike in that parents were intimate relatives in all three cases. Parents were considered intimate relatives by all the research couples even when they were not physically accessible. Although there appeared to be no very clearly formulated universal rules about rights of and obligations to kin such as one finds so frequently in small-scale primitive societies, all families expressed, directly or indirectly, the feeling that they had stronger obligations to parents than to any other type of relative. They felt that amicable relations should be kept up with parents even though they did not always like them. In fact some couples were glad that physical separation made frequent contact impossible so that they were able to avoid the awkwardness of open hostility.

In other respects the three families differed in order of intimacy with relatives according to genealogical connection. In all the research families there was an implicit assumption that women would usually be somewhat more active than men in keeping up kinship ties, but in the case of the Newbolts this tendency was extremely pronounced. The mother was the all-important relative

[1] Even in rural areas, however, kinship may only be recognized as far as first cousins (see Curle, 1952, and Harris, 1954). Such narrow range is probably linked to the restricted importance of kinship in economic affairs. A high emigration rate may also contribute to it.

and the mother-daughter link was the all-important relationship. Mrs Newbolt went to see her mother almost every day and her mother often came to visit her. They frequently helped each other with housework and with small loans. Mrs Newbolt's mother often cared for the children and Mrs Newbolt did her mother's shopping for her. Mrs Newbolt spoke of her mother far more frequently than of her father. She always said, 'I'm going round to Mum's', never 'I'm going round to my parents'. She spoke of her parents' home as 'Mum's home', and it was her mother who came to visit her rather than her mother and her father together. Similarly, Mr Newbolt spoke of his mother far more frequently than of his father. The Newbolts did not feel that they were unique in this respect. They took it for granted that the relationship between mother and child was closer than that between father and child not only in childhood but also in adulthood. They also took it for granted that in adulthood the relationship between a woman and her mother would be closer than that between a man and his mother and that the relationship between a woman and her mother would be closer than that between a woman and her mother-in-law. This meant that the maternal grandmother was expected to be a more intimate relative than the paternal grandmother. Mrs Newbolt's own maternal grandmother was alive and Mrs Newbolt visited her almost as often as her mother. The Institute of Community Studies reports these attitudes and practices as customary among families studied in Bethnal Green.

The effect of the close link between mother and daughter can be seen in the Newbolts' relationships with genealogically more distant relatives. With the exception of Mr Newbolt's parents, all their intimate kin were Mrs Newbolt's relatives. All their accessible but non-effective kin were his relatives. As Mrs. Newbolt said, 'David doesn't see so much of his family now except his Mum. When he married me he didn't only marry me, he married my family too, didn't you, David?' The Newbolts recognized that the relationship between a man and his mother-in-law was likely to be difficult. The claims of the husband on his wife and the mother on her daughter are likely to conflict so that the woman will be caught between conflicting loyalties. Mrs Newbolt felt she was very fortunate because her husband and her mother got along well together.

The Hartleys and the Daniels placed less stress on the mother as the all-important parent. When discussing past events they spoke of their fathers as often as their mothers; since their fathers had died some years before the interviews began, they were mentioned less frequently when events of the immediate present were being discussed. From what they said it seemed clear that the Hartleys and the Daniels conceived of their parents as more of a unit, as 'parents' rather than as 'mother' and 'father' considered separately. Parents were of course differentiated and considered separately as well, but there was not the emphasis on the mother as the really important parent; there was a tendency for women to feel slightly closer to their mothers, men to their fathers. Other things being equal, it was expected that the wife's mother and the husband's mother would be equally intimate relatives. Furthermore, the Hartleys and the Daniels felt they owed their first loyalty to each other rather than to their parents; conflict with parents was to be avoided if possible, but if it was inevitable, the tendency would be to side with one's spouse at the expense of one's parents. Both wives expected their husbands to provide them with some of the domestic help and emotional support that Mrs Newbolt expected from her mother and other female relatives.

This comparatively even stress on the parents as equally important is reflected in the Hartleys' and the Daniels' relationships with more distant kin. Unlike the Newbolts, there was no preference for the wife's kin rather than the husband's or the mother's rather than the father's. There was a very rough order of intimacy: after parents came siblings, uncles and aunts on both sides, together with all the members of their households. These kin were likely to be effective relatives, although many were non-effective and some were unfamiliar. Cousins were likely to be non-effective or unfamiliar, although here too there were exceptions.

In brief, type of genealogical relationship accounts for some of the facts of contact but not all. It does not operate as a single, isolated factor.

4. The Connectedness of the Network of Kin

In all three cases discussed here the elementary family existed as a distinct unit clearly marked off and separated from its kin and from other institutions. Indeed among all the research families the norm was that each elementary family should form a household unit and should be financially independent of other families. The individuation of the elementary family was also expressed in the fact that informants thought of their kin in terms of families rather than individuals; they conceived of their relatives as a set of families or family-households linked through relationships between individuals. All elementary families thus existed as distinct units, but there were variations in degree of individuation, that is, in a family's expectation of governing its own affairs without help or hindrance from relatives. These variations were associated with the degree of connectedness of the kinship network.

In all cases the total set of kin recognized by a family formed a network rather than an organized group. Some members were in contact with one another; others were not. Although all the relatives recognized by a particular family were cognatically or affinally related to the particular family, some were not so related to one another and each had other relatives who were not recognized as kin by the family. Temporary groupings were drawn from the kinship network for certain activities such as weddings, funerals, and so forth, but the personnel of these groupings was not likely to be the same twice, and the individuals were brought together through their obligation to a particular kinsman or household-family.

There were marked differences in the connectedness of the kinship networks of the Newbolts, the Hartleys, and the Daniels. The Newbolts' network of kin was close-knit. Their forty intimate kin were in close contact not only with the Newbolts but also with one another. Fewer of the Hartleys' kin were in intimate contact with one another, although many were in effective contact. Still fewer of the Daniels' relatives saw one another independently of the Daniels.[1] These differences in connectedness are associated with differences in the type and amount of contact the three families maintained with kin. What I am suggesting here is that differences in frequency and intensity of contact between a family and their kin can be attributed, in part, to differences in frequency and intensity of contact of the relatives themselves with one another independently of the family. The more close-knit a family's network of kin, the greater the likelihood that the family will visit their kin. If kin see one another frequently, they are able to put consistent, almost collective, pressure on a family to keep up kinship obligations. If they hardly see one another at all, their social control of the family is fragmented and partial and likely to be inconsistent.

Thus it was difficult for anyone in the Newbolts' set of intimate kin to keep a secret or maintain his privacy, but members could rely on one another for help in case of sickness, unemployment, or other troubles. Out of their constant interaction, they had evidently developed a shared set of opinions and values; their shared values in turn facilitated their continued interaction. Because there was basic consensus among them, and because of the services they offered one another, they were able to put effective social pressure on the Newbolts and on one another to keep up kinship obligations. But even in the Newbolts' close-knit network, relatives were not compelled to take part in kinship activities. Escape was possible. But if one wanted to reap the benefits of companionship, emotional support, and aid in crises, one had to conform to the values of relatives. Families like the Hartleys and the Daniels

[1] Information on the amount of contact relatives had with one another, as distinct from their contacts with the couple we interviewed, is fairly complete for the Newbolts, the Hartleys, and the Daniels, but not complete or consistent enough to permit quantitative presentation. Ideally one should interview the relatives themselves as well as the couple with whom one is primarily concerned. In practice this would be very difficult in most cases but it would be possible to ask couples themselves more detailed and uniform questions about their relatives' independent contacts with one another. Unfortunately the importance of such questions was not realized until much of the field work had been completed.

found some of these services with friends, but Mrs Newbolt considered friends an unreliable substitute for relatives.

The Hartleys' network of kin was less close-knit than that of the Newbolts, but more close-knit than that of the Daniels. This difference in network-connectedness accounts, in part at least, for the fact that 40 per cent of the Hartleys' relatives were effective whereas only 20 per cent of the Daniels' were effective. Some of Mr Hartley's aunts and uncles saw one another and his mother, and together they put gentle pressure on the Hartleys to visit them. Their sanctions were not very strong, not nearly so compelling as those of the Newbolts' relatives, but nevertheless they did make the Hartleys feel that they should keep up kinship ties. The Hartleys paid duty visits to their uncles and aunts, but the people with whom they were most involved (in addition to his mother) were their friends and neighbours.

The Daniels' network of kin was even more loose-knit. They had less contact with one another so that they had still less basis for shared opinions and values and they put less pressure on the Daniels to visit relatives. In so far as they exerted any social pressure on the Daniels, their control was partial and fragmented. With the exception of their mothers and his sister, their intimate relationships were conducted with friends rather than with relatives.

The differences between the three families are illustrated by their own weddings and their attitudes toward them. Mrs Newbolt regretted very much that her wedding had, for various reasons, been a very small affair, attended only by parents on both sides. But she made up for it the following year by having a very large twenty-first birthday party to which a great many relatives came—'ever such a lot, I couldn't count them or remember'.

The Hartleys were married in church, 'with me in a white dress and all the trimmings', as Mrs Hartley put it. The wedding guests consisted of six relatives, five friends, and two friends of parents. The relatives consisted of Mr Hartley's mother and Mrs Hartley's brother (the other parents were dead and Mr Hartley has no siblings) two cousins of Mr Hartley and a second cousin of Mrs Hartley's father together with this cousin's wife.

The Daniels got married in a registry office. The only relative who came was Mr Daniels' sister. All the other guests were friends. Although the Daniels got along well with their parents, and had introduced each other to their respective parents before they married, they did not feel it was essential for their parents to come to the wedding. Their parents were living in the country at the time.

The contrast suggests that the Daniels conceived of the wedding purely as their personal union, not as a bringing together of their relatives. Friends rather than relatives were needed as an audience for the establishment of the new relationship. The Newbolts felt that weddings were occasions for large groups of relatives to be brought together. Friends were hardly mentioned. The Hartleys stood somewhere between.

In the Newbolts' network of relatives there was a nucleus of women consisting of Mrs Newbolt's maternal grandmother and several of the grandmother's daughters, including Mrs Newbolt's mother. Mrs Newbolt was the eldest of the third generation, but her cousins were growing up and marrying and it seemed likely that they would soon begin to join in the activities of their mothers and aunts. Each of these women brought her children and to some extent her husband into relationship with the other members of the nucleus. It was these women who organized the large gatherings of kin at weddings, funerals, christenings, and so on, it was usually these women who persuaded male relatives to help one another get jobs, and it was the women who did most of the visiting and small acts of mutual aid. This nucleus of female kin was so close-knit and so well integrated that it should perhaps be considered an organized group rather than a network. Such groups have been reported in detail by Young and his colleagues in Bethnal Green (Young, 1954a, and 1956; Young and Willmott, 1957; Townsend, 1955a, 1955b, and 1957), and there are suggestions that they occur in other working-class areas as well (Gorer, 1955, pp. 45-6; Jephcott and Carter, 1955; Kerr, 1955; Shaw, 1954; Sheldon, 1948). There were no groups of this sort in the kinship networks of the Hartleys and Daniels, although there was a tendency in their networks, as in those of all the research families, for women to be slightly more active than men in keeping up kinship ties.

Three questions may be asked here. First, why are women more active than men in keeping up kinship ties? Second, why is this tendency so much more pronounced in the case of the Newbolts? Third, why are there groups of women in the Newbolts' network but not in those of the other families?

First, in all families the wife has a greater emotional investment in the family than the husband and she is more concerned with the children, especially when they are very small. When the children grow up they still have a slight tendency to feel closer to the mother. This is likely to be a little more marked in daughters than in sons. Daughters expect, like their mothers, to be more family-centred than their brothers, more involved in relationships with parents and with other relatives, more concerned with the prospect of getting married themselves, whereas their brothers are more concerned with their jobs and careers.

In Chapter III it was pointed out that families in loose-knit networks tend to have a joint role-relationship between husband and wife, whereas families in close-knit networks tend to have a more segregated conjugal role-relationship. If people have been brought up in a family with a joint conjugal relationship, in which the mother and father shared the tasks of child care, differences in attitude towards the parents and sex differences in orientation towards the family and relationships with kin are likely to be minimized. If, in addition, relatives are scattered all over the country, it becomes increasingly unlikely that many close ties will be kept up by relatives at all either by men or by women.

In the case of the Newbolts, the emphasis on women as specialists in kinship affairs was greatly exaggerated. I suggest that this is related to experience of growing up in a family that has sharp segregation of parental roles. To a child in such a situation the mother is the all-important parent. The father is likely to be away from home much of the time, and he is a somewhat distant figure—an occasional disciplinarian, a source of entertainment sometimes, not a very close person although obviously important as the source of financial support for the family as a whole. As a son grows older he is weaned away from his mother, perhaps not only by positive identification with his father, which psycho-analysis has shown to be so important, but also by positive identification with a peer group. For, from the age of three on-wards, such boys spend a great deal of time with groups of boys in the local neighbourhood and these relationships may continue over a considerable number of years, even into adulthood. From what we could gather from the Newbolts, girls were drawn out of the home much less than boys by friends and jobs and they maintained closer relationships with their mothers in adulthood. Mother and daughter had more in common than mother and son or father and son.

But the psychological consequences of being brought up in a family having marked segregation of parental roles does not of itself produce groups of women within a kinship network. All it produces is a close emotional tie between mother and children, particularly between mother and daughter. Before there can be a group there must also be several related women in the same place at the same time. If groups of grandmother, mothers, and daugh-ters are to be formed, women should get married young, they should have plenty of children, preferably girls, they should live for a long time, and all the women concerned should continue to live in the same local area. The formation of such groups also depends on certain negative factors—on the absence of rights to land or other economic advantages through the father and his relatives. And it also depends on psychological factors, for the advantages of matrilateral ties and female solidarity may be out-weighed by personal dislike.

To phrase the discussion in general terms: whenever there are no particular economic advantages to be gained by affiliation with paternal relatives, and whenever two or preferably three genera-tions of mothers and daughters are living in the same place at the same time, a bilateral kinship system is likely to develop a matri-lateral stress, and groups composed of sets of mothers and daughters may form within networks of kin. But such groups are only possible, not necessary. Quarrels between matrilateral kin, preference for the husband's relatives, and a host of other similar factors may upset the pattern.

In the case of the Newbolts and similar families, these groups of female kin were perhaps reinforced by a desire for economic security. Husbands and fathers might die or desert, but women could use their maternal kin as an informal insurance policy for themselves and their children. These groups had a strong hold over their members, who could get from one another many of the emotional and material satisfactions that other women had to get from their husbands. In Chapter III I have argued that such extra-familial relationships permit segregation in the role-relationship of husband and wife. For the children, such segregation leads in turn to the development of conscious and unconscious attitudes appropriate to the continuation of grandmother-mother-daughter groups, and so it goes on. But these groups of mothers and daughters have no structural continuity. They do not last for several generations; they are not named; they tend to break up when the grandmother dies, and they are readily dissolved if their members are separated from one another.

The question remains that some families have more closely knit kinship networks than others. This is related, among other factors, to occupational similarities and common residence.

Eighty-two per cent of the Newbolts' relatives had occupations roughly similar in status to that of Mr Newbolt (semi-skilled or unskilled); many of the Newbolts' relatives worked in local industries. Two-thirds of the Newbolts' relatives lived in the same or adjoining boroughs so that they were accessible not only to the Newbolts but also to one another. As stated above, residential propinquity facilitates a high degree of network-connectedness although it does not require it. Similarly, as I shall discuss below, it is *felt* social similarities that are important in affecting relationships with kin, and such felt similarities do not always coincide with objectively assessed similarities of occupational status.

The Hartleys' relatives were more dispersed than the Newbolts' both occupationally and geographically. Only 44 per cent of their relatives had occupations similar to that of Mr Hartley and only one-seventh of their relatives lived in the same or adjoining boroughs.

The Daniels' relatives were even more dispersed. Forty-three per cent had occupations roughly similar in status to that of Mr Daniels, and none of their relatives lived in the same borough as the Daniels themselves. There was a residential difference between the Hartleys' and the Daniels' relatives that gives some geographical basis for the greater degree of connectedness in the Hartleys' network of kin. The Hartleys' relatives were clustered in two sets, one in the south of England and the other in the north, and there was a good deal of contact within each set, particularly within the set in the south of England. The Daniels' relatives were much more scattered geographically.

But connectedness does not depend on occupational similarities and residential propinquity alone. As described in Chapter IV, it is the complex resultant of countless decisions made by all members of the network according to particular combinations of personal need and situational factors—presence or absence of economic ties among relatives, common residence, opportunities to form relationships outside the local area and outside the kinship network, and a complicated set of factors involved in physical and social mobility.

5. The Presence and Preferences of Connecting Relatives

The four factors discussed so far—economic ties among relatives, residence and physical accessibility of kin, type of genealogical relationship, and connectedness of the kinship network—explain many but not all of the facts of contact between the three families and their relatives. They do not explain, for example, why the Newbolts were in intimate contact with two maternal aunts but in only effective contact with other maternal aunts. Similarly they do not explain why the Hartleys saw some cousins and not others. Some of these anomalies may be attributed to the presence and preferences of 'connecting relatives'.

All intimate and effective kin are socially connected with one another, but some relationships are direct whereas others are maintained more indirectly through an intervening relative. A person may see his aunts and uncles because the aunts and uncles see his parents. Or he may see his cousins because he visits his aunt. Such intervening relatives are here called 'connecting relatives'.[1] They direct the flow of relationships between other kin, sometimes helping to bring them together, sometimes discouraging them from seeing each other. Among the research families, the most important connecting relatives were usually parents, particularly mothers, and grandparents if they were alive, although in some cases this role was filled by an aunt.

The Newbolts' chief connecting relatives were Mrs Newbolt's mother and her maternal grandmother. When Mrs Newbolt visited her mother she saw not only her mother, her father, and her siblings, but also the relatives who came to visit her mother, these being chiefly her mother's sisters and their children. Similarly when she visited her grandmother she saw not only her grandmother but all the other people who lived in the grandmother's house, namely her grandfather, two aunts, the husband of one of the aunts, an uncle, and a cousin. She also saw all the people who came to visit her grandmother, most of these being the grandmother's children. To a very much lesser extent, Mr Newbolt's mother also acted as a connecting relative, bringing the Newbolts into contact with her sisters and their children.

Many of the discrepancies in the order of intimacy according to genealogical relationship can be attributed to the personal preferences of the Newbolts' connecting relatives. Thus Mrs Newbolt's mother had two sisters whom she did not like, and these women and their households were only effective relatives for the Newbolts instead of being intimate. On the other hand, she was fond of two of her husband's sisters so that these women and their households were intimate kin for the Newbolts. Or again, Mr Newbolt's mother was particularly fond of the wife of one of her

[1] Cf. Firth's concept of 'pivotal relatives' (Firth, 1956), and Lewin's concept of the 'gatekeeper' (Lewin, 1948).

husband's brothers so that when this family moved to a new housing estate, considerable effort was made to keep up the relationship, and the Newbolts saw this uncle and aunt occasionally when they visited Mr Newbolt's mother. Personal likes and dislikes are thus important, but at this point it is the personal preferences of the connecting relatives that matter rather than the likes and dislikes of the couple themselves. Whether the Newbolts would continue their present pattern of contact with kin if their connecting relatives died one cannot tell, but it seems likely that it would be drastically altered. This had in fact happened in the case of two of the other research families who had formerly had very close-knit networks of kin.

The Hartleys and Daniels do not provide a very good contrast to the Newbolts since their fathers were dead and only their mothers could act as connecting relatives. But in all the research families there was a tendency for mothers to play this role more frequently than fathers.

Mr Hartley's mother was the Hartleys' most important connecting relative. She had come originally from Ireland and had no relatives in England so that she brought the Hartleys into contact with her own relatives only on the rare occasions when they came to England. But she was active in encouraging the Hartleys to visit her late husband's sisters and their children in London and the south of England. The Hartleys explained that they would not have had independent contact with their cousins unless they had liked them personally and shared the same interests, but since Mr Hartley's mother saw the cousins' parents and since they were all living within fairly easy reach of one another, it was natural that they should see a good deal of their cousins as well as their aunts. The Hartleys had more independent relationships than the Newbolts. About one-quarter of their relationships with effective kin were carried on without the encouragement of connecting relatives. These independent relationships were conducted chiefly with Mrs Hartley's relatives; both her parents were dead and no one else in her network had taken over the role of connecting relative for her.

In the case of the Daniels' there was no difference between the intimacy maintained with his mother and that maintained with hers, although they were not able to visit her mother so frequently because she lived further away. It was difficult for their mothers to be very active as connecting relatives because they were also living at some distance from most of their relatives so that it was almost as difficult for them to visit relatives as it was for the Daniels themselves. But here again, the Daniels did see more of those relatives with whom their mothers maintained relationships. Mrs Daniels said that although her brothers and sisters did not see much of one another at the present time, she doubted if there would be any contact among them at all after her mother died. Mr Daniels' mother brought the Daniels into relationship with some of the uncles and aunts. These uncles and aunts acted as secondary connecting relatives for their children, the Daniels' cousins. But these more indirectly connected relatives were much less intimate than the uncles and aunts. The Daniels explained that cousins were not important once one had grown up; one had to see them when one was a child because one met them when one visited uncles and aunts, but once the cousins had left home one would not bother about them at all unless one shared many interests with them other than the mere kinship tie. This view was shared by other families with loose-knit networks.

For all families, parents and grandparents had acted as connecting relatives in the past when our informants were children, bringing them into contact with some relatives and ignoring others. The residues of the past could be seen in the present; the effective kin of our informants were usually those whom they had known and visited in childhood. There were many cases in which formerly effective kin had become non-effective but there were very few cases in which kin who had been non-effective in childhood had become effective in adulthood, except for brief periods during the war.

A family is thus not related to its kin in a uniform way. Some relationships are kept up directly by the family; others are maintained more indirectly through the medium of connecting relatives.

Connecting relatives are to a kinship network what a leader is to an organized group. They control and direct the flow of activities and social relationships. The role of connecting relative is not obligatory and inevitable, however. Some individuals have more talent and liking for it than others, and there are no formalized rules about how the role should be carried out and no strong sanctions compelling a person in the appropriate position to carry it out in a particular way. Within the limits set by economic ties, residence, and obligations to parents, personal likes and dislikes are allowed free expression so that families are affected not only by their own preferences, but also by those of their connecting relatives.

6. *The Effect of Perceived Similarities and Differences in Social Status*

It was obvious among the research families that personal likes and dislikes played a large part in the choice of whether to associate with kin or to ignore them. The problem here is whether one can find any general social basis for these likes and dislikes, both on the part of the couple themselves and on the part of their connecting relatives, although attention will be devoted primarily to the couple's own preferences.

It seemed likely that similarities and differences in social status might reveal a general basis for likes and dislikes. An examination was accordingly made of type of contact with kin in relation to similarities and differences of social status between the couple and their various relatives. Similarities and differences in status were estimated, as a first approximation, on the basis of occupation; for this purpose all the members of a family-household were considered to have the same social status as the chief breadwinner. The results are shown in *Table 7*. The association is not as close as one might expect. In the case of the Newbolts, all their intimate kin were of the same occupational status as themselves, but so were most of their effective and non-effective kin. In the case of the Hartleys, their only intimate relative, Mr Hartley's mother, was of lower status than themselves. (Status of widows was based on the occupation formerly held by the husband.) In the choice of

· TABLE 7

TYPE OF RELATIONSHIP MAINTAINED WITH KIN OF SIMILAR
AND DIFFERENT OCCUPATIONAL STATUS

Relationship with kin	Newbolt			Hartley			Daniels		
	Number of kin whose occupational status was								
	Same	Differ-ent	Un-known	Same	Differ-ent	Un-known	Same	Differ-ent	Un-known
Intimate	40	—	—	—	1	—	2	1	—
Effective	22	7	—	14	5	2	7	7	—
Non-effective	52	4	7	7	8	6	25	36	—
Unfamiliar	—	—	7	2	—	7	5	4	3
Totals	114	11	14	23	14	15	39	48	3

effective kin, the Hartleys showed a slight prejudice in favour of
kin of similar occupational status; their non-effective kin were
evenly divided. In the case of the Daniels, his mother and sister
were of roughly the same status as themselves, whereas her mother
was of slightly lower status. Status considerations did not seem to
have entered into their choice of effective relatives, since half were
of the same status and half were different. Similarly, status did not
seem to have been very important in their choice of non-effective
relatives, for about two-fifths of these were of the same status,
and three-fifths were different.

In brief, objectively assessed differences in occupational status
do not seem to have much effect on choice of contact with kin.
Qualitative analysis of the material suggests that such objectively
assessed status differences are important only when the differences
are very great, and that they affect relations with genealogically
distant relatives more than those with close relatives.

Nevertheless, there were many indications in the interview
records that subtle status considerations did play some part in
people's feelings of like and dislike for their relatives. There were
many people who made remarks such as the following, 'We like
my mother's people better than my father's because—well, I don't
like to sound snobbish, but they are a better sort of type, if you
know what I mean.' In many of these cases there was no very

great difference in occupation between the approved and the rejected relatives. In other words, it was the couple's own concepts of status and prestige that were immediately relevant, not the judgements of an external observer.

As I explain in the next chapter, implicit and explicit definitions of prestige and class varied from one informant to another and even a single informant shifted his definition according to changes in the immediate context of comparison and evaluation. This variability made it difficult to track down exactly which concepts of class people were using when they talked about their relatives. It would have been helpful if we had asked informants what class they would place certain relatives in, but we felt that such questions about relatives would have made most of the couples so resentful and embarrassed that they would hardly have been willing or able to answer. As the Hartleys pointed out, it makes one feel disloyal to talk openly about the class position of one's relatives, particularly if their position is felt to be lower than one's own. We therefore took what was offered spontaneously but did not probe if informants did not talk about status differences of their own accord. Our information on this matter is therefore uneven.

In the case of the three families chosen here as examples, a knowledge of what they thought of the class position of their relatives does contribute something to an understanding of their contacts with kin. The Newbolts strongly condemned all relatives 'who think they are posh'. But whether the Newbolts thought the relatives considered themselves posh did not depend on whether the relatives had been occupationally mobile. The two families who were most strongly condemned for thinking themselves posh had not been occupationally mobile. There were four families who had moved up the occupational ladder but who were not felt by the Newbolts to consider themselves posh. Class sentiments emerged most strongly about relatives who had moved away from the old neighbourhood to new housing estates. If the Newbolts felt a family had moved primarily because of the housing shortage they remained in effective contact, regardless of whether the family had·been occupationally mobile. If the family had moved so as to 'better themselves', they were condemned for being posh and contact became non-effective.

In the case of the Hartleys, things were more complicated. First, Mr Hartley had been occupationally mobile, and his style of life at the time of interviewing was rather different from that of his parents when he was a child. But his mother was their only intimate relative, and they were both very fond of her. When Mr Hartley's mother first came to London, her husband's sisters (Mr Hartley's paternal aunts) had looked down on her a little bit for being a simple country girl; one of the sisters was married to a taxi-driver and another to a head waiter. Mr Hartley's success meant a good deal to his mother, for she could show off her son and daughter-in-law to her sister-in-law with considerable pride. The sisters also had socially successful children and the three old ladies spent a good deal of time comparing notes on their children's progress. The aunts found the Hartleys 'modern' and slightly shocking. The Hartleys thought the aunts were amusing in small doses. In terms of their concepts of class, the aunts were 'lower middle-class', whereas they themselves were 'middle middle-class', although they were reluctant to say this directly. They thought their cousins were middle middle-class like themselves but that they were a bit tedious and conventional, and they saw each other chiefly because their mothers were in close contact.

The Hartleys had less contact with Mrs Hartley's relatives because most of these relatives lived in the north of England and because her parents were dead, so that there were no very important connecting relatives. Such effective relatives as Mrs Hartley had, however, were on her father's side. Her father they described as having been middle middle-class, like themselves. Her mother's people appear to have been of somewhat lower social status and even when her parents were alive Mrs Hartley had less contact with her mother's relatives than with her father's. Concepts of status and prestige had thus been important, but her parents' concepts mattered more than her own. Concepts of class do not explain Mrs Hartley's relationship with her brother. He was felt to be middle middle-class like Mrs Hartley, but they had had a quarrel several years before the interviews began and there had been no contact between them since that time.

The Hartleys had thus kept in contact with several relatives whom they felt to be of lower social status than themselves. With regard to his mother, they felt their own success was a positive thing for her as well as for themselves. Seven other families in the research set had been socially mobile, and they too had kept in intimate contact with their parents. It appears that the parent-child relationship transcends social as well as physical separation. But the Hartleys were also keeping up effective contact with several more distant relatives of lower social status. They appeared to be doing this as an affirmation of their own status, partly on their own behalf, but much more for his mother's sake.

By the Daniels' definition, none of their relatives shared their own class attitude for, in their view, they themselves were middle-class by occupation and income, but they identified themselves with the working class. They had several relatives with occupations similar to their own, but they did not have much in common with them because their class interests lay elsewhere. In this respect the Daniels had far more in common with their friends than with their relatives. Their concepts of class do not account for the differences in type of contact with Mr Daniels' relatives, for all these relatives were felt to be different from the Daniels themselves. It appears that Mr Daniels' mother used to have rather more contact with her husband's relatives than with her own when Mr Daniels was a child; her feelings about status may have had something to do with her preference, but the fact that her husband's relatives lived nearer was probably the most important factor. The effect of her preferences on the Daniels was shown at the time of interviewing in the fact that the Daniels had rather more effective contacts with his father's relatives than with his mother's. Mrs Daniels' political views may have had something to do with the fact that she hardly ever saw six of her brothers and sisters, for the only sibling with whom she kept in touch shared her opinions to some extent. Like other families, the Daniels kept in touch with parents regardless of their feelings about their parents' status.

Judging from these families, personal likes and dislikes cannot be explained in terms of independently assessed measures of status. They can be explained partly, but not entirely, in terms of the individuals' own concepts of status. But people kept in touch with their parents even when they thought their parents were of a different social status from themselves. Felt status differences were more important in affecting contact with more distant relatives, although even here the preferences of connecting relatives sometimes overrode the couple's own preferences.

7. *Some Psychological Mechanisms Affecting Attitudes Towards Relatives*

Not all likes and dislikes of kin can be attributed to perceived differences in status. On the basis of status similarity (and the other five factors previously discussed) one would expect Mrs Hartley's brother to be at least an effective relative, but in fact he was non-effective. Similarly one would expect Mrs Daniels to be in effective contact with her brothers and sisters but in fact she was in effective contact with one only. Even the Newbolts seemed to be beginning to express their own personal preferences instead of following the lead of their connecting relatives entirely, and their preferences cannot be explained wholly or even chiefly in terms of perceived status differences.

Personal likes and dislikes stand out clearly as a separate factor when other factors work in the opposite direction, but of course such preferences operate in all relations with kin. Thus the Newbolts liked many of their intimate relatives, even though the pressure applied by their connecting relatives would probably have made them visit their intimate kin in any case. Indeed, in all societies people doubtless like some relatives better than others. But among the research families such likes and dislikes could frequently be made the basis of choosing whether or not to associate with relatives, whereas in many other kinship systems emotions concerning relatives cannot so readily be translated into action; they are more likely to be institutionalized and directed into socially defined channels so that purely personal likes and dislikes are not so important as an independent factor affecting type of contact with kin. In order to examine this factor it is necessary to consider some of the psychological mechanisms involved in attitudes towards relatives.

The same psychological mechanisms operate in relationships with extra-familial kin as in other relationships. But kinship relationships have a peculiar importance because of their permanence. They are particularly useful to the individual as a field for expressing and coping with feelings, unconscious as well as conscious.[1] The implicit assumption appears to be that relatives are in some way parts of oneself and one is part of them, even if one had never seen them. One can break off a friendship but one cannot break off a 'blood' relationship. Contact with a relative may be stopped, but in a sense the relationship is still there, something is still shared. Relatives are links with the past and the future. They give a feeling of continuity. One must die oneself, but one's family, in the broadest sense, goes on.

Thus most couples seemed to feel that they were somehow responsible, however slightly, for the behaviour of their relatives. Their relatives' successes were their successes and their relatives' failures were their failures. Nearly all couples maintained a 'there but for the grace of God go I'' sort of attitude to some relatives, and a feeling of 'if only I had had his luck' (or sometimes 'ability' or 'gifts') towards others. Everyone uses relatives as a basis of comparison and contrast with his own way of life.

As stated above, socially mobile couples tend to regard their success as a positive thing for their parents as well as for themselves. Unconsciously such success may be felt as a reparation to parents for any harm that is unconsciously felt to have been done to them. Similar reparative feelings may be extended to more distant relatives.

[1] Cf. Elliott Jaques' examination of the way individuals use social institutions as a defence against unconscious anxiety (Jaques, 1953).

A few people interviewed in the course of the research seemed to be consciously trying to behave like a particular relative whom they admired. But this sort of identification may also take place unconsciously. People sometimes acted as if they had qualities that they attributed to a relative, even when they were not aware of the resemblance.

In many cases attitudes towards one relative may be displaced on to another. Thus one may be able to see one's father as a kindly helpful person partly because one can find the ferocious authoritarian side of his nature (or what one unconsciously feels is his nature) in an uncle or some other relative. Or one may find in other relatives desirable qualities that one's own parents are felt to lack. Ambivalent feelings towards parents can be split and expressed separately towards more distant relatives; one can feel unadulterated hatred for one relative and idealized devotion for another, especially if one has only intermittent contact with them. What the relatives are really like is another problem; we are concerned here with the mechanisms by which people cope with their feelings about relatives regardless of whether such feelings are realistic and justifiable or not.

Parts of one's own self may also be put into relatives unconsciously so that one can express such parts vicariously without having to act that way oneself. Sometimes it is qualities that are felt to be bad that are projected; castigating one's own faults in others is an easily recognized form. But good qualities may be projected too. Thus several research couples seemed to feel that their own spirit of adventure and exploration had somehow been satisfied by those relatives who had gone away to America, the Dominions, and the Colonies. But feelings of envy, resentment, and loss also seemed to be implied occasionally in descriptions of kin who had emigrated. By a similar mechanism of projection a rather priggish couple may get considerable satisfaction from disreputable relatives who act more spontaneously than they do themselves. In such cases of displacement and projection, lack of direct contact with relatives sometimes makes the relatives more rather than less useful psychologically, for the less direct one's knowledge of the relative, the less chance there is of checking one's fantasies against the reality.

These few examples give only the barest indication of the many unconscious factors affecting feelings towards relatives and of the many ways such factors may be combined in individual cases. To analyse these psychological mechanisms in detail would require a full discussion of psycho-analytic concepts, which I do not propose to attempt here.[1] But as an example of how these various mechanisms may be combined in a particular case, I shall describe inferences about the Daniels' unconscious attitudes towards their relatives.

Mr Daniels spoke of his relatives at length and seemed to be interested in describing them. At the same time, he made very few personal comments about them. He did not describe their characters and he was very guarded about criticizing them directly. He was freer in expressing his special liking for his grandparents and one of his aunts, and in one of the later interviews he indicated that they were interesting and exciting in contrast to his parents who were more neutral. He said that his father's father came from Wales and set up a grocery shop in a small town in Shropshire. His father became a lieutenant-commander in the first war, and then the manager of a small canning factory. He lost his job during the depression. His father's brothers became businessmen; one of them had only some slight success whereas the other became wealthy. Mr Daniels described his cousins as rather weak men who depended on their father for financial security; one of them he described as a 'spiv'. He said that his mother's people were mostly in the Army; several became officers but most belonged to other ranks. Some of the cousins on his mother's side were clerks and minor professional people. Others he described as spivs, meaning that they had money, large houses, and cars, but that they had little education and few intellectual or artistic interests. There was also a suggestion that they did not really deserve

---

[1] For a statement of the theory of psychological mechanisms in general followed here, see the works of Melanie Klein, especially *Psycho-Analysis of Children* (1932), *Contributions to Psycho-Analysis* (1948), and *New Directions in Psycho-Analysis* (1955). For briefer statements see Klein and Riviere (1937), Segal (1952), Heimann (1952), and Jaques (1953).

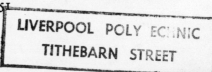

their wealth, that they had acquired it through sharp practices, and that in any case they did not lead the kind of life he cared for.

In presenting his relatives, he appeared to be expressing several themes. The first concerned the careers of his father and his father's father. Both had been very successful at their work when they were young but both had had difficulties in middle age. His grandfather lost his customers because of his left-wing beliefs. His father lost his job during the depression. Mr Daniels said these events had been very important in shaping his own political opinions and his belief that security lay in group solidarity and group action. The helplessness and social injustice experienced by his father and grandfather were things he wanted to avoid at all costs. He had got himself a secure job and he was determined that he and his family would weather his middle age without mishap in spite of his left-wing political views.

He found in his grandparents and some of his aunts and uncles exciting relatives who compensated for what he felt to be the dullness of his parents. It was these aunts and uncles with whom he maintained some contact at the time of interviewing. One cannot tell what his parents were really like, but one of his main methods of coping in the present with people and situations about which he has strong feelings is to feel neutral about them, so that there is some likelihood that he has neutralized his parents and located their exciting aspects in other relatives.

He talked a good deal about those relatives who had become businessmen, partly because his mother kept him informed about them and partly because their way of life provided such a contrast to his own. He himself chose a professional occupation and he was relieved that he was not a businessman. He said his successful uncle seemed to have an empty, meaningless life that reminded him of *Death of a Salesman*. He also expressed some interest in and yet distaste for his spiv relatives. 'I suppose you might say I was envious of them', he remarked on one occasion. From his total pattern of statements it is possible to infer that at least unconsciously he would like to have been a spiv himself, though he was afraid of the idea at the same time. But nothing could have been further from his actual behaviour. Our inference is that he could express such wishes vicariously through his spiv relatives, thus freeing himself from the need to express them directly. At the time of interviewing these spiv relatives were non-effective kin. He did not like them and made no effort to see them, although he knew a certain amount about them through his mother. But lack of contact did not make them less interesting and significant to him.

Mrs Daniels spoke of her relatives with less caution and restraint. Her chief remark was that hers was not a united family. She said several times, 'Mine is the sort of family that gets scattered to all four winds in each generation.' Her father's parents died young and all the children were brought up in orphanages so that they lost contact with one another and Mrs Daniels knew very little about them. Her mother's family was disrupted by the early death of the grandfather who left the grandmother with ten young children. Mrs Daniels never met her grandmother, but she had collected stories about her from one of her aunts. Apparently her grandmother took to drink, squandered her inheritance, used her children's money, and pawned their possessions. At the same time she was a majestic woman and she really enjoyed herself. Several of her children left home for good. Mrs Daniels said she thought her own mother disapproved of the grandmother, although her mother never talked about her. At any rate, Mrs Daniels described her mother's character as quite the opposite of the grandmother—sober, responsible, unable to express her feelings or respond to things spontaneously. One of the aunts seemed to be a more harmless version of the grandmother, having her enjoyment of life but not her greediness and selfish capacity to harm others. This aunt was one of Mrs Daniels very few effective relatives at the time of interviewing. Two of the uncles were musicians and one had considerable success. Two other uncles went into the Navy, most of the cousins were black-coated workers. The theme of scattering was repeated by Mrs Daniels' siblings. She said that most of them either disliked one another or felt indifferent, and that they had stopped seeing one another as soon as possible. She said there was very little brotherly love in the family, except between herself and one of her brothers when they were children.

There were several themes that seemed to be important in Mrs Daniels' presentation of her relatives. The first was her stress on the family being scattered. Such scattering was not uncommon among the research families, but few informants felt it so keenly as Mrs. Daniels. When I remarked on this, she said she thought there really was more scattering in her family than in most, for some of her brothers and sisters had commented on it too. She added that she thought I was making too much of it, for after all it was my questions about it that had made her reflect on the matter and talk so much about it. She gave me the feeling that she had a sense of loss about her relatives, loss not only for herself but also on behalf of her relatives, expecially her father, who had been deprived of proper family life. Some of her stress on the scattering of distant relatives may have been a displacement of her concern about the scattering of close relatives, for she seemed to feel a little sad about the estrangement of her brothers and sisters from herself and from one another and said she wondered if it was normal. But she also seemed to be finding, or rather stressing, something in her relatives that was also represented unconsciously in herself. There was a good deal of evidence suggesting that she had several contradictory aims and wishes; at times she felt herself to be scattered among them, although usually she could organize her life so that her various wishes could be satisfied, but still they were kept together by the mere fact of genealogical relationship. She was also sometimes worried by what she felt to be some malign potentiality in herself and in her relationships with people, especially by what she felt as her inability to express positive feelings easily. In the scattering of her relatives she found disturbing evidence of broken relationships. The implicit questions seemed to be: 'Were they all like me?'; 'Can't I be different?'; 'Is it my fault?' From time to time she had seriously tried to find out about her relatives from her aunt and her mother, as if she were recovering her lost past and, so to speak, putting her relatives harmoniously together again.

Another important theme was her picture of her grandmother, particularly in contrast to her mother. She was amused and pleased by her grandmother, especially by her gusto and disregard of convention. In practice Mrs Daniels was more like her mother, although every now and again she gave a hearty laugh that suggested her grandmother. In her grandmother she seemed to have located the greedy, demanding, self-indulgent parts of herself that she could not express directly for fear of hurting people and turning them against her. The 'grandmother' part of her was controlled in practice but expressed vicariously.

It is obvious that this sort of analysis requires discretion. It would be absurd to say that because a man's uncle murdered someone, the man himself felt he had committed murder vicariously and was thus relieved of the necessity of doing it himself. Whether this was the case or not would be shown by the way he talked about his uncle, not by the bare facts of the case. In other words, the facts themselves are not so important as the way people present them. It would be helpful if one had an independent check on the facts so that one could gauge how much informants were distorting the picture, but in most cases such information is not available, particularly for past events. In any case whether the facts are distorted or not, the way they are presented is expressive of the individual's personality. In making these inferences, however, we have used not only the material concerning relatives but also material collected in other contexts in which similar themes were expressed.

Other families would combine these various psychological mechanisms in other ways, with differing consequences for their likes and dislikes of relatives. Thus, just as one can show how various factors affect choice of contact with kin but one cannot predict exactly what choices any particular family will make, so one can describe the various psychological mechanisms involved in relations with extra-familial kin, although one cannot tell in advance exactly how these mechanisms will be combined in the case of any particular individual.

C. OTHER FACTORS AFFECTING CONTACT WITH KIN

Several important factors affecting type of contact with kin have been omitted from the preceding analysis.

Variation in kin contacted according to the type of activity involved has been ignored because it was incorporated into the definition of types of contact. Each activity, however, has its own kin personnel; the range of kin who visit each other frequently is usually narrower than the range of those who attend a wedding, a funeral, or a christening. New activities and new situations may change the pattern of contact. There were many examples among the research families of people who had made new contacts with kin during the war, when long-lost cousins turned up from overseas; non-effective kin became effective, at least temporarily. On a smaller scale this sort of thing goes on all the time, and it should not be thought that the categories of intimate, effective, non-effective, and unfamiliar kin are rigid and unchanging.

The phase of development reached by the family has been held constant, since all the research families were families with young children. In comparing families of different phases or individuals of different ages, however, this factor would become very important, for it is obvious that a young person will have fewer descendants and therefore a narrower range of knowledge of kin than an older person, and that a family tied down by young children will be less able to keep up contact with geographically distant relatives than a family with older children. To judge from the couples we interviewed, it appears that contacts with kin go through several phases of expansion and contraction as the individual and the family develop. Most of our informants said that in childhood they had had some contact with their grandparents and with the families of their uncles and aunts as well as with their own parents and siblings. Most people indicated that in late adolescence and early adulthood they had broken away from their parents and siblings to some extent, and contacts with extra-familial kin were dropped or greatly reduced. After people had married, and particularly after they had had children of their own, they often began to see more of their parents again if they could, but contacts with other kin were not picked up again to the same extent except in cases like the Newbolts where many of the other kin lived nearby. In fact couples with young children are probably more affected by where their kin live than any other type of family, since their children tie them down so much that they cannot make frequent visits away from home. Since we did not study families in later phases of development, we have no precise information on further changes in the amount and type of contact with kin.[1]

Factors connected with religious and ethnic group membership were also held constant in this analysis, since all the families were British and were of mainly Protestant background.

Household composition is an important determinant of which kin one will see; when one visits a relative one sees not only that particular relative but also the other people who live in the house. Because of the importance of household composition, it would perhaps be advisable to count the household as one unit for purpose of analysis instead of using the individual relative as the unit. Certainly this procedure would be closer to the informants' conception of their kinship network as a set of elementary families linked to one another through relationships between individuals. In effect this procedure has been followed throughout this chapter, although the quantitative material has been presented in number of individuals rather than in number of family-households.

Gross numbers of kin recognized and contacted depend not only on the various factors discussed in this chapter, but also of course on the biological existence of the kin. It is also possible that birth order might be another significant factor, although a brief comparison yielded no significant results with our data.[2] The relative age gap between generations is also significant, chiefly because it is one of the factors affecting the presence of

[1] These later phases are being studied comparatively by Peter Townsend (1955a, 1955b, and 1957).

[2] Birth order is an important factor in the Bethnal Green families studied by the Institute of Community Studies, where eldest daughters appear to have an appreciably different pattern of contact with kin from that of youngest daughters (Young and Willmott, 1957).

connecting relatives. Thus Mrs Newbolt's mother married young and so did Mrs Newbolt. Since her grandmother was still alive and active, the Newbolts had a very important connecting relative that other families, with greater age gaps between the generations, did not have.

SUMMARY

In conclusion, all three families' relationships with kin followed the bilateral pattern in which persons are affiliated in the same way, actually or potentially, with their mother's and their father's kin. But the Newbolts had a great deal of contact with kin, the Hartleys had less, and the Daniels still less. Similarly the Newbolts' kin had a great deal of contact with one another, the Hartleys' had less, and the Daniels' still less. These variations were not random and unpredictable. The effects of ecological, social, and psychological factors have been considered in turn. These factors are interdependent and no one factor can explain all behaviour towards kin. Any given instance of such behaviour is affected by several factors, sometimes operating to the same end, sometimes in conflict with one another. The relative weight of each factor depends on the particular configuration of the combination.

CHAPTER VI

Norms and Ideology:
Concepts of Class

In the preceding chapters it has been pointed out many times that a family does not live directly in the total society, or even, in many cases, in a local community. The effective social environment of a family is its network of friends, neighbours, relatives, and particular social institutions. This is its primary social world. But this does not mean that families have no ideas about their society as a whole or about families in general. The research couples differed widely in their views on these matters. These differences are interpreted here as a result of varying social experience and personal needs.

The couples' ideas about class structure give a good, though by no means complete, indication of their conception of the society as a whole and their own place in it. Much of the literature on class suggests that social classes are concrete entities in the sense of being actual groups, and that most members of a society agree in their description of what these entities are and what criteria should be used to describe them. Our data suggest, on the contrary, that people disagree profoundly in their views on class, so much so that we sometimes wondered if they were talking about the same society. Our conclusion is that in certain important respects they were not. Although a finisher in Bermondsey and an account executive in Chelsea are both members of the larger British society, they live in different worlds; they have different jobs, different friends, different neighbours, and different family trees. Each bases his ideas of class on his own experience, so that it is hardly surprising that each has a different conception of the class structure as a whole. In these circumstances it would be naïve to assume that people's ideas about class will be a valid representation of the 'real' or 'objective' class structure of the society as a whole. Their ideas do, however, reveal information about the people themselves and their primary social experience. In this chapter an attempt is made to describe how people construct their ideas about class and how they use them in making comparisons and evaluations.

Questions about class were asked as part of a general inquiry into each couple's *Weltanschauung*. Various matters associated with class, prestige, and power came up spontaneously in the course of conversation about other matters. Direct questions about class were asked towards the end of the interviews. Information was sought on seven topics:

1. What classes each couple thought there were.
2. What criteria they were using in defining these classes and also what criteria they used to place individuals in them.
3. What they thought about the mobility of individuals.
4. What they thought about changes in the class structure as a whole in the past and probable changes in the future.
5. Where they placed themselves.
6. What aspirations they had for their children.
7. Whether they thought family life varied according to class.

The material on class ideology was not central to the main aim of the investigation, so care was taken not to put an unnecessary strain on the relationship between the field worker and the couple for this purpose. As a result, four early families were not asked about class at all. Of the remaining sixteen, five were not asked about self-placement because the field worker thought the couple would be too anxious to deal with such a question without embarrassment. The spontaneous material is therefore uniformly rich and detailed, but the systematic probing of this material by direct questioning could not be carried out to the same degree in all cases.

As noted in Chapter II, the research families varied considerably in socio-economic status, although there were no unskilled workers. The incomes of the husbands before tax ranged from £330 to over £1,800. The occupations of the husbands in families with loose-knit networks were: deputy fire manager of an insurance firm, pottery designer working as an occupational therapist in a mental hospital, statistician in a welfare agency, account executive in an advertising agency—he was in charge of relations with several important clients—and temporary clerk in the Gas Board. The occupations of husbands in families with medium-knit networks were: skilled repairer of optical instruments, establishments officer in Public Health Department of a local authority, sundry supplies buyer for a medium-sized industrial firm, manager of health food shop, clerk in insurance firm, painter and decorator, general commercial manager of a light engineering firm, self-employed repairer of radio and television sets, and police constable. The husband in the family with the most close-knit network was a finisher in a large boot and shoe repair firm. The occupations of the husbands in families with transitional networks were: draughtsman in a firm of architects, clerk in a large department store, W.E.A. lecturer, owner-operator of a small tobacco and sweet shop, and plumber.

A. THE PROCESSES BY WHICH INDIVIDUALS DEVELOP THEIR CONCEPTS OF THE CLASS STRUCTURE

In this chapter I discuss only class ideology, not the class structure of the society as a whole. The method adopted did not provide the data necessary for a study of class structure as such, and as the study progressed it became clear that a detailed knowledge of the class structure of the society as a whole was not a necessary prerequisite for understanding the way in which individuals construct and use their own ideas about class. If one's aim were to compare and contrast the class ideology of a large number of informants, it would be helpful to use some measure of their position in the total class structure as a yardstick against which their class ideology could be compared. Various theories and definitions of class might be used for this purpose. In my opinion no one of these theories is valid for all purposes although each is appropriate to particular problems. If one is studying social and economic change, a useful definition is the Marxian one of classes as actual or potential corporate groups recruited on the basis of position in relation to the means of production. If one is studying the distinctions of prestige in a small community, Warner's definition of social class is useful (Warner and Lunt, 1941). If one is comparing the attitudes of a large sample of people one is likely to treat class as a socio-economic category. For the purposes of the present study, however, the most important point about the class structure is its extreme complexity. The various institutions and groups involved in social differentiation are not tightly fitted together so as to form a small number of closed, corporate classes easily identified by all members of the society. It is this complexity and loose articulation that makes possible the variation in class ideology that was found among our informants.

There have been several studies, notably that of Centers, in which political and social attitudes have been compared with 'objective' class position and with 'subjective' self-placement in a pre-defined class (Centers, 1949 and 1952). Hammond has extended this approach very considerably by comparing people's ideology about class with their objective class position. Instead of asking his informants to place themselves in pre-defined classes, he asked what they thought the classes were and then compared the different types of ideological model with objective class position (Hammond, 1952). His results are in line with the present study, but instead of concentrating on large-scale comparisons of ideology with objective position, the aim here is to understand the processes and mechanisms by which particular individuals arrive at their ideas of class.

To tackle such a problem, it is not enough to know the individual's position in a socio-economic category or objectively defined class. People do not experience their objective class position as a single, clearly defined status. They do not report any direct, immediate experience of belonging to a class as a membership group, except on the now rare occasions when classes act as corporate groups. But people do have direct experience of distinctions of power and prestige in their places of work, among their colleagues, in schools, and in their relationships with friends, neighbours, and relatives. In other words the ingredients, the raw materials, of class ideology are located in the individual's various primary social experiences, rather than in his position in a socioeconomic category. The hypothesis advanced here is that when an individual talks about class he is trying to say something, in a symbolic form, about his experiences of power and prestige in his actual membership groups and social relationships both past and present. These experiences have little intrinsic connection with one another, especially in a large city, and each of the groups and networks concerned has its own pattern of organization. The psychological situation for the individual, therefore, is one of belonging to a number of unconnected groups each with its own system of prestige and power. When he is comparing himself with other people or placing himself in the widest social context, he manufactures a notion of his general social position out of these various experiences. He reduces them all to a sort of common denominator. This is not a very accurate procedure. The experiences are not differentiated and related to one another; they are telescoped and condensed into one general notion. But it is accurate enough for orientating him in a complex society.

Most people are hardly aware of performing these acts of social conceptualization. Thus a plumber, whose class ideology is reported in detail below, combined together his experiences in several groups to arrive at a general model of two interdependent but conflicting classes. The most important experiences he was using in constructing this model were his membership in a closely integrated neighbourhood during his childhood, his experience of unemployment, his experience in his present job, with his colleagues, with his superiors at work, with neighbours, with acquaintances in various clubs, together with some more indirect information about the 'idle rich'. But he was not aware of the precise contribution of each of these separate group memberships, even though he had talked about each of them separately and agreed with the field worker's suggestion that his experience in them provided the basis of his own view of the class structure.

Very occasionally an informant pointed out that the various group contexts were separate and should not really be combined into a notion of general status or class. Thus the clerk in an insurance firm dealt with the situation by saying that prestige depended on the context of evaluation. Quoting from the interview record:

'... He went on to say that it made a difference if you were looking at the thing nationally or locally. If you looked at a man's position from the point of view of his neighbourhood, any professional man would be at the the top of the tree. But if you looked at the profession as a whole, from the national point of view, it might not be the top of the tree. ... Most doctors work in one local area and live in another. Among other doctors, their position would depend on how well they did their work, etc. In their neighbourhood, it would depend on where they lived. Take Golders Green, for example. That was predominantly a Jewish neighbourhood. Also it was mostly an area of professional people. He said it wouldn't give a man any particular prestige to be a doctor in Golders Green because everyone else was a doctor there too.'

Most informants reduced their own unconnected relationships and group memberships to a notion of general position without worrying about such niceties of evaluation, and many individuals seemed to be hardly aware of the fact that they were using their own experiences as a basis for their model of the class structure.

The individual performs a telescoping procedure on other people as well as on himself. If they are people who have the same, or similar, group memberships as himself, he is likely to feel that they have the same general position and belong to his own class. If they are outsiders, his knowledge of them will be indirect and incomplete so that there is plenty of room for projection and distortion. Thus several individuals who placed themselves in the 'middle class' made two or three differentiations in their own class but spoke of the 'working class' or 'manual labourers' as an undifferentiated mass. Similarly some people who placed themselves in the 'working class' made differentiations within it but lumped together everyone else as 'the rich'. The more remote the people of another class, the less opportunity there is for checking fantasy against fact, so that the individual can see in such people what he wants to see, and what he wants to see will depend on his perception of their position relative to his own.

In brief, the individual constructs his notions of social position and class from his own various and unconnected experiences of prestige and power and his imperfect knowledge of other people's. He manufactures classes, assigns norms and values to them, and then uses them in various contexts to make comparisons and evaluations. He is not just a passive recipient assimilating the norms of concrete, external, organized classes. He creates his own model of the class structure and uses it as a rough-and-ready means of orientating himself in a society so complex that he cannot experience directly more than a very limited part of it.[1]

B. THE CONCEPT OF REFERENCE GROUP
IN RELATION TO CLASS IDEOLOGY

Although the term 'reference group' has been very rapidly adopted by sociologists and social psychologists during the past ten years, there appears to be considerable disagreement over its definition.[2] I use it to mean *any group, real or fictitious, that is*

[1] Cf. Bartlett's general theory that perceiving and remembering are active processes in which the individual not only receives information but also constructs it in accordance with his own attitudes (Bartlett, 1932).

[2] Hyman, who introduced the term, uses it to mean any group with which the individual compares himself (Hyman, 1942). Newcomb uses it to mean any group with which the individual is identified; the identification may be positive, negative, or ambivalent but cannot be neutral (Newcomb, 1948, 1950; and 1952). Merton and Kitt use the term very generally, to refer both to groups used for comparison and to groups with which the individual is emotionally identified (Merton and Kitt, 1950). Sherif restricts the term to groups with which the individual is positively identified (Sherif, 1953). Keller and Stern use it only for groups to which the individual does not belong (Keller and Stern, 1953). Eisenstadt is concerned with the way norms and values become linked to a particular

thought by an individual to have a real existence and is employed by him to compare or evaluate his position with that of others, and to justify or explain his actions. He may belong to the reference group; he may not. He may be positively identified with it and want to belong to it; he may not. The 'group' concerned may not even be a real group; it may be a category constructed by the individual. At this point I go beyond the literature, for most authors assume that reference groups exist *sui generis* apart from the individual. Such sociologically real groups have independent norms that can be internalized by the individual, and that can then be used by him in perceiving and evaluating himself and other people; the norms of the external group become the attitudes of the individual. I think the reverse process occurs too; individuals do, of course, internalize norms that exist in actual external groups, but they also project some of their own attitudes and values back into the external situation. Re-interpretation and projection occur to some extent in all cases of assimilating norms, but such processes are particularly important in the construction and use of classes as reference groups.

Many authors have mentioned in passing that individuals use classes as reference groups. Newcomb goes into the matter in some detail in discussing the work of Centers and Steiner (Newcomb, 1950, pp. 228–32). According to the work of Centers, one can predict political attitudes from the individual's subjective class identification about as well as from his occupational status as objectively defined (Centers, 1949 and 1952). According to Steiner, students who are middle-class by objective criteria but working-class by self-placement have attitudes similar to those of students who are working-class both by objective and subjective criteria. In the language of reference group theory, one would say that the individual expresses attitudes that are in accordance with the norms of the class which is a positive reference group for him. If

group (Eisenstadt, 1954). Kelley points out that the term is sometimes used to mean any group with which the individual compares himself, sometimes to mean any group with which he is emotionally identified (Kelley, 1952). I find it convenient to use the term in the most general sense, adding qualifying adjectives where necessary.

he uses his own class as a positive reference group, he will adhere to its norms. If he uses another class as a positive reference group, he will express attitudes in accordance with this group of which he is not a member.

Such an interpretation assumes that classes are actual groups with interlocking social roles and distinctive norms, so that norms can be directly internalized by the individual. This amounts to a reification of the concept of class; classes, at least as defined in the above studies, appear to be categories rather than actual groups, so that their norms cannot be internalized directly. My suggestion is that there are three steps in an individual's creation of a class reference group: first, he internalizes the norms of his primary membership groups—place of work, colleagues, friends, neighbourhood, family—together with other notions assimilated from books and the various mass media; second, he performs an act of conceptualization in reducing these relatively unconnected and often contradictory norms to a common denominator; third, he projects his conceptualizations back on to society at large. This is not a conscious, deliberate process; it happens for the most part unwittingly. Moreover, modifications and revisions are constantly being made, and there are often inconsistencies and contradictions between the constructions made at different times and for different purposes. The main point is that the individual himself is an active agent. He does not simply internalize the norms of classes that have an independent external existence. He takes in the norms of certain actual groups, works them over, and constructs class reference groups out of them.

It is useful to make a distinction between *direct reference groups* and *constructed reference groups*. *Direct* reference groups are those in which the referent is an actual group with interlocking roles and distinctive norms that can be directly internalized by the individual; there is a relatively small amount of construction of the group and projection of norms into it by the individual. Such direct reference groups may be membership groups, or they may be non-membership groups whose norms have been internalized by the individual. The crucial point is that they are actual groups that exist independently of him. *Constructed* reference groups are those in which the referent is a concept or social category rather than an actual group; in this case the amount of construction and projection of norms into the constructed group is relatively high.

Classes are constructed reference groups. They are used by individuals to structure their social world and to make comparisons and evaluations of their own behaviour and that of other people. Although these concepts may not be objectively real, they are psychologically real, in the sense that they affect the behaviour of the individual. Among the research families, there was considerable variation in the extent to which people believed in the external reality of their class reference groups. Some informants were deeply convinced that classes had a real, objective, external existence; others were very sceptical and said that classes were really figments of people's imaginations; the most common attitude, although not expressed in these words, was that classes were rather like stereotypes, not to be taken too seriously, but virtually indispensable for making comparisons and evaluations.

·C. THE USE OF CLASS REFERENCE GROUPS AND MODELS OF THE CLASS STRUCTURE

All the research couples made some use of class reference groups in the course of informal conversation. In addition, most couples produce a model of the total class structure in reply to our direct questions. There were two wives who denied the existence of classes, but they did it so vehemently as to suggest that they thought classes existed, but wished for various reasons that they did not. Several people were hardly aware that they were operating a model of the class structure, and they experienced some pain in the course of making it explicit and realizing that it was full of contradictions and inconsistencies. Many couples pointed out that the various criteria of class membership they were using—occupation, income, control of people through wealth or industrial power, education, family background, manners, accent, etc.—did not fit together closely so as to form a neat hierarchy, and they were not sure which should be given first priority. At this point several people remarked that classes were not real groups and that people who believed in them were snobbish and unpleasant.

In ordinary conversation, people never used their whole model. They used bits and pieces of it as reference groups in particular contexts of comparison and evaluation. Nearly everyone talked about classes when discussing the society as a whole and the social and political changes in it. Classes were also used for placing strangers and for contrasting other people's social lot with one's own in a wide social context. Apart from these universal usages, couples varied greatly in the extent to which they used class reference groups in ordinary conversation. The couples who used them most frequently were those who were dealing with unfamiliar situations, making relationships with new people in different social or physical surroundings. Some had been mobile socially, some only physically, but they were all faced with the problem of sorting people out, of placing themselves in relation to other people. They were all structuring their social world. Couples who were more settled talked about prestige and power in more particular terms without generalizing them into concepts of class.

It appears, then, that everyone operates a model of the class structure, but that the models are fluid and variable and are used differently in different social contexts. It is this fluidity which explains the fact that one gets such different results about class ideology when using different methods of inquiry. Several studies show that if a large number of people are asked to rank occupations and to place them in pre-defined classes, they will agree, more or less, in their rankings (Centers, 1949 and 1952; Form, 1946; Hall and Caradog Jones, 1950; North and Hatt, 1947). In spite of some contradictions between these studies, it seems clear that there is some general agreement about the social status of occupations, but it is difficult to tell how much of this agreement is a function of the methods used and how much is a reflection of social stereotyping or of genuine consensus. In any case, such agreement does not necessarily mean that these rankings or classes are used by the rankers in their everyday social life.[1]

Our method of open-ended questioning, like Hammond's (1952), turned up far more variation than studies made by questionnaire. Although some features were common to all versions, and it is possible to define several main types of model, each version had some unique features of its own. Furthermore, it is always necessary to remember that an informant's responses were strongly influenced by his immediate social situation, particularly by his relationship with the field worker. At times this was very obvious, as when a woman revealed her snobbishness, or what she thought was snobbishness, and then asked if the field worker thought the same way. On another occasion one of the field workers asked a man what type he meant by 'semi-professionals' and was told,'Well as a matter of fact I was thinking of you. You aren't an ordinary office worker, but you aren't like a lawyer or a doctor either.' At other times people were less consciously aware of the immediate situation. But it always had some effect on the presentation of the model and it was necessary for the field worker to use his understanding of it in the analysis of each couple's ideas about class.

In ordinary conversation, as has been stated above, people used only parts of their model. There were sometimes discrepancies between these bits and pieces and the tidied-up version presented in reply to direct questions, but the differences were usually variations in emphasis and detail. For example, the sundry supplies buyer and his wife used a model of upper, middle, and working class with three subdivisions in the middle class, placing themselves in the 'middle middle-class'. On other occasions when

[1] Cf. Eysenck's statement that answers to forced-choice questions need not represent the subject's attitudes as expressed in more unstructured interviews. 'It has generally been assumed that stereotyped replies to questions on "national characteristics" indicate stereotyped thinking on the part of the respondents; our results suggest *per contra* that the majority of respondents have no particular views on the subject at all, and are perfectly aware of the fact that any replies they can make are merely the result of cultural and social indoctrination. In other words, the results of studies of this kind are predetermined by the methodology used; when we look for stereotyped views, and give the subject no chance to reply in any non-stereotyped fashion, we should not be surprised that the answer we get is a stereotyped one' (Eysenck and Crown, 1948).

they were discussing general social and political changes and comparing certain neighbourhoods, they spontaneously used the terms 'middle class' and 'working class' much as they used them when formally outlining the whole model. Sometimes they used the phrase 'the lower income groups'—always spoken with inverted commas—as a synonym for 'working class', partly as a gentle dig at surveys and research work, and partly as a way of getting around the embarrassment of talking directly about people lower in the hierarchy than themselves. In talking spontaneously about friends, neighbours, and colleagues, they introduced a number of additional concepts: 'suburbanites', 'bohemians', 'intellectuals', and 'intelligent people'. All of these concepts were concerned with social status to a greater or lesser degree, and all had some connection with their class reference groups; they were refinements within the middle-class reference group, although they cut across the three sub-divisions within the middle class.

In brief, people use class reference groups for making both comparisons and evaluations in the widest social context, but their usages vary according to the immediate social situation and the specific purpose of the comparisons and evaluations. It follows that there is no one valid way of finding out what people *really* think about class, for each method will reveal slightly different reference groups, although there is a strain of consistency and continuity running through each couple's usages at different times.

D. DISCUSSION OF FIELD MATERIAL

1. *Points of General Consensus among all Informants*

As has been stated above, all the couples used class reference groups, and everyone operated a model of the class structure, at least implicitly. With two exceptions, informants agreed that classes existed and that society could be divided up into layers differing in power or prestige, or both. In spite of all the individual variations, there was some general consensus about these layers, particularly about contrasts between extremes. Thus, most informants said, or implied, that very rich people or big industrialists or professionals belonged in different classes from people who worked with their hands. There seemed to be some agreement, too, about the terms 'middle class' and 'working class', although not everyone used the words, and the usages were not precise. There were two common definitions of 'the working class'; first as 'anyone who works for a living', and second as 'people who work with their hands', although there were several informants who included clerks in this second category. It was more difficult to find any general agreement on the term 'the middle class'; it usually meant people above the working class, and those people who used the term generally thought there was an upper class as well.

Consensus disappeared when informants began to deal with occupations or people who were close together.. Should clerical workers, for example, be included in the 'working class' or the 'middle class'? Is a doctor in the same class as a large factory manager? Is a small shopowner in the same class as a highly skilled tradesman? In such cases, which were brought up by various informants, there was no general agreement; different individuals dealt with these problems in different ways.

There was general agreement that occupation was the most important criterion of an individual's class membership, although some informants did not mention it directly and a few insisted that money income was more important than occupation. (These were individuals who considered themselves to be relatively well-off financially.) In spite of the agreement on occupation, however, it soon became evident that informants meant different things by the term; some thought of occupation as a source of power, others were thinking of its general prestige, others of the income attached to it. Three informants distinguished the occupational placement of individuals from the industrial and occupational system in general, but most informants did not bother about the causes of the class system as distinct from the placement of individuals in it; similarly they did not distinguish sharply between the mobility of individuals and changes in the class structure as a whole.

All informants agreed that there had been a great deal of 'levelling-up' and that this was a good thing, especially for the working class. A few couples spoke rather regretfully of their loss of income and domestic servants, comparing their situation with that formerly enjoyed by their parents. (None of the families had severe current problems concerning taxation and industrial investment.) The levelling-up was variously attributed to the war, to the militant activities of trade unions and the Labour Party, to the Welfare State, to full employment, or to national solidarity in the face of England's decline as an international power. The most cautious statement was that the old classes remained but the economic and social inequalities between them were less sharp; the most radical version was perhaps the statement by one of the clerks to the effect that 'there used to be a middle class but it seems to have gone out now'. Descriptions of levelling-up depended on the experiences of the speaker. Thus the wife of the sundry supplies buyer mentioned the rise of the working·class and then went on to say that, as regards the middle class, it used to be a terrible thing to be 'in trade' but it didn't matter now, and the wife of the occupational therapist said that before the war you would not have been accepted socially (in her parents' class) if you had an accent even if you had money, but that nowadays accent and manners did not matter so much. People who placed themselves in the working class were more inclined to discuss the decline of the bosses' power and the breakdown of the distinctions between clerks, skilled workers, and unskilled workers. Before the war, the clerks in particular were said to have lived in a different world; now they earned about the same amount of money as manual workers, or even less, lived in the same housing estates, and sent their children to the same schools. Indeed, although only one or two informants mentioned the increase in numbers of clerical workers, many people talked about their uncertain status and about general flux in the class structure as a whole. Several people made remarks such as the following:

'It might have been simple in the Middle Ages, everything being so definite you knew exactly what your place was and did not expect to be anything else. Now it is all uncertain and you don't even know what your place is.'

Such were the main areas of general agreement. The data do not provide enough cases or suitable conditions of contrast to allow conclusions to be drawn about the conditions under which people's class models will resemble one another. It seems likely that the degree of resemblance will vary directly as the degree of similarity in primary social experience. If people have radically different experiences, they will have different class reference groups. If their experiences are similar, they are more likely to have similar class reference groups. But if their experiences are not only similar but also shared—that is if they form a close-knit network or an organized group—they are even more likely to converge on a common definition. Thus one would expect to find more consensus in a mining village than in a mixed working-class area where experiences were similar but not shared.

2. *Varieties of Model*

Four models of the total class structure were used by the informants:

a. Two-valued power models.
b. Three-valued prestige models.
c. Many-valued prestige models.
d. Mixed power and prestige models.

These four models are sufficient to explain the views of the sixteen couples who were questioned about class ideology. More extensive interviewing would doubtless lead to modifications and additions.[1]

---

[1] Cf. Hammond (1952) whose method of comparing class models with 'objective' position for a larger number of subjects is more appropriate to this type of analysis. The models discussed in the present paper are similar to Hammond's, although there are some differences in definition and criteria. For example, many of his 'composite frameworks' would probably be included in the 'prestige models' of the present paper rather than in the 'mixed power and prestige models'. Hammond also places less stress on numerical valuation as an intrinsic component of the different types of model.

a. Two-valued power models were used by people who identified themselves strongly with the working class and felt no desire or compulsion to be socially mobile. They conceived of classes as interdependent but conflicting groups; their idea of bettering their position was by organizing the working class to get more out of the bosses, although they usually added that the boss class had lost a good deal of its power because of full employment. The use of the two basic classes is a logical consequence of using the ideas of power, conflict, and opposition, since two units represent the smallest number required for a conflict. However many classes are actually mentioned, these models are basically two-valued. For example, one man made an overall division into two classes and then made a further sub-division within his own class—again in terms of conflicting opposites; another man made a sub-division in the boss class in which professionals were allied with the bosses proper. Neither of these men felt any embarrassment about placing themselves in the lower of the two classes. They did not feel that the other class was morally superior—it had more power but not more prestige.

Two-valued power models were used by the plumber, the tobacconist, and, by implication, the radio repairer. It is possible that the wife of the radio repairer was beginning to operate a prestige model, although she denied the existence of classes.

b. Three-valued prestige models were used by people who placed themselves in the middle class. They divided society into three classes, upper, middle, and working, with two or three sub-divisions in the middle class. If they made three sub-divisions in the middle class they put themselves in the middle division. If they made two, they put themselves in the upper division. No mention was made of class conflict, nor indeed of any relationship between classes as organized groups. Individuals were never described as acting on behalf of their class. It was assumed that individuals could move from one class to another without being traitors. Although classes were described as 'groups', it is evident that they were conceived as categories. Each category was thought to be composed of similar people, and each differed from the others in sub-culture and prestige. The categories were arranged one on top of the other to form a prestige hierarchy. Attention was focused on the placement of individuals in these categories, i.e., their position in the hierarchy. The basic idea seemed to be that individuals in one class, if they happened to meet, might associate with one another as equals in informal interaction. Various criteria of class membership were used, but all were aimed at defining those similarities of taste and interest that would determine the boundaries of social equality and possible friendship. The women tended to place most stress on manners, accent, taste, and social acceptability, whereas the men talked about occupation and income. The women were thinking primarily of entertaining, whereas the men were thinking about their occupations and colleagues as well. But both men and women suggested that individuals bettered themselves by acquiring the education, occupation, sub-culture, and personal friendship of people in a superior class. Over half the informants who used this model remarked on the lack of fit among the various criteria of class membership. Nearly all of them also said that snobbishness was bad and that people who thought about class all the time were snobbish.

If the basic criterion of potential friendship had been systematically followed out, the class structure would have been conceived as an interlocking network of relations among friends. But in place of this conception one finds a notion of three separate classes. The use of a three-valued model is a logical consequence of thinking in terms of prestige. In order to conceptualize prestige —not only general class status but any form of prestige—one must represent one's equals, one's superiors, and one's inferiors. Three groups is the natural number for such a representation. All informants put themselves in the middle group. No one put himself in the bottom group or the top group; two informants put themselves in the upper division of the middle group. All informants were making a symbolic representation of their own status together with their equals in the middle position, with their social

superiors above and their inferiors beneath.[1] Status was not conceived in relative terms as a continuum. Each class was given a
specific sub-culture. By endowing each of the three groups with a
distinctive set of norms and values that distinguishes it from the
others, one gives concreteness and substance to the symbolic
expression of superiority, equality, and inferiority, so that rela-
tivity is removed from the system.

Three-valued prestige models were used by the commercial
manager, the W.E.A. lecturer, the sundry supplies buyer, the
draughtsman, and one of the clerks. By implication, the statistician and his wife also used this model, although they denied the
existence of classes. In all these cases both husband and wife used
the same sort of model. While, however, the wives of the account
executive and the occupational therapist used three-valued
prestige models, their husbands used mixed power and prestige
models.

c. *Many-valued prestige models* were used by people who placed
themselves in the working class but felt some incompatibility in
their position. In three cases they said they were working-class by
occupation, but regarded themselves as intellectually and culturally different. Intellectuals and professional people were their
positive reference groups; businessmen and rich people were
ignored or given lower status. In one case a man placed himself
in the working class though he admitted some obligation to be
mobile at least physically if not socially, and had to justify his
desire to stay where he was. All four couples thought of class in
terms of prestige rather than power, but they did not use the
three-valued model. They listed from four to eight classes, and
put themselves in the class second from bottom.

I think they multiplied the number of classes because of their
adherence to the points of general consensus mentioned earlier.

[1] Cf. Barnes.'I think that in some, at least, of the many instances in which people of
widely varying economic position say that they belong to the middle class in a system of
three (or more) social classes, they are merely stating that they are aware of these three sets
of persons. (Superiors, equals, inferiors.) It does not of itself imply that society can be
divided into three groups with agreed membership' (Barnes, 1954, p. 46).

The term 'middle class' is not completely relative; it carried an agreed absolute connotation such that these individuals did not feel justified in placing themselves in it. If they had used the three-valued prestige model, they would then have had to place themselves in the bottom class, and this is something that no one was willing to do, presumably because it would have meant acknowledgement of absolute rather than relative inferiority. The solution adopted was multiplication of the number of classes with self-placement in the class second from the bottom. The process was not conscious and deliberate.

Many-valued prestige models were used by two of the clerks, the optical instrument repairer, and the painter and decorator.

d. Mixed power and prestige models were the most complex. No basic numerical value appeared, one individual using three classes, another four, and another eight. All were 'intellectuals' and they discussed the causes of the class system in general. They phrased their explanations primarily in terms of economic power. In informal conversation, however, they often talked about particular forms of status and skill in terms of equality, superiority, and inferiority, and traces of this prestige framework appeared in their formal presentations of class structure. Their models were not only complex but also unstable. Even in the course of presenting the model in reply to direct questions, these informants tended to shift from a mixed model to a two-valued power model or a three-valued prestige model.

Models of this type were used by the occupational therapist and the account executive, although their wives used three-valued prestige models. Both the deputy insurance manager and his wife, however, used a mixed model.

3. *A Comparison of Two Models*
Two models will be presented in detail in order to illustrate the way people used their experiences and group memberships in the construction and use of class models and class reference groups. Both of the husbands were skilled tradesmen and both placed themselves in the working class, but in other respects their social

experience was different and their class reference groups were correspondingly different. The first couple used the many-valued prestige model, the second the power model.

The Jarrolds

The Jarrolds had three children, had been married for eight years, and lived on a socially heterogeneous housing estate. Mr Jarrold worked at a factory repairing optical instruments for a gross salary of £8 per week. He had a war disability pension of £2 16s. and Family Allowances of 16s., so that the total family income was £11 12s. He enjoyed his work very much, but thought he should be paid more for it.

Mr Jarrold was an orphan, or at least he knew nothing about his parents except that his father was a manual worker in a north-country town and that he himself was found abandoned at the age of one. He was in and out of five foster homes until he settled down in a country town with a family he described as 'working-class and respectable'. He left school at fourteen, was a delivery hand and sales clerk, then joined the Army and became a mechanic, After the war he took a Government-assisted course in ophthal-mic and optical instrument manufacture and repairs.

Mrs Jarrold said that she came from an 'ordinary working-class London family'. Mr Jarrold was inclined to doubt this statement. What one might say is that her grandparents were 'ordinary working-class people' but that most of her uncles and aunts had been occupationally mobile. Her father was a greengrocer. Mrs Jarrold had suffered considerable frustration of her educational ambitions, partly because of circumstances and partly, she said, because she did not try hard enough. She wanted to go to a university and become a journalist. She got a scholarship to a public school but failed the medical examination. Her father died at this time, which more or less finished her chance of going to university, and so she matriculated and became an office worker. After a succession of office jobs she married an Army lieutenant whom she divorced in 1944, after which she married Mr Jarrold.

The first two or three years of their marriage were difficult. Mr

Jarrold developed cysticercosis towards the end of the war and the resulting fits began to be seriously incapacitating so that he could not hold any job for very long. They moved to the country for the sake of his health and lived in seven different places in six months together with their two children. Eventually he began to recover and took a training course in ophthalmic and optical instrument repairs. He then returned to London, where he worked in several instrument repair factories for a time, found a flat, and finally obtained his present job. They began to feel settled and Mrs Jarrold started attending a University Extension Course, but she became pregnant again shortly afterwards and had to stop.

At the time of interviewing they had a large number of friends scattered over London and the south of England. The friends, whose occupations showed considerable variety, ranged from minor professional people to skilled workers like Mr Jarrold. They also had friendly relations with a large number of people on the housing estate. They were both active in various voluntary associations. Mr Jarrold spent a good deal of his spare time producing plays and acting in a local drama group. He had formerly belonged to the local branch of the British Legion but decided it was doddery and stopped attending meetings. They had also resigned from the Tenants' Association on the housing estate because there seemed to be a lot of squabbles. Mr Jarrold was an active member of his trade union. They both belonged to the Labour Party. Mrs Jarrold went to church occasionally and they both admired the vicar. She intended to join the Local History Society when the children were a little older.

In brief, they were a busy couple. The clinical interviewers reported that they were both very intelligent, and that each had a good deal of artistic and dramatic talent. Without making a fuss about it, they seemed to feel they had come through their trials and misfortunes rather well. According to the field worker, they felt they were giving their children a much better upbringing than either of them had had. They were aware that they wanted their children to fulfil their own unfulfilled ambitions. Mrs Jarrold was not worried about their occupations so long as they were well-educated people with wide interests; she wanted a child who would go to a famous school and a university. Mr Jarrold wanted his son to be properly trained as an engineer. At the same time they felt parents should not put their ambitions on their children in this way, and that in fact the children would do what they themselves wanted to do, particularly if they continued to be as independent as they were at the time.

When asked directly about class, Mrs Jarrold did most of the talking as if she had thought about it before. Mr Jarrold took an active part in the discussion, filling in details and pointing out discrepancies. He asked her repeatedly, 'What class are we in?'

1. *The Real Blue-Bloods.* She said there weren't many of them and they weren't very important now. He said he was old-fashioned enough to believe that the aristocracy should remain the aristocracy.

2. *The Leaders of Fashion and Popular Influence.* These were people who had earned their wealth and position rather than inherited it. She said they were not always rich. She would include various scholars like Bertrand Russell. (She said she knew he was a blue-blood, but that it was unimportant and he had forgotten about it himself.) They thought the B.B.C. had had a big influence here because it provided the means for these people to make contact with the public. Both the Jarrolds—but particularly Mrs Jarrold—expressed approval of this group.

3. *Professional People.* Doctors, lawyers, higher civil servants, officers in the Services. This group would include some wealthy people because rich people were scattered over quite a range and did not form a class. She expressed general approval of this group, particularly for the 'higher professionals'.

4. *The Upper Middle Class.* Rich people, but not necessarily highly educated. Wealthy business people. Their main values were concerned with material things. She expressed disapproval.

5. *The Poorer Middle Class.* The first interview on class reports that Mrs Jarrold said she thought this group was nicer than any of the others. In a later interview, she revised this, saying that

the groups she valued most highly were the intelligentsia and higher professionals. She did not think of the poor middle class as a group; it was rather that most of the nice people she knew were members of the poor middle class. Mr Jarrold asked if they would include themselves in the poor middle class. She said they were with them in spirit at least. Later on she talked about suburban people as members of the poor middle class. She also included lesser civil servants, various kinds of office workers and clerical workers. In another interview she talked about her dislike of office work, but she did not say that she disliked office workers.

6. *The Rich Working Class.* 'These are the people who have TV, fur coats, rocking horses, and cars.' Mrs Jarrold said all this very emphatically. Mr Jarrold looked surprised and said, 'Darling, I didn't know you felt like this,' and she said, 'Well, I do,' and went on with rather a tirade about Covent Garden porters earning £20 a week and said, 'I don't think it can take much brains or training to be a Covent Garden porter.' Again Mr Jarrold asked where they would place themselves and she said in the next class.

7. *The Poor Working Class.* These were the majority, she said. She did not differentiate within this group or describe them in any detail. Later on she said that she didn't think occupation was a terribly good criterion of class because even though you might be working in a factory this didn't condemn you to be a type. You could work in a factory and still listen to the Third Programme. Later on when they described the working class of the old pre-war days they always spoke of them as 'they' rather than 'we'.

8. *The Floaters.* Unstable people who lived from hand to mouth and just muddled along.

Mr Jarrold asked about self-placement twice more. His wife said that in spirit they were with the poor middle class, but by occupation and income they belonged in the poor working class. Discussing mobility, she said that for men it depended on their jobs, getting promotion, and so on. He said he thought intelligence was a help, and she said that intelligence helped at school and the kind of job you did depended on your education. She also said that women always moved to their husband's class. He took this as meaning that she had married down. She disputed this, saying that she had come from an ordinary working-class family. He seemed a bit dubious about this, said he thought they were on the way up, and then suggested that perhaps he and she had met half-way.

On being asked about general change in the system, Mrs Jarrold said she thought there were more in-between grades now and that the working class was smaller. They did not make the usual point about levelling up, perhaps because she did not feel she had gained in status or income, although they both felt the quality of their personal relationships was an improvement on those of past generations.

The Jarrolds' statements about class indicated that they felt they used their notions of class mostly to place people when they first met them:

> '. . . when you know somebody and like them because of what they are you regard them somehow as a person in their own right and you don't think of them as having a class position.'

At the end of the discussion on class the field worker recorded:

> 'They went on to talk about national stereotypes, as similar to class stereotypes, but indicating that they thought the national ones were pretty unreal. They are things which exist in your own mind rather than in the people you think about.'

In addition to their class reference groups, they had two other notions that were partly linked to class and partly independent. These were whether people were 'common' or 'naice'. Mrs Jarrold was embarrassed about these terms—hence the mispronunciation—and found them difficult to define, but the general idea was that common people were vulgar, materialistic, and self-important whereas 'naice' people were people who were actual or potential friends. She said 'common people' were to be found in every class although they were perhaps particularly prevalent in the 'rich middle class' and the 'rich working class'. 'Naice' people were interested in artistic, intellectual, and mechanical matters, without being pompous, and they were not confined to any particular class. They also used several other concepts spontaneously, 'intellectuals', 'intelligent people', 'technicians', and 'creative people' being the most important. Again these concepts were concerned with status but were not entirely synonymous with their class reference groups.

The Butlers

When the interviewing began, the Butlers were both in their mid-thirties and had been married for nine years. They had two children. Mr Butler was a plumber, earning a gross weekly wage of £7 10s. The Family Allowance of 8s. brought the family income up to £7 18s.[1] Mr Butler belonged to the local branch of his trade union. Both he and his wife had been brought up in tightly knit working-class neighbourhoods and they had both belonged to close-knit networks. Both had experienced a good deal of unemployment during the depression. They had mixed feelings about living on a heterogeneous housing estate. They felt life had been easier for working people since the war, but that they had lost the excitement, friendliness, and community solidarity of their old neighbourhoods. Quoting from the interview record:

'Before the war there was a little bit of slum clearance and other people saw it and realized what they might have and put on the pressure and got things started. Nowadays people have got the new flats and houses, but somehow we do not appreciate them . . .

'People live more together now but they are miles apart.

[1] This was in 1951. Subsequent cost-of-living bonuses brought his wages up to £8 4s. 3d. per week. He had also taken on a temporary evening job for which he was paid £3 per week. Increase in Family Allowance and the arrival of a third child brought the Family Allowance up to 16s. In 1954 the total family income was £12 0s. 3d. per week.

You do not get neighbours coming in so much for a ding-dong [sing-song]. Nowadays people tend to be frightened of their neighbours. At one time if you wanted something you would just go and knock at the door across the road and get it, nowadays people do not like letting on what goes on in their homes . . .

'We have been coming into something new from an old type of life but they [our children] will be used to the new way and they will see the mistakes we have made.'

Mr Butler used class reference groups a good deal in ordinary conversation, particularly in contrasting himself with the 'administrators' and 'black-coated workers' on the housing estate. He also talked spontaneously about the 'administrators' and 'technicians' at work, saying they did not really know the job in the way the old craftsmen knew it, and that they were always having to ask his advice about things on which they were supposed to be instructing him.

The Butlers wanted their children to reproduce their own style of life. Mr Butler wanted the children to have a trade, not necessarily office work. 'I am all for production, something where you can see what it is you do and what you have made.' He thought the girls would probably get married anyway, and he had no particular plans for his son, but rather wanted him to become a plumber.

Mr Butler did most of the talking in reply to the direct questions about class, although he appealed to his wife for confirmation and she gave it. In his view there were two classes only, there was no middle class left. The top classes were 'the utter snobs, the few idle rich, the people who control everything' and the other class was 'the rest, a very mixed bag'. The old middle class, in his view, comprised the ordinary factory boss and the building boss; they had lost their power because of full employment.

The mixed bag was composed of a series of parallel occupations such as woodworkers, miners, engineers, teachers, and so on, all of equivalent status. Within each occupation, he made a division into producers and administrators; the producers really did the work whereas the administrators just supervised and got paid more for it. He pointed out that administrators and producers were dependent on each other, but at the same time they were always in conflict. The administrators were the modern substitute for the old bosses; they could not fire people, but they did not really do any work. Their authority rested on paper qualifications rather than on real knowledge of the job.

Quoting from the interview record:

'. . . he said that first of all there was a division between the production and administration sides. The administration people do not always remember that it is the others who bring them the wealth, and if it was not for the producers there would not be anything to administer. On the other hand the workers ought to know that it is necessary to have someone to organize them and give the orders. The trouble is that as things are now there are about six administrators to about every one producer. He went straight on to talk about himself. "Me, I am not a producer. I am really in between the two. I keep what the producers have made in use, keep things going while we wait for them to produce more. Miners and engineers are the production people, the ones who are turning out the goods, but I suppose we are part of the producers." I put a question here, something about different levels, and he said that over him there was a charge-hand and then a general foreman and then the clerk of the works and technical advisers and rent collectors. Mrs Butler interposed, "You know as much as all them put together." Mr Butler went on to say that he and his mate knew what to do, but had to ask all these people first. "They do not actually do anything, not even turn a spanner, but we have the pleasure of really doing something." He went on to make another remark about the necessity of some administration but said he thought paper work ought to be cut by half. Mrs Butler went into a long complaint about people like technical advisers, etc., who have never been properly trained on the job that they are giving advice about. Mr Butler said that as you improve yourself you do less production. He does not know what the solution to this is unless it is to make the producer's money higher so that there would then be less fighting for administrative posts, but he does not know if this would work.'

At this point he perhaps began to wonder about the field worker for the field notes continue: ·

'He went on to enlarge on this, illustrating from what he supposed to be my situation. He explained that I am a producer because I am at work on producing a book, and of course there will be the printers and so on who will have a hand in this, but in between is my governor who does not have anything directly to do with this. He just says, "Go out and write the book," and does not do anything towards it. He just sits there and gives orders and probably gets twice as much for it as you do.'

After some more discussion about administrators and producers, the field worker began to ask him if there were differences between occupations, and Mr Butler said that each one had its own ladder, and that all occupations were equivalent. The field worker pressed him hard on this point, but Mr Butler insisted that all the feet of the ladders were on a level, and at the bottom of each ladder were the producers and at the top were the administration people who got paid more for doing less. At the end of the discussion he remarked that he had a hard time reading through a technical paper by the field worker, but that he supposed the field worker wouldn't understand if he were told to go ahead and make a leadburned joint.

He conceived of mobility as moving up one of these ladders. He said people moved across from one ladder to another only in times of unemployment when they could not stick to their preferred trade. Quoting from the interview record again:

'Take engineering, for example, you start off with a shop boy and then you come to the machinists who are the producers, and then if you like to go to evening school or something you can get into the drafting office or become a skilled engineer and a specialist. Then you can become a foreman or an overseer and you drop work on the machines altogether and just take over looking after other people. Then you can become shop manager and so on up into the management line. If your face still fits, then you get into one of the higher offices with a secretary to do your writing for you and all you have to do is give verbal orders and sign your name.'

He gave similar examples for woodworking and schoolteaching.

On change in the class system in general, he said that the old middle class, the boss class, had disappeared because:

'. . . there is now so much work to be done and so little unemployment so if the boss rattles at you or threatens you with the sack you can just up and leave. There is no poverty any more so that makes a lot of difference. The working people are better off and the bosses have lost a lot of their grip.' The people he is talking about, he says, are the 'ordinary factory boss and the building boss. The only bosses now are the snob class, the high-ups, senior civil servants, directors and such.'

In addition he added that there were fewer differences in class because all children mixed together in the same school and that his children had an equal chance with the bosses' children.

DISCUSSION

The most obvious difference between these two couples was that the Jarrolds wanted to be mobile whereas the Butlers wanted to continue in their present position. The Jarrolds' idea of bettering their condition was to become members of the poor middle class; Mr Butler's idea of bettering his position was to organize the producers to control the administrators and reduce the difference in pay between the two groups. The Jarrolds operated a model of classes as prestige groups, the Butlers as power groups. Mrs Jarrold made as much differentiation at the top of the scale as she did at the bottom, but Mr Butler divided the society into two groups and then differentiated only within his own; the differentiation within his own class was made on the basis of power and conflict. Mrs Jarrold used the 'poor middle class' and the intelligentsia as positive class reference groups, whereas Mr Butler used the producers. The Jarrolds also approved of producers, but they did not conceive of them as a class. But each model had other aspects that cannot be entirely explained in terms of their mobility orientations. In fact their feelings about mobility were in turn derived from their experiences in present and past membership groups.

Mrs Jarrold was trying to conceptualize several experiences— her own family background, her frustrated educational ambitions, her husband's occupation, and their wide scatter of friends. In her description of the lower levels of the system she tried to do justice to her direct knowledge of these people and at the same time to her own feeling of frustration. Class status, she said, *ought* to depend on intelligence and skill; actually it depended on income and occupation. But in the upper levels of the system all this was put right. First there was a decaying but harmless aristocracy, then an intellectual *élite*, then the professional people; the rich businessmen were relegated to fourth place. She seemed to be using the distant upper reaches of the system to solve the problem she presented in the lower levels. Finally she used 'common people', 'nice people', and 'intellectuals' as reference groups that cut across the class groups, to show that it was personal qualities that mattered, not just status in the public eye.

Mr Jarrold's chief interest in the class question was in terms of, 'Where do we belong, where do I belong?'—which was perhaps a way of asking what must have been a very important question to him, 'Who am I, who were my parents?' But it was also a question about his relationship with his wife, and about his rapid occupational mobility in the past and his own and his family's destination in the future.

Mr Butler seemed to be trying to fit together three main experiences: his upbringing in a closely integrated working-class neighbourhood together with his experience of unemployment; his current position at work and in his union; his new situation on the housing estate. The legacy from his past was found in his conception of a power struggle between bosses and producers, but the struggle had assumed a new shape. The immediate bosses were gone and in their place were the administrators whose authority rested on paper qualifications rather than on power to give people the sack. Furthermore, since the war the administrators of different occupations had not formed a compact group in opposition to all producers; the conflict went on within each occupation, and all occupations were separate but equal. In other contexts, however, he grouped all administrators together into a class and equated them with the office workers on the housing estate. Their presence was partly responsible for his feeling of discontent with life on the estate. The enemy had penetrated the home territory: he felt their presence made it difficult to organize all the tenants in effective opposition to the housing authorities. He also resented the fact that the office workers looked down on him for wearing old clothes and not trying to keep up appearances.

It is perhaps unusual for a man in Mr Butler's position to insist so firmly that there are no status differences between occupations. His attitude seemed to be that he could get along with anyone who was his equal, that all producers were equal regardless of occupation, and that anyone he liked must be an equal and, therefore, a producer. This was a characteristic attitude that he expressed in many contexts, but perhaps his relationship with the field worker was particularly important in the interviewing situation, because he made him into a producer, and he stressed the fact that although he did not entirely understand the field worker's productions, the field worker would not understand his either.

In summary, both the Jarrolds and the Butlers operated models of the class structure, and used classes as reference groups in comparing themselves with other people and in evaluating themselves and other people as well. In spite of similarity in occupational level, their models of the class structure were different. Each made use of other personal experiences, worked them over, and put them back into the external situation in a symbolic form.

Any model of the class structure applies to the whole society, but neither the Jarrolds nor the Butlers—nor anyone, for that matter—can possibly know everything about the society as a whole. Distortion is inevitable. People must make use of their personal experience to reach a working definition of the class structure, and their personal needs and wishes enter into it too. Concepts of class are used for general orientation in the society at large, for placing strangers, and for evaluating one's own position and that of others. But the definitions are flexible. They are often internally inconsistent, but since they are used differently in different contexts and for different purposes, individuals need not be made aware that their concepts are not completely logical and consistent.

CHAPTER VII

Norms and Ideology: The Normal Family

In the last chapter it was shown that there was not complete consensus on class ideology among the research couples. Their concepts of class varied according to their personal experience. In the present chapter the same sort of analysis is applied to the couples' ideas about what constitutes a normal family. Here again, people differed in their views. An attempt is made to account for the variations and to discuss the way in which norms are arrived at.

A. INTRODUCTION

In any group discussion, lay or technical, of family life, people are quick to agree that there is no such thing as a 'normal' family. No one, they argue, is perfect and no family is perfect either. But at some later point the phrase usually creeps back into the discussion, though its meaning may have changed slightly; from being the 'perfect' family it has become the 'average' family. The label may be changed too; words like 'average' or 'ordinary'—our own choice—may be used instead of 'normal'. In common-sense usage the word 'normal' and its various substitutes are thus very ambiguous. They may mean perfect, average, or customary, according to context. But it is impossible to get away from using the idea of normality. One must have some sort of base-line, some standard against which variations can be compared. So the concept of the normal family continues to be used in spite of its ambiguity. And, in fact, its very ambiguity is useful in casual discussions; the same word and the same basic idea can be used with different meanings according to the context of comparison.

In technical discussions it is still necessary to have a yardstick, a standard of comparison. People who study grossly abnormal families are particularly in need of some understanding of the 'normal' family so that they may know how and to what degree the abnormal families they study are deviant. But in technical work the ambiguity of the term 'normal' leads to confusion. It ceases to be convenient. It is therefore necessary to distinguish verbally between the various meanings of 'normal' and 'norms', and to relate them to one another. In some work, as I suggest later in this chapter, it is most useful to compare families against two or more different standards of normality.

First, there is normal in the sense of 'clinically ideal'. This is the meaning that most clinical psychologists and psycho-analysts use. The exact content of the ideal varies according to the psychological theory employed, but 'normal' in this sense is always an ideal which may be approached but never fully realized in practice.

Second, 'normal' may mean statistically average behaviour. For this I suggest the term 'behavioural mode'.

Third, 'normal' may mean behaviour that the informants themselves think is morally right or at least expected and customary. This is the usage with which I am chiefly concerned in this chapter.

Fourth, sociologists and anthropologists sometimes use the term 'norm' to mean a typical pattern, a sort of generalized model of conduct, which they abstract from informants' behaviour as well as from their stated ideals and expectations. (See Nadel, 1951, p. 94; Parsons and Bales, 1955, p. 106; Radcliffe-Brown, 1940.) I do not use the term in this sense. Of all the various usages, I find this the most vague and confusing, for its precise empirical referents are seldom made clear.

In this chapter I chiefly discuss norms in the third sense, that is, *people's ideas about what behaviour is customary and what behaviour is right and proper in their social circle.* These norms are social. They are views that informants assume they share with the other members of their social circle. They are not views that informants think are personal attitudes of their own. If expected behaviour is not felt to be ideal, or if ideal behaviour is not expected, I make a distinction between *ideal norms* and *norms of expectation*. If the expected and the ideal coincide, I do not use a qualifying adjective.

It is often assumed that there is a large measure of agreement on the social norms of family life in the society as a whole, and that these norms are embodied in the teachings of churches and the rulings of courts of law. Such a view implies that given individuals will recognize that these agreed-upon external standards exist and that they will be able to make the norms explicit without difficulty. It seems to me that this view of social norms is much more appropriate to a small-scale homogeneous society than to a large-scale society with a complex division of labour. In a small-scale society, where many people know one another, where there are few strangers, and most relationships serve many interests, agreement on familial norms develops out of constant interaction, and individuals know what the norms are. Most anthropologists report that their informants have little difficulty in making explicit the approved and customary rules of conduct between members of elementary families and between more distant kinsmen. Behaviour does not always conform to norms, but at least people know what the norms are and when they are deviating from them. If such societies have courts of law, most laymen are familiar with court procedure and know the norms on which the court will draw to make judgements. Similarly everyone will know what norms of familial conduct are embodied in religion. But recent work shows that even in primitive societies norms should not be regarded as a precise, consistent set of rules. Gluckman points out that the Lozi have some very precise rules ('a husband must not go to his wife's granary') but that others are vague ('a husband should treat his wife properly') (Gluckman, 1955). This very vagueness leaves room for flexible adjustment to varying circumstances. Similarly, norms may contradict one another, which permits selection to suit personal and social convenience. Although there is a fairly high degree of consensus on what the norms are, they are rarely made explicit except in times of conflict or crisis, when people use them to justify their own behaviour or to pass judgement on that of others.

Even in a small-scale society, then, norms are not precise and consistent. But in a large-scale society the situation is much more complicated, especially where familial norms are concerned. How much agreement on the social norms of family life one would find if one interviewed a representative sample of the general population I cannot say, for I have not been engaged in that kind of study. Among the research couples there were some points of agreement; most of these were very vague and general and did not give a precise blueprint for action. On many points there was considerable variation from one couple to another. Furthermore, not only was there variation among the families interviewed, but several couples also drew attention to the fact that there was variation among the people they knew personally. Two couples also pointed out that there must be variation in the society at large, if one could believe the wireless, television, newspapers, books, and so forth. But most couples did not even mention such sources of information. They discussed only their own little world of the people they knew personally or had known in the past.

Another fact emerged clearly in our interviews: informants found it very difficult to make familial norms explicit at all. There were several reasons for this, which are discussed below, but in the present connection the relevant point is that inability to make norms explicit was closely associated with awareness of variation. It was the couples who drew attention to variation who said they could not make generalizations about customary and proper ways of familial behaviour. Difficulty in generalizing depended also on the context and the situation. People were reluctant to generalize when asked direct questions about norms, although they made many implicit generalizations when talking spontaneously.

In this chapter I attempt to interpret these two findings: first, that there was less consensus on familial norms than is commonly assumed, and second, that many informants found it difficult to state norms explicitly. Perhaps one should not speak of social norms at all in this situation. If consensus is made essential to the definition of social norms, then the research families had only a few very general social norms concerning familial roles. Most of their views on the subject would have to be described as personal opinions. But the data suggest that there is an intermediate stage between complete consensus and random variation. Informants *thought* there was agreement even when there was not. Or, to be more accurate, in some contexts they thought there was agreement and in other contexts they thought there was variation.

Some refinement of terminology is necessary. In ordinary usage the term 'social norms' has a double connotation. It means norms that are in fact agreed on by some group or category of persons; it also means norms that individuals think are current in some group or category. I find it necessary to distinguish these two aspects. I use the term *social norms* to refer to the norms people think are current in some group or category. I suggest the term *norms of common consent* for norms on which there is in fact consensus. I use the term *personal norms* for those ideals and expectations that informants think are their own private standards, different from those they attribute to other people.

B. DISCUSSION OF FIELD MATERIAL

For the first eight or ten interviews, we did not ask any direct questions about the norms of conjugal roles. Such questions were left until the last two or three interviews. In the course of the earlier interviews it became clear that each couple had a fairly consistent set of standards by which they were judging their own and other people's performance as husbands and wives. The field workers picked up these codes very quickly almost without being aware of doing so. Indeed, I was so convinced that such standards existed that I thought informants had made explicit statements about how husbands and wives should behave. It was only when I went carefully over the field notes again that I realized nothing had been said directly; everything was conveyed by implication, by complimentary or derogatory remarks about friends, neighbours, and relatives. Very few general comments were made until direct questions were asked, and even then, many couples were reluctant to make any generalizations.

I. *Variations in Content of Norms*

On the basis of their spontaneous statements and replies to direct questions, it is possible to summarize the norms the couples adhered to.

There were a few general points of agreement, that is, there were a few norms of common consent. All the couples took it for granted that each elementary family should be financially independent of relatives and friends and should have its own dwelling. All couples took it for granted that there should be a basic division of labour between husband and wife in which the husband was primarily responsible for supporting the family financially and the wife was primarily responsible for looking after the children and seeing that housework and cooking were done. The world would be upside down if the woman went out to work and the husband stayed home to care for the house and the children, although it was recognized, with varying degrees of disapproval and approval, that husbands sometimes helped with child care and housework and wives sometimes went to work. All couples took it for granted that adultery was a serious offence. It was assumed that parents were obliged to care for their children until they could look after themselves, although the standards of good care differed from one family to another.

These norms were not explicitly stated in so many words. They were simply taken for granted. I think one may say that these general points of agreement arise from similarities in familial tasks and *general* similarity of social environment. Most of these norms of common consent were very vague and general so that a considerable variety of behaviour could be encompassed within the bounds of conformity.

Many norms varied according to network connectedness. Variations in content have been discussed in Chapter III and need be only briefly summarized here. Couples in close-knit networks expected husbands and wives to have a rigid division of labour. There was little stress on the importance of shared interests and joint recreation. It was expected that wives would have many relationships with their relatives, and husbands with their friends. Both partners could get help from people outside the family, which made the rigid division of labour between husband and wife possible. Successful sexual relations were not considered essential to a happy marriage.

In contrast, families in loose-knit networks had a less rigid division of labour, stressed the importance of shared interests and joint recreation, and placed a good deal of emphasis on the importance of successful sexual relations. They were more self-conscious about how to bring up their children than couples in close-knit networks. They were aware that the people they knew had a great variety of opinions on this subject and they were worried about which course they themselves should follow.

In addition to these variations according to connectedness of the family's network, there were many idiosyncratic variations. One couple carried the idea of joint sharing of tasks to a point that almost denied the basic division of labour between husband and wife. They stated their views more strongly on some occasions than others. In the most emphatic statement they said wives and mothers should be able to work if they wanted and that it was quite all right for women to work in the same field as their husbands, to be better at their jobs, and to earn more. They implied that this view was generally accepted in their social circle. Another couple with a similar sort of loose-knit network had very different norms on the role of the mother. They said that people in their social circle thought mothers of small children should not work, although in some cases they had to. Each couple recognized that the issue of whether mothers should work or not was highly controversial, but each regarded his own solution as the right course of action and indicated that the other people in their social circle held similar views although they did not always adhere to them in practice.

There were other more subtle variations. Couples with loose-knit networks, for example, generally stressed the importance of joint decision-making by husband and wife. But one wife implied that men were generally more dominant in fact, although not in theory, whereas another wife implied that men were more dominant in theory, although not in fact. Each was attributing to other people what was in fact the case in her own household. Again, a wife suggested indirectly that women in general were more sensitive than men and better at dealing with children and smoothing over difficulties between people. Here she seems to have been attributing to people in general not what was actually the case in her own family but what she would have liked to have been the case. In our judgement her husband was more skilful at handling interpersonal relations than she was. In another case a wife made a similar statement, but here it seemed that she was in fact generalizing from her own behaviour. In another case a husband maintained, in the face of protests from his wife, that his handling of the family finances was the usual and the right procedure among his friends and among families in general.

In brief, there was a tendency for people to treat their own behaviour and standards as the norm for other people as well as for themselves. In some cases people implied that the exact opposite of their own behaviour was the general norm—a sort of wish-fulfilment about their own behaviour. It seems from these cases that people sometimes treat their personal views as social norms. Ideally, of course, one should interview the people with whom the couple identify themselves to see if they would acknowledge the conjugal standards attributed to them—to see whether the social norms of the couple are in fact norms of common consent. In practice this is very difficult when couples live in networks. And in some cases it would be impossible because, as I describe below, some couples identify themselves with abstract categories of person. But from statements made by the couples in other contexts, it often appeared that there was a good deal of variation among the members of their networks, not only in behaviour but also in norms, so that in setting up one sort of behaviour as the norm, the couple were making a considerable over-simplification. In consideration of these cases of displacement and projection of one's own norms on to other people, I have come to the conclusion that the usual sharp separation of personal attitudes from social norms does not do justice to the facts of the situation. The research couples assumed they shared certain standards of conjugal behaviour with other people, but some of these social norms were partly a thing of their own creation. Doubtless they had assimilated norms from experience with other people. But they also seemed to have selected some expectations and ideals rather than others, and they sometimes attributed their own personal version of norms to people in general or to some group or category of their own choosing without being aware of doing so.

2. *How Norms Were Expressed*
a. *The difficulty experienced by informants in making norms explicit.*
I have mentioned above that although informants continually expressed norms indirectly in spontaneous discussion, they made very few explicit generalizing statements. In the last two or three interviews we asked several direct questions that were intended to get people to talk about norms more directly. We found many of these questions difficult to ask and informants found them difficult to answer so that certain questions were often left out. The questions were these:

  1. What do you think the main changes in the family have been in the last fifty years or so? The aim of this question was to find out not only what people thought about social change, but also how they would characterize modern families in general.
  2. How would you describe the rights and duties of husband and wife?
  3. How would you describe the ideal husband, the ideal wife, the ideal child?
  4. How do you feel your own ideas on how to run a family resemble those of people you know, or are different from them?

5. When you got married, did you have a clear idea of what family life would be like? Have your ideas changed?
6. What do you feel are the important things in keeping a family ticking over? What things make it difficult?

Couples found all of these questions, except the first, difficult to answer. Couples with loose-knit networks seemed to find the second question particularly difficult. Their usual reaction was either a prolonged uncomfortable silence—two minutes in one case—or an immediate reply to the effect that there was so much variation one could not generalize. Couples with more close-knit networks found the questions a little easier, although even they often remarked that no two people would agree on how husbands and wives should behave or customarily did behave.

I think there are several reasons for the difficulty people experienced in answering these questions. First, since the field workers belonged to the same society, more or less, informants may have felt that we had some ulterior motive for asking the questions. Otherwise why should we ask questions to which we must have answers of our own? We never became very successful in allaying this sort of anxiety or in asking direct questions skilfully. The question about ideal husbands and wives and children was particularly upsetting. Because we interviewed husband and wife together, it was interpreted as an invitation to comment on the other partner's conjugal deficiencies in his and the field worker's presence. This question did not produce much useful information on norms, but we kept asking it because it was useful to compare how people coped with the slight awkwardness of the situation. But although we did not fully realize it at the time, this question upset the atmosphere of the interview so much that people did not give their full attention to the questions that followed it. If we were asking direct questions about norms again, we should omit this question or put it at the end.

But our awkwardness in asking questions about norms cannot be the only factor, because however stupidly we asked about occupational roles, we always got straightforward answers.

Occupational roles are specific and easy to describe. Familial roles are diffuse; they cover many different activities, the organization of which is left to the discretion of the individuals concerned. People become so involved emotionally in familial roles that it is very difficult for them to separate themselves from the roles conceptually.

Another factor affecting difficulty in stating norms explicitly may have been the absence of overt crisis in the families. Norms are usually brought forth only in times of crisis and conflict, when they are used to justify one's own behaviour and to pass judgement on that of other people. When nothing much is going wrong, there is no need to state what the norms are.

The fact that couples in close-knit networks found the questions easier to answer suggests another factor. Many of the people they knew were known to one another, so that out of their constant interaction a general measure of consensus had been reached. The family knew, more or less, what the agreed standards were and could make them explicit. Couples in loose-knit networks were more aware of variation. Since many of the people they knew were not acquainted with one another, there were fewer norms of common consent. It was impossible for such couples to reply to the questions without making gross over-simplifications. Perhaps some of their discomfort and hesitation when asked direct questions sprang from a realization that they made such generalizations implicitly in spontaneous discussion all the time, but that their generalizations were not very accurate.

b. References to individuals, groups, and categories. Most spontaneous expressions of norms took the form of comments on friends, neighbours, and relatives. Very occasionally couples also referred spontaneously to groups or categories of person, although these more general references were made much more frequently in replies to direct questions about norms.

No one referred to religious teaching on the family and no one mentioned legal rules. Indeed, although we did not ask enough questions on this point, it was our impression that most of the research couples were almost totally ignorant of their legal rights and obligations as members of a family. Some expressed surprise at the strange rules of familial behaviour the courts enforced. Unless informants had had direct experience of the law, they thought it was something they did not need to know about, something very far removed from their everyday life. Similarly there were very few references to reports of family life in newspapers and other media of mass communication, and none of the couples expressed the anxiety shown in public statements about divorce, delinquency, the decline of religion, and the moral decay of the family. Of course the fact that there were so few explicit references to religion, law, and the media of mass communication in spontaneous discussion or in reply to our direct questions about norms does not mean that people's conceptions were entirely unaffected by such institutionalized expressions of norms. Our data were not collected to show how public expressions of norms influence people's own views, but it does seem likely that they are highly selective in assimilating such information, taking in what fits in with their own personal experience and ignoring or reworking most of the rest. Similarly it seems very likely that expression of norms varies according to the social situation and the research technique used. The norms expressed in the group discussions we attended were much closer to those of newspapers and the church than to those expressed by the research couples in interviews. If we had used questionnaires or highly structured interviews with the research families, we should probably have been given a rather different view of familial norms. I would suggest that there is no single correct way of getting at the truth about norms. Different techniques will reveal different aspects of it.[1]

[1] At first I thought replies to direct questions were less 'true' than spontaneous conversation. I now regard this as an error. Except for cases of conscious lying, I now think people express their views quite differently in different contexts without being aware of it. They may even hold different views in different contexts. This exemplifies Max Gluckman's point that flexibility and inconsistency in norms make them more rather than less useful socially; they can be adapted to suit immediate circumstances (Gluckman, 1955).

Informal discussions with other family sociologists suggest that they have fallen into the same error. In cases where questionnaires and unstructured interviews with the same informants have yielded very different results, research workers have tended to regard one

In spontaneous discussion all couples made indirect expressions of norms in talking about particular individuals they knew. Of all these specific individuals, parents were the most important referents. Parents provided the basic models of family life that the couples we were interviewing were trying to emulate or improve on. There were also many references, usually negative, to friends, neighbours, and other relatives besides parents. A wife, for example, remarked that her brother-in-law was a good bread-winner but neglected his wife and children so that his was not a happy family. Implicitly she was drawing a contrast with her own husband, who was not a great success at his job but did enjoy the company of his wife and children. Or again, a wife remarked that one of the neighbours had ridiculed her own husband in public, with the clear implication that such behaviour was very disloyal and ill-mannered. One husband, in the midst of an argument with his wife, went straight through a list of all his friends to show her that all men were difficult to live with and that she was expecting far too much of him. As we got to know families better, we began to be told their gossip. Gossip is one of the chief means by which norms are stated and re-affirmed.

Informants referred to groups or categories of person as well as to specific individuals, especially when replying to our direct questions about norms. Many different reference groups were selected. There was no one group or category that everyone chose as a matter of course. This contrasts with the situation in a small-scale society, in which the group referent is clear; the norms apply to everyone in the society, or at least to everyone in a clearly de-fined sub-group within the society. When a family is not con-tained in an organized group, but only in a network, especially a loose-knit network, the referent of the norms becomes much less predictable and more complicated.

When informants were trying to generalize about standards of

technique as right and truth-revealing and the other as wrong and false. It would be more rewarding to regard both sets of results as 'true' in the sense of revealing what people think in different research situations. The two sets of results could be compared closely to see if there were a consistent bias. Such a procedure would lead to greater understanding of the effects produced by different research techniques.

conjugal behaviour, I think most of them were considering primarily their own personal experience, their informal social network of friends, neighbours, and relatives. But no one referred to this set of people as such, presumably because it is difficult to conceptualize a network, since it has no beginning and no end. Some couples referred to local areas. Others tended to choose sets of friends or some kind of abstract category such as 'people like us' or 'our social circle' or 'our kind'. Such choice depended partly on the connectedness of the family's network. If a couple had a close-knit network, they usually talked about local areas, although they sometimes also referred to the conjugal practices of other generations or social classes. If they had a loose-knit network, they referred primarily to sets of friends or to abstract categories. In Chapters III and IV it was noted that the most close-knit networks were found where most of a family's friends and relatives were living in the same local area as the family itself. It is hardly surprising that such families conceptualized their network as the local area in which most of the members lived. Families with loose-knit networks did not choose a local area as a reference group, for their relatives and friends were scattered all over England. The closest they could come to a concrete reference group was a set of friends. When they were trying to generalize more broadly they referred to more abstract categories such as 'people like us' and 'our social circle'. In the cases where we thought to ask whom informants were thinking of when they used such phrases, it was clear that the meaning shifted according to context. Sometimes it meant 'people of our general class and style of life'; sometimes it meant 'people of our age and style of life'; sometimes it meant 'our friends' or 'potential friends'. People who used such words shifted imperceptibly from one meaning to another, and often reference to the category was followed by references to specific individuals who came within it.

People also referred to groups and categories in which they did not place themselves. Families who had had experience of close-knit networks in the past often referred to the local areas in which they had formerly lived. Families with loose-knit networks

usually referred not to local areas but to other classes and generations. All couples contrasted their own conjugal standards occasionally with those of the older generation and 'Victorian families'.

The patterns of selection described above were only general
tendencies. Couples varied greatly in choice of reference groups
and in feelings towards them. Thus one couple identified themselves with the local area in which they lived and subscribed almost completely to the standards of conjugal behaviour they
attributed to the people in it. They contrasted it favourably with
conjugal behaviour in other areas. Another couple of similar
occupational status and general background (but a more loose-
knit network) said they liked their local area and would never
leave it, although they did not approve of all the local standards
of conjugal behaviour. They said it was terrible the way the wives
gossiped about their husbands and the way husbands never spent
any time at home. They felt they themselves had personal standards that were different and better. At the same time, they condemned the conjugal practices of other areas and other classes.

Many couples used several different reference groups. Thus the
plumber and his wife contrasted the confused and variable conjugal standards of their present local area with those of the areas
in which they had been brought up. They also contrasted themselves with the households that the husband encountered in the
course of his work. Their evaluation of themselves varied according to the context of comparison. Some couples rejected almost
completely the norms they attributed to the group with which
they identified themselves. Thus one couple acknowledged that
they were similar in occupation to their neighbours and relatives
but said they had a totally different outlook. They criticized their
neighbours and relatives and identified themselves with an abstract category of nice people who had high standards of cleanliness, orderliness, and good manners. At the same time, in the
course of spontaneous discussion they revealed that they visited
their relatives and neighbours more than this sweeping condemnation implied. Some other couples who rejected the standards

they attributed to their local area or friends did not bother to identify themselves positively with some other group or category. They were content to present themselves as deviants above the norms of the category in which they placed themselves. But not all couples selected reference groups in such a way as to make themselves appear in the best light. A few couples went to some trouble to make themselves appear average—that is, they chose categories in which they were placed in the middle when they might easily have chosen categories of such a kind that they would have been at the top.

I do not mean to suggest here that the couples we interviewed were deliberately distorting the norms of sets or categories of people. In nearly all cases, we felt their descriptions were consistent and probably reasonably accurate when they were describing concrete individuals with whom they had had direct experience. Of course we cannot be sure of this because we could not interview all their friends, neighbours, and relatives. But when they were asked to generalize about norms, over-simplification and distortion were inevitable. Families with loose-knit networks had a particularly difficult time here, since the variation among the members of their networks was greater. In brief, when families live only in networks, when there is no organized group that they must almost inevitably use as a reference group, they must construct reference groups. They must generalize from their varied social experience to reach some simplified description, which is inevitably distorted. If they choose, they can identify themselves or contrast themselves with categories that show off their own behaviour and standards in a favourable light. If they choose, they may select categories that will make them seem average. If they have a close-knit network, they will probably choose categories that are fairly close to their everyday experiences with friends, neighbours, and relatives, although they are not compelled to do so. If they have a loose-knit network, their categories are likely to be more abstract and generalized. And the more remote the reference group from their everyday experience, the greater is the opportunity for unfettered exercise of imagination.

Expression of norms thus varied according to the context and the particular individual or group that was being evaluated and compared with the couple's own standards of behaviour. Couples had a considerable range of choice in selecting the group or category with which they identified or compared themselves. This ability to choose one reference group rather than another makes it easy for informants to treat personal norms as social norms, for it is not difficult to find or construct some abstract category of person who shares one's own views.

3. *Deviance and Conformity*

Variation and flexibility of norms make it difficult to say what is deviance and what is conformity. In the course of the research I have come to the conclusion that it is impossible to make general, universally applicable assessments of levels of family functioning, which is a major aim of much research on the family. Such an aim assumes that there are many norms of common consent about familial roles. Too often the norms selected as the standard are those that the research worker thinks are current in his own social circle. Even if they are accurate for this category of person, they may be quite inappropriate for other types of family. I am not asserting here that families must never be measured against some standard, only that one should realize that the standard is arbitrary and that many families will not subscribe to it.

I think it is necessary to distinguish between *felt deviance* and *externally defined deviance*, felt deviance being lack of correspondence between the family's behaviour and their own social norms, externally defined deviance being lack of correspondence between their behaviour and some standard chosen by the research worker. It is very difficult to determine felt deviance, partly because people have trouble in conceptualizing norms, partly because they do not like to talk about deviance unless they think they are above their norm rather than below it, partly because they often use several different reference groups, and partly because they may be at or above their norms in some respects and below in others.

At the risk of considerable over-simplification, I have tried to infer felt deviance for the research families, with the following results. Seven families conformed in most respects to the norms they attributed to their most frequently used reference group. Seven thought they were better in some respects. Three thought they were worse in some respects. Three thought they were different without being better or worse. There were only two cases in which internal inconsistencies suggested that the couple were seriously misrepresenting their own behaviour and that of the people in their most frequently used reference group. Both these couples placed themselves above their norm.

Felt deviance can be compared with various types of externally defined deviance. If one takes conformity to the very general norms agreed on by all families, the norms of common consent, only two families were below these norms and even these families were below only in some respects, not in all. Both families tacitly acknowledged their deviance in the relevant respects.

If the norms of each set of families with similar degrees of network-connectedness are taken as the standards, there were fourteen cases in which felt deviance (or conformity) and externally defined deviance (or conformity) coincided and six cases in which they did not agree. These six cases include the two couples mentioned above who probably misrepresented their own behaviour and the norms of their reference groups. In the other four cases, the social norms of the families were slightly different from those of other families with similar types of network.

If one uses Burgess's 'companionship' family as the standard (Burgess and Locke, 1953) only nine families conformed. Of the eleven deviant ones, the behaviour of two was at their own norm, six were above, one was below, and two were different without being above or below.

In brief, if one uses different standards, one gets different measures of deviance. Perhaps in situations in which there are only a few norms of common consent it would be convenient to determine what might be called *average norms*. These would consist of a quantitatively determined mean of the social norms expressed by the members of some category or set of persons selected by the research worker. Such an average measure would permit comparison of particular informants' social norms against a general standard, admittedly an artificial one, even when there were few norms of common consent.

If one must evaluate families, I do not think it matters greatly what standard is used, provided it is relevant for the immediate problem and provided one bears in mind that there is not likely to be consensus on this standard among one's informants. But in almost any evaluative study, I should think it would be instructive to compare felt deviance with externally defined deviance. This permits one to do justice to the families' own standards and to the fact that their ideas of right and wrong, of the customary and the unusual, may be quite different from those of the research worker. But at the same time, it allows the research worker to use a fixed standard against which all variations, both in norms and in behaviour, can be compared.

4. Conflicts of Norms

Among the research families there were many examples of inconsistencies between norms. A wife should be able to work; a wife should stay home to look after her children. Among the families with comparatively close-knit networks (including here some of those that were classed as medium-knit in Chapter III), there was a conflict for the wives between obligations to the mother and obligations to the husband. In several cases ideal norms and norms of expectation conflicted with each other. Couples in close-knit networks said that husbands ought to give their wives a liberal housekeeping allowance, but they did not really expect such generosity. One wife complained about her husband's stinginess and another wife constantly stressed how fortunate she was in having a generous husband. The first wife thought most other women suffered as she did, whereas the second thought her husband was most unusual, but in both cases it was clear that the norm of expectation was that husbands would not give enough.

It is sometimes assumed that discrepancies and conflicts of norms are a sign of social change—an assertion that assumes the 'normal' state of social systems to be one of harmony and consistency. But, as I have stated above, norms are seldom consistent even in small-scale societies that are changing slowly, and it seems likely that certain types of conflict are endemic in a social system. It is difficult to imagine that conflict of norms about loyalty to one's mother and to one's husband could be eliminated from families with close-knit networks. It may disappear if the family moves, but then the whole organization of external and internal relationships is altered.

Conflicts between norms need not, as is sometimes suggested, lead to personal and social conflict. In favourable circumstances people may be able to reconcile the requirements of conflicting norms. Thus one of the wives with a close-knit network was able to fulfil her obligations both to her husband and to her mother, partly because of her own skill and tact, but also because her husband and her mother got along well together. In other cases wives were both working and fulfilling their obligations to their children, to their own and their husbands' satisfaction. Individuals may also cope with discrepancies of norms by constructing their own solution as an ideal norm and projecting it on to their social circle or some other reference group of their own choosing. This does not solve the problem on a social level but it does sort things out for the individual.

As I have stated above, people do not usually make norms explicit spontaneously except in situations of interpersonal conflict, and we were not able to witness many such disputes. The research families knew they were being studied as 'ordinary' families, so that it is not surprising that they did not display their conflicts before us. After the first few interviews, when they had lost much of their uneasiness about revealing the fact that they did not always get along well together, they would describe rows they had had in the past or might have in the future. But only one couple had a row in the presence of one of the field workers. In this case each partner asserted that he was behaving correctly and that the other was in the wrong. Each proclaimed different norms and tried to show that his own view was generally accepted in their social circle. It did not happen, as it often does in small-scale societies, that the disputants agreed about the norms in principle but disagreed over whether and how they had conformed to them.

C. CONCLUDING DISCUSSION

In this chapter I have reported more variation in the norms of familial roles than is commonly assumed, and I have also shown that many of the people we interviewed found great difficulty in making norms explicit. I have suggested that both facts can be interpreted in terms of the immediate social environment in which the research families lived. The argument may be most clearly summarized by contrasting the position of families that are encapsulated within organized groups with those in close-knit networks and those in loose-knit networks.

In an organized group in which members are in constant interaction, one is likely to find a large number of norms of common consent. Constant interaction corrects individual idiosyncrasies of ideology. The norms I have defined as social norms, that is, the norms people attribute to the group with which they identify themselves, are likely to be more or less the same as the norms of common consent. In other words, there is little variation in the norms various members of the group attribute to it. Members of the group will find it easy to make norms explicit. Almost inevitably members will use the group itself as a reference group when discussing familial norms. Individual members may of course have discordant personal views, but they will be aware of the discrepancy between their own views and those of other members of the group, just as they will soon find out if their own behaviour is ·deviant. Opportunities for treating personal norms as social norms are reduced to a minimum. This does not mean, of course, that group norms never change. They may change in response to changed external conditions and through internal upheavals in which the personal views of individual members may play an important part.

In a close-knit network the group situation is approached, but there is more variation in norms, since not all members of the network interact with one another. If one could interview all the members of a close-knit network, I should predict that one would find a fairly large number of norms of common consent: the social norms of the various members would be in fairly close agreement with one another. There would be more variation than in a group, less than in a loose-knit network. People in close-knit networks are likely to be intermediate in ability to state norms explicitly; they will have more difficulty than people in organized groups, less difficulty than people in loose-knit networks. People in close-knit networks are likely to use their networks as reference groups, although they conceptualize them as local areas. But they are not compelled to make this selection. They may also choose abstract categories or groups of which they have no direct experience. In such a situation, people have some opportunity to treat their personal norms as social norms, but if they are in constant interaction with the members of their network, and if the members of their network are in constant interaction with one another, they are likely to be made aware that their social norms are not norms of common consent.

In a loose-knit network fewer members know one another and there is less interaction. More variation in norms is likely to develop. There will be fewer norms of common consent, more variation in social norms from one member of the network to another. Informants find it difficult to make norms explicit, especially when their attention is focused on variation by direct questions. But, at the same time, they do assume implicitly that they share their standards of conjugal behaviour with other people. By my definition they have social norms, although there are few norms of common consent. People in loose-knit networks have considerable opportunity to treat personal norms as social norms, to assert that the standards they follow are those that are current in their social circle or in some other similar reference group. The referent of their social norms, although derived from experience with their friends, neighbours, and relatives, is likely to be an abstract category. Because they have so much experience of different standards among the people they know, their reference groups must be generalized and over-simplified, and they have a considerable range of potential reference groups to choose from.

The suggestion that personal norms may unwittingly be treated as social norms raises the question of how norms are acquired by individuals. The psychological mechanisms of this process are very complex, and I shall do no more here than suggest some points that merit further reflection and inquiry.

In the literature of social psychology, much stress is placed on the internalization of norms through interaction with other people (Sherif, 1936; Newcomb, 1950). This interpretation of the individual as a passive recipient of external norms is too simple for the data I have reported here. When individuals and families live in networks rather than in groups, the process of norm formation becomes more complicated. I would suggest that individuals internalize other people's standards from their experiences with them, but that this is not the end of the matter. If the internalized standards agree with one another, which tends to happen in organized groups and in close-knit networks, there is little necessity for selection and internal rearrangement. If many different and contradictory norms are internalized, individuals select some rather than others and construct their own version in accordance with their personal needs. They may attribute this personal version, or certain aspects of it, to other people besides themselves, and they have a wide range of reference groups or categories from which to choose the recipient of their norms. In brief, projection and displacement play as important a part as internalization in the acquisition of norms.

I would suggest, then, that both psychological mechanisms, introjection (internalization) and projection, are always involved in the acquisition of norms. Indeed, recent findings of psychoanalysis explicitly stress the importance of projection as well as introjection in all learning processes (Heimann, 1952; Klein, 1948). This view is also implicit in the work of George Herbert Mead (Mead, 1934). In the case of couples in loose-knit networks, the separate effects of the two mechanisms are comparatively easily distinguished. In close-knit networks or organized groups it is much more difficult to separate the two mechanisms. Errors of projection and of introjection are more rapidly corrected by constant interaction, so that a common standard is reached both internally and externally.

CHAPTER VIII

Summary and General Discussion

An attempt has been made in this book to analyse several types of variation—variation in conjugal roles, in network-connectedness, in behaviour towards kin, and in concepts of class and norms of conjugal roles. I should like now to summarize the analysis and to discuss some of the problems that have arisen in the research.

Variation in the performance of conjugal roles has been discussed in terms of the extent to which husband and wife carried out their activities and tasks separately and independently of each other. Some couples had considerable segregation between them in their conjugal role-relationship. Such couples had a clear differentiation of tasks and a considerable number of separate, individual interests and activities. At the other extreme were couples who had as little segregation as possible between them in their conjugal role-relationship. Such husbands and wives expected to carry out many activities together with a minimum of task differentiation and separation of interests. There were many degrees of variation between these two extremes. In Chapter III it has been suggested that one set of factors affecting these variations in degree of conjugal segregation is the pattern of relationships maintained by the members of the family with external people and the relationships of these external people with one another.

The immediate social environment of an urban family consists of a network rather than an organized group. A network is a social configuration in which some, but not all, of the component external units maintain relationships with one another. The external units do not make up a larger social whole. They are not surrounded by a common boundary.

In all societies elementary families have a network of social relationships. But in many small-scale societies with a simple division of labour, elementary families are also contained within organized groups that control many aspects of their daily activities. Urban families are not completely encapsulated by organized groups in this way. As individuals, members of the family may belong to organized groups. As a family, some aspects of their activities may be controlled by a doctor, by a church, by a local borough council and other government bodies. But there is no organized group that regulates all aspects of a family's life, informal activities as well as formal. Urban families are not isolated, since members maintain many relationships with individuals and groups outside the family. But they are more 'individuated' than families in relatively small, closed communities. Many of the individuals and groups to which an urban family is related are not linked up with one another, so that although each external individual or group may control some aspect of familial activity, social control of the family as a whole is dispersed among several agencies. This means that each family has a relatively large measure of privacy and of freedom to regulate its own affairs.

The networks of urban families vary in degree of connectedness, namely in the extent to which the people with whom the family maintains relationships carry on relationships with one another. These variations in network-connectedness are particularly evident in informal relationships between friends, neighbours, and relatives. Such differences in connectedness are associated with differences in degree of segregation of conjugal roles. The degree of segregation in the role-relationship of husband and wife varies directly with the connectedness of the family's social network. Four sets of families have been described in Chapter III, and the relationship between the connectedness of their networks and the degree of their conjugal role segregation has been discussed.

217

It has been suggested that if husband and wife come to marriage with close-knit networks, and if conditions are such that this pattern of relationships can be continued, the marriage is superimposed on the previous relationships and each partner continues to be drawn into activities with outside people. Each gets some emotional satisfaction from these external relationships and demands correspondingly less of the spouse. Rigid segregation of conjugal roles is possible because each partner can get help from people outside. But if husband and wife come to marriage with loose-knit networks, or if their networks become loose-knit after marriage, they must seek in each other some of the emotional satisfaction and help with familial tasks that couples in close-knit networks can get from outsiders. Joint organization becomes more necessary for the success of the family as an enterprise.

It seems to me that many clinical workers, doctors, and family research workers take it for granted that joint organization is the natural and normal form for familial behaviour to take. Advice based on this assumption must be rather bewildering to families in close-knit networks, as Michael Young has suggested (1956). And behaviour that might correctly be interpreted as overdependent or defensively authoritarian in families with loose-knit networks should be interpreted differently if it occurs in families with close-knit networks. I do not mean to say that such behaviour should be accepted as 'normal' in the clinical sense simply because it is culturally acceptable to certain types of family, but I think that one should be prepared to see whether it has different psychological meanings and effects for the people concerned.

I do not believe it is sufficient to explain variations in conjugal segregation as cultural or sub-cultural differences. To say that people behave differently or have different expectations because they belong to different cultures amounts to no more than saying that they behave differently because they behave differently—or that cultures are different because they are different. It is for this reason that I do not think it would be illuminating to attribute differences in conjugal segregation to social class differences even if the correlation were high. This is only a first stage of analysis, a preliminary classification on a descriptive level. It is essential to push the analysis further, to find out what factors in social class are relevant to conjugal segregation and how they actually produce an effect on the internal role structure of families.

In my view a culture is specific to a particular social situation. In this book I have tried to show how certain sub-cultural variations in familial organization are associated with variations in patterns of social relationship with and among persons outside the family. The norms—or the culture, if one prefers that term—of conjugal segregation are appropriate to families in close-knit networks. If the family moves, or if for any other reason their network becomes loose-knit, a new culture becomes appropriate. I do not assert, however, that culture can be reduced to social relationships, or that it changes automatically when social relationships change. Some of the transitional families of the research set were finding it very difficult and painful to give up their old beliefs and practices and to develop new ones more appropriate to their changed situation.

I am sometimes asked if there are any differences in happiness or stability of marriage according to degree of conjugal segregation. Among the research families such differences were not marked. By their own standards, the Newbolts were one of the happiest families. So were several of the families with loose-knit networks, although they required different things for their happiness. They would not have been happy with the Newbolts' arrangements and the Newbolts would not have been happy with theirs.

With regard to stability of marriage, all families were stable in the sense that none of them were contemplating divorce. Further study would be required to answer this question in general terms. Existing divorce statistics do not tell one very much about the stability of different types of conjugal relationship. The most that can be done is to correlate divorce rates with income and occupation. In the United States the evidence suggests that people with lower incomes and occupations of lower status get divorced somewhat more frequently than those with higher incomes and occupations of higher status (Goode, 1951). The same correlation is reported in New Zealand (Nixon, 1954). But, as described in Chapter IV, income and occupation are not very good indicators of degree of conjugal segregation. Logically, one can point to factors that make for stability and instability in both joint and highly segregated relationships. Joint conjugal relationships might lead to conjugal stability because the emotional investment of both partners is so considerable; but on the other hand husband and wife expect so much of each other that disillusion and disappointment might drive them apart. In a highly segregated conjugal relationship the partners expect less of each other and would be less likely to part because of disillusionment, but on the other hand they get less from each other emotionally and might therefore leave each other more easily. But children are the most important deterrent to divorce, as the divorce statistics indicate (Cahen, 1932; Jacobson, 1950). It is very difficult for one person to bring up children and earn a living at the same time, regardless of type of conjugal relationship and type of social network. Possibly it might be easier for divorced people in close-knit networks to care for their children since they can get help from kin more easily.

In Chapter IV an analysis of the factors affecting connectedness was presented. Variations in network-connectedness cannot be explained in terms of any single factor. Such variations are made possible by the complexity and variability of the economic, occupational, and other institutional systems, which create a complex of forces affecting families in different ways and permitting selection and choice by the family according to their personal needs. It has been suggested that the connectedness of a family's network is a function on the one hand of a complex set of forces in the total environment, and on the other hand, of the family themselves and their reaction to these forces. Several situational factors possibly relevant to the connectedness of families' networks have been suggested, including the extent to which members of the network are bound to one another by economic ties, the type of neighbourhood in which they live, their opportunities to make relationships outside their existing networks, and their opportunities for physical and social mobility.

Connectedness is affected by factors associated with social class, but in a most complex way. The empirical resultant is that families with close-knit networks are likely to be working-class, but not all working-class families will have close-knit networks. It is only in the working class that one is likely to find a combination of factors all working together to produce a high degree of connectedness. The structure of the professions is such that this pattern of forces almost never occurs. But the fact that a man has a manual occupation does not automatically mean that he will have a close-knit network. He may live in a relatively heterogeneous area, for not all manual occupations are localized. He may live in one place and work in another. He may move. Similarly his friends and relatives may move or make new relationships with people he does not know. A high degree of connectedness may be found in association with manual occupations, but the association is not necessary and inevitable.

Considerable variation was found among the research families in the amount and intensity of contact with kin. In Chapter V an attempt has been made to analyse the general features of the kinship system and to account in detail for variation in frequency and intensity of contact between three families and their relatives, and, in so far as the data permit, of their relatives with one another.

In contrast to the bilateral kinship systems of small-scale 'primitive' societies, bilateral kinship in an urban industrialized society does not provide the basic framework of the social structure. The reduced importance of kinship in economic and political affairs is associated with a narrower range of kin recognition, with absence of corporate groups of kin recruited according to residence or some other non-kinship principle, with less highly connected kinship networks and correspondingly more individuation of elementary families, and with much variation in kinship behaviour and norms.

As stressed by Firth, kinship in an urban setting provides a field for personal selectivity and choice (Firth, 1956). It is the variable effect of situational factors that makes choice possible, but it is the families that make the actual decisions. The results of three families' choices have been described and an attempt has been made to analyse the factors affecting their choices, namely, economic ties among kin, residence and physical accessibility of kin, type of genealogical relationship, the connectedness of the kinship network, the presence and preference of connecting relatives, perceived similarities and differences in social status among relatives, and likes and dislikes based on an idiosyncratic combination of conscious and unconscious needs and attitudes.

In the case of the Newbolts, these factors were combined in such a way that the family, especially the wife and children, had a great deal of contact with relatives, and a group composed of grandmother, mothers, and daughters had formed within the total network of kin. This pattern of contact was associated with opportunities for relatives to help one another occupationally; minimal differences in occupational status among kin; residential propinquity of kin; the presence of three generations of mothers and daughters in the same place at the same time, each acting as connecting relative for her husband and children; and experience by husband and wife of segregation of parental roles in their families of orientation.

In the case of the Hartleys, the factors had combined in such a way that the family had a fair amount of contact with kin although there was no matrilateral stress. This pattern was associated with little opportunity for relatives to help one another occupationally; considerable scatter of relatives in type of occupation and occupational status; more geographical dispersal of relatives than in the case of the Newbolts but less than in that of the Daniels; no opportunity for grandmother-mother-daughter groups to form since the necessary women were not alive; considerable opportunity for the husband's mother and paternal aunts to act as connecting relatives; and experience by husband and wife, especially the wife, of relatively loose-knit networks in childhood and relatively slight segregation of parental roles in their families of orientation.

For the Daniels, these factors had combined so that they had very little contact with kin, no bias in favour of contact with the wife's relatives rather than the husband's or the mother's rather than the father's, and no group of female relatives within the total network of kin. This pattern was associated with few opportunities for relatives to help one another occupationally; considerable scatter of relatives in type of occupation and occupational status; marked geographical dispersal of relatives; no opportunity for grandmother-mother-daughter groups to form since only two generations of women were alive and they did not live in the same place; reduced opportunity for women to act as connecting relatives; and experience by husband and wife of little segregation of parental roles in the families of orientation.

In Chapter VI and VII an analysis of class ideology and conjugal norms has been presented. The basic argument of both chapters is that people do not acquire their ideology, norms, and values solely by internalizing them from outside. They also re-work the standards they have internalized, conceptualize them in a new form, and project them back on to the external situation. The more varied their social experience and the more unconnected the standards they internalize, the more internal rearrangement they must make. And the more loose-knit their networks, the greater the necessity for them to use constructed reference groups, abstract categories of person, as the referents of their norms and ideology.

The members of organized groups are likely to develop a high degree of consensus on norms and ideology because of their frequent interaction with one another. Errors of internalization and projection are rapidly corrected, and the membership group is almost inevitably used as a reference group. When the immediate social environment is a network, not all the people the family knows interact with one another, and considerable variation in norms and ideology is likely to arise. The greater the amount of such variation, the more difficulty people are likely to have in conceptualizing norms as a simple set of unambiguous rules. At the same time, the greater the variation in behaviour, norms, and ideology internalized from experience with other people, the greater is the opportunity for reinterpretation and reordering of internalized standards in accordance with personal needs. This personal version can be applied not only to oneself but also to other people, and one has considerable choice in selecting and constructing the reference groups to whom it may apply.

This means that considerable variation in norms and ideology is likely to arise not only within the same society, but even between people with roughly similar social experience. In Chapter VII I have suggested that separate terms should be used to distinguish norms that are social in the sense that groups or categories of person actually agree on them ('norms of common consent') from norms that are social in the sense that individuals think other persons or groups share them ('social norms'). Analysis of deviance is much complicated by the variation, flexibility, and projection of norms. I have suggested that 'felt deviance', that is, discrepancy between the family's social norms and their behaviour, should be distinguished from 'externally defined deviance', that is, discrepancy between their behaviour and some standard chosen by the research worker. If there are norms of common consent, the research worker would be most likely to use these norms as the standard. If there is much variation, he must use some more artificial measure.

There are several ways in which the analysis presented in this book might be carried further. The central hypothesis—the association between conjugal segregation and network-connectedness—should be tested on other cases, particularly on cases in which families live in organized groups or very close-knit networks.[1]

Fuller understanding of the association between social networks and organization of familial roles might also be reached by study-

---

[1] Miss Rosemary Harris of London University has made a comparison of two types of rural family and neighbourhood organization which tends to support the hypothesis (Harris, 1954). Dr Yonina Talmon-Garber, on the other hand, is making a study of the organization of families in collective settlements in Israel which suggests that the hypothesis will need some revision (Talmon-Garber, 1954 and 1956).

ing them in the process of change. Detailed study of moves to housing estates would be instructive. Families in old-established working-class areas have been compared with families on new housing estates (Young, 1954b; Young and Willmott, 1957; Mogey, 1955 and 1956), but there have been few studies of the actual process of transition, beginning with the family in the old area and following them through the move to the new area and the development of a different pattern of external relationships and internal organization.[1] Study of changes in families with loose-knit networks when they move to more homogeneous communities would also be rewarding.

It would be valuable to study the various phases of familial development and the associated changes in external relationships and internal organization. It would be more than a life's work to follow several families through the whole process of development from courtship to old age, but a more limited long-range study could be made with profit. It would be instructive to examine transitions from one phase to another, particularly that brought about by the birth of the first child, which transforms the family from a conjugal pair into a three-person group and entails radical changes of external relationships and internal organization. Phases of familial development could also be studied by comparing old and young families, but it would be very difficult to tease out the differences that were phase-conditioned from those that were the result of general social change. A good deal can be learned about change in familial roles from what informants say about the past, but since people reinterpret the past in the light of their present experience, it is unwise to take what they say entirely at face value. If an analysis of what they said were combined with an analysis of old empirical accounts and historical records, it might be possible to outline at least the general trends of change, although precise comparisons would be difficult to make except

[1] A study of this sort was begun in Edinburgh by Tom Burns and Mary McLean but it was unfortunately interrupted. A similar sort of study is being conducted by the London School of Hygiene and Tropical Medicine but this study does not consider the relation of changes in external social relationships to changes in internal familial roles.

for factors such as family size and income, of which exact records have been kept.

Further study could profitably be made of relationships between parents and children according to degree of conjugal segregation and type of social network. In the present research the children were not studied intensively and I have done no more than describe briefly a few of the differences in attitude towards children, child-rearing practices, and parenthood. In Chapter V some possible psychological consequences of being brought up in a family with pronounced segregation of parental roles have been suggested. This problem is worth further study.

In addition to further qualitative analysis of this sort, the hypothesis needs more precise formulation and testing in quantitative terms. A scale of segregation similar to that of Herbst could be devised (Herbst, 1952 and 1954). More precise information should be collected on connectedness so that it could be expressed in quantitative terms. Each family should be asked more detailed questions on the relationships of their friends, neighbours, and relatives with one another. All relationships should be graded according to degree of intimacy, which has been done here only for kin. Relationships with and among kin, neighbours, and friends need more precise comparison and contrast. Similarly, within the total network a more refined comparative analysis should be made of the joint and independent networks of husband and wife.

It would be most useful to interview all or at least some of the members of a family's network instead of relying entirely on what the family said about them. But this would be extremely difficult for, as noted above, acceptance by a family does not mean acceptance by all their friends, neighbours, and relatives. But at least some members of their network might be interviewed, especially if the inquiry were less intimate and detailed than the one reported here.

A more detailed examination should also be made of the factors affecting connectedness. I doubt if this part of the analysis could easily be refined and expressed quantitatively so as to permit precise prediction. Many factors are involved, and it would be necessary to determine their relationship to each other. It would be difficult to hold constant all factors but one so that the effects of that one factor could be examined; analysis of variance or multiple correlation would require the data to be quantified in a form amenable to statistical analysis, and many of the data do not fall easily into suitable categories.

Fuller understanding of the factors affecting connectedness might be gained, however, by making a systematic comparison of conjugal segregation and network-connectedness according to social class. Such comparative study would be most useful if the effect of the various factors associated with class—income, control of property, type of occupation, education, and so forth—were examined separately and compared with one another as much as possible.

Further study is required of the effects of physical and social mobility on connectedness. A study of urban neighbourhoods would also be most productive. A comparative study of neighbourhoods in which ecological analysis was combined with analysis of formal institutions and actual social relationships of families in the areas would fill an important gap in theoretical and factual knowledge. There is a growing number of empirical studies of families. There are studies of housing estates and local neighbourhoods on a 'community' level. But there is great need of a study that would put the two approaches together, a study that would analyse type of familial network in relation to type of local area.

In Chapter II it was noted that several changes of conceptual orientation took place in the research staff as the work progressed. At the beginning the research team wanted to 'integrate' sociological and psychological approaches to the study of families. During the third phase of the research they regarded such conceptual integration as the major aim of the research and spent much time in fruitless argument over concepts. Later on these discussions in the abstract were abandoned in favour of detailed analyses and comparisons of particular families, after which the combined use of psychological and sociological concepts became much easier. These changes in conceptual approach may now be summarized and expressed in general terms.

At the beginning of the research I hoped we might combine the two approaches of anthropology and psycho-analysis by analysing the implicit and unconscious aspects of familial roles. I thought it would be possible to analyse the formal role system of the elementary family and then to determine what psychological mechanisms members of that role system would be likely to use. Having defined the standard unconscious components of roles in this way, I thought it would then be possible to carry the analysis a step further by considering how real individuals actually behaved in their roles, thus finding out what sort of fit there was between their personalities and the explicit and implicit aspects of the roles they were playing. This approach had been used with great success by Trist in his study of the longwall method of coal-getting (Trist and Bamforth, 1951), and I saw no reason why it should not be applied to families. But as the work went on it became apparent that this method was easiest to apply when the roles were standardized, specific, and clearly defined. We could not define unconscious role components because we could not say what the standardized definitions of the roles were except in the most vague and general terms. There was variation not only in role performance from one family to another, but also in the very definitions of the roles. It proved impossible to define a single role system, a standardized set of precise, detailed norms that would be valid for all families. Without some such standard to work from, the method outlined above cannot be used.[1]

It was necessary to abandon the hope of finding in the data a single standard against which all the families could be compared. I then began to try to find some single factor in the social environment that would account for the differences in the families' norms and role expectations. I still thought that psychological concepts could not be used until I had found some external con-

[1] Parsons has used a similar approach in his recent book on the family (Parsons and Bales, 1955), but he has done so by using an *ideal type* of family as the basis for discussion. Empirically. as I have suggested above, there is more variation of conjugal roles than this ideal type indicates.

dition that would account for variations in norms. Role performance might vary according to psychological needs, but the definition of the roles themselves must come from outside the person, outside the family even. First I tried to explain differences in norms and definitions of roles in terms of class, then in terms of neighbourhood. Neither attempt was successful and I gave up this effort temporarily and turned to the analysis of class ideology. Here it was evident that personal experience and personal needs, both conscious and unconscious, were affecting people's concepts of class. Obviously such concepts were not entirely imposed from outside. Then I returned to the analysis of conjugal roles, but this time I related them to the form of the families' external networks. It was obvious that the form of the family's network could not be attributed to external factors alone; it also depended on the family itself. The personal needs, both conscious and unconscious, of the members of the family were one of the several sets of factors affecting the form of their network. Economic, geographical, and social factors were also important, but the effects of personality could not be ignored. I then turned to an analysis of the norms of conjugal roles, and here too it was evident that personality factors were affecting not only the performance but the very definition of the roles.

Two important changes had taken place in the method of analysis. First, psychological concepts were being used not only in the analysis of the *performance* of familial roles and of unconscious role components, but also in the *definition* of the roles themselves, and in the analysis of external social networks. Second, it was clear that role expectations and the form of networks could not be explained as the product of single factors.

In brief, I had to give up the attempt to interpret norms and roles as social and entirely externally determined and role performance as internal and psychologically determined. Sociological and psychological concepts were now used simultaneously at every stage of the analysis. To sum up the final position: Performance of familial roles depends on the personal needs and preferences of the members of the family in relation to the tasks they must perform, the immediate social environment in which they live, and the norms they adhere to. But the form of the immediate social environment and the norms of familial roles depend in turn on the personal needs and preferences of the members of the family in relation to a very complex combination of situational forces generated by the total social environment. The total social environment permits considerable choice among several potential arrangements of the immediate environment and of norms; the actual choices made by a particular family are shaped not only by situational factors but also by the personal needs of its members.

No claim is made here that psychological concepts must be used in every type of sociological analysis. In many inquiries it is possible to ignore or hold constant unconscious aspects of relationships or idiosyncratic variations in personal needs and attitudes. But in cases where there are many situational factors and much latitude for choice, consideration of the effect of personal needs can make the analysis more meaningful. It is not a simple matter for, as shown in Chapter V, personal needs are not a single factor. Examined closely, they turn out to be a complex resultant of various psychological mechanisms, and even if the mechanisms are understood, the exact resultant cannot be predicted. Once again it is necessary to deal with several factors whose individual weights depend on the particular configuration of the combination.

APPENDIX A

Outline of Topics
for Home Interviews

Note: The interviewing outline was changed considerably as the research went on. The version presented here was developed towards the end of the work. Departures from earlier versions are indicated at various points.

As described in Chapter II, the outline was used as a general guide by the field workers, and the inclusion, form, order, and wording of questions were left to their discretion.

A. BACKGROUND INFORMATION

1. *Genealogy*
   a. Age, occupation, residence, marital status, and general comments on all known relatives. (The amount of detail varied by family and by field worker.)
   b. Contact with relatives in childhood. (This information was collected systematically only with the last few families.)
   c. Contact with and among relatives at the time of interviewing. (This topic was often taken up later when friends and neighbours were being discussed.)

2. *Family of Orientation*
   a. Occupation of father. General history of parents.
   b. Physical moves of family when informant was a child.
   c. Siblings. Ages, schooling, careers, marriage, children, contact with siblings.

3. *Personal History*
   Schooling, jobs, service career, recreation in childhood and adolescence. (Most of the material on this topic was collected in clinical interviews.)

231

4. *First Phase of Family, and Second Phase before Contact with Research Team*
   a. *Courtship and wedding*
   How met, when, where. Who came to wedding. Place and type of wedding.
   b. *Occupational History*
   c. *Housing and Neighbourhoods*
   Neighbourhoods lived in since marriage. Feelings about them. Plans for moving, if any. How did they find flat or house.
   d. *Birth of Children*
   Dates were usually given here, but full discussion of children was usually postponed until child care was discussed.
   e. *General Comments on the Conjugal Relationship*
   Few direct questions were asked on this topic until it was raised in later discussions. Then we asked how the conjugal relationship had changed.

B. ORGANIZATION OF FAMILIAL ACTIVITIES

1. *Diary*
   Yearly, weekly, daily diary. We asked for an actual and for a typical week.

2. *Decision-making*
   We asked four families direct questions about decision-making in specific task areas. People found it difficult to answer these point-blank questions. Later we waited until the couple mentioned decisions and then we asked how particular decisions had been made, what decisions were considered important, how decisions should be made, what changes had occurred in decision-making since marriage.

3. *Financial Support of the Family*
   a. *The husband's job.* Type of job. Place of work. Permanent or temporary employment. Income. Ideas about job compared with past and future jobs. Overtime. Extra jobs. Friends at work. Union, if any. Attitudes towards employers. Special features of work, e.g. whether husband was away from home a lot. How much his wife knew about his work.
   b. *The wife's job.* Working now? Since children born? After marriage but before children born? Plans for future? Attitudes about working. Attitudes towards women working in general. Views of husband.

4. *Housework*
   At first we inquired about a list of specific items, asking who did each,

who was responsible for it, how decisions about it were made, and whether husband and wife had any disagreements about it. (Cf. Herbsr, 1952 and 1954). The queries about decisions were dropped (see above). The queries about disagreements were dropped because we felt they were tactless. The list of items was: cooking (breakfast, lunch and dinner, tea, snacks), laying the table, washing up, cleaning and tidying the house, hoovering, shopping, laundry, ironing, cleaning shoes, lighting fires, fetching coal, tending the boiler, closing up at night, getting up first in the morning, repair jobs, including carpentry, electrical and gas fixtures, plumbing, etc., gardening, decorating.

After the first six families we stopped using this specific list of items and asked what the couple thought the main tasks of housework were, who did which, which tasks were interchangeable, shared, and independent, whether outsiders helped, which tasks were liked and which were disliked. We usually followed up these general queries with questions about specific tasks that the couple had omitted. This method gave the couple a better chance to structure the discussion in their own way. But it made impossible any precise rating on degree of segregation of conjugal roles, since we were not sufficiently careful in checking up on the same items with each couple.

5. *Child Care*

a. *Items of child care and child training.* At first we asked specific questions on particular topics: pregnancies; births (including who helped immediately after birth of children, especially in caring for older children); feeding in past and present; cleanliness (when training was begun, how old the children were when they had learned, general attitudes about it); did children ask about sex and how were their questions answered; what was done about aggression to parents, siblings, other children, other adults; supervision of children inside and outside the home; how children were punished and what for; how they were rewarded, and what for.

Later we asked questions about pregnancies, births, and feeding, but raised the other topics in the context of general discussion. If any topic seemed difficult it was omitted and quite frequently we forgot some of the topics.

b. *General attitudes towards children and child care.* A direct question was asked: 'What is the most important thing about bringing children up?' We also asked what plans they had for the children's future education and employment. But there was no standardized question on this topic.

c. *Division of labour between husband and wife in child care.* With the first few families we asked specific questions about responsibility, decisions, and disagreements on the following specific items: getting the children up, getting them dressed, seeing them off to school, giving them their meals, taking them on outings, playing with them, supervising their contacts with other children, correcting their manners, putting them to bed, caring for them when parents were out.

Later we asked more general questions first and followed these by queries about items that had been neglected. We asked who did which task, which tasks were interchangeable or shared, whether outsiders helped, etc. Questions about attitudes towards child-rearing techniques and so forth were easily fitted into this discussion.

6. *Financial Management*

a. *Sources.* One or several? Type of payment.

b. *General amounts.* Total wages or salary per week, month, year. Bonuses. Tax. (We did not press for this information if couples were unwilling to give it.)

c. *Channelling.* Housekeeping allowance? Bank account? Joint account? Is money put into common fund or controlled by partners separately, or some combination of the two? Pocket money for children. Savings (bank, insurance, certificates, clubs). Hire-purchase. Saving for rainy day or specific items. (We did not press questions on any of these points if couples seemed uncomfortable.)

d. *Expenses.* Who spends which money, and how much. Budgets, sometimes precise and sometimes estimated, were collected from nearly all families. Items covered were: food, rent or payments for house (including rates, etc.), coal, electricity, gas, telephone, insurance (if not covered before), transport, laundry, toilet articles, entertainment, cigarettes, children's allowances, clothes, presents, holidays, new household items (how purchased, how often, how much), children's schools. Each family presented us with their idea of their budget and we asked about items they had not covered.

e. *Ideology about money.* Three direct questions were asked. 'What would you do if you had a little bit more money?' 'What would you need to live on comfortably?' and 'What would you do if you won £75,000 on a football pool?' (Robb always asked these questions at the end with the other questions on ideology. Bott asked them when discussing financial management.)

7. *Recreation*

a. 'What are your main forms of recreation?'

b. Specific probe on holidays, books, magazines, papers, radio, television, plays, films, ballet, concerts, etc., special classes, hobbies, pub, entertaining.

c. Who took part in recreation (husband alone, wife alone, husband and wife together, whole family). Attitudes towards joint and independent recreation.

d. Where did recreation take place, at home or away from home.

C. INFORMAL EXTERNAL RELATIONSHIPS

Discussions on this topic and on recreation often overlapped.

1. *Relatives*

a. Type of contact. With which relatives, how often, when, where. Mutual visiting. Help in crises. Care of children. Help with housework. Borrowing articles, money. Weddings, funerals, christenings, Christmas, summer holidays. Letters.

b. Who in the family took part. Husband alone, wife alone, children alone, husband and wife together, wife and child or children together, father and child, whole family.

c. Connectedness. Towards the end of the field work we began to ask specific questions about which relatives saw each other. But most of the information on connectedness with earlier families had to be inferred from information given spontaneously or in the course of answering questions above.

2. *Friends*

Same as for relatives, but we also asked who first met the friend, where they lived, their marital status. In several cases we also asked where and how the couple drew the line between friends and acquaintances.

3. *Neighbours*

Which ones count as friends. How much is known about the others (name, age, occupation, children, etc.). Type of contact, as for relatives. General attitudes. Contact of neighbours with each other.

D. FORMAL EXTERNAL RELATIONSHIPS

1. *School*

Contact with children's schools. Aspirations for children, if not covered above.

2. *Church*

Attendance, activities, beliefs. Attendance by children.

3. *Political Parties*

Membership, attitudes, activity. Joint or independent.

4. *Trade Unions and Professional Organizations*

5. *Clubs and Voluntary Associations*

Membership, activities, frequency. Joint or independent.

6. *Public Institutions and Professional Services*

Hospital, doctor, dentist, health visitor, maternity and child welfare clinic, school nurses, social workers, lawyers, insurance agents, etc., local government bodies. Frequency of contact, and by which member of the family.

E. IDEOLOGY

1. *On Social Change*

'What do you think the main social changes in England have been in the last fifty years or so?'

2. *On Class*

a. 'What do you think the most important groups are in England to-day?' Classes were usually mentioned because this question followed the one on general social change and 'levelling up' was nearly always mentioned as a chief social change. If class was not specifically mentioned, we suggested that some people thought it was important and asked what the couple thought about it.

b. 'What kind of people are in each class? What makes one class different from another?' Attitudes towards each.

c. 'Is it possible to move from one class to another? How does this happen?'

d. 'Do you think there will be any important changes in the class picture as a whole? How would such changes come about?'

e. If possible, we asked where the couple placed themselves, their most intimate relatives, their friends.

f. If this topic had not been covered previously, we asked about their educational and occupational plans and aspirations for their children.

g. Occasionally we asked if the couple thought family life varied by class.

DELETE

236

People often became uncomfortable in the course of the interviews on class, and questions were frequently omitted.

3. *On the Family*

  a. 'What do you think the main changes in the family have been in the last fifty years or so?' (Fifteen couples were asked.)
  b. 'How would you describe the rights and duties of husband and wife?' (Four couples were asked.)
  c. 'How would you describe the ideal wife, the ideal husband, the ideal child?' (Ten couples were asked.)
  d. 'How do you feel your own ideas on how to run a family resemble those of people you know or are different from them?' (Nine couples were asked.)
  e. 'When you got married, did you have a clear idea of what family life would be like? Have your ideas on it changed?' (Ten couples were asked.)
  f. 'What do you feel are the important things in keeping a family ticking over? What things make it difficult?' (Seven couples were asked.)

Development of Classification of Conjugal Organizations

This description of classifications is included to show the changes that took place as ideas were tried out on the data.

The initial classification was strongly influenced by the work of Talcott Parsons on kinship (1943) and on age and sex (1942), Kurt Lewin's ideas on differentiation (Appendix of *Field Theory and Social Science*, 1952), and Herbst's classification of conjugal relationships as autocratic, autonomic and syncratic (Herbst, 1952). It consisted of a division into unspecialized, differentiated, autonomous, and hierarchically organized activities. I soon found I was speaking of 'shared unspecialized activities' and 'autonomous unspecialized activities'; the dimension of autonomy was cutting across the others.

An attempt was then made to classify each activity according to how decisions about it were made and put into effect (authoritarian, joint, autonomous). Somewhat to my surprise, no couples clearly recognized the right of one spouse to direct the activities of the other. None of the research couples talked about the conjugal relationship in terms of authority; there was no assumption that the husband wielded authority and the wife had to accept it, or that she wielded authority and he had to accept it. In a more subtle sense it was often suggested that one or other partner had a stronger character and dominated the other, and some couples indicated indirectly that it was more natural for men to be domineering than women. But on the whole these differences appeared to be more a matter of personality characteristics than of role expectations. In any case most couples found it very difficult to describe how they made decisions. All couples said that important decisions should be made together and that in certain types of decision one partner's interests might receive more consideration than the other's. But when it came to describing how decisions had been made most people said they did not know, it had just happened. Or decision-making, like authority, was explained in terms of personality factors, not in terms that could be described as role expectations. Similar statements were made about conflicts and disagreements between husband and wife. In some families there were standardized, expected conflicts, but most conflicts between husband and wife were considered to be clashes of personality, and people could not describe any general rules about them.

For a time I tried to define the major tasks of families and to classify activities according to their contribution to the tasks (central, peripheral), and according to locus (internal, external). But at this stage it was impossible to work out satisfactory criteria of the importance of activities and tasks; such evaluation was premature.

I then revised the original classification of conjugal organization. The activities of husband and wife were classified according to whether they were different and complementary, different and independent, or the same or similar. Each of these types was further subdivided according to whether the activities were carried out by the husband and wife together or separately. This led to six types of organization, which are shown below, together with the labels that were attached to each type.

ORGANIZATION OF ACTIVITIES BY HUSBAND AND WIFE
(Activities that were finally defined as 'joint' are enclosed by the broken line.)

Type of Activity	Relation of Husband and Wife in Activity	
	Together	Apart
Different and complementary	'complementary together'	'differentiated' interdependence'
Different and independent	'parallel'	'autonomic'
The same or similar	'shared'	'interchangeable'

I found these classifications exceedingly cumbersome to apply. The sociological descriptions of each family grew so complicated that I could hardly understand them myself a week after I had written them. At first the distinctions did not seem to be leading to any new formulations of problems or data. But one important thing gradually began to emerge. Certain types of organization were usually found in close association, and the couples themselves seemed to think of them as a single type of behaviour. All activities carried out by husband and wife in each other's presence were felt to be

239

similar in kind regardless of whether the activities were complementary (e.g. sexual intercourse, though no one talked about this directly in the home interviews), independent (e.g. husband repairing a book case while the wife read or knitted), or shared (e.g. washing up together, entertaining friends, going to the pictures together). It was not even necessary that husband and wife should actually be together. As long as they were both at home it was felt that their activities partook of some special, shared, family quality. Interchangeable activities were also considered to be of the same general character as activities carried out together. For example, if a husband and wife took turns at doing the washing up, this arrangement was felt to be roughly similar in quality to activities that were done together. Similarly, if one spouse helped the other with any task, it was felt to be a shared activity even when the main responsibility for doing it rested with one partner.

I began to use the word 'joint' to refer to all these four types of organization that were felt to have something in common and were found in close association with one another. This reduced the number of types of organization to three: 'joint', 'differentiated', and 'autonomic'. I dropped the word 'autonomic' in favour of 'independent', and more recently the word 'complementary' has been substituted for 'differentiated'.

In the course of time it became clear that classification of organization could not be based merely on the form of the activity. It was also necessary to take into account what the couple thought and felt about it. Thus one couple might think of a wife's job as an independent activity, whereas another couple would construe it as helping her husband to support the family financially. The choice of one view or the other depended on the couple's general expectations about the role-relationship of husband and wife; if they had many joint activities they usually interpreted the wife's job as a joint activity; if they had many complementary and independent activities they usually interpreted it as an independent activity.

REFERENCES

ALBRECHT, R. (1953) 'Relationships of Older People with Their Own Parents.' *Marriage Fam. Liv.*, Vol. 15, No. 4, pp. 296–8.

ALBRECHT, R. (1954) 'The Parental Responsibilities of Grandparents.' *Marriage Fam. Liv.*, Vol. 16, No. 3, pp. 201–4.

ARENSBERG, C. M., and KIMBALL, S. T. (1948) *Family and Community in Ireland.* Cambridge, Mass: Harvard Univer. Press.

ARMSTRONG, W. E. (1928) *Rossel Island.* London: Cambridge Univer. Press.

BARNES, J. A. (1954) 'Class and Committees in a Norwegian Island Parish.' *Hum. Relat.*, Vol. 7, No. 1, pp. 39–58.

BARNES, J. A. (1955) 'Kinship.' *Encyclopaedia Britannica*, 1955 Printing.

BARTLETT, F. C. (1932) *Remembering.* London: Cambridge Univer. Press.

BARTON, R. F. (1919) *Ifugao Law.* Univer. California Publ. Amer. Arch. Ethnol., Vol. 15, No. 1.

BARTON, R. F. (1949) *The Kalingas.* Chicago: Univer. Chicago Press.

BOSSARD, J. H. S., and BOLL, E. S. (1946) 'The Immediate Family and the Kinship Group: A Research Report.' *Soc. Forces*, Vol. 24, No. 4, pp.379–84.

BROWN, J. S. (1952) 'The Conjugal Family and the Extended Family Group.' *Amer. sociol. Rev.*, Vol. 17, No. 3, pp. 297–306.

BURGESS, E. W., and LOCKE, H. J. (1953) *The Family: From Institution to Companionship.* (Second edition). New York: American Book Co.

CAHEN, A. (1932) *Statistical Analysis of American Divorce.* Columbia Univer. Stud. Hist. Econ. publ. Law, No. 360. New York: Columbia Univer. Press.

CENTERS, R. (1949) *The Psychology of Social Classes.* Princeton: Princeton Univer. Press.

CENTERS, R. (1952) 'The American Class Structure: A Psychological Analysis.' In Swanson, G. E., Newcomb, T. M., and Hartley, E. L. (Eds.) *Readings in Social Psychology.* New York: Henry Holt, pp. 299–311.

CODERE, H. (1955) 'A Genealogical Study of Kinship in the United States.' *Psychiatry*, Vol. 18, No. 1, pp. 65–79.

COLSON, E. (1954) 'The Intensive Study of Small Sample Communities.' In Spencer, R. F. (Ed.) *Method and Perspective in Anthropology*. Minneapolis: Univer. Minnesota Press, pp. 43–59.

CURLE, A. (1952) 'Kinship Structure in an English Village.' *Man*, Vol. 52, Article No. 100, pp. 68–9.

DAVIS, A. (1941) 'American Status Systems and the Socialization of the Child.' *Amer. sociol. Rev.*, Vol. 6, No. 3, pp. 345–56.

DAVIS, A. (1943) 'Child Training and Social Class.' In Barker, R. G., and others (Eds.) *Child Behavior and Development*. New York: McGraw Hill, pp. 607–20.

DAVIS, A. (1944) 'Socialization and Adolescent Personality.' *Forty-third Yearbook natl. Society Stud. Educ.*, Part I, Adolescence.

DAVIS, A., and HAVIGHURST, R. (1946) 'Social Class and Color Differences in Child Rearing.' *Amer. sociol. Rev.*, Vol. 11, No. 6, pp. 698–710.

DAVIS, A., and HAVIGHURST, R. (1947) *Father of the Man*. Boston: Houghton Mifflin.

DOLLARD, J. (1937) *Caste and Class in a Southern Town*. New Haven: Yale Univer. Press.

DOTSON, F. (1951) 'Patterns of Voluntary Association among Urban Working-Class Families.' *Amer. sociol. Rev.*, Vol. 16, No. 5, pp. 687–93.

EISENSTADT, S. N. (1954) 'Studies in Reference Group Behaviour: I—Reference Norms and the Social Structure.' *Hum. Relat.*, Vol. 7, No. 2, pp. 191–216.

EYSENCK, H. J., and CROWN, S. (1948) 'National Stereotypes: An Experimental and Methodological Study.' *Int. J. Opin. Attitude Res.*, Vol. 2, No. 1, pp. 26–39.

FAMILY DISCUSSION BUREAU (1955) *Social Casework in Marital Problems*. London: Tavistock Publications.

FIRTH, R. (1929) *Primitive Economics of the New Zealand Maori*. London: George Routledge and Sons.

FIRTH, R. (1955) 'Social Anthropology.' *Encyclopaedia Britannica*, 1955 Printing.

FIRTH, R. (Ed.) (1956) *Two Studies of Kinship in London*. London School of Economics Monographs on Social Anthropology, No. 15. London: Athlone Press.

FORM, W. H. (1946) 'Toward an Occupational Social Psychology.' *J. soc. Psychol.*, Vol. 24, pp. 85–99.

FORTES, M. (1949) *The Web of Kinship among the Tallensi*. London: Oxford Univer. Press.

FRAZIER, E. F. (1940) *The Negro Family in the United States*. Chicago: Univer. Chicago Press.

GEDDES, W. R. (1954) *The Land Dayaks of Sarawak.* Colonial Res. Stud., No. 14. London: H.M.S.O.

GLUCKMAN, M. (1950) 'Kinship and Marriage among the Lozi of Northern Rhodesia and the Zulu of Natal.' In Radcliffe-Brown, A. R., and Forde, D. (Eds.) *African Systems of Kinship and Marriage.* London: Oxford Univer. Press, pp. 166-206.

GLUCKMAN, M. (1955) *The Judicial Process among the Barotse of Northern Rhodesia.* Manchester: Manchester Univer. Press.

GOLDBERG, E. M. (1953) 'Experiences with Families of Young Men with Duodenal Ulcer and "Normal" Control Families. Some Problems of Approach and Method.' *Brit. J. med. Psychol.,* Vol. 26, Parts 3 and 4, pp. 204-14.

GOODE, W. J. (1951) 'Economic Factors and Marital Stability.' *Amer. sociol. Rev.,* Vol. 16, No. 6, pp. 802-12.

GOODENOUGH, W. H. (1955) 'A Problem in Malayo-Polynesian Social Organization.' *Amer. Anthrop.,* Vol. 57, No. 1, pp. 71-83.

GORER, G. (1955) *Exploring English Character.* London: Cresset Press.

HALL, J., and CARADOG JONES, D. (1950) 'Social Grading of Occupations.' *Brit. J. Sociol.,* Vol. 1, No. 1, pp. 31-55.

HAMMOND, S. B. (1952) 'Stratification in an Australian City.' In Swanson, G. E., Newcomb, T. M., and Hartley, E. L. (Eds.) *Readings in Social Psychology.* New York: Henry Holt, pp. 288-99.

HAMMOND, S. B. (1954) 'Class and Family (Part I).' Chapter XVIII of Oeser, O. A., and Hammond, S. B. (Eds.) *Social Structure and Personality in a City.* London: Routledge and Kegan Paul, pp. 238-48.

HARRIS, R. (1954) Social Relations and Attitudes in a Northern Irish Rural Area—Ballygawley. Unpublished M.A. Thesis, University of London.

HEIMANN, P. (1952) 'Certain Functions of Introjection and Projection in Early Infancy.' In Klein, M., Heimann, P., Isaacs, S., and Riviere, J. *Developments in Psycho-Analysis.* London: Hogarth Press, pp. 122-68.

HERBST, P. G. (1952) 'The Measurement of Family Relationships.' *Hum. Relat.,* Vol. 5, No. 1, pp. 3-36.

HERBST, P. G. (1954) 'Conceptual Framework for Studying the Family', 'Family Living—Regions and Pathways', and 'Family Living—Patterns of Interaction.' Chapters X-XII of Oeser, O. A., and Hammond, S. B. (Eds.) *Social Structure and Personality in a City.* London: Routledge and Kegan Paul, pp. 126-79.

HODGES, M. W., and SMITH, C. S. (1954) 'The Sheffield Estate.' In Liverpool University and Sheffield University Social Science Departments, *Neighbourhood and Community.* (Liverpool University Social Research Series) Liverpool: Liverpool Univer. Press, pp. 79-133.

HOPKINSON, T. (1954) 'Down Jamaica Road.' *The Observer,* March, 1954.

HYMAN, H. H. (1942) The Psychology of Status. *Archives Psychol.*, No. 269.

JACOBSON, P. H. (1950) 'Differentials in Divorce by Duration of Marriage and Size of Family." *Amer. sociol. Rev.*, Vol. 15, No. 2, pp. 235–44.

JAQUES, E. (1953) 'On the Dynamics of Social Structure.' *Hum. Relat.*, Vol. 6, No. 1, pp. 3–24.

JEPHCOTT, A. P., and CARTER, M. P. (1955) The Social Background of Delinquency. Unpublished manuscript, University of Nottingham, Department of Philosophy.

KELLER, S., and STERN, E. (1953) 'Spontaneous Group References in France.' *Publ. Opin. Quart.*, Vol. 17, No. 2, pp. 208–17.

KELLEY, H. H. (1952) 'Two Functions of Reference Groups.' In Swanson, G. E., Newcomb, T. M., and Hartley, E. L. (Eds.) *Readings in Social Psychology*. New York: Henry Holt, pp. 410–14.

KERR, M. (1955) 'The Study of Personality Deprivation through Projection Tests.' *Soc. econ. Stud.*, Vol. 4, No. 1, pp. 83–94.

KLEIN, M. (1932) *The Psycho-Analysis of Children*. London: Hogarth Press.

KLEIN, M. (1948) *Contributions to Psycho-Analysis*. London: Hogarth Press.

KLEIN, M., and RIVIERE, J. (1937) *Love, Hate and Reparation*. London: Hogarth Press.

KLEIN, M., and others (1955) *New Directions in Psycho-Analysis*. London: Tavistock Publications.

KUPER, L. (1953) *Living in Towns*. London: Cresset Press.

LEACH, E. (1954) *Political Systems of Highland Burma*. London: G. Bell and Sons.

LEWIN, K. (1935) *A Dynamic Theory of Personality*. New York: McGraw Hill.

LEWIN, K. (1936) *Principles of Topological Psychology*. New York: McGraw Hill.

LEWIN, K. (1948) 'Frontiers in Group Dynamics: II—Channels of Group Life; Social Planning and Action Research.' *Hum. Relat.*, Vol. 1, No. 2, pp. 143–53.

LEWIN, K. (1952) *Field Theory in Social Science*. (Dorwin Cartwright, Ed.) London: Tavistock Publications.

LOOMIS, C.P., MORALES, J. O., CLIFFORD, R. A., and LEONARD, O.E. (1953) *Turrialba*. Glencoe: Free Press.

MAAS, H. S. (1951) 'Some Social Class Differences in the Family Systems and Group Relations of Pre- and Early Adolescents.' *Child Developm.*, Vol. 22, No. 2, pp. 145–52.

MAYS, J. B. (1954) *Growing up in the City*. Liverpool: Liverpool Univer. Press.

MEAD, G. H. (1934) *Mind, Self and Society*. Chicago: Univer. Chicago Press.

MERTON, R. K. (1949) 'Patterns of Influence: A Study of Interpersonal Influence and of Communications Behavior in a Local Community.' In Lazarsfeld, P. F., and Stanton, F. N. (Eds.) *Communications Research 1948–1949*. New York: Harper and Bros., pp. 180–219.

MERTON, R. K., and KITT, A. S. (1950) 'Contributions to the Theory of Reference Group Behavior.' In Merton, R. K., and Lazarsfeld, P. F. (Eds.) *Continuities in Social Research. Studies in the Scope and Method of 'The American Soldier'*. Glencoe: Free Press, pp. 40–105.

MITCHELL, G. D., and LUPTON, T. (1954) 'The Liverpool Estate.' In Liverpool University and Sheffield University Social Science Departments, *Neighbourhood and Community*. (Liverpool University Social Research Series) Liverpool: Liverpool Univer. Press, pp. 15–77.

MOGEY, J. M. (1955) 'Changes in Family Life Experienced by English Workers Moving from Slums to Housing Estates.' *Marriage Fam. Liv.*, Vol. 17, No. 2, pp. 123–8.

MOGEY, J. M. (1956) *Family and Neighbourhood*. London: Oxford Univ. Press.

MORENO, J. L. (1934) *Who Shall Survive?* Washington: Nervous and Mental Disease Publishing Co.

MORRIS, H. S. (1953) *Report on a Melanau Sago Producing Community in Sarawak*. Colonial Res. Stud., No. 9. London: H.M.S.O.

MURDOCK, G. P. (1949) *Social Structure*. New York: Macmillan.

MCGUIRE, C. (1951) 'Family Backgrounds and Community Patterns.' *Marriage Fam. Liv.*, Vol. 13, No. 4, pp. 160–4.

MCGUIRE, C. (1952) 'Family Life in Lower and Middle Class Homes.' *Marriage Fam. Liv.*, Vol. 14, No. 1, pp. 1–6.

NADEL, S. F. (1951) *Foundations of Social Anthropology*. London: Cohen and West.

NEWCOMB, T. M. (1948) 'Attitude Development as a Function of Reference Groups: The Bennington Study.' In Sherif, M. *An Outline of Social Psychology*. New York: Harper and Bros., pp. 139–55.

NEWCOMB, T. M. (1950) *Social Psychology*. London: Tavistock Publications and New York: Dryden Press.

NEWCOMB, T. M., and CHARTERS, W. W. (1952) 'Some Attitudinal Effects of Experimentally Increased Salience of a Membership Group.' In Swanson, G. E., Newcomb, T. M., and Hartley, E. L. (Eds.) *Readings in Social Psychology*. New York: Henry Holt, pp. 415–20.

NIXON, A. J. (1954) *Divorce in New Zealand*. Auckland Univer. College, Bulletin No. 46, Sociology Series No. 1.

NORTH, C. C., and HATT, P. K. (1947) 'Jobs and Occupations: A Popular Evaluation.' *Opin. News*, Vol. 9, No. 1, pp. 3–13.

PACKER, E. L. (1947) 'Aspects of Working Class Marriage.' *Pilot Papers*, Vol. 2, No. 1, pp. 92–104.

PARSONS, T. (1942) 'Age and Sex in the Social Structure of the United States.' *Amer. sociol. Rev.*, Vol. 7, No. 5, pp. 604–16.

PARSONS, T., (1943) 'The Kinship System of the Contemporary United States.' *Amer. Anthrop.*, Vol. 45, No. 1, pp. 22–38.

PARSONS, T. (1949) 'The Social Structure of the Family.' Chapter X of Anshen, R. (Ed.) *The Family: Its Function and Destiny*. New York: Harper and Bros., pp. 173–201.

PARSONS, T., and BALES, R. F. (1955) *Family, Socialization and Interaction Process*. Glencoe: Free Press.

PHILLIPSON, H., (1955) *The Object Relations Technique*. London: Tavistock Publications.

RADCLIFFE-BROWN, A. R. (1929) 'A Further Note on Ambrym.' *Man*, Vol. 29, Article No. 35, pp. 50–3.

RADCLIFFE-BROWN, A. R. (1940) 'On Social Structure.' *J. roy. anthrop. Inst.*, Vol. 70, pp. 1–12.

RADCLIFFE-BROWN, A. R. (1950) 'Introduction.' In Radcliffe-Brown, A. R., and Forde, D. (Eds.) *African Systems of Kinship and Marriage*. London: Oxford Univer. Press, pp. 1–86.

REES, A. D. (1950) *Life in a Welsh Countryside*. Cardiff: Univer. Wales Press.

RIVERS, W. H. R. (1924) *Social Organization*. London: Kegan Paul, Trench, Trubner.

SCHNEIDER, D. M., and HOMANS, G. (1955) 'Kinship Terminology and the American Kinship System.' *Amer. Anthrop.*, Vol. 57, No. 6, pp. 1194–1208.

SEGAL, H. (1952) 'A Psycho-Analytical Approach to Aesthetics.' *Int. J. Psycho-Anal.*, Vol. 33, Part 2, pp. 196–207.

SHAW, L. A. (1954) 'Impressions of Family Life in a London Suburb.' *Sociol. Rev.*, Vol. 2 (New Series), No. 2, pp. 179–94.

SHELDON, J. H. (1948) *The Social Medicine of Old Age*. London: Oxford Univer. Press.

SHERIF, M. (1936) *The Psychology of Social Norms*. New York: Harper and Bros.

SHERIF, M., and SHERIF, C. W. (1953) *Groups in Harmony and Tension*. New York: Harper and Bros.

SLATER, E., and WOODSIDE, M. (1951) *Patterns of Marriage*. London: Cassell.

SUSSMAN, M. B. (1953) 'The Help Pattern in the Middle Class Family.' *Amer. sociol. Rev.*, Vol. 18, No. 1, pp. 22–28.

SUSSMAN, M. B. (1954) 'Family Continuity: Selective Factors which Affect Relationships between Families at Generational Levels.' *Marriage Fam. Liv.*, Vol. 16, No. 2, pp. 112–20.

TALMON-GARBER, Y. (1954) 'The Family in Israel.' *Marriage Fam.. Liv.*, Vol. 16, No. 4, pp. 343–9.

TALMON-GARBER, Y. 'The Family in Collective Settlements.' *Trans. Third World Congr. Sociol.*, Vol. 4, pp. 116–26. paper, the Hebrew University, Jerusalem, 1955.

TOWNSEND, P. (1955a) 'The Anxieties of Retirement.' *Trans. Ass. ind. med. Offrs.*, Vol. 5, No. 1, pp. 1–6.

TOWNSEND, P. (1955b) 'The Family Life of Old People: An Investigation in East London.' *Sociol. Rev.*, Vol. 3 (New Series), No. 2, pp. 175–95.

TOWNSEND, P. (1957) *The Family Life of Old People.* London: Routledge and Kegan Paul.

TRIST, E. L., and BAMFORTH, K. (1951) 'Some Social and Psychological Consequences of the Longwall Method of Coal-Getting.' *Hum. Relat.*, Vol. 4, No. 1, pp. 3–38.

VON HENTIG, H. (1946) 'The Sociological Function of the Grandmother.' *Soc. Forces*, Vol. 24, No. 4, pp. 389–92.

WARNER, W. L., and LUNT, P. (1941) *The Social Life of a Modern Community.* New Haven: Yale Univer. Press.

WILSON, A. T. M. (1955) 'A Note on the Social Sanctions of Social Research.' *Sociol. Rev.*, Vol. 3 (New Series), No. 1, pp. 109–16.

WILSON, C. S. (1953) 'The Family and Neighbourhood in a British Community.' Unpublished M.Sc. Thesis, University of Cambridge.

YOUNG, M. (1954a) 'Kinship and Family in East London.' *Man*, Vol. 54, Article No. 210, pp. 137–9.

YOUNG, M. (1954b) 'The Planners and the Planned—the Family.' *J. Tn. Plann. Inst.*, Vol. 40, No. 6, pp. 134–8.

YOUNG, M. (1954c) 'The Role of the Extended Family in a Disaster.' *Hum. Relat.*, Vol. 7, No. 3, pp. 383–91.

YOUNG, M. (1956) 'The Extended Family Welfare Association.' *Soc. Work*, Vol. 13, No. 1, pp. 145–50.

YOUNG, M., and WILLMOTT, P. (1957) *Family and Kinship in East London.* London: Routledge and Kegan Paul.

ZWEIG, F. (1952) *Women's Life and Labour.* London: Gollancz.

Reconsiderations

_____

Reconsiderations

'Perhaps the really lasting significance of Bott's study is that she has made impossible the proliferation of studies of the internal structure of the family which take no account of its social environment.'

C. C. Harris, *The Family*, 1969, p. 175

'The estrangements in the family are associated with the extension of ties to wider kinship groupings. These groupings support the family, but they are also inimical to the family. And they are important in building the cohesion of the larger society. . . .'

Max Gluckman, 'Estrangement in the Family', in
Custom and Conflict in Africa, 1955, p. 57

In their different ways these two quotations sum up what *Family and Social Network* is about. C. C. Harris deals with its general aspect, Max Gluckman with the particular. Harris's statement picks up a point that I consider basic to the understanding of any group, namely, its relationship to its environment. Max Gluckman's formulation concerns the basic nature of that relationship in the case of the elementary family. Marriage has a contradiction at its core—the sexual cleavage that divides as it unites. This combination of dividing and uniting is reproduced in the way in which networks ('groupings') articulate the family into the larger society.

This chapter consists of a general review of some of the work on families and networks that has been done since 1957 when *Family and Social Network* was first published. My own anthropological work since 1957 has been devoted to other problems, so that I have no further field data to contribute, only reflections on the work and criticisms made by other investigators.

In approaching the task of reviewing the relevant literature, I find myself suffering a peculiar sort of difficulty. *Family and Social Network* is generally thought of as a book about families, sometimes also as a book about networks. But to me the fact that it talks about families and networks is more or less incidental. The basic problem it deals with is the way a group, any sort of group, is related to its environment. My aim was (and still is) to understand how the internal functioning of a group is affected not only by its relationship *with* the people and organizations of its environment, but also by the relationships *among* those people and organizations. I think this basic approach could usefully be adopted in other problems than that of social variations in types of conjugal relationship. It could be applied, for example, to study of the relation of a complex organization to its environment, or to study of the differential effects of variations in the social environment on sub-groups within such an organization. The approach might prove useful in studying patterns of communication, interaction, and alienation in 'community' as well as organizational settings. Combined with study of phase change, it would be helpful in developing a sociology of friendship. It might also be of assistance in a comparative study of responses to geographical and social mobility.

In the course of reviewing the literature, however, I shall for the most part follow the lead of subsequent investigators in centring the discussion on families and on networks. I shall discuss the material under two main headings: I. Conjugal segregation and families' networks; and II. Further developments in the study of networks. When reading the literature on families, the basic things I have looked for are, first, further information on families' networks and the way they support and/or divide the family and the marital relationship; and, second, further information on factors such as geographical mobility, social mobility, class position, education, cultural, and ethnic differences, ecology, and so forth, factors that may affect conjugal norms and behaviour either directly, or indirectly through having an effect on families' networks. When discussing developments in the general conceptual analysis of networks, I look particularly for the social context in which the concept is used, for example whether it is used to analyse relations within groups, between groups, or in the creation of new groups.

But first, two points of terminology. Throughout much of the original text I used the term 'network' in what has come to be called the 'personal' or 'egocentric' sense, meaning that the network is conceptually anchored on a particular individual or conjugal pair (Mitchell, 1969, p. 12; Barnes, 1969a, pp. 56–60). But at various points in the present chapter I want to talk about the 'total network', which is *not* anchored on a particular individual or group. In order to avoid confusion in this chapter I shall use the adjective 'total' to distinguish the general network that is not focused on a particular person or group.

In the original text I use the term 'connectedness' to describe the extent to which the people known by a family know and meet one another independently of the focal family. No one seems to like this term; I do not like it either because it is jargon. Several authors use the term 'interconnectedness', which at least has the merit of sounding more ordinary even though it is longer. John Barnes objects to 'connectedness' on the grounds that my usage of the term is confusingly similar to but different from usage of the same term by graph theorists. Barnes suggests the term 'density', which I shall accordingly adopt throughout this chapter (see Barnes, 1969a and 1969b). But I shall continue to use the adjectives 'close-knit' and 'loose-knit' in the present chapter. In the text the original term 'connectedness' is still used.

I. CONJUGAL SEGREGATION AND FAMILIES' NETWORKS

My aim is twofold: first to review the literature, and then to discuss the issues that I now consider to be of central importance in this field, including the changes I would make if I were doing the study again.

A. REVIEW OF RELEVANT FAMILY AND COMMUNITY STUDIES

In this section I discuss the considerable number of studies that either cite and discuss *Family and Social Network* or provide relevant evidence, or both. I divide the studies into those of general relevance and those that specifically test or discuss the conjugal roles/networks hypothesis.[1]

It now appears to be widely accepted that in tribal, rural, and long-established working-class situations there are close-knit networks and marked conjugal segregation. Further, it is generally reported that geographical mobility makes a close-knit network more loose-knit, and that comparatively loose-knit networks are usually found in the middle class. But degree of conjugal segregation is found to be variable among families in loose-knit networks. Some studies also report that many couples, especially husbands, live in comparative social isolation, though the data are tantalizingly incomplete. Many recent kinship studies show that ties with parents and siblings remain strong in all social classes even in cases of geographical dispersal.

Whether and how network density is related to conjugal role-segregation is not yet agreed. Some authors accept my hypothesis more or less as it stands. I suspect that one factor in its acceptance has been a tendency to fill in the transitional phases with logic rather than facts. What I mean by this is that if the two extremes of the continuum seem to be empirically valid, and if one knows of some transitional cases that seem to fit, such as Young and Willmott's (1957) account of the changes produced in working-class families by moving from Bethnal Green to a

---

[1] I shall not attempt to summarize or discuss the reviews, most of which appeared in British journals. The main ones are: Chambers, 1958; R. N. Rapoport, 1957; Richmond, 1958; Davison, 1958; Whyte, 1958; *Brit. J. med. Psychol.*, 1958 part 2; *J. Roy. Society Health*, 1958; Thomson, 1961; McDougall, 1958; Rodd, 1968; Birley, 1969; La Fontaine, 1969; Packman, 1969; Perraton, 1969; Robottom, 1969.

For various reasons the book was not sent to American journals for review and knowledge of it seems to have spread by word of mouth. The central ideas of the book appeared first in *Human Relations* in 1954 and 1955, and then in Anderson (1956). Various sections of the book were reprinted in readings edited by Norman Bell and Ezra Vogel (1960), Ruth Laub Coser (1964), and Gerald Handel (1967). It was probably through these reprintings that the book came to be known by family sociologists, for example Goode, 1960 and 1964; Foote, 1961; Komarovsky, 1961; Mogey, 1962; Zelditch, 1964; Pitts, 1964. It is occasionally cited by students of families' relations with kin, for example: Sussman, 1965; Sussman and Burchinal, 1962a; Adams, 1967b; and Guterman, 1969. It is also referred to by various students of the American working class and 'lower' class, for example Gans, 1962; Cohen and Hodges, 1963; Blum, 1964; Rainwater, 1964; Rainwater and Handel, 1964. Four American attempts to test the central hypothesis are discussed below: Udry and Hall, 1965; Aldous and Straus, 1966; Nelson, 1966; Blood, 1969.

housing estate at Greenleigh, it then seems comparatively easy to
fill in all the gaps between the two extremes without bothering too
closely about whether actual empirical data fit the hypothesis or not.
Other authors, however, criticize or qualify the hypothesis. An
early and basic criticism was made by Harold Fallding (1961), the
essence of it being contained in the following quotation:

> 'It seems that what she is really demonstrating is the existence in
> certain cases of sex in-groups. These reinforce male and female
> in a distinctive conception of themselves and their roles, whether
> they are at home or away from it. The role-segregation of the
> sexes within the family goes with sexual segregation outside it.
> ... There thus appears to be a *sharp cleavage by sex right across the
> network*, so that it can hardly be called connected. . . . It is
> pointed out that an exception is made by having joint social
> participation with kin. But may we not presume that sexual
> segregation is observed and actively fostered here? It is as though
> the sexes can only trust themselves to one another in that family
> and kinship context where segregation is, one might say,
> actually being manufactured' (Fallding, 1961, p. 342).

Turner provides further evidence relevant to sexual segregation
outside as well as inside the family. Rosser and Harris (1965) and
Harris (1969) build on Fallding's basic criticism. Harrell-Bond
(1969) criticizes both my specific hypothesis and my general
approach. These various criticisms are further discussed below.

1. *Generally Relevant Studies*

Both Josephine Klein and Ronald Frankenberg, in their different
ways, make use of the conjugal role/networks hypothesis in
ordering their descriptions and analyses of community studies in
Britain (Klein, 1965; Frankenberg, 1966). Frankenburg uses the
idea of networks, along with several other concepts, in analysing
the process of urbanization.

(a) *Studies of networks and/or conjugal roles in the geographically non-mobile working class*

The pioneering studies of kinship in Bethnal Green by Michael

Young and his colleagues of the Institute of Community Studies have clearly established the importance of kin ties in stable working-class neighbourhoods, especially the importance of kin ties for women, through women, and for both sexes with the mother. The picture of the husband's social relationships other than those with kin remains a bit hazy (Young and Willmott, 1957; Townsend, 1957; and, later, Willmott, 1963). I was of course greatly helped by knowledge of the work of Young and his colleagues when I was doing my own study. I would have had some misgivings about building so much theory on the case of a single family, the Newbolts, if I had not known that there were many others like them. The work of Slater and Woodside (1951), John Mogey (1956), and conversations with Madeline Kerr also indicated that the Newbolts were not unique (see Kerr, 1958).

Rosser and Harris (1965) studied both working-class and middle-class families in Swansea. Among the working-class families they found the same sort of conjugal role-segregation and involvement with kin that Young and Willmott reported for Bethnal Green, but with indications of increasing dispersal of kin and lessening of role-segregation. Rosser and Harris briefly discuss my conjugal segregation/networks hypothesis, stating that they do not have the data to test it but criticizing it anyway and suggesting that both density of kinship networks and conjugal segregation can be attributed to the degree of a wife's 'domesticity' (p. 208), for which they are in turn criticized by Mogey (1966). (Rogers and Sebald's (1962) discussion of 'familism' would appear to be very relevant to the 'domesticity' thesis.)

Rosser and Harris refer to Fallding (1961) and make the point that one might find a joint marital relationship combined with a social network of common *friends*, but one is less likely to find couples belonging to a close-knit joint network of *relatives*. Like Young and Willmott (1957), Rosser and Harris stress the role of women in maintaining kin activities and relationships, and they emphasize that this pattern is just as prevalent in the middle class as it is in the working class.

Studies of the American working class have generally confirmed the picture of conjugal role-segregation and close-knit extra-familial networks when the families concerned are not geographically mobile. Walter Miller (1958) reports a study by participant observation of what he calls 'the lower-class subculture', defining 'lower class' by '. . . its use of the "female-based" household as the basic form of child-rearing unit and of the "serial monogamy" mating pattern as the primary form of marriage' (Miller, 1958, p.6n). He was primarily interested in delinquency and therefore in adolescents, but studied the general subculture that, in his view, was generating the delinquency. He describes the 'focal concerns' of this subculture, stressing its emphasis on masculinity and toughness, excitement, smartness, and the ambivalent mixture of objection to any authority combined with seeking out situations and institutions where control will be stringent. Miller makes it clear that sex segregation within the family is marked and that boys and men have groups of male peers. Adolescent girls evidently have gangs too, but the article is not very clear about the social relationships of women once they have children. It appears to be a general failing of all studies of the working class that they report entirely or mainly for one sex only or one generation only. This in itself is an indication of sharp social cleavages by sex and generation. It is virtually impossible for one field worker to be in touch with all camps, and even Miller, who had several assistants, gives a much more complete picture of adolescents, especially boys, than of adults.

Subsequent American studies make it clear that the 'lower-class' pattern described by Miller occurs in depressed areas in conditions of acute job uncertainty (see Gans, 1962). Rainwater (1964) reviews several community studies of poor rural and urban areas, also described as 'lower-class subcultures'. In all of them there is a pattern of highly segregated conjugal role-relationships with husband and wife each participating in relatively 'closed' social networks to which he or she can look for stability and continuity. The fact is noted that the husband's social relationships:

'. . . are outside the home, with other men, some of whom may be relatives, others not. His performance as a husband and father is more influenced by the standards they set than by his wife's desires, just as her behaviour is more influenced by the standards and expectations of her kin-based network' (Rainwater, 1964, p.228).

My work is then discussed.

Allowing for differences of orientation and method, Miller's description of lower-class subculture would apply also to depressed areas in Britain such as the 'Branch Street' area of London (Klein, 1965) and the 'Ship Street' area of Liverpool (Kerr, 1958). Shortly after Miller's account of the lower-class subculture, Rainwater, Coleman, and Handel (1959) reported on a study of working-class women which drew attention to the importance of their ties with kin.

S. M. Miller and Riessman (1961) discuss the subculture of the working class as distinct from the lower class, meaning by 'working class' people who are in stable manual employment. Among other things, the authors note the importance of relationships with kin.

Herbert Gans (1962) gives a lively and convincing account of a working-class neighbourhood of second-generation Italians in Boston. He stresses segregation between husband and wife, and describes how each spouse is attached to his (or her) own group of peers composed mainly of relatives but partly of friends. There are two ways in which the situation he reports differs from the English working-class pattern described by me for the Newbolts and by Young and his colleagues for Bethnal Green, Mogey (1956) for Oxford, etc. First, among Gans's Italians, parents and the older generation generally are not much respected, and they are not frequently visited or invited to visit the focal families; the intimate kin network is drawn from the universe of siblings and cousins. Second, men entertain their peers (relatives and friends) at home, although in a separate room from the wife and her peer group, whereas in Britain the men see their friends away from home. Gans thinks that these are distinctive features of Italian culture that have survived in the new environment. He notes the contrast of the Italian pattern with the Irish and the Jewish patterns (Gans, 1962, pp.237–242).

Unfortunately Gans does not give quite enough detail in this fascinating study for one to know exactly how the networks are structured. One cannot, for example, work out which parts of the network are 'joint' and which parts are separate for the husband and wife. By the 'joint' part of the network I mean not only those people whom husband and wife visit jointly but also people who have relationships with both spouses even though the contact may be conducted with one spouse at a time.[1] There are many points in Gans's account that arouse one's curiosity without gratifying it. One wonders what happens if a husband is very friendly with, say, one of his cousins, but his wife cannot stand the cousin's wife. One wonders, too, whether parents are really so unimportant, especially the wife's parents. And indeed Gans reports (p.47) a desire by some daughters to live near their mothers. Gans indicates that girls are much less addicted to the adolescent peer group than boys (pp.64–70) but he notes that it was hard for him to collect material on girls and women because of sexual and generational segregation (p.64n). Whatever the details of omission from his analysis, one must be grateful to Gans for doing a field study that brings a set of social relationships to life and makes them meaningful.

Cohen and Hodges (1963) also deal with the working class. They made a questionnaire study of 2600 men in the San Francisco area, which showed that the working-class men of their sample were involved separately from their wives in social networks of kin, neighbours, and peers, and that they had very patriarchal attitudes about the authority of the husband/father and the place of

[1] If, for example, a husband and wife went to visit another husband and wife, I would count it as a joint contact even if they split up into separate groups after arriving. And if a husband and wife visited the same person or household but on different occasions, I would include that person of household in the 'joint' region of the network. But if a husband characteristically went to visit one relative and his wife never or very rarely went with him, I would count that relative as a member of the husband's network only. Once one abandons the level of generalized description, it becomes apparent that the form and content of networks are exceedingly complex to map and difficult to quantify.

women. Blum (1964) puts forward the view that working-class people participate chiefly in primary relationships with people from the neighbourhood and are unlikely to join voluntary associations or make friends at work. (It would appear that working-men's clubs are not usual in the United States.) He suggests that working-class people withdraw from any relationships that conflict with their 'most salient' relationships. Like Cohen and Hodges, he discusses *Family and Social Network*. De Hoyos and de Hoyos (1966) describe the 'Amigo' system in a Mexican community where they conducted a questionnaire on the 'alienation' this system produces in the wife. The 'Amigos' are a strong male peer group established before marriage and persisting afterwards. The system is strongest in the working class, but the working-class wives are less alienated by it than middle-class women. Perhaps they have a compensatory network of kin or friends, but the authors did not try to find out if this was the case.

Several of these studies give some indication that the number of social relationships maintained by working-class people is not great. Gans (1962), on the other hand, paints a picture of constant visiting and intense interaction, similar to the situation described by Young and his colleagues for Bethnal Green (Young and Willmott, 1957).

In summary, these studies of geographically and socially non-mobile working-class families show that there is marked sexual segregation both inside *and* outside the elementary family. The husband has his relationships outside the family and the wife has hers. Usually when close-knit networks are reported in enough detail for one to know who is in them, one finds that kin play an important part, although friends may be included too. There are apparently some cultural/ethnic variations: in some cases the women's network consists almost entirely of kin (Young and Willmott, 1957), whereas in others her network includes friends (Gans, 1962). In all cases *except* that reported by Gans, contact with parents is more frequent than contact with siblings and cousins. There are variations in the place where men's social activities take place—at home in the case of Gans's Italians, in pubs in Bethnal

Green. I suspect that there are variations too in the composition of the 'joint' region of the network. But on all these matters, even in the case of basic data about who has relationships with whom, the data reported are still very sketchy and generalized.[1]

(b) *Studies containing information about networks and conjugal roles in middle-class families*

So far as I know there are no studies that specifically devote themselves to analysis of social networks and conjugal roles in middle-class families. Josephine Klein (1965) summarizes current studies, using a lot of material from *Family and Social Network*. Colin Bell's book *Middle Class Families* (1969) does not discuss conjugal roles, though it illuminates social and geographical mobility. There are, however, a considerable number of studies that produce relevant and suggestive material.

Willmott and Young (1960) report that the middle-class couples they interviewed in Woodford were home-centred; the husband shared in domestic work and did many 'male' household tasks especially of the do-it-yourself variety. The husband/wife relationship, in other words, was more joint than it was in Bethnal Green. Kinship ties were looser than in Bethnal Green, fewer kin lived locally, and friendship was more important than in Bethnal Green. Somewhat to their surprise, the authors found a 'female core' to the kinship system. The activities and relationships were maintained on the initiative of the women, as in Bethnal Green. They also found the suburb unexpectedly friendly; middle-class people, they conclude, have a certain capacity for making friends, or at least the people of Woodford had it. Gans, in yet another important study, gives a similar report of the middle-class families in a newly established American suburb (Gans, 1967).

Much of the literature on middle-class families is concerned with their relationships with kin. Rosser and Harris (1965) discuss the role of kinship in Swansea for the middle class as well as for

---

[1] Doubtless there are other studies of the working class with pertinent material. I particularly regret that I was unable to obtain M. Komarovsky's (1962) *Blue Collar Marriage*.

the working class. They define the extended family (wisely in my view) as '. . . a variable, amorphous, vague social grouping within which circulate—often over great distances—strong sentiments of belonging. . . .' (Rosser and Harris, 1965, p. 228). They note the increased dispersal of the extended family, and then state that 'The key relationship within the extended family is that consisting of wife's mother—wife—husband—husband's mother' (p. 289). Like Willmott and Young they stress the role of women and relationships through women, saying that middle-class families were not distinct in this respect. Like Goldthorpe and Lockwood (1963) they think that the 'trend of change . . . is in the direction of a *convergence* in behaviour between the social classes' (p. 291).

Since Firth's original studies of kinship (Firth, 1956) and Young and Willmott's study of Bethnal Green (1957) and then Woodford (1960), there have been a large number of kinship studies both in England and in the United States. In England the main studies are: Firth, 1956, 1961, and 1964; Hubert, Forge, and Firth, 1968; Firth, Hubert, and Forge, 1969; Young and Willmott, 1957; Willmott and Young, 1960; Young and Geertz, 1961; Townsend, 1957; Marris, 1958; Lancaster, 1961; Loudon, 1961; Willmott, 1963; Hubert, 1965; Crozier, 1965a and 1965b; Rosser and Harris, 1965; Colin Bell, 1968 and 1969.

The American literature on kinship contacts is enormous. It appears to have been developed initially mainly by Sussman and Litwak, and much of it is devoted to showing that the nuclear family is not 'isolated' as Parsons is supposed to have claimed. (See Parsons, 1943 and 1949. Actually he said the nuclear family was *structurally isolated*, which some of his antagonists appear to have misinterpreted as *actually* isolated.) Much of this literature is summarized and cited by Sussman and Burchinal (1962a). The main studies I consulted were: Sussman, 1953, 1959, and 1965; Sussman and Burchinal, 1962a and 1962b; Litwak, 1959, 1960a, 1960b, 1965; Levy and Fallers, 1959; Cumming and Schneider 1961; Greenfield, 1961; Aldous, 1962 and 1967; Reiss, 1962; Robins and Tomanec, 1962; Stuckert, 1963, who strikes a slightly dissenting note to the effect that socially mobile women of all classes are less involved with kin and are more socially isolated generally than are non-mobile women; Schwarzweller, 1964; Back, 1965; Kerckhoff, 1965; Rosow, 1965; Furstenberg, 1966; Adams, 1967b; Guterman, 1969. Several studies are collected together in Shanas and Streib, 1965, and in Farber, 1966.

The general picture that emerges from these studies, both the English and the American ones, is that middle-class children are geographically mobile relative to each other so that kin are dispersed. According to Crozier, (1965a and 1965b), this is a traditional pattern, prevalent also in the nineteenth-century middle class, at least in the Highgate region of London. But in those days there were what Crozier calls 'patrinominal kin nuclei', namely, kin recruited for employment in family businesses from a kin universe consisting of descendants through male lines from a common male ancestor (Crozier, 1965a). In the absence of descendants through males, descendants through females might be recruited. Crozier also found kin nuclei in the Home and Indian civil services, but these were multilateral, including both paternal and maternal kin of many different patrinominal families. By the 1960s such kinship recruitment to businesses and professions was less obvious in the middle class of Highgate (Hubert, 1965; Firth, Hubert, and Forge, 1969).

Nevertheless, both in Britain and in the United States middle-class married children keep up relationships with their parents and siblings even when physically separated from them. Kin provide a major (perhaps *the* major) sense of identity and belonging; they provide mutual help and services, sometimes amounting to substantial financial aid in the case of the parent-child relationship, assuming that at least one partner in the relationship is well-off. Gifts are asked for and given, however, with great subtlety so as not to infringe upon the ideology of independence for each elementary family. When distance is controlled, interaction with parents is much more frequent than interaction with siblings, and interaction with both is much more frequent than with other kinds of kin (see especially Hubert, 1965, and Reiss, 1962). Reiss, like Willmott and Young (1960) and Rosser and Harris (1965), stresses the role of women in operating the kinship system in the middle class.

Colin Bell, however, reports a different finding among the middle-class families he studied on two housing estates in Swansea (Bell 1968 and 1969). He says:

'I found that over and over again where there had been aid from the extended family the important structural link between members of the extended family was the father-in-law/father-son/son-in-law link' (Bell, 1969, p. 91).

It was through this link that aid flowed to the elementary family. Another important finding was that social mobility affected the functioning of the extended family (meaning here particularly the giving of financial aid by the parental family) much more than geographical mobility, for the amount of aid given to those from middle-class backgrounds (whose parents were presumably well-off financially) was naturally greater than for those from working-class backgrounds (Bell, 1969, p. 95).

Perhaps the two emphases—on the mother/daughter/mother-in-law ties and the father/son/father-in-law ties are not inconsistent. Perhaps women arrange visits and certain minor types of mutual aid, but when large sums of money are involved, the men take over.

I found only two studies that specifically deal with the role of friendship in the networks of middle-class families (Babchuk and Bates, 1963, and Adams, 1967a). Babchuk and Bates used a questionnaire method to discover whether husbands or wives were 'dominant' in determining who became the joint friends of the husband and wife as a couple. With such an unexplored problem I wish they had used an observation/unstructured interview sort of approach instead of a questionnaire, but the results are instructive and suggestive in any case. The authors take it for granted that middle-class couples 'consider themselves a unit with respect to friends' but, when interviewed separately, the husband and wife often failed to agree in their listings of mutual friends. The authors were surprised by the small number of mutual friends (mean 3, mode 2) and by the fact that few friendships were made after marriage. (The couples of this study were aged 20 to 40.) As the authors had anticipated, husbands rather than wives were the initiators of most of the mutual friendships that had continued since the marriage. (I think this would also be correct for my research families.) Another striking finding is that one-third of the mutual friends listed were not living locally. The authors say:

'. . . our couples talked about non-local friends in such vivid language that we thought such persons had only recently moved to other areas and were surprised later in the interview, to find there had been no face-to-face contact and little correspondence between some such friends for many years' (Babchuk and Bates, 1963, p. 384).

It seems rather a pity that they did not also collect information on the husbands' and wives' *separate* friends, both local and non-local, for such information is essential to analysis of the role of friendship *vis-a-vis* marriage.

Fallding (1961) also reports that old friends were important to his couples even if they were not seen for long periods, and he interprets it as an indication that old friends confirm the continuity of ones' identity. My middle-class research families expressed similar attitudes, though I did not emphasize this point sufficiently in my analysis.

In a questionnaire study of 799 people in Greensboro, North Carolina, Adams (1967a) finds that the essential feature of friendship is that it is voluntary and based on shared interests and consensus (also stressed by Lazarsfeld and Merton, 1954, by Y. Cohen, 1961 and Litwak and Szelenyi, 1969), as compared to kinship, in which concern and obligation are the focal elements. He does not find marked class differences in the content of friendship and kinship; unfortunately he does not give any data on class differences in frequency of contact with relatives and friends or on differences in numbers of relationships maintained with kin compared to those with friends. He does report that women manifest higher percentage scores on affection and consensus with kinsfolk than men do. Like Babchuk and Bates, he was surprised to find that 'intimate communication' was *not* a feature of close friendship. But this is not really surprising, because all his informants were married, and the 'intimate communication' aspect of friendship is likely to be sharply curtailed after marriage, though this in itself is a subject that has not been thoroughly studied.

It seems to me that in spite of the many studies, our knowledge of middle-class families is far from complete. Several studies provide potential starting-points for extending it. Merton (1957) contrasts 'local' and 'cosmopolitan' orientations within the middle class. Watson (1957) contrasts 'burgesses', who are locally based, and 'spiralists', who move about the country in pursuit of their careers. Daniel Miller and Swanson (1958) contrast an 'individuated-entrepreneurial' with a 'welfare-bureaucratic'orientation and examine associated methods of child care. Gans (1962, pp. 246–249) contrasts 'middle-class subculture' in general and the 'professional upper-middle-class subculture' in particular. Both subcultures are built around the elementary ('nuclear') family; in both the man's work is conceived as a career and education for children is thought important; in both there is contact with friends and close relatives; and in both the outside world is not alien territory as it is for working-class people. According to Gans, the distinctive features of the upper-middle-class subculture are first, that it places 'greater emphasis on the independent functioning of its individual members' so that work is an achievement and a social service as well as a means of supporting the elementary family, and, second, that the family is adult-directed rather than child-centred (middle class) or adult-centred (working class).

None of these dichotomies exactly duplicates the others, but it seems likely to me that there are affinities among them. Cosmopolitans are likely to be spiralist bureaucrats of the upper-middle-class subculture, and locals are likely to be burgess entrepreneurs of the middle-class subculture. Further, it seems likely that our research families with intermediate networks, particularly those living in homogeneous neighbourhoods, were of the local/burgess/middle-class subculture variety, though some of them were 'entrepreneurs' and some were 'bureaucrats'. All the research families with very loose-knit networks and joint conjugal norms were cosmopolitan/spiralist/bureaucrats/ of the upper-middle-class subculture. However, various indications in the literature suggest that, in the upper reaches of the managerial and professional class, the career of the husband may become so time-consuming and involving that the marital relationship becomes segregated in fact even if not in ideology. Mowrer (1969), for example, indicates that marital role differentiation increases as social status increases. Double careers (Rapoport and Rapoport, 1969) are hard to launch without the support of the husband, which means a joint ideology, but are likely to lead to increased behavioural segregation and perhaps eventually to an acceptance of segregation as 'normal'.

In brief, much work remains to be done in putting together the ideas of various types of class and family study.

(c) On changes of class, networks, and conjugal roles

Two studies report cases of the persistence of conjugal segregation in the face of external factors that one might have expected to lead to more joint conjugal norms and behaviour. Since in both cases the social networks remained more or less unaltered, these cases of non-change lend some support to the conjugal roles/networks hypothesis.

Little and Price (1967) report a study of marriage among educated West Africans. It appears that Little's informants accepted the idea of a 'joint' marriage in principle because of their Western education, but when it came to putting it into practice they ran into difficulties because they got involved in lineage obligations. In other words, change in ideology is not enough. It needs to be backed up by an appropriate social situation. Mogey and Morris (1960 and 1965) report a study in which a 'rough' group of families who had squatted in huts after the war were eventually given new houses on the same site. The authors conclude that rehousing in itself does not promote more joint relationships between husband and wife. If the basic structure of the community is left unaltered, only 'fringe' members are likely to undergo internal familial changes.

The analysis of change, both trends of social change and studies of geographical and social motility, is of crucial importance to the conjugal roles/networks hypothesis, for according to my expectations geographical mobility *alone* should be enough to disrupt the sort of close-knit networks one finds in homogeneous working-class areas, and such disruption should be accompanied by greater jointness in the husband-wife relationship.

On the whole, empirical research confirms this expectation. Young and Willmott's initial study (1957) reported the disruption of the wives' kin relationships when the family moved away from Bethnal Green to a housing estate. Relations with the new neighbours were hostile. Husbands were expected to help their wives more often than in Bethnal Green. Willmott's later study of Dagenham (1963) shows that eventually (forty years after the establishment of the estate) close-knit networks of kin and neighbours can grow up again, at least in the Dagenham sort of economic and social situation.

Tallman (1969), Rainwater and Handel (1964), and Handel and Rainwater (1964) report very similar findings for American working-class families. They stress the break-up of close-knit networks by geographical mobility, an increase in home-centredness, more joint relationships between husband and wife, more mutuality in the sexual relationship, more marital tension as a result of the new expectations and isolation from old networks, and, finally, the report that parents emphasized the importance of education for children; like Young and Willmott (1957), Rainwater and Handel stress families' increased susceptibility to the mass media once they had moved away form their close-knit networks (Rainwater and Handel, 1964). But Berger (1960) provides a welcome reminder that not all geographical mobility is traumatic for working-class families. He studied 100 families who had shifted from a city to a working-class suburb to which the Ford factory in which they worked had been moved. Berger's general finding was that the families were not upset and did not change their ways of life very much. They did not become middle class and their most important social contacts were with their relatives in the neighbourhoods they had left. Evidence about friendly contacts with their new neighbours was contradictory, but they did not show the hostility and uneasiness of the Bethnal Green people who moved to Greenleigh. One of the important facts about Berger's families was that this was not their first move. They were people who were migrants already, or whose parents had been migrants. They were not undergoing the break-up of very close-knit networks or the destruction of a traditional and solidly working-class neighbourhood.

Several authors raise the question whether there is a permanent trend among working-class families in the direction of greater 'family-centredness' and more joint husband-wife relationships at the expense of the collective solidarity of the working class, and, on a more limited level, at the expense of families' close-knit networks.

The major paper in this field is a scholarly analysis by Goldthorpe and Lockwood, who conclude that there is a trend towards 'normative convergence' by certain sections of the working class and the middle class, convergence on what they call 'instrumental collectivism' and 'family-centredness' (Goldthorpe and Lockwood, 1963). The working class are becoming less collective, with family-centredness as a byproduct. Certain sections of the middle class are becoming less individualistic, with instrumental collectivism as a byproduct. Affluence alone does not diminish the solidarity of the working class; it must be accompanied by changes in work, community, and family life which are in turn related to prosperity, advances in industrial organization, demographic trends, and mass communication.

Recently Toomey (1969) has used Goldthorpe and Lockwood's ideas in distinguishing working-class parents who are 'involved' with the education of their sons. The best predictors of such involvement were whether the husband spent his leisure-time at home and/or with his wife; for wives it was the amount of contact they had outside the elementary family. Home-centred families are child-centred and education-centred.

I find myself wondering whether these studies of class change pay sufficient attention to the effect of geographical mobility in producing family-centredness and weakening collective loyalties both to the working class in general and to the husband's network of 'mates' and the wife's network of kin and neighbours. It may be that it is geographical mobility that distinguishes the 'new' working class. Or it may be that living from birth in a mixed-class neighbourhood such as Woodford (Willmott and Young, 1960) has the same sort of effect on working-class families as geographical mobility has.

Watson's (1957) work on spiralists (geographically mobile) and burgesses (geographically stable) in the middle class and Merton's (1957) differentiation of cosmopolitans and locals give at least a starting-point for the analysis of geographical mobility and stability in the middle class. It seems to me highly likely that middle-class 'burgesses' will have closer knit networks and more conjugal role segregation than 'spiralists', but this has not been adequately studied as yet.

Colin Bell has used Watson's ideas in his study of middle-class families on two Swansea housing estates; teasing out the effects of geographical as distinct from social mobility has paid him handsome rewards in understanding social interaction on the housing estates he studied (Bell, 1969). (One of the most striking findings was that there was not one family that was socially mobile but not geographically mobile.) But Bell did not study variations in conjugal norms and behaviour, since this was not his main research interest.

In any case the effects of different sorts of move on both networks and conjugal roles need more study. Berger's work (1960) described above indicates that moving need not be traumatic for working-class families if they have already had their networks streamlined for moving, so to speak, by previous experience of moving. When people from Bethnal Green moved to Greenleigh, on the other hand, the wives' networks of kin and neighbours were broken up but the husbands' male networks were left more or less intact, provided they went back to Bethnal Green to work. The Greenleigh wives were very discontented. What happens when *both* husband and wife leave their close-knit networks at the same time? In what circumstances can they establish new networks? Is it easier for husbands to do so than wives? Barbara Harrell-Bond presents interesting material that bears on this problem, which I discuss below (Harrell-Bond, 1969).

(d) *Studies of family and work*

Since 1957 a new and interesting field of investigation has developed—study of the relation of family structure to work and the industrial system. It is of course closely linked with the analysis of family, class, and work discussed above, especially that of Goldthorpe and Lockwood (1963). I have not attempted to follow this literature, but I think it represents a corrective to the earlier tendency to talk about the family as if it existed in isolation. It is also a corrective to my own emphasis, overemphasis perhaps, on informal ('primary') social relationships.

Parker (1967) summarizes studies relevant to industry and the family. Daniel Miller and Swanson (1958) and Gold and Slater (1958) produced two of the earliest reports in this field. Both were concerned with the effects of certain types of occupation on families, though without companion study of their social networks. The Rapoports have established themselves authoritatively in this field (Rapoport, 1964; Rapoport and Rapoport, 1965 and 1969). Blood and Wolfe have examined the ways husbands and wives manage the work-family relation (Blood and Wolfe, 1965; Wolfe, 1963).

(e) *Comparative, rural, and tribal studies*

In his Preface (above) Max Gluckman discusses the relevance of the conjugal roles/networks hypothesis to the study of tribal and rural societies. I shall mention a few studies that clarify particular points.

Yonina Talmon-Garber (1962) gives a fascinating analysis of variations in the elementary family in three different environmental situations in Israel. On the kibbutzim, especially at the beginning, the elementary family was thought to menace collective solidarity, and various measures were taken to weaken it.

On the moshavim, the traditional corporate extended family of North African Jews flowered at the expense of both the elementary family *and* community solidarity. But the European refugee families living in the cities were isolated, turned in on themselves, and unwilling to make relationships with outsiders. This sort of family reaction to trauma is also described, in a less acute form, by Schelsky for post-war German families (Schelsky, 1966). It is not unlike the initial reaction of Bethnal Green families, particularly the wives, when removed to the Greenleigh estate (Young and Willmott, 1957). Presumably conjugal role-playing and role expectations may become more joint for a time, though Talmon-Garber thinks the urban refugee families clung to whatever sort of husband/wife relationship had been traditional to them. Unfortunately, as she notes, her study does not include information about the role expectations or role-performance of husband and wife.

Matthews (1965) discusses an intriguing contrast between two sections of a rural 'hill' community in Tennessee. Following Murdock's terminology Matthews describes both sections as belonging to the same 'deme', that is, an endogamous territorially based grouping of kin (Murdock, 1949). In one section (Lower Ridge) of 31 families, husband/wife roles were markedly segregated and the family was 'open' to neighbours and kin. In the other section ('Upper Ridge') the role-relationship of husband and wife was joint, and the family was 'closed' to outsiders. The reason for the contrast, apparently, was that whereas the Lower Ridge families grew tobacco and had work groups consisting of several neighbouring men, the Upper Ridge families owned secret, illegal, and profitable moonshining stills with access to public highways and lorries. The moral seems to be that you can trust your friends with tobacco but not with whisky. It is a special case of the influence of an occupational and ecological factor on network formation, a factor so specific that it appears to have led to differences in network formation and to emphasis of different values even between people not only of the same culture but of the same extended kinship category.

Changes in certain tribal societies lend some support to the conjugal roles/social networks hypothesis. Plotnicov (1962) discusses change in families in urban situations in Africa, his general argument being that in 'fixed membership' 'gemeinschaft' groups like the family, experimentation with new cultural forms can readily take place; cultural principles will be sacrificed in order to maintain the membership of the group, whereas in 'flexible membership' 'gesellschaft' groups based on cultural principles, group members are likely to be sacrificed in the interests of preserving the cultural purpose of the group. Although Plotnicov does not cite *Family and Social Network*, part of his discussion is very reminiscent of it.

'The privacy of the urban family of tribal origins has another aspect. . . . Assuming, for example, that the husband and wife come from a tradition that regards males as superior, the urban couple, being more dependent upon each other for mutual physical and emotional support than in the tribal situation, will tend to acquire a greater degree of mutual equality. In the city, the privacy of the couple also means that they have no sure external source of help. Consequently, the spouses must depend more upon each other for carrying out familial tasks; they must seek in each other the emotional satisfactions that cannot be derived from their new, loosely-knit social networks' (Plotnicov, 1962, p. 102).

Pauw says that the urban Africans he studied tended to have more loosely knit networks and less conjugal segregation than the rural members of the same tribe, and that white-collar urban Africans had more loosely knit networks and more joint conjugal relationships than town dwellers 'of simpler culture'. But he thinks that both network and marital changes are to be explained as the result of changes in education (Pauw, 1963, pp. 187–193).

We have seen from the account of Little's work, however, that Western education alone is not enough to produce an effect without some corresponding change in the structure of corporate kin groups (Little and Price, 1967). Education for joint relationships in marriage needs at least a moderately appropriate social framework before it can be realized.

Philip Mayer (1961, 1962, and 1964) reports a division between 'Red' and 'School' Xhosa—a division based on community and kin-group decisions more than a hundred years ago about whether or not to change from traditional practices. The traditionally oriented 'Red' Xhosa who migrate to East London have more closely knit networks than the 'School' Xhosa. Further, the Red Xhosa migrants confine their friendships in town to other Red Xhosa, and their networks extend into the rural area too. It is thus possible for a migrant to maintain a strong rural orientation even when he spends much of his life working in town. The School Xhosa have looser-knit networks that include some town-oriented people, and they take part in town-based activities.

Lynn Oeser (1969), in a study of Port Moresby women from various New Guinea cultural groups, reports that she found no relation between network density and conjugal role performance. It is difficult to compare my qualitative analysis with her quantitative scores. It seems likely, however, that we are in substantial agreement that most of the women she studied had segregated role-relationships with their husbands but that her method of measuring density is so different from my idea of density ('connectedness') that the results are not comparable. To me the most interesting feature of her study is that the women were going through a crisis situation of adapting to a radically changed environment—Greenleigh ten times magnified. Oeser describes a socialization sequence that may apply to other situations of urbanization. The women started with contacts with relatives, progressed to individual contacts with other members of their own language group, then to informal group activities with their own language group, then to informal groups composed of women from more than one language group, and finally to formal 'urban' groups whose members were drawn from several language groups.

My own field of experience in Tonga lends support to the conjugal roles/networks hypothesis. Conjugal roles are sharply segregated in Tonga, though with different content in the sexual

271

division of labour from that of our society. Contrary to generally accepted belief in anthropological circles, there are no unilineal descent groups, though each spouse is involved in a large and close-knit network of kin and friends.

(f) Network therapy

My work has been cited by a psychiatric team who practice what they call 'network therapy' (Speck, 1967; Speck and Rueveni, 1969; and also Attneave, 1969). In my capacity as a social anthropologist the therapeutic use of network ideas is interesting though not of crucial relevance to anthropology. But as a psycho-analyst I feel some misgiving about this particular application of the network idea. The method consists of asking a family to assemble as many friends and relatives as possible and then conducting a form of group therapy with them. It is not that I think psychoanalysis is the only effective therapy—there is room for many sorts of treatment in this field, and psycho-analysis would probably not be practicable with the sort of patient and social situation described. My uneasiness is based on fear of arousing more anxiety than one therapeutic team could deal with, particularly since it is the therapists who take it upon themselves deliberately to produce a change in the form of social relationships by bringing the various members of the patient's network together. If one is prepared to interfere with society to this extent, one should accept the consequences in responsibility, and that would mean a very long-term contact. 'Family therapy' (Speck, 1964) and what Attneave (1969) calls 'tribal' therapy seem to me to be different, for in both cases the therapist deals with a pre-existing group that has sufficient corporate identity to enter into or opt out of a therapeutic contract.

2. Studies that Specifically Discuss or Test the Conjugal Roles/ Network Hypothesis

In *Family and Social Network* I said that before the hypothesis could be proved or disproved, it would have to be quantified and tested, which several research workers have subsequently tried to do. I realize now that if one is serious about accurate replication of a study, one ought to make one's own experiments in quantifying one's definitions. Turner (1967) describes my concepts as 'intuitive definition(s) based on considerable empirical evidence,' which seems accurate to me. Of all the reported studies, his is the only one about which I feel fairly sure that we were talking about the same things and using similar criteria. Certainly the other authors cannot be blamed for discrepancies between their criteria and mine, because I gave no guidance about how my definitions should be quantified.

The quantitative studies cannot be compared with one another, for, as Barnes notes, they all used different methods of measuring density (Barnes, 1969b). Further, accurate measurement of marital behaviour and norms is also a very difficult task. (Brown and Rutter, 1966, devote a detailed paper to certain aspects of it.) In family studies it is customary to use some measure of marital satisfaction and/or task segregation, but behaviour and norms in different regions of family life may be so complex and variable that it is not meaningful to use simple measures of marital segregation/jointness. (See especially Platt, 1969, and Harrell-Bond, 1969, but also Zelditch, 1964.) For example, what is one to do about couples who have what looks like a comparatively rigid household division of labour, though one knows that they adhere to a joint ideology and that the rigid division of labour would be easily changed if either partner asked for help, got ill, etc.? Platt, in a sensitive discussion of problems of measuring jointness of conjugal roles, notes:

'The main substantive conclusion is that there is some reason to be sceptical about the unidimensionality of jointness/ segregation of conjugal roles, even after the possibility that couples may show greater jointness in some respects than in others has been taken into account.
'. . . It is always advisable to collect data on both norms and behaviour, and imperative to do so when the situation studied is one of unusual individual mobility or general change. . .
'. . . it may as a matter of research tactics be more suitable to use

qualitative and partly impressionistic measures, since the intervening variables may be so diverse that it will be impossible to hold them constant without an impracticably large sample' (Platt, 1969, p. 295).

Udry and Hall (1965) examined marital segregation and the density of partial networks of 43 middle-class couples who were the parents of students in a sociology class at a California Public College. Each student asked his parents separately to list the four persons with whom the parent had had the most frequent social contact in the previous year. The people named were then asked whether they knew the other three, and how well. Scores were assigned: two points for 'know well', one point for 'know', and zero for 'don't know', with a possible score range for each parent of 0 to 24. The score of the wife was then added to that of the husband, giving a possible range from 0 to 48 for each couple. This method of measuring density is so far away from my idea of network density that I am not sure if it is meaningful or not. Marital role segregation was measured by a schedule of 25 items concerning which partner did various activities, but the article does not say which regions of family activity were included. The couples were divided into three groups according to their segregation scores.

In this sample and with this method, role segregation was not related to network density. The lowest degree of marital segregation was found in couples in which the wife was highly educated and working outside the home. (It seems probable to me that these two factors were connected.) Compared to the 'high' role segregation couples, the 'medium' role segregation husbands had *greater* network density, the 'medium' role segregation husbands and wives listed more relatives as contacts, they had more children still living at home, and they had lived in their respective areas longer. This is a curious pattern, but without further empirical data on the connection of the various items of information with one another in the case of particular families, I do not think one can do much to further one's understanding of it.

Aldous and Straus (1966) also had negative results when trying to test the hypothesis on 252 women, some rural and some urban, and with some of higher and some of lower socio-economic status in each residential category. Each woman was asked to name the eight women she most often visited socially (rather a large number, I should have thought), and then to say which of them knew one another. The general level of network density was low, especially for the urban 'blue-collar' women. A sex role activities index was constructed on the basis of performance of male tasks, female tasks, and child socialization. A marital task differentiation index was also devised based on the women's replies to questions asking whether the husband or the wife performed certain household tasks.

In conjunction with place of residence, network density *did* result in significant differences in marital task differentiation scores, but the cell means indicated only small differences and failed to reveal the expected pattern. The authors suggest that the hypothesis might hold only for extreme cases, that is, for families in very close-knit or very loose-knit networks. They also make the valuable suggestion that one should investigate whether the networks of husband and wife are separate and segregated or joint and shared, and, having done so, whether it is possible to have a joint but close-knit network or to have separate but loose-knit networks. To rephrase their point somewhat, one needs to analyse, for each family, total network density, the density of their joint network, that is, the part of the total family network that the husband and wife share, and the density of their separate networks.

In both cases I think one would need to know more about how the various factors fitted together in the case of particular families before one could get any ideas about how to interpret the data of these two studies. Perhaps the complexity of the social situation allows families much latitude for choice. Perhaps the couples are very similar and the investigators were looking for differences when it would have been more appropriate to look for similarities. It is very difficult to tell when there is no standard of comparison. The crudeness of the measuring instruments also complicates the task of comparison, for one may not be measuring the same things even when using the same scales. I think that if I were still working in this field, I would continue with an empirical descriptive approach until I got a clearer idea of which factors were important and of how to interpret them.

Nelson (1966) examined the marital segregation and a measure of network density of 131 working-class married women living in New Haven. He developed an ingenious measure of getting at close-knit networks by asking the women to list the four people with whom they had most frequent contact, and then asking how often they saw two or more of the four *together*. Women who saw two or more of their contacts once a week or more often were said to have 'clique' as opposed to 'individualistic' contact.

This time, even with these very crude measures, the expected results occurred. Wives who had 'clique' contacts had more segregated marital relationships than the women with individualistic contacts. The 'clique' women were also less likely to expect 'companionate' (joint) marriage. Nelson also reports the interesting (and to me satisfying) finding that the wife's satisfaction with the husband and the marriage was greater with either the companionate/individualistic pattern or the traditional (segregated)/clique pattern, but was somewhat lower with the traditional/individualistic pattern and with the companionate/clique pattern. But one needs to know more about the husband and his network, which has a considerable effect both on the wife's satisfaction and the use she makes of her social resources. One wonders in passing what factors affected choice of these four patterns. Closer study of geographical mobility, occupation, and the families' relation to their neighbourhoods might provide interesting material on variation and choice.

More recently *Robert Blood* (1969) reports an analysis of marital solidarity and contact with kin for 731 married women constituting a representative sample of intact households in Detroit. He says the results support my hypothesis, but I think he somewhat distorts my rendering of it. He says that 'role segregation' is the same thing as lack of solidarity (Blood, 1969, p. 173) whereas I would say that it is a different sort of solidarity. In my view role segregation is sometimes solidary, sometimes not. My point is that it is a different *type* of solidarity (of whatever degree) from that which arises in a joint relationship. The distinction goes back to the comparison Durkheim drew between organic and mechanical solidarity. If one compares the two dimensions of degree of solidarity and whether the relation is based on difference of similarity, one produces four possibilities.

	Solidary	Not Solidary
Segregated (relation based on difference)	interdependence	conflict or withdrawal
Joint (relation based on similarity)	sharing	competition and rivalry

Blood defines marital solidarity in terms of the wife's satisfaction with her husband's role performance '. . . the companionship he provides her, the love and affection he gives her, his understanding of her problems and feelings, the standard of living his earnings provide, and number of children they have borne' (Blood, 1969, p. 174). The bias is thus in favour of a solidary joint relationship rather than a solidary segregated relationship.

I also find Blood's notion of network 'closure' difficult to work with, though he is by no means the only author who uses the term closure when discussing networks. Networks, in the sense I am using the term, cannot be closed except conceptually when one draws a mental boundary around all the people a given individual and/or couple knows and says this is their network. But this is evidently not what Blood means, because he appears to speak of 'closed' network where I would say 'close-knit' network.

In spite of the conceptual and terminological differences, I find Blood's paper interesting and important. It demonstrates that conjugal role segregation (his measure is based on household tasks only) increases as the proportion of relatives living in the neighbourhood increases. But his findings also demonstrate the seemingly contradictory finding that role segregation is greatest when kin helpfulness is least, and conversely that role segregation is least (and wife's satisfaction greatest) when kin helpfulness is greatest.

His conclusion is that:

'. . . intensive interaction with kin impairs marital solidarity, but that kinship interaction in lesser amounts may positively support the husband-wife relationship' (p. 173).

I would rephrase his conclusion somewhat: intensive interaction with kin is found to be associated with behavioural segregation of husband and wife in performing household tasks. Moderate or less than moderate interaction with kin is found to be associated with joint or shared performance of household tasks. I would reserve judgment on whether the wife's satisfaction with the companionship and love etc. provided by her husband is an adequate measure of solidarity. I would prefer a measure less biased in favour of a joint relationship.

I think that Blood's study, like mine and Turner's and several others, gives empirical realization to the idea put forward by Max Gluckman (1955a) and quoted at the beginning of this chapter, namely, that external groupings both support *and* divide the family against itself.

Barbara Harrell-Bond's study of conjugal roles on a housing estate in Oxford is not exactly, as she points out, a test of the conjugal roles/networks hypothesis (Harrell-Bond, 1969). She describes it as an attempt to explain negative instances, which she does by reference to the couples' cultural backgrounds, and though she gives details only for financial management, to the tendency for couples to pattern their behaviour on that of their parents, or, in the case of financial management, to depart from that of their parents. She also notes, like Platt (1969), that different regions of family life may be differently organized (washing up; routine child care; the spending of leisure; financial management) and she suggests that how leisure is spent may be the best indicator of 'mutuality'.

She does not present information on the couple's networks,

which was not part of the research design, but she concludes that I would have defined the families' networks as loose-knit because there were many immigrants to Oxford from other parts of the country and from abroad, and because the estate was isolated from the city where local kin lived. I think it might have helped her analysis to have examined conjugal segregation in the light of the respective families' geographical mobility, even though the results might well have been complex and inconclusive. Without empirical data it is impossible to tell what the families networks would have been like, but with so much variation in geographical mobility and different degrees of availability of kin, I would anticipate a considerable variation in density of social networks and in what one might call 'culture shock'—meaning the upheaval of a move for families who are not used to it and have not developed the requisite social skill to establish new contacts in unfamiliar settings. As noted above, one move, even a comparatively short move (from Bethnal Green to Greenleigh), will be a social and psychological upheaval for a family if it involves the break-up of close-knit networks, whereas families who have moved before or who have been brought up to expect geographical mobility will be much less upset (Berger, 1960).

Harrell-Bond disapproves strongly of my using the assumption that there is a 'limited fund of sociability', with its concomitant propositions that if people have discontinuous relationships outside their elementary family they will seek help, a sense of identity, and continuity within the family, and vice versa. I agree that this is a crude psychological assumption. I made it, in the fashion of Gluckman and Devons (1964), so that I could get on with my sociological analysis. If I were studying emotional investment as such, I would set about it quite differently. (I am now no longer so sure that I would draw what Gluckman and Devons call 'the limits of naivety' at this particular point, but that is another matter.)

I would dispute, however, Harrell-Bond's assertion that I am implicitly committed to an ideal of increased mutuality in marriage. I do think that norms of 'mutuality' will be found whenever couples move around a lot before and after marriage, and that if economic and social conditions are such that individuals and families move around more and more, I would expect an increase in the proportion of couples, particularly wives, who expect to have a joint relationship. Whether their norms will be realized or not is another matter, and one that has not been thoroughly studied. It seems to me probable that joint norms are more difficult to put into practice than segregated norms. Actually the notion of 'ideals' in marriage seems to me rather unreal—whose ideal, and whose norms? I thought that I had made it clear enough in Chapter VII on The Normal Family and in the last chapter (p. 218) that it is inappropriate to apply the norms of one social situation to families in another.

I find two points in Harrell-Bond's paper particularly interesting. First is the fact that informants spontaneously mentioned their experiences in other parts of the country. I think this exemplifies the way people use reference groups to orient themselves in a new situation and to explain and justify the way they are doing things now in relation to the way things were done in their childhood or in other places of which they have knowledge.

The second point of particular interest is the fascinating differences between the Irish and the English families (see Harrell-Bond, 1969, pp. 86–87). The families with Irish husbands displayed marked segregation of roles, largely, one gathers, because the husbands willed it so, though Harrell-Bond does not explicitly say so. At the same time, the husbands recreated a close-knit male network similar to the one they had had at home in Ireland.

'The majority of the men from Southern Ireland had work-mates of other male Irish immigrants as their leisure-time companions and their wives tended to mention neighbours with whom they had become acquainted since coming to Oxford. . . . there seemed to be a very general tendency among the men to build up a social network of other men from Southern Ireland. . . . they encapsulate themselves in a social environment which largely replicates the way of life in Ireland' (Harrell-Bond, 1969, p. 87).

For their wives, however, things were different. The local English wives who married Irishmen 'were often in close contact with their own relatives and friends outside the neighbourhood of the estate'. But the Irish wives were differently situated.

'It was my impression that generally Irish women expressed feelings of dissatisfaction and unhappiness which apparently their husbands did not share' (Harrell-Bond, 1969, p. 87).

And:

'The wives, on the other hand, by virtue of an absence of other Irish women in their immediate neighbourhoods usually find their associates among English women' (Harrell-Bond, 1969, p. 87).

And:

'I did not observe that their wives tended to choose their friends from among other Irish women even though certain activities in the estate would have permitted them to do so' (Harrell-Bond, 1969, p. 87).

I think that for women, finding Irish friends is clearly not enough. For women who have been brought up in close-knit kin networks, it is their female *kin* that provide the counterbalance to what Tiger calls 'male bonding' (Tiger, 1969).[1] And it looks as

---

[1] I find Tiger's work on male bonding stimulating and worthy of further study. The term 'male bonding' is especially convenient because it gives a generic name for attachment that covers kinship, friendship, shared group memberships, and so forth. For a time I toyed with the idea of adopting the term myself but have thought better of it because I think there is a danger that ethologists and ethological anthropologists may allow themselves to be lulled into the belief that if other animals behave in a particular fashion, that fashion is part of our animal/human inheritance and therefore can be dismissed as understood. Whether or not male bonding is part of our genetic inheritance is a matter I find interesting in itself but not sociologically crucial, for it occurs in a great variety of forms, each of which needs sociological understanding and analysis in its own right, and as yet few empirical studies have been specifically devoted to this problem. Further, one must also be prepared to analyse the social conditions in which 'female bonding' occurs, that is, solidary female groups as distinct from female pair relationships of the mother/child, sibling/sibling, and 'best friend' variety. On the positive side I think that ethology and the ethological school of anthropology have shaken us out of our sociological complacency and have reawakened our interest and concern in comparative analysis.

if it is easier for men to establish a new network of friends with men of their own cultural background than it is for women to create something that would take the place of the lost kin network. Friends are more replaceable than kin.

Another important finding reported in Harrell-Bond's paper is a discrepancy between what the English husbands would *like* to do with their leisure and what they *actually* do. Fifty-six per cent of the English husbands defined their idea of a really enjoyable evening in such a way as to make it clear that they would not spend it with their wives. But in reality, only 37 per cent managed to spend their leisure away from their wives. Among the Irish husbands, 73 per cent wanted separate recreation and 72 per cent got it. It looks, in short, as if the English husbands would like a bit of 'male bonding' too, but they do not get it. The data presented, however, do not tell one how social pressure was brought to bear on the unfortunate Englishmen. I would agree with Harrell-Bond's conclusion that if conjugal organization becomes less segregated '. . . it is the man who must make the most radical changes in his conjugal role performance' (p. 88).

I agree with Harrell-Bond that cultural background and experience in one's parental family are important factors shaping conjugal expectations and one's expectations about how relationships with people outside the elementary family should be conducted. As I discuss in the text (p. 219), particular cultural expectations are associated with particular patterns of social relationship, but when the social relationships change, the cultural expectations do not change automatically, and the change is often painful. But I would not give cultural background pride of place in shaping conjugal norms and behaviour. It becomes meaningful only when understood in combination with other factors—the family's current situation including their type of network, geographical mobility, social mobility, ecological factors, and so forth.

Turner (1967) studied 115 families and their social networks in a rural community. His study is particularly important to my hypothesis, because it is the only one in which the investigator has had independent and detailed information about network density.

He did not carry out the study to test the conjugal roles/networks hypothesis, but did the work in the course of a community study. It was Ronald Frankenberg who suggested that he might use the material to make a more precise examination of my hypothesis.

Turner notes (accurately) that I was discussing the density of interconnections between family-households. He first determined the composition and density of the husband's network and of the wife's network considered separately, and then aggregated the two networks and calculated the density for all the households involved. (Barnes, 1969b, observes that in all these calculations the focal household or individual was omitted from the analysis.) Turner distinguished three degrees of network density and three degrees of conjugal segregation. His measure of conjugal segregation was based on his observations of how couples behaved in three areas of marital organization: leisure activities outside the home, domestic tasks, and child rearing. If all three were joint, the relationship was considered joint; if all three were segregated, the overall relationship was considered segregated; if there was any discrepancy between sub-area classifications, the conjugal role relationship was counted as intermediate.

The results are statistically significant in the expected direction, but the distribution is not as I would have expected, especially in the middle range, for there is no close association between medium-knit networks and an intermediate degree of role segregation.

Turner adds to our understanding of close-knit networks, confirming but also modifying Fallding's statement that there is 'a sharp cleavage by sex right across the network. . . .' Turner reports that husbands and wives tended to include the same kinfolk in their respective separate social networks. '. . . When kinfolk are excluded, thirty-two couples could be unambiguously identified for whom the husband's friends constituted a close-knit male network, and the wife's friends a close-knit female network. These thirty-two couples also demonstrated a high degree of conjugal role segregation' (Turner, 1967, p. 125).

In other words, there is not a sharp cleavage right across the network, for the kin part of the husband's and the wife's network is shared. (This was also the case for the Newbolts (p. 68) though she visited relatives much more than he did.)

The only thing I find surprising about these rural families with close-knit networks is that wives have independent networks of *friends* as distinct from relatives. Studies of the urban working class in Britain stress that married women have close-knit networks of kin and some attenuated relationships with female neighbours who are seen in the street but are not entertained at home, but that after adolescence is over married women have virtually no close female friends who are not also relatives. It will be recalled, however, that the Italian wives studied by Gans had friends as well as relatives (Gans, 1962). Perhaps the various investigators of working-class families, including myself, have been too bedazzled by kinship to take proper note of friendship. At my request Turner has amplified his statement:

'Farmers or farmers-to be show a marked preference for farmers' daughters as marriage partners. (Indeed the local ideology stresses that a town girl will be "no wife".) Farmers' daughters and other rural girls in this area tend to develop small close-knit female peer networks before marriage.

'Re girls: Friends are small in number and I think there is a tendency to *change* friends before marriage, but to consolidate friends—especially married friends—after marriage. *Residence* appears to shape the post-marriage networks, as one would expect' (Turner, personal communication, 1970).

As he suggests, in a farming community residence and propinquity are particularly important as determinants of social relationships, more so than in any sort of urban situation where work-place and living-place are separated.

Turner next points out that 'When the (individual) networks of husband and wife show considerable overlap, no distinctive pattern of conjugal role relationship appears to be associated with them' (Turner, 1967, p. 125). This is an important finding and an important way of mapping out the data, for if it should prove to be the case in other studies, further attention should be paid to

284

understanding variations in the degree of conjugal segregation among families who have this type of network formation.

Since degree of network density provided only a partial prediction of the form of the conjugal role-relationship, Turner went on to investigate other factors, of which occupation and geographical mobility were the most important.

There was a marked tendency for farm families to be close-knit and segregated (27 out of 35). *All* the loose-knit/joint families were non-farm. There was a marked tendency for the families of joint and intermediate degrees of conjugal segregation to be non-farm (45 non-farm out of 50 joint and intermediate), but about one-third (26 out of 71) of the non-farm families had segregated relationships. Of these 26 non-farm families with segregated relationships, 14 were 'Dalesfolk', that is, both husband and wife had been born and brought up in the local area.

Turner also analysed his families according to whether the husband and wife were both Dalesfolk, both incomers, or mixed.[1] Dalesfolk, particularly *farm* Dalesfolk, tended to have close-knit networks and conjugal segregation. Incomers tended to have loose-knit networks and joint conjugal relationships. Mixed marriages showed a wide spread of both network density and conjugal segregation. Turner adds in a letter:

'The major factor underlying variations, I suspect, is in-migration. But most in-migrants in the past, with one or two notable periods of exception have been drawn from adjacent areas, and it is only fairly recently that in-migrants could be classified into 1) in-marriers and in-migrants from adjacent localities with a similar social structure, 2) special in-migrants who are locally expected to be different, e.g. ministers, doctor, etc., 3) old in-migrants from urban/suburban/rural arable areas, and 4) young in-migrants with children to be brought up locally. At the same time out-migration, especially if it is over any

[1] There is a discrepancy in this part of Turner's paper, p. 127, between Table 3 and the text. In a personal communication Turner says the penultimate paragraph on p. 127 should read: 'When both spouses are Dalesfolk but currently fall into the non-farm category . . . etc.'

distance, can play havoc with established network patterns, and there has been almost continuous depopulation since 1880, which means that the losses from the local born population must have been substantial' (personal communication, 1970).

To my surprise, Turner's families showed no tendency towards greater segregation as they became older. He has since explained (again in a personal communication) that he thinks this finding is a statistical artifact for the non-farm families but a genuine finding for the farm families. In the case of the farm families, he thinks that different factors operate at different phases of the life cycle to maintain similar patterns both of close-knit male and female networks and of conjugal role segregation.

With the exception of a few professional and business families, data on education were too uniform to account for variations in networks or conjugal roles. An analysis of nine couples with a 'cosmopolitan' orientation (Merton, 1957) failed to reveal any single conjugal and network pattern.

Turner's work suggests that close attention should be paid to geographical mobility in future studies. He suggests a multivariate research design and indicates several relevant variables: network size and composition; network density; occupation, geographical mobility; stage of developmental cycle; educational level; cosmopolitan or local orientation. He himself, however, has gone on to analyse the processes of network structuring both for individual families and historically for the community and its network patterns. He ends a recent letter with a statement that will be painfully familiar to anyone (like Fallding) who has done exploratory research:

'I only wish I had more cases so that it would make sense to tabulate the data by all the variables at the same time. If I had my time over again I think this is how I would start, but at the time I would not even have known how to do it, never mind have had the patience' (Turner, personal communication, 1970).

So far as I can discover, these are the main empirical studies that attempt to test the conjugal roles/network hypothesis. Before concluding I will briefly discuss Fallding's (1961) and Harris's (1969) general criticisms. Several other criticisms have been noted in the course of the discussion.

I have already quoted *Fallding's* basic criticism, that sex segregation within the family is an intrinsic part of sex segregation in general, which of course means outside the family. But he adds a second and important point.

'. . . One wonders whether *general* network connectedness has much to do with the case. It does seem to resolve itself very much into *kinship* solidarity, in which milieu sex role segregation is enforced' (Fallding, 1961, p. 342).

He goes on to note that a considerable number of his research families were primarily devoted to kin but gave a second place to stable friendships; although the parents had very little time to cultivate friends, friends were valued because they shared with kin the primary function of confirming the continuity of one's identity. This finding is consistent with the work of Babchuk and Bates (1963) on friends and with the growing number of kinship studies that indicate the importance of continuing relationships with parents and siblings for *all* types of family.

I agree with Fallding's basic criticism that it is not just network density *per se* that is crucial, but that where conjugal segregation is found to be marked inside the family, one will also find that the husband belongs to a close-knit network of men outside the family and that the wife similarly belongs to a close-knit network of women outside the family. I regard this as the basic criticism of the way I formulated the central hypothesis, a criticism which is also voiced by Rosser and Harris (1965), Aldous and Straus (1966) and Harris (1969).

However, unlike Fallding, I do think that general network connectedness has a great deal to do with the case, because it is only in areas where the 'total network' is relatively dense that sexual segregation of this sort develops. (As described above, I am here using the phrase 'total network' to mean a network that is not anchored on a particular individual or group.) In other words, close-knit but sexually segregated networks develop in areas where interactional clustering is dense and relatively enduring. Other factors may enter into the generating of sexual segregation, a problem that needs further study—but dense and relatively enduring total networks are certainly required.

Further, I agree with Fallding that kin are of special importance, although I do not think it is correct to say that general network density resolves itself *entirely* into kinship solidarity. Male networks and sometimes female networks include friends who are not always relatives. Both kinship and friendship should be analysed to see not only how they support but also how they are inimical to conjugal relationships. I make a first attempt at this sort of analysis in the next section of this chapter.

Harris's (1969) book *The Family* is particularly notable for its discussion of the extended family and the 'family process' (Harris, 1969, pp. 67–68), but it also examines my ideas on networks and conjugal roles at some length (pp. 169–175). I think Harris makes some minor misinterpretations of my meanings, but, these aside, he seems to make two main points, if I understand him correctly. The first is that the things I call close-knit networks should properly be called groups because the people in them develop shared norms through interaction. Such shared norms are the crucial criterion in his definition of group, and they make possible the development of capacity for acting together.

'When a set of people interact with one another over a period of time they come to share expectations about the way in which *each other* will behave. When a set of people share expectations of this sort we may describe them as a group' (p. 67).
'... a group—that is to say come to share valued ways of acting (norms) and a capacity for acting together' (p. 172).

So, if I have grasped the argument, husband and wife belong to groups, not close-knit networks, and their relationship is segregated because agreed norms of segregation exist in their respective 'groups', the 'groups' having developed the shared norms through prior interconnectedness.

I think the important thing in the process is the development of shared norms and social control of the spouses, which can only take place when network density is high. Where one draws the line between a close-knit network and a groups is somewhat arbitrary, and depends, as Boissevain (1968) puts it, on whether one is an 'interactionist' or a 'corporationist'. My own definition of group was more 'corporationist' than 'interactional'— 'common aims, interdependent roles, and a distinctive sub-culture' (see above, p. 58). What I did not stress sufficiently in this formal definition was 'common boundary', that is, agreement by all members of the group on who is and who is not a member. In my usage it is this lack of common boundary that is the hallmark of networks, even close-knit ones. While on the subject of definitions, I would distinguish a corporate group from groups in general by the criterion of ability to act as a unit, though not necessarily together in face-to-face action. And I find it useful to reserve the word 'grouping' as a general and inclusive term for entities on the borderline between a social category and a group or on the border-line between a network and a group.

Harris's second main comment is a development of Fallding's point that sex-role segregation within the family goes with sexual segregation outside it.

'Control over the spouses will be facilitated by a close-knit network. The formation of norms and groups will be facilitated by the existence of a close-knit network. Where such groups or sets of relationships are mono-sex, their members are likely also to share norms of marital role segregation which derive both from the fit of ideas and from the conditions under which marital roles are performed. If the roles are defined as segregated and cannot be performed without resources provided by external relationships, then those relationships will be between persons of the same sex. Hence we should expect to find an irregular relationship between network interconnectedness and role segregation, but a strong relationship between membership of mono-sex networks and marital role segregation. This is what the only satisfactory attempt to verify Bott's hypothesis found [i.e. Turner]' (Harris, 1969, pp. 174–5).

Harris concludes with the statement quoted at the beginning of this chapter, and he continues:

'She explicitly recognizes the implications of Parsons' description of the nuclear family—its segregation *qua* family from wider groups and the autonomy of the spouses as a couple—while recognizing that this does not imply that the family is isolated in the sense that its members, *individually*, are isolated. This is of course obvious *once it has been said*' (Harris, 1969, p. 175).

I often find Harris's argument difficult to follow, but I think his book raises, as did he and Rosser in 1965, an important point that deserves further empirical investigation, namely, what is the nature of the relation between network density and the *content* of norms? Is it possible, for example, to find a close-knit network that leads to consensus on *joint* instead of segregated conjugal norms? Like Gluckman, one is led on to ask what is the effect of a network composed mainly of kin compared to a network composed largely of friends.

B. CURRENT REFLECTIONS ON THE CONJUGAL ROLES/NETWORKS HYPOTHESIS

What, then, do all these studies add up to? Is the hypothesis established or disproved? Neither, I think.

The weight of empirical evidence and conceptual argument is that the hypothesis holds in the case of dense networks and segregated conjugal relationships, but that, when networks become more loose-knit, the type of conjugal relationship becomes unpredictably variable. The factors involved and their relations to one another have not been fully studied and are sure to be complex. It is in this area that there is much need for further understanding and imaginative research.

It seems to me that much rudimentary field research remains to be done, particularly in the realm of accurate mapping of network regions (i.e. shared or individual) and sectors (kin, friends, etc.); in studying the relation between norms and network density; in exploring the differential effects (if any) of different types of network density (e.g. multiplex as compared to simplex); in analysing further the relations between network formation and familial relationships, parent/child as well as conjugal; and in studying the relations of both networks and familial relationships to occupation, geographical mobility, social mobility, cosmopolitan/local orientation, various ecological factors, cultural background, education, phase of family development, and use of reference groups. We still, in other words, need to know a lot more than we know now about how the elementary family as a group is articulated to other groups and institutions and to the society at large.

There are three ways I would approach the field if I were still involved in it. The first is a technical matter concerning the mapping of networks. The second concerns the comparative analysis of network sectors, especially kinship compared to friendship. The third concerns the unpredictable variability of the relation between network formation and conjugal expectations once one leaves the extreme pole of close-knit network formation and a marked degree of conjugal segregation.

The problem, as always, is to think of research designs that will allow a fruitful marriage of ideas and field data so that one will be led on to new and better ideas and to new methods of extending and eventually testing them. What follows is a mixture of fact, hunch, and conjecture evoked by reflections on our original research and on the subsequent work by other people.

1. *The Mapping of Networks*

As I suggested in the original text (pp. 93–94 above) I would make maps of the husband's separate network and the wife's separate network, preferably by interviewing each partner alone; I would also plot out their joint network as described by them in a joint interview. Provisionally I would include in the joint network not only the contacts mentioned by the couple in the joint interview, but also any individuals who were listed separately by both husband and wife even if such individuals were not mentioned as joint contacts. Basically this was the procedure used by Turner (1967), and, one gathers, by Kapferer in the analysis referred to by Max Gluckman in his Preface. As Firth (1964) observes, if one is studying families and not just marriage, one should also include children's contacts.

In an urban situation one has to do most of this by interview. In an anthropological community study one can observe as well as inquire, though I think that even in a rural or tribal situation one would have to supplement observations by detailed interviewing with several families to get the sort of material required. The fieldwork would be tedious at best, and I doubt if many fieldworkers would be disposed to do it in the necessary detail.

I would differentiate relationships with kin, friends, neighbours, and with people met in voluntary associations only, so that these types of relationship could be mapped according to whether they occurred in the joint or separate sectors of the network.

I would also introduce a qualitative dimension by distinguishing between intimate, effective, and extended contacts within each category, as I did in Chapter V of the text in the case of kinship, though the analysis in that chapter was far from complete. Here one would need to use both some 'objective' measure based on frequency of contact in relation to physical propinquity, and some 'subjective' measure of felt closeness of involvement. Both types of measure are important, the 'objective' because it allows comparison of families within the research series, and the 'subjective' because it does justice to each family's personal definitions, but the two measures should be kept separate so that they can be usefully compared.

I doubt the usefulness of trying to collect lists of people in the more remote reaches of the 'extended' category. In the field of kinship, particularly, this exercise takes a great deal of time and tells one comparatively little. Perhaps it is worth doing for all types of relationship with a small number of families to make sure that one is not missing something of importance.

I would think it important to note the size of the various sectors of the network and to study size in relation to intensity, for the existing evidence is contradictory. Several students of the American working class appear to suggest that primary networks are small, whereas Young and Willmott (1957) and Gans (1962) suggest that kin networks in the working class are both large and, in their crucial relationships, intense. Babchuk and Bates (1963) were surprised at the small numbers of mutual friends listed by their middle-class married couples, and Rapoport and Rapoport (1969), writing about double-career families of the upper middle class, note that these couples did not have time to see friends. Gans (1967), on the other hand, notes that various students of suburbia have commented on the immense amount of informal social activity that goes on in middle-class suburbs, and Willmott and Young (1960) also comment on the friendliness of the middle-class families in the English suburb they studied. I suspect that many families have large numbers of comparatively 'superficial' relationships. It seems possible that there might be a relatively simple explanation or partial explanation for these seemingly contradictory findings, an explanation to do with ecological factors such as whether, regardless of class, families live in a relatively homogeneous neighbourhood. But so far as I know the problem has not been approached from this angle.

I would inquire into network density, that is, into which of the people in the various regions of a family's network knew each other. In a community study like Turner's (1967) the investigator has an independent check, but in an urban situation, and especially with families with loose-knit networks, I doubt if the effort of starting a fresh research contact with each individual or family/ household would be worth the immense trouble involved. Moreover, several of the non-focal family/households might well refuse to be interviewed. Even so, I think the research effort might well be worth the trouble, but I do not think that anyone will do it. Asking the focal couple who knows whom is a poor substitute, but it is the most that any research worker is likely to attempt.

I would calculate density according to Barnes's method for

293

each sector of the network: the husband's, the wife's, the joint sector, and their overall network is that, *all* the people with whom husband and wife (or all members of the family) were in contact jointly or individually. (For the method of calculating density, see Barnes, 1969b. Briefly it consists of actual relationships expressed as a percentage of possible relationships. The focal family (the 'root') is included in the calculations.) Later on it might appear that it is not necessary to go to all the trouble of collecting so much information and calculating density so meticulously, but I would rather err initially in the direction of too much material rather than too little.

Turner (1967) found that among families who had a large area of joint or overlapping network relative to the separate husband and wife sectors there was no consistent pattern of conjugal relationship. I suspect that this may prove to be the case in other families, in which case it would offer a convenient way of locating the families who need closer study.

2. Kinship and Friendship

Kinship and friendship are the most important types of primary social relationship, neighbours and voluntary associations being important largely in that they provide a pool of potential friends and may overlap with the kinship and friendship categories.

The definition of 'friend' is an important empirical problem. I think it best to start by using the definitions of one's informants; in questionnaire studies one should also remember that 'friend' may mean very different things to different people.

A main concern here is to understand the properties of kinship and friendship and their respective effects on conjugal and familial relationships. One important matter that deserves attention is the question of where kin and friends are located in the sort of network map described above. For example, in the case of the working-class families described by Young and his colleagues, by Mogey, and by myself, it seems likely that the husband's network of peers is composed largely of friends, of whom some are kin, whereas the wife's network is composed mainly of kin. Further,

I suspect that there is a substantial area of overlap between the wife's kin network and the joint network of husband and wife. More precisely, the wife visits female kin independently; the husband and wife together visit these same female kin *and* their respective husbands. In the case of the close-knit networks described by Gans (1962), however, the kin/friend composition in relation to the joint and separate sectors of the network would presumably have been rather different.

It appears likely that where close-knit networks exist, the husband's and the wife's networks will be differently related to and will have different effects on the conjugal relationship. At least, I think this is a question that deserves further study. It seems likely that the wife's female network both supports *and* divides the marriage, whereas the husband's male network only divides and does not support the conjugal relationship—except in the sense that it may produce a more satisfied man who is thereby a more satisfactory husband. However, the question is complicated by the question of whether the respective male and female networks are composed of kin, or friends, or both, and whether they include people of more than one generation. Generally speaking, friends of one spouse have little interest in maintaining that person's conjugal relationship, whereas kin will have a double interest, both in maintaining the marriage *and* in breaking it up.

(a) *Kinship*

One implication that emerges from the studies since 1957 is that *kin* are of special importance in any type of network. The importance of kinship is threefold. First, kin are especially likely to know one another, so that the kinship region of the network is likely to be more close-knit than other sectors. Second, relationships with and among close kin are relatively permanent. Third, kin play an important double role, not only supporting but also dividing the marriages of the families in a network.

In his Preface Max Gluckman draws attention to the close association between network density and kinship. Certainly, as he notes, in tribal societies kinship is the basic social relationship, and there can be little doubt that families' networks are usually denser in tribal societies than in most sectors of Western society. But Gluckman goes further, for he says he suspects that whenever networks are close-knit, kinship relationships will be found at their core. The essential features, as he sees them, and I would agree, are that kin should live and work together. Given these conditions, networks will be close-knit and both conjugal segregation and general sexual segregation will be marked. Within the network the categories 'kinsman', 'friend', 'neighbour', and 'workmate' will tend to overlap, and relationships will become what Gluckman has elsewhere (1955b) called 'multiplex'. There is of course another aspect of kinship that contributes to network density, an aspect so obvious that one takes it for granted, namely, that consanguineal kin are likely to know one another independently of the focal family because of the biological basis of the relationship.

Relations with close kin are enduring, at least compared with relations with friends and neighbours. When network density begins to decline either because the focal family moves or because of out-migration or in-migration in a local area, relationships with very close kin are the most likely to survive. Relations with neighbours are the most readily dropped. Close friendships remain in memory but not in current interaction. Interaction with and among distant kin becomes infrequent. But relations with and among parents and siblings are maintained, even over great distances. One can find new friends and neighbours but not new kin.

The importance of the kin region of the network lies not only in its density and relative permanence but also in the fact that it both supports *and* is inimical to the husband/wife relationship. Normally much of the kin region of a family's network is joint, that is, shared by husband and wife and by children too. Kin are related to all members of an elementary family, whereas friends and neighbours may be involved in a relationship with one family member only. Overlapping occurs between the kin cited and visited by the wife and those cited and visited by the husband, and joint visits are paid to kin, particularly on ceremonial occasions. Close kin support each other by mutual aid and sometimes by substantial gifts. In certain situations the support of the wife by kin balances and makes tolerable the husband's solidarity with his male friends. I believe that such overlapping and joint visiting of kin holds for all social classes and for all degrees of network density, though there may be marked variations in the size of the kin region of the network and in the proportion of 'joint' kin compared to 'separate' kin.

Within this 'joint' kin region, however, there is always a basic fault line of division between the husband's kin and the wife's. If the husband and wife disagree, the husband's kin may support the wife and her kin may support the husband in the interests of maintaining the marriage and its solidarity. But it is more likely that the kin of each spouse will support their own kinsman against the other spouse, and in some cases may also make demands on their kinsman that conflict with marital loyalty and obligations. This is of course the source of many classic jokes about in-laws.

Fallding (1961) draws attention to the double function of kinship in both expressing solidarity and manufacturing segregation (Fallding, 1961, p. 342). Even on normal occasions when there is no question of marital strife, joint visiting to kin ceremonially states the existence of and solidarity of the conjugal tie, but may also generate sexual segregation at the same time, for husband and wives may separate into mono-sex groups after they have arrived together.

(b) *Friendship*

Friendship, like kinship, can both divide and unite a marriage and a family. The role of friendship in different classes and the changing role of friendship at various stages in the life cycle of the individual and the family are topics that have not received the sociological attention they deserve.

Long ago Talcott Parsons contributed the idea that 'youth culture', which involves intense friendships with both sexes, helps to get children out of their families of orientation and into families of procreation (Parsons, 1942), an idea that is elaborated and given depth in a forthcoming psycho-analytic work by Donald Meltzer on psychosexual development. Fallding (1961) emphasizes the importance of old friends in giving a sense of the continuity of one's identity. Babchuk and Bates's (1963) study shows that only a few close friendships are made after marriage and that old, absent friends are felt by informants to be of great importance. Adams (1967a) contributes the important idea that the basic properties of kinship are concern and obligation expressed in mutual aid and ceremonies, whereas the basic property of friendship is consensus (shared interests) manifested in voluntary social activities. Both Babchuk and Bates and Adams comment with surprise on the fact that exchange of intimate confidences was not considered by their informants to be a characteristic activity of close friends. I believe this finding occurred because all their informants were married, and their results would have been quite different if their respondents had been unmarried.[1] However, no one appears to have done a study of phase changes in friendship, and, so far as I could find, no one has linked up all the findings about friendship into a comprehensive sociological analysis.

Putting together the various field studies and bits of information from specific studies of friendship, I think the general pattern of phase change is fairly clear. Close friendships are forged in the crucible of identity formation in adolescence and early adulthood. This includes both mono-sex and heterosexual friendships. Mating emerges out of these relationships and is not fully compatible with their continuation. How the conflict is resolved depends on a number of social and ecological factors acting in concert.

The development and resolution of the conflict is fairly clear for the two extreme ends of the continuum of network formation and conjugal segregation, that is, the role of friendship in relation

[1] Other, but for my immediate purposes less directly relevant, studies of friendship include: Lazarsfeld and Merton, 1954; Eisenstadt, 1956; Bell and Boat, 1956–1957; Axelrod, 1956; Bates and Babchuk, 1961; Cohen, 1961; Sutcliffe and Crabbe, 1963; Wolf, 1966; Paine, 1969; and Litwak and Szelenyi, 1969, who compare relationships with friends, neighbours, and kin, but chiefly on one dimension, that of giving help of varying duration.

to marriage is now moderately well understood in the case of families with very close-knit networks and in the case of families with very loose-knit networks. The pattern in the 'middle range' is more problematic. But first, the extremes.

In working-class neighbourhoods with close-knit total networks, boys and girls experience sexual segregation at home in their parents' relationship.

Max Gluckman comments, and I would agree, that close-knit networks are accompanied not only by segregation between the sexes but also by segregation between the generations, so that the gulf between parents and children is much more marked in families with close-knit networks than is the case with families having very loose-knit networks. Children grow up in mono-sex peer groups whose solidarity becomes very strong during adolescence, particularly among boys. Such children are taught at school by teachers who expect different things of marriage, of work, of individual achievement, and of friendship, but teachers have little impact when their teaching contradicts both parents and peer groups.

When boys go to work they do not have to change their place of residence, so the friendships of adolescence can be continued into adulthood to form an adult peer group; it consists of friends, most of whom are neighbours, some of whom are kin, and some of whom may be workmates. It is balanced by close-knit female networks of kin and sometimes friends (Gans, 1962; Turner, 1967). I suspect that a girl's relationships with her friends are of great importance until she has her first child, after which she will probably turn more and more to her kin. If she lives in a homogeneous neighbourhood, she will probably turn also to neighbours, who can provide her with short-term minor services that she did not need before. So far as I know, no detailed study of this phase change has been published. (Jane Hubert, however, is currently writing up a study of the role of kinship during the phase of the birth of the first child.) To my knowledge, the circumstances in which a wife's independent relationships with her female friends are continued or dropped have not been studied.

Children who are brought up in families with very loose-knit networks, which are likely to be middle class, experience at home at least the ideology if not also the behaviour of a joint conjugal relationship. Social distance between parents and children is less than in the case of families in close-knit networks, and parents usually know about their children's friends and their activities together. Peer groups exist, but are not so cut off from the family. Further, children are trained from an early age, though unintentionally, to expect friendships to be discontinuous; they also experience geographical mobility and its effects early in life. They may attend schools in different neighbourhoods from the one in which they live; they proceed through school and higher education in various places leaving a trail of friendships behind them, which gives them experience in managing a loose-knit network. The content of their education is also relevant, for they are taught a body of knowledge that is comparatively 'sex-free', shareable by men and women. Their teachers take joint relationships between the sexes for granted. Normally their teachers are devoted to an ideology of sexual equality and self-realization in career and creative achievement, somewhat unevenly combined with goals of self-realization in 'femininity' or 'masculinity' as the case may be. The pressure for achievement is considerable, both at home and at school. Implicitly the whole situation of higher education suggests that somewhere, in a personal relationship, a person will find a haven of security where he will be valued for what he is rather than what he can do; and this belief is the carrot that leads him to hope that in the shared intimacy of love he will find understanding and solace for the rigours of the pursuit of truth and success. Thus, although the ethic of a joint conjugal relationship is not explicitly taught, all the values appropriate to it are tacitly conveyed.

In brief, for middle-class children in loose-knit networks several factors work together to develop the skills necessary for operating a joint relationship and a loose-knit network. The ability to make friends is an important aspect of these skills.

Adolescence is a time of intense identity-seeking, sometimes also of revolt against parental complacency. For a brief period intense attachments to peer groups may be combined with hetero-sexual relationships, but soon mating pairs differentiate themselves out, and pursuit of careers disperses the peer groups. Friends are 'trimmed' so that they can be joint, with the husband probably dominant in the trimming. The intense relationships of late adolescence remain, reminders, as Fallding says, of the continuity of one's individual identity, or of the couple's identity if the friend is mutual. But most 'mutual' friends were originally the friends of one or other spouse, and the mutuality of the friend-ship is somewhat precarious. These intense identity-giving friends tend to be conveniently absent so that they do not threaten conjugal loyalty. Brief visits add spice to life; constant residence near such a friend is somewhat awkward. Henceforth new friend-ships are joint, but very much diminished in intensity. Joint acquaintanceship succeeds individual friendships.

Between these two extremes of friendship in the close-knit and the loose-knit network, there is a vast and incompletely known territory. We know something about the role of friendship for families of the 'middle range', but not enough, and, particularly, not enough about how friendship supports and divides the conjugal relationship.

3. Unpredictable Variability in the Relation of Conjugal Segregation to Loose-knit Network Formation

The cumulative evidence, however methodologically inadequate and incomplete, indicates that there is not a close association be-tween network density and conjugal segregation except in the case of close-knit networks, which are typically found in associa-tion with marked conjugal segregation. I shall discuss three issues: first, the question of network density in relation to sex segregation in general as well as conjugal segregation in particular; second, the variables relevant to network density and conjugal segrega-tion; and, third, research strategy.

(a) Total network and sex segregation

In the 1957 edition of *Family and Social Network* I treated network density as an intervening variable. Degree of conjugal segregation depended on degree of network density, which in turn depended on a great variety of social and economic factors, which I attempted to describe though not to study (see Chapter IV). I now think this tidy formulation is too simple. For if Fallding and others are right that conjugal segregation is a particular manifestation of sex segregation in general, it becomes important to know in what circumstances sex-role segregation will be marked and when it will be minimized. As Max Gluckman says in his Preface, the problem of conjugal segregation is pushed one stage further back.

In 1957, and to a considerable extent still today, I think that sex segregation in general will arise whenever people stay in one place long enough to get to know each other really well. But now I would add something. If people stay in one place for several generations they are likely to become kin to one another. I would agree with Max Gluckman that kinship is likely to be at the heart of total network density *and* general sex segregation. And I would agree, too, that both sex segregation and network density are increased when kin work together at shared tasks.

Such working together is of course very marked in tribal societies. It also occurs in rural areas of Western societies, as Gluckman's quotation from Arensberg (1937) shows. It may occur also to a lesser degree in industrial settings as in the coalmining village studied by Dennis, Henriques, and Slaughter (1956). Even when kin do not work together, male solidarity is somewhat enhanced if men, including some kin but also fellow neighbours or friends, work at *similar* occupations, as in the case of Bethnal Green and certain other erstwhile working-class areas of London. Gans's monograph indicates that conditions in American cities are similar (Gans, 1962).

Sex segregation probably also increases when men own or control economic resources, as in the case of Arensberg's and Turner's farmers (Arensberg, 1937; Turner, 1967).

Perhaps poverty and occupational uncertainty may increase male solidarity, for W. Miller (1958) and Rainwater (1964) appear to be describing situations of acute economic uncertainty and deprivation which lead to unstable marriage but not to unstable male peer groups. Adolescent gangs flourish, especially gangs of boys, and they evidently persist into adulthood.

Male solidarity, network density, and sex segregation are all decreased by geographical mobility and population turnover. They are also decreased by occupational and economic conditions that engender competition rather than cooperation, even in conditions of low population turnover that in other respects would favour the development of sex segregation and close-knit total networks. Italians in Southern Italy, for example, are thrown into competition and rivalry with each other in such a fashion that solidary ties outside the elementary family do not develop. (Gans, 1962, and Harris, 1969, summarize some of the relevant literature, which is itself somewhat contradictory.)

The density of the total network in a neighbourhood, male solidarity, and sex segregation all appear to decrease when the occupational heterogeneity of that neighbourhood increases. Occupational heterogeneity is itself a complex construct, and much study needs to be made of the relation between different sorts of neighbourhood structure and the economic system, and of the relation between different sorts of neighbourhood structure and the density of total networks, before one will be able to understand the position of families in loose-knit networks.

Sex segregation appears to decrease when women's economic power and independence increase.[1] However, this too is a complex

---

[1] Somewhat paradoxically, marital instability may be widespread when women are not dependent on men's earnings. In the situation of the 'lower class' in an American city described by W. Miller (1958), the government was evidently acting rather like a tribal matrilineage, in that it was supporting the women and their dependent children, thus making it possible for the women to have a succession of lovers who produced children but did not maintain them. What is cause and what is effect in this situation is difficult to say, but it does seem unlikely that the government is consciously attempting to induce men to be financially irresponsible. It seems more likely that current job uncertainty combined with a cultural background in which job uncertainty, sex segregation, and male solidarity are 'normal', work together to make men both fatalistic about security and easily bored by the prospect of permanence in job or sex. Leaving home is presumably made easier by the knowledge that the 'Welfare' will support the woman, but everything suggests that men would leave anyway even if the government did not step in. Miller does not discuss how this situation might be altered, though he is very critical of the naivety of the poverty programme of the 1960s (Miller, 1969).

problem requiring further study of the position of women in the labour force and the effect of their employment on sex and conjugal segregation, both directly and perhaps also indirectly through affecting and being affected by the network formation.

Thus in attempting to study total network density, density of familial networks, and general sex segregation, I would use these four factors as starting-points: geographical mobility in the neighbourhood and the network; occupational competition in the neighbourhood and the network; occupational diversity in the neighbourhood and the network; and loss of exclusive economic control by men.

(b) *Variables immediately relevant to network density and conjugal segregation*

Thanks to the various studies described above in Part A, especially perhaps that of Christopher Turner, we now have a good idea of the variables involved in network density and conjugal segregation. They are:

occupation
geographical mobility
social mobility
ecological factors
subculture and ethnic group
education
phase of individual and family development
various reference groups based on the above factors

In each case, study should be made of the effect of each variable not only on families' networks but also directly on conjugal segregation. This is a change from my 1957 position, for I was then loath to admit that anything could affect conjugal segregation except through the medium of its effect on the family's network.

Each of these so-called variables is in fact immensely complex, and considerable empirical study would be needed to discover which aspects were most relevant. Many aspects of *occupation* are likely to be relevant, for example: Is the occupation 'entrepreneurial' or 'bureaucratic'? (Daniel Miller and Guy Swanson, 1958.) Does it require or encourage cooperation among colleagues or workmates? Or among members of a family's network or kin network? Does it encourage workmate/colleague solidarity against some outside group? Does it encourage competition among workmates/colleagues? Is it a career, and if so, does it involve geographical mobility? (Watson's 'spiralists' and Merton's 'cosmopolitans'.) Does it promise security? Is it boring or absorbing? Can it be done on behalf of the family, or can it be treated as a legitimate excuse to escape family commitments? Can it be shared, talked about at home, seen by one's wife and children? Does it confer wealth, or high status, and in whose eyes?

Does the wife work? For money, and if so, money for the family or herself? Or does she work for interest, or as a counterbalance to her husband in some way or other?

What effect do the occupational activities of husband and wife have on contact with kin, friends, neighbours, and voluntary associations, and, conversely, what effect do network ties and network density have on pursuit of occupation?

Geographical mobility is likely to affect the conjugal relationship in the main indirectly through reducing network density. One needs some measure of population turnover in the local neighbourhood, so that this factor is closely associated with the next, namely, ecology.

For particular families, one needs to know how often the family has moved in the past, what sort of moves they were, and how often husband and wife moved as individuals before marriage. Even this seemingly 'factual' information is not as straightforward as it looks, for even a short move away from a close-knit network and a familiar neighbourhood may have a much greater effect on a family than would a number of moves on a family brought up to expect geographical mobility.

Information about the moves of relatives and friends is also important. The effect of geographical mobility on the kinship, neighbour, and friend regions of the husband's, the wife's, the joint, and the overall family network needs more precise study.

Geographical mobility should be studied in relation to occupation. Watson's 'spiralists' (Watson, 1957) are bound to develop more loose-knit networks than 'burgesses' of equivalent social status. As described above, Watson's classification has affinities with Merton's cosmopolitan/local distinction (Merton, 1957), and with Daniel Miller's bureaucratic/entrepreneurial distinction.

Social mobility should be conceptually distinguished from geographical mobility and studied in relation to it. Colin Bell (1969) has done much of the groundwork here but not with the full detail of network form, conjugal relationships, and other variables. It would be instructive to examine both types of mobility in relation to occupational type.

Under the general rubric of *'ecology'* I would include not only the physical structure of the neighbourhood but also its social composition: whether it approaches having a 'community' identity; whether it is relatively homogeneous in socio-economic level and/or occupation; whether it is heterogeneous. I would include also information on rates of out-migration and in-migration, as well as calculating which members of a particular family's network live in the neighbourhood, in nearby areas, in the metropolis, and in more distant areas.

Subculture, class, and ethnic group. I acknowledge a general bias in favour of economic and socio-structural rather than cultural interpretations. Explaining norms or behaviour as the result of cultural differences can amount to little more than saying that cultures are different because they are different. Hence the subcultural descriptions of W. Miller (1958) and Gans (1962) and others become fully meaningful to me only when they are related to economic and occupational factors. However, I am now more willing than I was in 1957 to acknowledge that social and economic determinism can be naive too. It assumes that economic or political values take priority, which should be a matter for empirical study, not for *a priori* assumption.[1]

---

[1] This is one of the difficulties I find with Barth's (1966) terse and brilliant exposition of generative models. How does one identify the relevant 'values'? Does one take one's informants' word for it? Or infer the values from their behaviour? Or both?

To do justice to the empirical complexities of conjugal segregation, I think one would have to give both culture and social situation their due. It is when change has occurred that discrepancies between cultural background and current social situation are thrown into relief. For example, working-class families who have moved away from a close-knit network face a new social situation for which they have little or no cultural preparation. They are likely to find themselves both very isolated, because they have not learned how to develop and maintain casual acquaintanceships with strangers, and at the same time very segregated conjugally even when they would both like to develop a joint relationship, because their cultural background did not include any practice in conducting a joint conjugal relationship. Thus Daniel Miller (personal communication) reports a pattern of working-class families with marked conjugal segregation living in near social isolation after moving geographically. I suspect that some of Barbara Harrell-Bond's (1969) segregated couples with loose-knit networks were similarly living in relative isolation after moving geographically. Perhaps Goldthorpe and Lockwood's (1963) 'privatized' workers were also isolated and segregated, though 'home-centredness' bespeaks the eventual development of at least some aspects of a joint relationship.

It would also be instructive to study what happens when families with cultural expectations of joint conjugal relationships and loose-knit networks move into a situation in which their networks become more closely knit. Middle-class academics who move to university towns would be a case in point. Do the closer-knit networks tend to enhance consensus about the pre-existing norms of joint conjugal relationships, or does the content of the norms change in the direction of segregation? Or do the norms remain joint in theory while behaviour becomes segregated in practice? It might also be helpful to study other situations where networks are likely to become close-knit: army posts, company towns, special research establishments, etc. All of these are structurally similar to but culturally different from the usual tribal, rural, or settled working-class situation in which close-knit networks and segregated conjugal relationships are typically found.

Certainly one thing that happens in situations of change is that people are likely to become consciously aware of norms and behaviours that were implicit in the past. This heightened awareness is accompanied by increasing use of families of orientation and neighbourhoods of orientation as reference groups, which is one of the first steps in assessing the meaning of the change and working out some sort of adaptation to it.

Daniel Miller provisionally reports another type of family constellation that he thinks is determined more by the husband's background than by the family's current situation. These are middle-class families that have large and loose-knit networks in which neither the husband nor the wife is much involved emotionally. Conjugal segregation is very variable, and appears to depend not on network formation but on the conjugal behaviour of the husband's father, on which the family tends to model itself. One can but await details, but I would like to have more information about occupation in relation to geographical and social mobility.

Education affects conjugal relationships both directly through explicit and implicit teaching of the ethic appropriate to a joint relationship and indirectly through its effect on networks. Both types of influence have been discussed above.

Phase of individual and family development. Phase changes occur both in network formation and in conjugal segregation. They are hard to study because they are easily confused with irreversible change. It is often asserted, for example, that conjugal relationships are generally becoming more joint (Young and Willmott, 1957; Rosser and Harris, 1965; Gorer, 1970). But, in contrast, some of Turner's unpublished work suggests that changes in norms may be considerable while changes in actual behaviour are slight.

Work on family crises has done something to clarify the nature of phase changes (Caplan, 1969 and 1964; Rhona Rapoport, 1963). I have described above some of what I think are probable changes in friendship and its relation to the husband/wife tie during the phase change from adolescence to the first phases of marriage. Jane Hubert's work should clarify the role of kinship in the phase change from childless couple to family-with-child. Peter Townsend's studies have done much to illuminate the role of kinship for old people. But much work remains tó be done in collating the various types of study and generalizing from them.

Reference groups. All the variables discussed here are likely to be used by families as points of references for some purpose or other. I have described above the frequent use of families of orientation and neighbourhoods of orientation, and reference groups are further discussed in the text in Chapters VI and VII.

(c) *Research design*

How is one to set about studying a field of such complexity? The anthropological method basically consists of messing about with a lot of variables and bits of information in a condition of acute uncertainty, in the hope that eventually one will see relationships one had not thought of before. This is quite a different method from that of starting with a formulated hypothesis that one tests. I think both methods should be used, first the qualitative, then the quantitative, then the qualitative again, until things are more clearly formulated. This is in effect what has happened in the family/network field. The conjugal roles/social networks hypothesis was formulated as the end point of a qualitative anthropological study. It has since been 'tested' as well as used qualitatively. It is now clear that further investigation is needed of families with medium-knit and loose-knit networks.

I think it would be most productive to continue for a time to examine all variables qualitatively in relation to one another in particular cases, in the hope that patterns of relationship between variables will begin to emerge. (This is what Daniel Miller is doing in his current study of internal and external relationships of families in London). Ideally, such qualitative study should lead to testable hypotheses. The task of working out methods of quantifying concepts should be done, if possible, by the same person who worked out the qualitative hypothesis and its related concepts.

The task of devising valid measurements in this field is very difficult. Zelditch (1964) discusses the virtual immeasurability of marital 'power'. Platt (1969) and Harrell-Bond (1969) discuss some of the pitfalls of trying to measure conjugal segregation. Both touch on what to me is a point of great importance, namely, that conjugal segregation is not unidimensional. Further, both norms and behaviour are important, and, I would add, most important of all is the relation between them. Once one has had several interviews with a family one gets a good idea of what their implicit norms of marital and parent/child behaviour are. But I do not think one could devise a questionnaire that would elicit information of similar completeness and subtlety. Further, *behavioural* measures of conjugal segregation, or rather informants' answers to questions about their behaviour, are surely inadequate because the relationship between behaviour and norms is unpredictable, particularly in situations of social change. I would agree with Platt that in some situations the best research strategy may be to rely on impressionistic measures, however open this leaves one to accusations of being 'unscientific'.

As for network density, only Turner (1967) has really attempted to measure it in anything like the form I had intended. The other studies arbitrarily fix the number of people in the network (Udry and Hall, 1965; Aldous and Straus, 1966; and Nelson, 1966).

It may be that there is a real dilemma, that one will be forced to choose between impressionistic methods that can never be replicated, and quantitative methods that do not measure the crucial variables. I do not think we have yet reached the point of such choice. Meanwhile I hope that investigators who work in this field will look for methods to suit the conceptual and empirical problems instead of choosing problems according to whether they can be solved by existing methods.

In addition to qualitative and subsequently quantitative study of the variables discussed above, several other types of study could be designed to contrast types of family and thus to pin down particular variables.

Upper-class families. Here the intriguing thing is that, among aristocrats and upper-class politicians and businessmen, one will probably find close-knit networks, particularly of kin, with ties of property and ties of potential political influence and power. But I suspect that conjugal relationships are joint and sex segregation relatively slight, so that all the factors involved in developing and maintaining shared interests should be studied.

Networks, norms, and *marriage in university towns.* Studies in university towns could clarify whether there is an intrinsic connection between high network density and segregated conjugal norms. As I have suggested above, in university towns conjugal norms are presumably joint but network density is probably high. Networks are composed mainly of friends and colleagues rather than kin. Further, networks are probably 'single-stranded' or 'simplex' rather than 'multiplex' (Gluckman, 1955b). Hence one might devise an intriguing contrast between the multiplex dense networks of settled working-class areas and the simplex dense networks of university towns. Personal knowledge of such towns suggests that behind a façade of 'jointness' there is a tendency for recreation to become segregated, with wives rather resenting the situation and husbands guiltily liking it. Development of the full-blown pattern of high density network and conjugal segregation is inhibited, however, by population turnover in the academic community and by the continued importance of each family's relationships with kin, colleagues, institutions, and friends outside the local community.

Studies of one ethnic group in different situations. Here the aim would be to disentangle ethnic subculture from immediate social and economic situation, and to relate both to conjugal roles and social networks. Studies of Southern Italians in Italy, the United States, Canada, and Britain would be instructive. Similar comparative studies could be made of Irish, Jewish, West Indian, African, Indian, and Pakistani families in their respective home communities and in their various host countries.

Occupational type and geographical mobility. Existing evidence suggests that 'entrepreneurs' maintain segregated parent/child relations (D. Miller and G. Swanson, 1958). But it also seems likely that entrepreneurs are geographically stable and live in closer-knit local networks than 'bureaucrats' of similar socio-economic status. One should therefore compare geographically stable entrepreneurs (Watson's 'burgesses', 1957) with geographically mobile entrepreneurs to see whether the conjugal and parent/child segregation has more to do with network formation or with occupation and its conjugal and characterological requirements.

Similarly it might be fruitful to compare geographically mobile entrepreneurs and bureaucrats and geographically stable entrepreneurs and bureaucrats.

Geographical and social mobility. Contrast studies have been suggested above in the course of discussing geographical and social mobility.

Uprooted families. It would be valuable to carry further the work of Young and Willmott (1957) and Harrell-Bond (1969) on uprooted families to see what happens to them after they have recovered from the initial trauma. Do they ever develop the habits of general sociability and the culture appropriate to a joint conjugal relationship, or is it left to the next generation to develop such skills? Or are the results variable, and if so, what factors affect the variations?

Negative cases. Throughout any study I would keep a careful eye out for negative cases because they are likely to show one which variables are crucial and how they operate.

Fallding (1961) and Rosser and Harris (1965) report cases of families with joint conjugal roles living in close-knit networks, though Turner (1967) found only 8 such families out of 115. I suspect that joint conjugal relationships combined with a close-knit network of *friends* is a common though short-lived state of affairs among young couples, especially in the case of a group situation such as a university. To a lesser extent it may continue in comparatively homogeneous middle-class areas like Woodford (Willmott and Young 1960) and Colin Bell's housing estates (Bell, 1969).

The combination of loose-knit networks with segregated conjugal roles evidently occurs fairly frequently and requires further study. Turner (1967) found only four such families out of 115, but

Harrell-Bond (1969) and D. Miller both report the pattern. The crucial factor may be isolation rather than loose-knittedness.

In summary, the original hypothesis holds for cases of high network density, which is typically found to be associated with a marked degree of conjugal segregation in both norms and behaviour. But the relationship between networks and conjugal roles becomes unpredictably variable once one steps outside the realm of families living in close-knit networks; several ways of studying the relationship more closely have been suggested. Methods of mapping networks have also been described, together with discussion of the respective roles of kinship and friendship in unifying and dividing families.

II. FURTHER DEVELOPMENTS IN THE STUDY OF NETWORKS

The idea of using the concept of network systematically rather than metaphorically was first developed by John Barnes in his analysis of a Norwegian fishing village (Barnes, 1964). The empirical material he described could be partially analysed with the customary concepts of 'field' and 'corporate group', but he developed the network idea to assist in the analysis of what he called the 'third field' (unnamed) of kinship, friendship, and social class in which the concept of corporate group did not seem applicable. He made it clear that in extending the use of the term network, he was building on the metaphorical usage of Radcliffe-Brown (1940) and on Fortes's idea that kinship and affinal ties provide a 'web' uniting unilineal descent groups (Fortes, 1940).

I also found the network idea necessary because the familiar concepts of group and corporate group of tradititional anthropology were not entirely adequate to the field data I was dealing with. The research families did not live in groups. They 'lived' in networks, if one can use the term 'lived in' to describe the situation of being in contact with a set of people and organizations some of whom were in contact with each other and some not. From this point I was led on to consider how differences in types of network might be related to differences in the families' internal organization.

Since 1957 a considerable amount of work has been done on networks, particularly in Britain. I shall first consider the history of the concept since 1957 in the United States and in Britain. Then I shall discuss the proliferation of terms. Finally I shall consider the status of the concept in sociological theory and the uses to which it has been put.

A. HISTORY OF THE CONCEPT OF NETWORK SINCE 1957

1. History of the Concept in the United States

In the United States the network concept is not yet, as of 1970, sociologically fashionable, even though all the requisite conditions for its adoption seem to be present. There is a lively tradition of experimental research with small groups and with forms of communication in them; there are many studies of diffusion and communication flow (partly summarized by E. Katz, Levin, and Hamilton, 1963, and by Mitchell, 1969); there is a great body of literature on graph theory (summarized by Barnes, 1969b and Mitchell, 1969); there are many questionnaire studies of kinship (which I have referred to above), a few studies of friendship (Lazarsfeld and Merton, 1954; Eisenstadt, 1956; Y. Cohen, 1961; Bates and Babchuk, 1961; Babchuck and Bates, 1963; Sutcliffe and Crabbe, 1963; Adams, 1967a), and a few studies in which relations with neighbours and friends are studied as well as those with kin (Axelrod, 1956; W. Bell and Boat, 1956–1957; Wilensky, 1961; Adams, 1967a; and Litwak and Szelenyi, 1969). But so far as I have been able to discover, only F. Katz (1958 and 1966), Cohen and Marriott (1958), Hammer (1963–1964), Jay (1964), and Adams (1967a), have written explicitly about social networks called by that name. Lesser (1961) makes a closely related point, namely, that for diffusion to occur, there must be 'patterned relationships between societies' though he relates this to Barnes' use of the term 'field' and not to the network idea. Of these various authors only Katz (1966) and Jay (1964) seem to be fully aware of the scope of the British studies, and Jay seems to me to add to the existing confusion by reversing the meanings Barnes had assigned to 'field' and 'network'.

This comparative neglect of the network idea is the more odd in view of the fact that as long ago as 1955 Caplow wrote a brief analysis of networks which, although theoretical in content, was applicable to field situations; he used the word 'ambience' instead of 'network'. He described many of the properties of networks (size, density, articulation, elasticity, duration, and homogeneity). He classified networks according to the origin of the contact, that is, place of residence, work, or voluntary association. He contrasted the overlapping of these regions in the networks of people in primitive societies with the separation of these regions of the network among people in complex societies. At the time, none of the British workers, including myself, nor the Americans who were working on kinship and related topics seemed to have realized that Caplow's work was so relevant to their own (Caplow, 1955).

More recently another American sociologist, Charles Kadushin, has written insightfully about networks, or rather about a closely related concept, the 'social circle', evidently without realizing the relevance of the work of the British social anthropologists to his own. Nor have British social anthropologists known about his work, probably because he uses the term 'social circle' instead of network (Kadushin, 1966 and 1968). His work is of special importance in the study of 'total networks', that is, networks that are *not* defined by selection of a particular person or group as the focal point or 'ego'. Kadushin deals with clusterings of interaction based on and contributing to emerging shared interests concerning cultural goals, power, and influence. Rather more than the British investigators, he stresses that networks ('social circles') exist because their members share or potentially share common interests. He starts from the shared interests and then moves on to locate the people involved, whereas most British workers start with the people, either with certain people already in relation with one another on a fairly permanent basis, or with the people involved in a particular social situation.

It seems inevitable that the kinship and friendship studies in the

United States and the conceptual work of Katz, Kadushin, and Adams will lead to more studies of the general patterning of informal and formal relationships and to more conceptualization of the network idea.

Further, although American anthoropologists have not been quick to adopt the network idea, at least one recent study makes full use of it in analysing Navajo ceremonial cooperation.

'The notion of "group", defined in terms of one or more of these attributes, and employed as an analytical tool, does not adequately characterise the ways in which Navajo organise activities.

'. . . Navajo social organisation, beyond the domestic group level, has the properties of a network rather than a system of large corporate groups' (Lamphere, 1970, p. 40).

2. *History of the Network Concept among British Social Anthropologists*

When we first used the idea of network I do not think that either John Barnes (1954) or I realized it would become fashionable in British social anthropology. The fact that our work has been recognized and used by other British anthropologists was at least initially the result of Max Gluckman's influence, for no one who worked in anthropology at Manchester after 1955 can have been unaware of networks. In fact it was while he was a Simon Fellow at Manchester that Barnes originally worked out the idea of networks, and Max Gluckman's seminar was very helpful to me. As Clyde Mitchell puts it in the dedication of his recent book (1969), Max Gluckman is the 'point source of our network'. But it has been Mitchell himself who mobilized use of the network idea in a variety of field situations, particularly in Africa while he was at the University College of Rhodesia and Nyasaland.

In 1961 Epstein reworked some of his field material on an African urban situation, which led him to make a useful distinction between the close-knit 'effective' region of an urban individual's network and the looser-knit 'extended' region; according to his analysis, the norms and values appropriate to urban life are clarified, redefined, and reaffirmed through gossip by the people in the 'effective' region of networks of the urban elite, and the norms then percolate through to the people in the extended part of the network, thus eventually reaching the non-elite (Epstein, 1961 and 1969). Meanwhile Philip Mayer and his colleague Pauw were finding the idea of network useful in analysing the different responses of 'Red' and 'School' Xhosa to urban experience (P. Mayer, 1961, 1962, and 1964; Pauw, 1963). At about the same time Southall used the idea of networks to order some of his field data on a suburb of Kampala (Southall, 1961).

Then came Adrian Mayer's studies of electioneering in India, and his development of the idea of the 'action-set'—a temporary group recruited through various channels to serve some short-term end (A. Mayer, 1962, 1963, and 1966). At about the same time Srinivas and Béteille wrote a brief article on the usefulness of the network concept in analysing complex societies that are undergoing rapid change, such as India, where the boundaries of traditional groups are changing and networks link individuals and groups in the village to external organizations and individuals. Srinivas and Béteille make the point that networks are becoming more loose-knit in India (Srinivas and Béteille, 1964). They also observe that networks exist in *all* societies. Barnes also stresses this point, which is an intrinsic part of his definition of network; he rightly criticizes me (in 1969a) for a careless comment I made in a popular article (Bott, 1964, p. 103) in which I wrote as if networks were an exclusive property of urbanized societies. Like Barnes and Srinivas, I also maintain in my more alert moments that networks of social relationship exist in all societies.

Meanwhile Ronald Frankenberg was using the idea of network formation, along with concepts of class, status, role, and 'social redundancy', to analyse the process of urbanization (Frankenberg, 1966).

In 1964 Boissevain published a brief analysis of factions and political parties in a Maltese village; he followed this by a general conceptual contribution in 1968 which treats personal networks as the general social matrix out of which various forms of quasi-group and eventually group and corporate group may be differentiated in certain circumstances. I find his formulation generally very useful, though Lucy Mair subjected it to a short sharp criticism (Mair, 1969).

In 1966 Wolf wrote an article that used the idea of network though not the word. He talks about 'supplementary interpersonal sets' in several types of complex society and discusses their importance in linking corporate groups and institutional structures. He also discusses differences that occur in the form of friendship when corporate kin groups are present and when they are not. Philpott (1968) writes about the networks of Montserratian immigrants to Britain and relates the density and exclusiveness of their networks to their fulfilment of financial and social obligations to the relatives they have left behind. Arnold (1969) gives an overall summary of the use of the network concept in the study of complex societies.

Under the aegis of Clyde Mitchell, a group of anthropologists working in Zambia and Rhodesia, most of them in towns, began to use the idea of networks to help order their complex material (see Mitchell, 1966). Several of these studies are included in *Social Networks in Urban Situations* (1969) which Mitchell edited and for which he wrote a general theoretical paper linking empirically based network studies with graph theory. Wheeldon (1969) analyses a challenge to the leadership of a voluntary association in a Eurafrican community—very reminiscent of politics in academic departments and learned societies. Kapferer (1969) analyses an argument between workers on the job and shows how each worker mobilized support. Boswell (1969) describes the action-sets that were developed to deal with three funerals in Lusaka. Harries-Jones (1969) shows how links of common rural origin, kinship, and proximity were used to establish a local branch of a political party in a Copperbelt town and how the various political leaders involved mobilized action-sets for particular purposes.

B. THE PROLIFERATION OF NETWORK TERMS AND DEFINITIONS

The concept of network has thus been used in several types of empirical study, and the definitions used and emphases given vary considerably from one study to another. When one contemplates the language—total network, personal network, ego-centric network, set, action-set, reticulum, quasi-group, field, star, zone, personal community, ambience, social circle, faction, party, clique, grouping, group, and corporate group—one feels oneself teetering on the brink of terminological if not conceptual disaster. I will first try to summarize the main current usages. In the next section I consider the field situations in which the terms have been developed, in order to discover the general preoccupations, the genotypes, as it were, that I think underly the phenotypical disorder.

First, *network* is sometimes still used metaphorically as Radcliffe-Brown used it (1940). In a recent article Yehudi Cohen uses it in a very loose sense to mean virtually any kind of social entity (Cohen, 1969). I now find this usage very confusing.

Second, network is used in the sense of Barnes's *total network* (Barnes, 1969a, p. 56) though he does not define it other than by the O.E.D. definition of 'an interconnected chain or system of immaterial things'. He then continues:

'. . . whatever it is, it is a first-order abstraction from reality, and it contains as much as possible of the information about the whole of the social life of the community to which it corresponds. I call it the total network. . . .' (Barnes, 1969a, p. 56).

'By "partial network" I mean any extract of the total network based on some criterion applicable throughout the whole network' (Barnes, 1969a, p. 57).

Barnes then gives examples: the cognatic web of kinship, networks of marriage, political networks, religious networks. He continues:

'. . . It seems to me preferable to use the term "network" only when some kind of social field is intended, for there has been much confusion about ego-centric and socio-centric extracts from the total network. In my usage we can never speak of an ego-centric network, and I shall suggest special terms for ego-

319

centric extracts or properties of the network' (1969a, p. 57).

I also use the term network in this overall sense and so do Adrian Mayer (1962 and 1966), Srinivas and Béteille (1964), and Frankenberg (1966).[1]

In the *third usage* a network is defined as all or some of the social units (individuals and groups) with whom a particular individual or group is in contact. Mitchell (1969) calls this a 'personal' or 'egocentric' network. I also use the term network in this sense as well as in the more general 'total network' sense, and so do Epstein (1961 and 1969), Boissevain (1968), Wheeldon (1969), Harries-Jones (1969), Adams (1967a), Katz (1966)—virtually everyone, in fact, except Barnes, who thinks it important to distinguish this type of extract from the total network by a special term, *star* (Barnes, 1969a, pp. 58-60). He also used the term *zone* to mean the set of all relationships between two persons, each of whom is either ego (the core person whose network it is) or one of ego's contacts. In other words, ego's 'star' consists of the people ego knows, and ego's 'zone' is the same set of people *plus* their interrelationships. Barnes distinguishes primary (people ego knows directly) and secondary (people ego knows through one intermediary step) stars and zones, tertiary stars and zones, etc. Most writers do not distinguish carefully between star and zone even conceptually let alone terminologically. I agree with Barnes that it is important to be clear whether one means total network, star, or zone, but I am afraid it is too late to introduce new terms. Like Mitchell (1969), I think the term network has become too well entrenched in the ego-centric sense to be abandoned, and this fact, combined with the different meaning of the word 'star' in common speech as well as in sociometry, makes it unlikely that Barnes's terms will be readily adopted. My own solution is to use the word 'network' in all three senses (total network, star, and zone), but

[1] In a recent personal letter Barnes says that because of our interest in different problems, he and I use the term 'total network' differently. He writes: 'You contrast the ego-centred network with the total network, so that "total" comes to refer to the social area that is under consideration. . . . I contrast the "total network" with a "partial network" so that "total" refers to the fact that relations of all kinds—kinship, work, leisure, politics, everything—are being considered and not merely relations of one kind.'

to use adjectives to distinguish them where necessary, for example, 'total network', and 'personal network'. But I have not found a good adjective to distinguish 'zone' from 'star'.

The terminological proliferation does not stop here, for several authors have used other terms instead of 'personal network'. Caplow called it 'ambience' (Caplow, 1955). Jules Henry calls it 'the personal community' (Henry, 1958). Jay (1964) calls it 'field'.[1] Adrian Mayer, if I understand him rightly, calls a personal network a 'set' (Mayer, 1966). Kapferer calls it 'reticulum' (Kapferer, 1969). But 'network' is still the most commonly used term.

As I note above, Barnes criticizes my use of the term 'connectedness' and says the correct work to use according to graph theory is 'density', which I have now adopted. (My only reservation is that the term 'density' conveys to me an idea of how many people are in a given space but does not suggest how many relationships exist among them. I hope this is a private meaning not shared by those others who, like me, are not graph theorists.) Barnes describes methods of measuring density and interactional clustering by expressing the *actual* relationships between the people in a selected extract of a network as a percentage of the *possible* relationships (Barnes, 1969b). This method should prove extremely useful if generally applied, though the fieldwork necessary to do it even for a simple network is unfortunately very great.

Adrian Mayer (1966) introduced the term *action-set* (suggested to him by P. H. Gulliver) meaning a temporary set of people recruited through various channels to serve some short-term goal. I think everyone welcomes this idea and the label for it. Although Mayer does not labour the point, this sort of group has often been called a 'grouping' in the past, for example in describing temporary gatherings of people at funerals or for housebuilding or planting, etc. Mayer's use of the term 'action-set' frees the term 'grouping' from some of its ambiguity so that it can now be reserved for collectivities on the borderline between groups and

---

[1] Jay appears to reserve the term 'network' for a particular type of social activity and the relationships that go with it (Jay, 1964). Barnes and most other writers use the term 'field' in this sense and I think they have anthropological tradition on their side.

categories (such as the 'extended family' in British society; see Rosser and Harris, 1965).

But when Mayer goes on to discuss 'sets' in general and 'quasi-groups' I find his argument somewhat unclear, for he evidently thinks that quasi-groups arise in situations where the same or similar action-sets are mobilized on successive occasions. He uses the term 'core' for the more constant members closest to ego. A core may crystallize into a group or, at the least, into a 'clique' (A. Mayer, 1966). I think Mayer is perhaps restricting his terms too closely to his Indian election experience, though I find the emphasis on processes of development a most valuable ideal.

I regard Boissevain's arrangement of labels as perhaps of more general applicability (Boissevain, 1968). He uses 'network' (meaning personal network, though) as the general interactional matrix from which what he calls 'quasi-groups' and groups may be differentiated out.[1] 'Quasi-group' he thinks of as a generic term for any sort of coalition recruited out a network; it may be an action-set, a faction, a clique, and probably the sort of dense clustering described by Barnes, though Boissevain does not specifically mention this intensified area of interactional density. If a quasi-group develops long-lasting consciousness of kind, routinized methods of recruitment, and common norms, it has become a group.

In the present state of affairs I doubt if any set of definitions will be universally adopted, however clarifying and precise. 'Network' is suffering the fate of some other basic sociological concepts such as 'status' and 'role'. It is being used for so many purposes that it will take some time before we get a sense of what it is really most useful for. In the meantime I suggest we put up with the muddle and keep the possibility of eventual clarification in mind. At the same time efforts like those of Mitchell (1969) and Barnes (1969a and 1969b) to link empirically based network theory

---

[1] Boissevain notes that his use of 'quasi-group' is different from Adrian Mayer's (1966) [successive action-sets] and from Pospisil's (1964, pp. 34–37) [temporary unions on behalf of a common ego, that is, action-sets], and also different from Ginsberg's (1934, p. 40) usage of 'quasi-group' to mean 'social category'.

with graph theory and sociometry can alert us to things we might otherwise miss. Mitchell's discussion of the morphological properties of networks (anchorage, reachability, density, and range) and their interactional properties (content, directedness, durability, intensity, and frequency of interaction) is particularly important. It seems likely that further empirical work will make it imperative for us to be more precise about the general forms that networks assume. The 'chain' sort of structure, for example, has very different effects from the sort of 'ego-centric network' (Barnes's 'star') in which there is a focal ego who is by definition in contact with everyone else in the network. There is of course some danger of 'network-ology'—getting lost in classificatory exercises for the fun of it, but so long as one is firmly rooted in empirical field studies one is unlikely to indulge in classificatory games.

C. THE STATUS OF THE NETWORK CONCEPT IN SOCIOLOGICAL THEORY

To understand the status of the network concept it helps to ask when and why the idea was adopted. I think it was adopted because it seemed to offer a way out of the stalemate that social anthropology appeared to have got into by the late 1950s. The structural/functional vein had been thoroughly mined by the elegant studies of Evans-Pritchard, Fortes, Gluckman, and their numerous colleagues and students. Discontent was in the air. What about social change? What about complex societies? What about variability, choice, and the choosing individual? Why stick to equilibrium models? Firth (1954), Eisenstadt (1961), and others discuss many of these problems.

Gluckman's 'extended case study' method (Gluckman, 1961), van Velsen's 'situational analysis' (van Velsen, 1967), and Reader's 'sociological history' (Reader, 1964) suggest new approaches and methods. Barth (1966) and Boissevain (1968) indicate a more radical departure from traditional structural/functionalism; their method is based on the concept of the interacting individual, who, in the course of attempting to maximize his 'values', may generate new social forms. But these are not the only trends of development. Lévi-Strauss's work has attracted the attention of several British social anthropologists, most notably Edmund Leach. The approach of ethology has also won several adherents, and ethologists as well as 'ethological' anthropologists sometimes report their more general findings in anthropological journals. (See, for example: Tiger and Fox, 1966; Freeman, 1966; Reynolds, 1966 and 1968; Fox, 1967; Chance, 1967; and Tiger, 1969).

Examination of the way in which the concept of networks has been used suggests, at least to me, that it is not in itself a new approach. It can be and has been used in conjunction with any of the basic conceptual orientations of social anthropology. I think it has been used in three main ways: first, as a method of studying social linkages within the basic unit of study; second, in the study of system-environment relations; and third, in studies of social process and the generating of social forms.

1. Use of the Concept of Network in the Study of Linkages within Local Communities or Social Categories

In his original paper (1954) Barnes uses the network idea to characterize social relations in the 'third field' of friendship, kinship, and social class. He now (1969a) asserts, rightly, I think, that networks cut across *all* social fields, including those in which corporate groups operate.

Frankenberg's (1966) comparative study of rural and urban communities uses the concept of networks, among others, to analyse the process of urbanization.

M. G. Smith (1965) uses a method of analysing 'cliques' of the elite in Grenada as part of his complex and meticulous analysis of the basis of actual and imputed stratification in Grenada.

Kadushin's method of analysing 'social circles' also has a particular universe as the focus of interest, with the 'social circles' arising or being analysed within that universe. But the universe of interest is a social category not a local community. In his first paper, 'The Friends and Supporters of Psychotherapy' (1966), he is concerned to discover a set of people who share interests, have indirect chains of interaction, and no leadership or formal structure. The people were selected from the category of persons who applied to psycho-analytic clinics in New York. Two social circles appeared to be important: the psychiatrically sophisticated and the 'culturally' sophisticated (theatre-goers and so forth), with the 'Friends and Supporters of Psychotherapy' being particularly likely to be found where the two circles overlapped.

His second article (1968) is reflective and conceptual rather than empirical. He discusses power and some general notions about social circles and then describes methods of using the social-circle idea and method to study power and influence. He describes three basic techniques, all based on what he calls an 'open-ended sociometric' and all involving a 'snowball' technique. In the 'reputational' method, selected members of an elite are given a list of elite, and asked to rank them and to add others, who are in turn asked to do the ranking. This method is very similar to that used by M. G. Smith (1965). In the 'decisional' technique the same basic procedure is followed, but informants are asked to say who was involved in a particular decision or decisions. In the 'positional' method informants are asked whom on the list they know.

I have described certain aspects of Kadushin's method in some detail because, as he suggests, I think it useful in studying both clusterings in total networks and the economic and governing elites of comparatively small societies. Kadushin seems unaware of, however, or at least does not mention, the immense practical difficulty involved in carrying out this sort of analysis in a real society where it may be impossible to gain the confidence of opposed groups, let alone to gain access to the elite at all. Perhaps M. G. Smith knows the ins and outs of this sort of problem particularly well. Barnes (1963) also discusses some of the practical difficulties and implications.

In all these types of study the focus of interest is on the ways in which social networks link and divide individuals and groups within the local group or social category that is the basic unit of study, or at least the unit within which the study takes place. Because of their central interest in the social category or in the local community as a whole, authors who study this sort of problem use the term network (or 'social circle' in Kadushin's case) in the 'total network' sense.

2. Use of the Concept of Network in Studies of System-Environment Relations

Typically anthropologists who approach problems from this point of view use the idea of network both in the 'total network' sense *and* in the 'personal network' sense. The 'system' they identify as their focal interest varies. Sometimes it is a local group, sometimes a particular type of group within a society, such as families in the case of my own work, and sometimes it is individuals, not in their own right, but as representatives of a social category.

(a) *Studies using the concept of network to establish links between one group or sets of groups and the individuals in them to groups and individuals defined as external to the unit under study*

Cohen and Marriott (1958), Srinivas and Béteille (1964), and Wolf (1966) all use the idea of network to cope with this sort of problem. Further, I would place my own work in this category, even though the group I was concerned with was the family, not a village or sub-caste, and I was more concerned than any of the above authors with the analysis of the effect of the form of the external network on role expectations within the group under study.

In this connection it is worth noting that although many authors regard the individual as the unit of network formation, several authors specifically note that the groups may be the units of the network (Barnes, 1954; Jay, 1964; Poggie and Miller, 1969; Boissevain, 1968). Mitchell (1969, pp. 14-15) states that a group itself is an abstraction, and that 'A link connecting one group to another can only mean that the groups as wholes are in some sort of relationship to each other'. I would agree, but I have also found it necessary to study the way groups are connected to external groups and individuals through the ties of the individuals who compose them. This is a thread running through much of the argument of *Family and Social Network*: the family as a whole is not contained within any larger group, nor does it really 'belong' to anything, and rarely enters into relationships with other groups as a whole. Nevertheless the family is not isolated in the sense of having no external relationships at all. It is linked to other individuals and groups, but through its component individuals, and also through the relationships maintained by husband and wife as a pair. Similarly, in studying the relationship of a mental hospital to its environment, I found that although the hospital conducted some relationships as a corporate group, many of its links to its environment consisted of ties through individuals acting as individuals not primarily as representatives of the hospital as a corporate group.

(b) *Studies involving redefinition of group and environment*

It seems to me that the migration studies of Philip Mayer (1961, 1962, and 1964), Pauw (1963), Philpott (1968), and to some extent Harries-Jones (1969), all deal with special cases of the linking of two different types of group and social situation, rural 'home' and 'city', and they use the concept of network to elucidate different responses to the possibilities the situation presents. In other words, I think these migration studies are a special case of the more general type of problem described above, namely, of the way groups are linked to other groups defined as 'external' to the system under study. But in these migration studies the definition of what is group and what is environment shifts; the home base and the town (or foreign country) to which people migrate are part of one social system, at least for a time. For analytical purposes either the urban area, or the rural area, or the two together may be treated as the unit of study.

(c) *Diffusion studies*

As Lesser (1961) observes, all diffusion requires 'patterned relationships' between societies, between groups, or between innovators and recipients. But it is not often that studies are made of the actual networks of existing and developing relationships in the relevant field of activity. A classic study by Coleman, Katz,

327

and Mendel (1957) showed that the rate of adoption of a new drug by physicians was associated with the networks of personal and professional relations among the physicians. Katz, Levin, and Hamilton (1963) summarize some of the very considerable literature on diffusion. They emphasize 'communication flow', and stress that interpersonal channels of communication should be viewed as elements of the social structure, but they do not make very explicit use of the concept of networks.

(d) *Studies of the individual in his social environment*

Most of the American studies of 'primary groups' or 'primary group behaviour' are studies of the relationships of *individuals* to their environment of friends, neighbours, and relatives. The earlier studies tended to examine all types of informal relationship (Axelrod, 1956; Bell and Boat, 1956–1957). Then came a large number of kinship studies (cited above). More recently there have been more systematic attempts to relate different types of informal social participation to each other and sometimes to work and career patterns Wilensky, 1961; Adams, 1967a; Litwak and Szelenyi, 1969). In these studies the emphasis is not usually psychological, that is, the aim is not to understand the individual as such. Sometimes it is the nature of the informal interaction that is the focus of interest–friendship or kinship as such. In many studies the interest is in social class, and the individual and his informal primary group behaviour are studied as representative of 'blue-collar' or middle-class society.

3. *Use of the Concept of Network in Studies of Social Process and the Generating of New Social Forms*

These studies use the concept of network as part of an examination of the social processes that keep groups going in their current state or lead to the emergence of new social forms and the decay of old ones, through the manoeuvrings of interacting individuals. Some studies of this sort are done by 'conventional' social anthropologists who, through use of the extended case study method (see especially Gluckman, 1961, and van Velsen, 1967) and what

Reader (1964) calls 'sociological history', find themselves involved in studying social process. Other studies such as those of Boissevain (1964 and 1968) are more frankly conceived as departures from the structural/functional approach. Such students adopt the idea of the interacting individuals as the basic unit of study and of society. In the course of pursuing some goal or value, the interacting individuals generate new social forms (compare Barth, 1966).

(a) *Studies of the recruitment of action-sets*

Adrian Mayer describes the workings of electioneering action-sets in India (A. Mayer, 1962, 1963, 1966). Boswell describes the mobilization of people to conduct three funerals (Boswell, 1969). (Barnes 1954) briefly describes the recruitment of fishing crews, which, like other action-sets, were recruited through various channels but with special attention to technical competence; while the fishing was actually going on the 'action-set' functioned as a corporate group.

(b) *Studies of political manoeuvring within groups*

Wheeldon's (1969) study of a Eurafrican voluntary association, Kapferer's (1969) study of an argument on a shop-floor, and some of Frankenberg's (1957) discussion of the wrangles over recreation in Glynceiriog are examples. Although the manoeuvring within the group is the immediate forcus of interest, all the studies bring certain aspects of the environment into the analysis. Authors dealing with this sort of problem tend to define network in the ego-centric sense because they are dealing with the way individuals mobilize support and manage conflict.

(c) *Studies of the generating of quasi-groups and groups out of social networks*

Adrian Mayer's idea of action-sets developing into something more organized is an example of this sort of approach (A. Mayer, 1966). So are Boissevain's studies (1964 and 1968) of action-sets developing into factions and cliques and then into corporate groups.

In Conclusion

There is nothing revolutionary about the idea of social networks. It is the sort of concept that can be used in many conceptual frames of reference. It has been used in conjunction with traditional structural/functional theory, in the analysis of societies and groups as open systems, and in conjunction with situational analysis, sociological history, and the construction of 'generative models'. What the concept can do is to provide a slight enlargement of the conceptual repertoire. Perhaps we can now see things we might not have looked for before 1954.

REFERENCES
TO SECOND EDITION

ADAMS, B. N. (1967a) 'Interaction Theory and the Social Network.' *Sociometry*, Vol. 30, pp. 64–78.

ADAMS, B. N. (1967b) 'Occupational Position, Mobility and the Kin of Orientation.' *Amer. sociol. Rev.*, Vol. 32, pp. 364–77.

ALDOUS, J. (1962) 'Urbanization, The Extended Family, and Kinship Ties in West Africa.' *Soc. Forces*, Vol. 41, pp. 6–12.

ALDOUS, J. (1967) 'Intergenerational Visiting Patterns: Variation in Boundary Maintenance as an Explanation.' *Fam. Process*, Vol. 6, pp. 235–48.

ALDOUS, J., and STRAUS, M. A. (1966) 'Social Networks and Conjugal Roles: A Test of Bott's Hypothesis.' *Soc. Forces*, Vol. 44, pp. 576–80.

ANDERSON, N. (Ed.) (1956) *Studies of the Family*. Tübingen: J. C. B. Mohr (Paul Siebeck).

ARENSBERG, C. (1937) *The Irish Countryman*. London: Macmillan.

ARNOLD, K. (1969) 'Network Analysis in Complex Societies.' Unpublished paper.

ATTNEAVE, C. L. (1969) 'Therapy in Tribal Settings and Urban Network Intervention.' *Fam. Process*, Vol. 8, pp. 192–210.

AXELROD, M. (1956) 'Urban Structure and Social Participation.' *Amer. sociol. Rev.*, Vol. 21, pp. 13–18.

BABCHUK, N., and BATES, A. P. (1963) 'The Primary Relations of Middle Class Couples: A Study in Male Dominance.' *Amer. sociol. Rev.* Vol. 28, pp. 377–84.

BACK, K. W. (1965) 'A Social Psychologist Looks at Kinship Structure.' In Shanas, E., and Streib, G. F. (Eds.) (1965) *Social Structure and the Family: Generational Relations*. New Jersey: Prentice-Hall, pp. 326–40.

BARNES, J. A. (1954) 'Class and Committees in a Norwegian Island Parish.' *Hum. Relat.*, Vol. 7, pp. 39–58.

BARNES, J. A. (1963) 'Some Ethical Problems in Modern Fieldwork.' *Brit. J. Sociol.*, Vol. 14, pp. 118–34.

BARNES, J. A. (1969a) 'Networks and Political Process.' In Mitchell, C. (Ed.) (1969) *Social Networks in Urban Situations*. Manchester: Manchester Univ. Press, pp. 51–76.

BARNES, J. A. (1969b) 'Graph Theory and Social Network: A Technical Comment on Connectedness and Connectivity.' *Sociology*, Vol. 3, pp. 215-32.

BARTH, F. (1966) *Models of Social Organization*. Occasional Paper No. 23, Royal Anthropological Institute, London.

BATES, A. P., and BABCHUK, N. (1961) 'The Primary Group: A Reappraisal.' *Sociol. Quart.*, Vol. 2, pp. 181-91.

BELL, C. (1968) 'Mobility and the Middle Class Extended Family.' *Sociology*, Vol. 2, pp. 173-84.

BELL, C. (1969) *Middle Class Families*. London: Routledge and Kegan Paul.

BELL, N. W., and VOGEL, E. F. (Eds.) (1960) *A Modern Introduction to the Family*. Glencoe, Illinois: The Free Press.

BELL, W., and BOAT, M. D. (1956-57) 'Urban Neighbourhoods and Informal Social Relations.' *Amer. J. Sociol.*, Vol. 62, pp. 391-98.

BERGER, B. M. (1960) *Working-Class Suburb*. Berkeley: Univ. of California Press.

BIRLEY, J. L. T. (1969) Review of *Family and Social Network* in *Brit. J. Psychiat.*, Vol. 115, No. 520, p. 367.

BLOOD, R. O. (1969) 'Kinship Interaction and Marital Solidarity.' *Merrill-Palmer Quarterly*, Vol. 15, No. 2, pp. 171-84.

BLOOD, R. O., and WOLFE, D. M. (1965) *Husbands and Wives*. New York: The Free Press.

BLUM, A. F. (1964) 'Social Structure, Social Class, and Participation in Primary Relationships.' In Shostak, A. B., and Gomberg, W. (Eds.) (1964) *Blue Collar World*. New Jersey: Prentice-Hall, pp. 195-207.

BOISSEVAIN, J. (1964) 'Factions, Parties, and Politics in a Maltese Village.' *Amer. Anthrop.*, Vol. 66, pp. 1275-87.

BOISSEVAIN, J. (1968) 'The Place of Non-Groups in The Social Sciences.' *Man*, Vol. 3, pp. 542-56.

BOSWELL, D. M. (1969) 'Personal Crisis and the Mobilization of the Social Network.' In Mitchell, C. (Ed.) (1969) *Social Networks in Urban Situations*. Manchester: Manchester Univ. Press, pp. 245-96.

BOTT, E. (1964) 'Family, Kinship, and Marriage.' In Douglas, M. et al. (Eds.) (1964) *Man in Society: Patterns of Human Organization*. London: Macdonald, pp. 82-103.

Brit. J. med. Psychol. (1958) Abstract of Family and Social Network, Vol. 31, Part 2, p. 138.

BROWN, G. W., and RUTTER, M. (1966) 'The Measurement of Family Activities and Relationships.' *Hum. Relat.*, Vol. 19, pp. 241-63.

CAPLAN, G. (1960) 'Patterns of Parental Response to the Crisis of Premature Birth: A Preliminary Approach to Modifying Mental Health Outcome.' *Psychiatry*, Vol. 23, pp. 365-74.

CAPLAN, G. (1964) *Principles of Preventive Psychiatry*. New York: Basic Books; London: Tavistock Publications.

CAPLOW, T. (1955) 'The Definition and Measurement of Ambiences.' *Soc. Forces*, Vol. 34, pp. 28–33.

CHAMBERS, R. (1958) Review of *Family and Social Network* in *Brit. J. Sociol.*, Vol. 9, pp. 186–7.

CHANCE, M. R. A. (1967) 'Attention Structure as the Basis of Primate Rank Orders.' *Man*, Vol. 2, No. 4, pp. 503–18.

COHEN, A. K., and HODGES, H. M. (1963) 'Characteristics of the Lower-Blue-Collar-Class.' *Soc. Problems*, Vol. 10, pp. 303–34.

COHEN, Y. A. (1961) 'Patterns of Friendship.' In Cohen, Y. A. (Ed.) (1961) *Social Structure and Personality: A Casebook*. New York: Holt, Rinehart and Winston, pp. 351–86.

COHEN, Y. A. (1969) 'Social Boundary Systems.' *Current Anthrop.*, Vol. 10, pp. 103–26.

COHN, B. S., and MARRIOTT, MCK. (1958) 'Networks and Centres in the Integration of Indian Civilisation.' *J. soc. Research* (Bihar), Vol. 1, pp. 1–9.

COLEMAN, J., KATZ, E., and MENDEL, H. (1957) 'The Diffusion of an Innovation among Physicians.' *Sociometry*, Vol. 20, pp. 253–70.

COSER, R. L. (Ed.) (1964) *The Family: Its Structure and Function*. New York: St. Martin's Press.

CROZIER, D. (1965a) 'Kinship and Occupational Succession.' *Sociol. Rev.* Vol. 13, pp. 15–43.

CROZIER, D. (1965b) 'History and Anthropology.' *Inter. soc. sci. J.*, Vol. 17, pp. 561–70.

CUMMING, E., and SCHNEIDER, D. M. (1961) 'Sibling Solidarity: A Property of American Kinship.' *Amer. Anthrop.*, Vol. 63, pp. 498–507.

DAVISON, E. H. (1958) Review of *Family and Social Network* in *Soc. Work.*, Vol. 15, p. 472.

DE HOYOS, A., and DE HOYOS, G. (1966) 'The Amigo System and Alienation of the Wife in the Mexican Conjugal Family.' In Farber, B. (1966) *Kinship and Family Organization*. New York: Wiley, pp. 102–15.

DENNIS, N., HENRIQUES, F. M., and SLAUGHTER, C. (1956) *Coal is our Life*. London: Eyre and Spottiswoode. Second edition (1969) London: Tavistock Publications.

EISENSTADT, S. N. (1956) 'Ritualized Personal Relations.' *Man*, Vol. 56, No. 96, pp. 90–5.

EISENSTADT, S. N. (1961) 'Anthropological Studies of Complex Societies.' *Current Anthrop.*, Vol. 2, pp. 201–21.

EPSTEIN, A. L. (1961) 'The Network and Urban Social Organization.' *Rhodes-Livingstone Journal*, Vol. 29, pp. 29–62. Reprinted in Mitchell, C. (Ed.) (1969) *Social Networks in Urban Situations*. Manchester: Manchester Univ. Press, pp. 77–116.

EPSTEIN, A. L. (1969) 'Gossip, Norms and Social Network.' In Mitchell, C. (Ed.) (1969) *Social Networks in Urban Situations*. Manchester: Manchester Univ. Press, pp. 117–27.

FALLDING, H. (1961) 'The Family and the Idea of a Cardinal Role.' *Hum. Relat.*, Vol. 14, pp. 329–50.

FARBER, B. (1966) *Kinship and Family Organization*. New York: Wiley.

FIRTH, R. (1954) 'Social Organization and Social Change.' *J. roy. anthrop. Inst.*, Vol. 84, pp. 1–20.

FIRTH, R. (Ed.) (1956) *Two Studies of Kinship in London*. London: Univ. of London, Athlone Press.

FIRTH, R. (1961) 'Family and Kin Ties in Britain and their Social Implications.' *Brit. J. Sociol.*, Vol. 12, pp. 305–09.

FIRTH, R., HUBERT, J., and FORGE, A. (1969) *Families and Their Relatives. Kinship in a Middle Class Sector of London: An Anthropological Study*. London: Routledge and Kegan Paul.

FOOTE, N. (1961) 'New Roles for Men and Women.' *Marriage Fam. Liv.*, Vol. 23, pp. 325–9.

FORTES, M. (1949) *The Web of Kinship among the Tallensi*. London: Oxford University Press.

FOX, R. (1967) 'In the Beginning: Aspects of Homonid Behavioural Evolution.' *Man*, Vol. 2, pp. 415–33.

FRANKENBERG, R. (1957) *Village on the Border*. London: Cohen and West.

FRANKENBERG, R. (1966) *Communities in Britain*. Harmondsworth: Penguin Books.

FREEMAN, D. (1966) 'Social Anthropology and the Scientific Study of Human Behaviour.' *Man*, Vol., 1, pp. 330–42.

FURSTENBERG, F. F. (1966) 'Industrialization and the American Family: A Look Backward.' *Amer. sociol. Rev.*, Vol. 31, pp. 326–37.

GANS, H. J. (1962) *The Urban Villagers*. New York: The Free Press of Glencoe.

GANS, H. J. (1967) *The Levittowners*. London; Allen Lane, The Penguin Press.

GINSBERG, M. (1934) *Sociology*. London: Thornton Butterworth.

GLUCKMAN, M. (1955a) *Custom and Conflict in Africa*. Oxford: Basil Blackwell.

GLUCKMAN, M. (1955b) *The Judicial Process Among the Barotse of Northern Rhodesia*. Manchester: Manchester Univ. Press.

GLUCKMAN, M. (1961) 'Ethnographic Data in British Social Anthropology.' *Sociol. Rev.*, Vol. 9, pp. 5–17.

GLUCKMAN, M., and DEVONS, E. (Eds.) (1964) *Closed Systems and Open Minds.* Edinburgh: Oliver & Boyd.

GOLD, M., and SLATER, C. (1958) 'Office, Factory, Store—and Family: A Study of Intergration Setting.' *Amer. sociol. Rev.*, Vol. 23, pp. 64–74.

GOLDTHORPE, J. H., and LOCKWOOD, D. (1963) 'Affluence and the British Class Structure.' *Sociol. Rev.*, Vol. 11, pp. 133–63.

GOODE, W. J. (1960) 'Norm Commitment and Conformity to Role-Status Obligations.' *Amer. J. Sociol.*, pp. 246–58.

GOODE, W. J. (1964) *The Family.* New Jersey: Prentice-Hall.

GORER, G. (1970) 'The Sex-War Truce.' *The Sunday Times* Report on Sex and Marriage, Part 2. *Sunday Times* 22 March, 1970.

GREENFIELD, S. M. (1961) 'Industrialization and the Family in Sociological Theory.' Reprinted in Farber, B. (Ed.) (1966) *Kinship and Family Organization.* New York: John Wiley and Sons. pp. 408–17.

GUTERMAN, S. S. (1969) 'In Defense of Wirth's "Urbanism as a Way of Life."' *Amer. J. Sociol.*, Vol. 74, pp. 492–99.

HAMMER, M. (1963–64) 'Influence of Small Social Networks as Factors on Mental Hospital Admission.' *Hum. Organization*, Vol. 22, pp. 243–51.

HANDEL, G. (Ed.) (1967) *The Psychosocial Interior of the Family.* Chicago: Aldine Publishing Co.

HANDEL, G., and RAINWATER, L. (1964) 'Persistence and Change in Working-Class Life Style.' In Shostak, A. B., and Gomberg, W. (Eds.) (1964) *Blue Collar World.* New Jersey; Prentice Hall, pp. 36–41.

HARRELL-BOND, B. E. (1969) 'Conjugal Role Behaviour.' *Hum. Relat.*, Vol. 22, pp. 77–91.

HARRIES-JONES, P. (1969) ' "Home-Boy" Ties and Political Organization in a Copperbelt Township.' In Mitchell, C. (Ed.) (1969) *Social Networks in Urban Situations.* Manchester: Manchester Univ. Press, pp. 297–347.

HARRIS, C. C. (1969) *The Family.* London. Allen and Unwin.

HENRY, J. (1958) 'The Personal Community and its Invariant Properties.' *Amer. Anthrop.*, Vol. 60, pp. 827–31.

HUBERT, J. (1965) 'Kinship and Geographical Mobility in a Sample from a London Middle-Class Area.' *Inter. J. comparative Sociol.*, Vol. 6, pp. 61–80.

HUBERT, J., FORGE, A., and FIRTH, R. (1968) Methods of Study of Middle-Class Kinship in London. Occasional paper of the Department of Anthropology, London School of Economics and Political Science.

JAY, E. J. (1964) 'The Concepts of "Field" and "Network" in Anthropological Research.' *Man*, No. 177, pp. 137–9.

J. Roy. Society Health (1958) Abstract of *Family and Social Network*, Vol. 78.

KADUSHIN, C. (1966) 'The Friends and Supporters of Psychotherapy: On Social Circles in Urban Life.' *Amer. sociol. Rev.*, Vol. 31, pp. 786–802.

KADUSHIN, C. (1968) 'Power, Influence and Social Circles: A New Methodology for Studying Opinion Makers.' *Amer. sociol. Rev.*, Vol. 33, pp. 685–99.

KAPFERER, B. (1969) 'Norms and the Manipulation of Relationships in a Work Context.' In Mitchell, C. (Ed.) (1969) *Social Networks in Urban Situations.* Manchester: Manchester Univ. Press, pp. 181–244.

KATZ, E., LEVIN, M. L., and HAMILTON, H. (1963) 'Traditions of Research on the Diffusion of Innovation.' *Amer. sociol. Rev.*, Vol. 28, pp. 237–52.

KATZ, F. E. (1958) 'Occupational Contact Networks.' *Soc. Forces*, Vol. 37, pp. 52–5.

KATZ, F. E. (1966) 'Social Participation and Social Structure.' *Soc. Forces*, Vol. 45, pp. 199–210.

KERCKHOFF, A. C. (1965) 'Nuclear and Extended Family Relationships: A Normative and Behavioral Analysis.' Chapter 5 of Shanas, E. and Streib, G. F. (Eds.) (1965) *Social Structure and the Family: Generational Relations.* New Jersey: Prentice-Hall, pp. 93–112.

KERR, M. (1958) *The People of Ship Street.* London: Routledge and Kegan Paul.

KLEIN, J. (1965) *Samples from English Cultures.* London: Routledge and Kegan Paul.

KOMAROVSKY, M. (1961) 'Class Differences in Family Decision-Making.' In Foote, N. *Household Decision-Making.* New York: New York University Press, pp. 255–65.

KOMAROVSKY, M. (Ed.) (1962) *Blue Collar Marriage.* New York: Random House.

LA FONTAINE, J. S. (1969) Review of *Family and Social Network* in *Man*, Vol. 4, pp. 490–1.

LAMPHERE, L. (1970) 'Ceremonial Co-operation and Networks: A Reanalysis of The Navajo Outfit.' *Man*, Vol. 5, pp. 39–59.

LANCASTER, L. (1961) 'Some Conceptual Problems in the Study of Family and Kin in the British Isles.' *Brit. J. Sociol.* Vol. 12, pp. 317–33.

LAZARSFELD, P. F., and MERTON, R. K. (1954) 'Friendship as Social Process: A Substantive and Methodological Analysis.' In Berger, M., Abel, T., and Page, C. H. (1954) *Freedom and Control in Modern Society.* New York: van Nostrand, pp. 18–66.

LESSER, A. (1961) 'Social Fields and the Evolution of Society.' *Southwestern J. Anthrop.*, Vol. 17, pp. 40–8.

LEVY, M. J., and FALLERS, L. A. (1959) 'The Family: Some Comparative Considerations.' *Amer. Anthrop.*, Vol. 61, pp. 647–51.

LITTLE, K., and PRICE, A. (1967) 'Some Trends in Modern Marriage among West Africans.' *Africa*, Vol. 37, pp. 407-24.

LITWAK, E. (1959) 'The Use of Extended Family Groups in the Achievement of Social Goals: Some Policy Implications.' *Soc. Problems*, Vol. 7, pp. 177-87.

LITWAK, E. (1960a) 'Occupational Mobility and Extended Family Cohesion.' *Amer. sociol. Rev.*, Vol. 25, pp. 9-21.

LITWAK, E. (1960b) 'Geographic Mobility and Extended Family Cohesion.' *Amer. sociol Rev.*, Vol. 25, pp. 385-94.

LITWAK, E. (1965) 'Extended Kin Relations in an Industrial, Democratic Society.' In Shanas, E. and Streib, G. F. (Eds.) (1965) *Social Structure and the Family: Generational Relations*. New Jersey: Prentice Hall, pp. 292-323.

LITWAK, E., and SZELENYI, I. (1969) 'Primary Group Structures and Their Functions: Kin, Neighbours, and Friends.' *Amer. sociol. Rev.*, Vol. 34, pp. 465-81.

LOUDON, J. B. (1961) 'Kinship and Crisis in South Wales.' *Brit. J. Sociol.*, Vol. 12, pp. 333-50.

MAIR, L. (1969) 'Correspondence on Groups and Non-Groups'. *Man*, Vol. 4, p. 134.

MARRIS, P. (1958) *Widows and Their Families*. London: Routledge and Kegan Paul.

MATTHEWS, E. M. (1965) *Neighbour and Kin*. Nashville: Vanderbilt Univ. Press.

MAYER, A. C. (1962) 'System and Network: An Approach to the Study of Political Process in Dewas.' In Madan, T. N., and Sarana, G. (Eds.) (1962) *Indian Anthropology*. London: Asia Publishing House, pp. 266-78.

MAYER, A. C. (1963) 'Municipal Elections: A Central Indian Case Study.' In Philips, C. H. (Ed.), (1963) *Politics and Society in India*. London: George Allen and Unwin, pp. 115-32.

MAYER, A. C. (1966) 'The Significance of Quasi-Groups in the Study of Complex Societies.' In Banton, M. (Ed.) (1966) *The Social Anthropology of Complex Societies*. A.S.A. Monograph No. 4. London: Tavistock Publications, pp. 97-122.

MAYER, P. (1961) *Townsmen or Tribesmen*. Cape Town: Oxford University Press.

MAYER, P. (1962) 'Migrancy and the Study of Africans in Town.' *Amer. Anthrop.*, Vol. 64, pp. 576-92.

MAYER, P. (1964) 'Labour Migrancy and the Social Network.' In Holleman, J. F. (Ed.) (1964) *Problems of Transition*, Proceedings of The Social Science Research Conference 1962, Pietermaritzburg: Natal Univ. Press, pp. 21-51.

MERTON, R. K. (1957) *Social Theory and Social Structure*. Glencoe, Illinois: The Free Press.

MILLER, D. R., and SWANSON, G. E. (1958) 'Changes in Society and Child Training in the United States.' In Miller, D. R., and Swanson, G. E. (1958) *The Changing American Parent*. New York: Wiley, pp. 30–60. Reprinted in Shostak, A. B., and Gombert, W. (Eds.) (1964) *Blue Collar World*. New Jersey: Prentice-Hall, pp. 359–77.

MILLER, S. M., and RIESSMAN, F. (1961) 'The Working-Class Subculture: A New View.' *Soc. Problems*, Vol. 9, pp. 86–97. Reprinted in Shostak, A. B., and Gomberg, W. (Eds.) (1964) *Blue Collar World*. New Jersey: Prentice-Hall, pp. 24–36.

MILLER, W. B. (1958) 'Lower Class Culture as a Generating Milieu of Gang Delinquency.' *J. soc. Issues*, Vol. 14, No. 3, pp. 5–19.

MILLER, W. B. (1969) 'The Elimination of The American Lower Class as National Policy: A Critique of the Ideology of The Poverty Movement of the 1960s.' Chapter 10 of Moynihan, D. P. (Ed.) (1969) *On Understanding Poverty: Perspectives from the Social Sciences*. New York: Basic Books, Inc.

MITCHELL, C. (1966) 'Theoretical Orientations in African Urban Studies: Methodological Approaches.' In Banton, M. (Ed.) (1966) *The Social Anthropology of Complex Societies*, A.S.A. Monograph No. 4. London: Tavistock Publications, pp. 37–68.

MITCHELL, C. (Ed.) (1969) *Social Networks in Urban Situations*. Manchester: Manchester Univ. Press.

MITCHELL, C. (1969) 'The Concept and Use of Social Networks.' In Mitchell, C. (Ed.) (1969) *Social Networks in Urban Situations*. Manchester: Manchester Univ. Press, pp. 1–50.

MOGEY, J. M. (1956) *Family and Neighbourhood*. London: Oxford University Press.

MOGEY, J. (1962) 'Introduction' to 'Changes in the Family.' *Int. soc. sci. J.*, Part one of Vol. 14, pp. 411–24.

MOGEY, J. (1966) Review of Rosser, C., and Harris, C. C. (1965) *The Family and Social Change* in *Amer. Sociol. Rev.*, Vol. 31, pp. 300–1.

MOGEY, J., and MORRIS, R. (1960) 'Causes of Change in Family Role Patterns.' *Bulletin on Family Development*, Research Centre on Family Development, Community Studies Inc., Kansas City 6, Missouri, Vol. 1, pp. 1–10.

MOGEY, J., and MORRIS, R. (1965) *The Sociology of Housing*. London: Routledge and Kegan Paul.

MOWRER, E. R. (1969) 'The Differentiation of Husband and Wife Roles.' *J. Marriage and the Family*, Vol. 31, pp. 534–40.

MURDOCK, G. P. (1949) *Social Structure*. New York: Macmillan.

MCDOUGALL, K. (1968) Review of *Family and Social Network. Case Conference*, Vol. 15, p. 156.

NELSON, J. (1966) 'Clique Contacts and Family Orientations.' *Amer. sociol. Rev.*, Vol. 31, pp. 663–72.

OESER, L. (1969) *Hohola: The Significance of Social Networks in Urban Adaptation of Women in Papua.* New Guinea Research Bulletin No. 29. Canberra: Australian National University.

PACKMAN, J. (1969) Review of *Family and Social Network* in *Soc. Work*, Vol. 26, pp. 28–9.

PAINE, R. (1969) 'In Search of Friendship: An Exploratory Analysis in "Middle-Class" Culture.' *Man*, Vol. 4, pp. 505–24.

PARKER, S. R. (1967) 'Industry and the Family.' in Parker, S.R., Brown, R. K., Child, J., and Smith, M. A. (1967) *The Sociology of Industry.* London: Allen and Unwin, pp. 42–53.

PARSONS, T. (1942) 'Age and Sex in the Social Structure of the United States.' *Amer. sociol. Rev.*, Vol. 7, No. 5. Reprinted in Parsons, T. (1949) *Essays in Sociological Theory Pure and Applied.* Glencoe: The Free Press, pp. 218–32.

PARSONS, T. (1943) 'The Kinship System in the Contemporary United States.' *Amer. Anthrop.*, Vol. 45, pp. 22–38.

PARSONS, T. (1949) 'The Social Structure of the Family'. In Anshen, R. N. (Ed.) *The Family: Its Function and Destiny.* New York: Harper and Row, pp. 173–201.

PAUW, B. A. (1963) *The Second Generation.* Cape Town: Oxford Univ. Press.

PERRATON, J. K. (1969) Review of *Family and Social Network, J. Town Planning Institute*, Vol. 55, p. 39.

PHILPOTT, S. B. (1968) 'Remittance Obligations, Social Networks and Choice Among Montserratian Migrants in Britain.' *Man*, Vol. 3, pp. 465–76.

PITTS, J. R. (1964) 'The Structural-Functional Approach.' Chapter 3 of Christensen, H. T. (Ed.) (1964) *Handbook of Marriage and the Family.* Chicago: Rand-McNally, pp. 51–124.

PLATT, J. (1969) 'Some Problems in Measuring the Jointness of Conjugal Role-Relationships.' *Sociology*, Vol. 3, pp. 287–97.

PLOTNICOV, L. (1962) 'Fixed Membership Groups: The Locus of Culture Process.' *Amer. Anthrop.*, Vol. 64, pp. 97–103.

POGGIE, J. J., and MILLER, F. C. (1969) 'Contact, Change and Industrialization in a Network of Mexican Villages.' *Hum. Organization*, Vol. 28, pp. 190–98.

POSPISIL, L. (1964) *The Kapauku Papuans of West New Guinea.* New York: Holt, Rinehart and Winston.

RADCLIFFE-BROWN, A. R. (1940) 'On Social Structure.' *J. roy. anthrop. Inst.*, Vol. 70, pp. 1–12.

RAINWATER, L. (1964) 'Marital Sexuality in Four Cultures of Poverty.' *J. Marriage and the Family*, Vol. 26, pp. 457–66. Reprinted in Heiss, J. (1968) *Family Roles and Interaction*. Chicago: Rand McNally.

RAINWATER, L., COLEMAN, R. P., and HANDEL, G. (1959) *Workingman's Wife*. New York: Oceana Publications.

RAINWATER, L., and HANDEL, G. (1964) 'Changing Family Roles in the Working Class.' In Shostak, A. B., and Gomberg, W. (Eds.) (1964) *Blue Collar World*. New Jersey: Prentice-Hall, pp. 70–6.

RAPOPORT, RHONA (1963) 'Normal Crisis,' Family Structure and Mental Health.' *Fam. Process*, Vol. 2, pp. 68–80.

RAPOPORT, R. N. (1958) Review of *Family and Social Network*, in *Man*, Vol. 58, Article No. 243, pp. 182–3.

RAPOPORT, R. N. (1964) 'The Male's Occupation in Relation to his Decision to Marry.' *Acta Sociologica*, Vol. 8, pp. 68–82.

RAPOPORT, R., and RAPOPORT, R. N. (1965) 'Work and Family in Contemporary Society.' *Amer. sociol. Rev.*, Vol. 30, pp. 381–94.

RAPOPORT, R. N., and RAPOPORT, R. (1969) 'The Dual Career Family.' *Hum. Relat.*, Vol. 22, pp. 3–30.

READER, D. H. (1964) 'Models in Social Change with Special Reference to Southern Africa.' *African Studies*, Vol. 23, pp. 11–33.

REISS, P. J. (1962) 'The Extended Kinship System: Correlates of Attitudes on Frequency of Interaction.' *Marriage Fam. Liv.*, Vol. 24, pp. 333–9.

REYNOLDS, V. (1966) 'Open Groups in Hominid Evolution.' *Man*, Vol. I, pp. 441–52.

REYNOLDS, V. (1968) 'Kinship and the Family in Monkeys, Apes and Man.' *Man*, Vol. 3, pp. 209–23.

RICHMOND, A. H. (1958) Review of *Family and Social Network*, *Brit. J. Psychol.*, Vol. 49, pp. 171–2.

ROBINS, L. N., and TOMANEC, M. (1962) 'Closeness to Blood Relatives Outside the Immediate Family.' *Marriage Fam. Liv.*, Vol. 24, pp. 340–46.

ROBOTTOM, M. (1969) Review of *Family and Social Network* in *Medical Soc. Work*, Vol. 21, pp. 255–6.

RODD, C. S. (1968) 'Recent Books on Sociology.' Review of *Family and Social Network* in *The Expository Times*, Dec. 1968, pp. 69–70.

ROGERS, E. M., and SEBALD, H. (1962) 'A Distinction between Familism, Family Integration, and Kinship Orientation.' *Marriage Fam. Liv.*, Vol. 24, pp. 25–30.

ROSOW, I. (1965) 'Intergenerational Relationships: Problem and Proposals.' In Shanas, E., and Streib, G. F. (1965) *Social Structure and the Family: Generational Relations*. New Jersey: Prentice-Hall, pp. 341–78.

ROSSER, C. and HARRIS, C. (1965) *The Family and Social Change*. London: Routledge and Kegan Paul.

SCHELSKY, H. (1966) 'The German Family and Opposed Developmental Tendencies in Industrial Society.' In Farber, B. (Ed.) (1966) *Kinship and Family Organization*. New York: Wiley, pp. 83–7.

SCHWARZWELLER, H. K. (1964) 'Parental Family Ties and Social Integration of Rural to Urban Migrants.' *J. Marriage and the Family*, Vol. 26, pp. 410–16.

SHANAS, E., and STREIB, G. F. (Eds.) (1965) *Social Structure and the Family: Generational Relations*. New Jersey: Prentice-Hall.

SLATER, M., and WOODSIDE, M. (1951) *Patterns of Marriage*. London: Cassell.

SMITH, M. G. (1965) *Stratification in Grenada*. Berkeley: Univ. California Press.

SOUTHALL, A. W. (1961) 'Kinship, Friendship, and the Network of Relations in Kisenyi, Kampala.' In Southall, A. W. (Ed.) (1961) *Social Change in Modern Africa*. London: Oxford Univ. Press, pp. 217–29.

SPECK, R. V. (1964) 'Family Therapy in the Home.' *J. Marriage and the Family*, Vol. 26, pp. 72–6.

SPECK, R. V. (1967) 'Psychotherapy of the Social Network of a Schizophrenic Family.' *Fam. Process*, Vol. 6, pp. 208–14.

SPECK, R. V., and RUEVENI, U. (1969) 'Network Therapy—A Developing Concept.' *Fam. Process*, Vol. 8, pp. 182–90.

SRINIVAS, M. N., and BÉTEILLE, A. (1964) 'Networks in Indian Social Structure.' *Man*, Vol. 64, No. 212, pp. 165–8.

STUCKERT, R. P. (1963) 'Occupational Mobility and Family Relationships.' *Soc. Forces*, Vol. 41, pp. 301–7.

SUSSMAN, M. B. (1953) 'The Help Pattern in the Middle Class Family.' *Amer. sociol. Rev.*, Vol. 18, pp. 22–8.

SUSSMAN, M. B. (1959) 'The Isolated Nuclear Family: Fact or Fiction?' *Soc. Problems*, Vol. 6, pp. 333–40.

SUSSMAN, M. B. (1965) 'Relationships of Adult Children with their Parents in the United States.' In Shanas, E., and Streib, G. F. (Eds.) (1965) *Social Structure and Family: Generational Relations*. New Jersey: Prentice-Hall, pp. 62–92.

SUSSMAN, M. B. and BURCHINAL, L. (1962a) 'Kin Family Network: Unheralded Structure in Current Conceptualizations of Family Functioning.' *Marriage Fam. Liv.*, Vol. 24, pp. 231–40.

SUSSMAN, M. B., and BURCHINAL, L. (1962b) 'Parental Aid to Married Children: Implications for Family Functioning.' *Marriage Fam. Liv.*, Vol. 24, pp. 320–32.

SUTCLIFFE, J. P., and CRABBE, B. D. (1963) 'Incidence and Degrees of Friendship in Urban and Rural Areas.' *Soc. Forces*, Vol. 42, pp. 60–7.

TALLMAN, I. (1969) 'Working-Class Wives in Suburbia: Fulfillment or Crisis?' *J. Marriage and the Family*, Vol. 31, pp. 65–72.

TALMON-GARBER, Y. (1962) 'Social Change and Family Structure.' *Inter. soc. sci. J.*, Vol. 14, pp. 468–87. Reprinted in Farber, B. (Ed.) (1966) *Kinship and Family Organization*. New York: John Wiley and Sons, pp. 88–101.

THOMSON, L. (1961) Review of *Family and Social Network* in *Canadian Welfare*, Vol. 37, p. 254.

TIGER, L. (1969) *Men in Groups*. London: Nelson.

TIGER, L., and FOX, R. (1966) 'The Zoological Perspective in Social Science.' *Man*, Vol. 1, pp. 75–81.

TOOMEY, D. (1969) 'Home-Centred Working Class Parents' Attitudes towards their Sons' Education and Careers.' *Sociology*, Vol. 3, pp. 299–320.

TOWNSEND, P. (1957) *The Family Life of Old People*. London: Routledge and Kegan Paul.

TURNER, C. (1967) 'Conjugal Roles and Social Networks: A Re-Examination of an Hypothesis.' *Hum. Relat.*, Vol. 20, pp. 121–30.

TURNER, C. (1970) Personal Communication.

UDRY, J. R., and HALL, M. (1965) 'Marital Role Segregation and Social Networks in Middle-Class Middle-Aged Couples.' *J. Marriage and the Family*, Vol. 27, pp. 392–5.

VAN VÉLSEN, J. (1967) 'The Extended-Case Method and Situational Analysis.' In Epstein, A. L. (Ed.) (1967) *The Craft of Social Anthropology*. London: Tavistock Publications, pp. 129–49.

WATSON, W. (1957) 'Social Mobility and Social Class in Industrial Communities,' in Gluckman, M., and Devons, E. (Eds.) (1964) *Closed Systems and Open Minds*. Edinburgh: Oliver & Boyd, pp. 129–57.

WHEELDON, P. D. (1969) 'The Operation of Voluntary Associations and Personal Networks in the Political Processes of an Inter-Ethnic Community.' In Mitchell, C. (Ed.) (1969) *Social Networks in Urban Situations*. Manchester: Univ. of Manchester Press, pp. 128–180.

WHYTE, M. B. H. (1958) Review of *Family and Social Network* in *Mental Health*, Vol. 17, pp. 110–11.

WILENSKY, H. L. (1961) 'Orderly Careers and Social Participation: The Impact of Work History on Social Integration in the Middle Mass.' *Amer. sociol. Rev.*, Vol. 26, pp. 521–39.

WILLMOTT, P. (1963) *The Evolution of a Community*. London: Routledge and Kegan Paul.

WILLMOTT, P., and YOUNG, M. (1960) *Family and Class in a London Suburb*. London: Routledge and Kegan Paul.

WOLF, E. R. (1966) 'Kinship, Friendship, and Patron-Client Relations in Complex Societies.' In Banton, M. (Ed.) *The Social Anthropology of Complex Societies*. A.S.A. Monograph No. 4. London: Tavistock Publications, pp. 1–22.

WOLFE, D. M. (1963) 'Power and Authority in the Family.' In Winch, R. F., McGinnis, R., and Barringer, H. R. (Eds.) (1963) *Selected Studies in Marriage and the Family*. London: Holt Rinehart.

YOUNG, M., and GEERTZ, H. (1961) 'Old Age in London and San Francisco: Some Families Compared.' *Brit. J. Sociol.*, Vol. 12, pp. 124–41.

YOUNG, M., and WILLMOTT, P. (1957) *Family and Kinship in East London*. London: Routledge and Kegan Paul.

ZELDITCH, M. (1964) 'Family, Marriage, and Kinship.' In Faris, R. E. L. (1964) *Handbook of Modern Sociology*. Chicago: Rand McNally, pp. 689–733.

AUTHOR INDEX

Adams, B. N., 251n., 260ff., 298, 314f., 320, 328
Albrecht, R., 115
Aldous, J., 251n., 259, 287, 310
Allcorn, D. H., xxviii
Anderson, N., 251n.
Arensberg, C. M., xx, xxi, 115, 302
Armstrong, W. E., 59n.
Arnold, K., 318
Attneave, C. L., 272
Axelrod, M., 298n., 314, 328

Babchuk, N., 261ff., 287, 293, 298, 314
Back, K. W., 260
Bailey, F. G., xiii
Bales, R. F., 81n.
Barnes, J. A., xvin., xxvi, 59n., 116, 117n., 250, 273, 283, 293f., 313ff., 319ff., 324ff., 329
Barth, F., 306n., 323
Bartlett, F. C., 165n.
Barton, R. F., 117
Bates, A. P., 261–2, 263, 287, 293, 298, 314
Bell, C., 258, 259, 261, 267, 306, 312
Bell, N., 251n.
Bell, W., 298n., 314, 328
Berger, B. M., 265–6, 276, 279
Béteille, A., 317, 320, 326
Blood, R. O., xxiin., 251n., 268, 276–8
Blum, A. F., 251n., 257
Boat, M. D., 298n., 314, 328
Boissevain, J., xxvn., 289, 317–18,

320, 322f., 326, 329
Boll, E. S., 115
Bossard, J. H. S., 115
Boswell, D. M., 318, 329
Bowlby, J., xvi
Brown, G. W., 273
Brown, J. S., 115
Burchinal, L., 251n., 259
Burgess, E. W., 209

Caplan, G., 308
Caplow, T., 315, 321
Caradog Jones, D., 169
Carter, M. P., 64, 65, 111
Caser, R., 251n.
Centers, R., 162, 166, 169
Chambers, R., 251n.
Chance, M. R. A., 324
Codere, H., 115
Cohen, Y. A., 251n., 256f., 262, 298, 314, 319
Cohn, B. S., 314, 326
Coleman, J., 328
Coleman, R. P., 255, 327
Colson, E., xiv, 9n.
Crabbe, B. D., 298n., 314
Crown, S., 170n.
Crozier, D., 259, 260
Cumming, E., 259
Cunnison, I. G., xiii
Curle, A., 115, 129n.

Davis, A., 64, 111

344

346

SUBJECT INDEX

Action-sets, 317, 321, 329
Administration of Estates Act, 116
Alienation, 249
Ambience, 315, 321
Amigo system, 257
Anonymity, of research couples, 11, 18
Anthropological techniques, 8, 24, 48, 49
Anthropology, xv, xxii, 36, 48, 115
Anxieties, 32, 47
Authoritarianism, male, 64, 150, 256

Behavioural mode, 193
Behavioural segregation, 264
Behaviour,
  analysis of, 31-3
  conjugal standards of, 204-6
  convergence of, between classes, 259
  definition of term, 4, 5
  evaluation of, by research couples, 49, 168
  group, 31
  variability of in industrial societies, 118
  wish-fulfilment and, 199
Bethnal Green study of kinship, 116, 125, 130, 135, 157n., 251ff., 255, 257-8f., 265ff., 269
Bilateral kinship system, *see under* kinship
Boredom, of housewives, 84, 89
'Branch Street' area, study of, 255
'Bureaucrats', 264, 311

'Burgesses', 263, 267, 306, 312
Butler family,
  and concepts of class, 184-8, 188-91
  and conjugal role-segregation, 90-1

California Public College, study of students' parents, 274
Case conferences, 26-7
Case study technique and method, 8, 48, 50
Caste and the Economic Frontier, xiii
Chicago University, 43, 44
Child/parent segregation, xxvii, 299
Children,
  aspirations for, 160, 180-1, 185
  care of,
    advice on, 43
    discussed by groups, 27, 29
    in division of labour, 22, 54, 79
    and extra money, 74
    in intermediate families, 87-8
    by other mothers, 72
    by relatives, 69, 71
    in transitional families, 91
    variations in, 81
  education of, 72-3, 76
  effect of on conjugal relationship, 55-6, 77, 93
  met during interview, 17, 24
  middle-class, 260, 300
  personalities of, 50
  punishment of, 72, 81
  relationship of with parents, *see under* relationship

349

Personality theory, 50
Personal needs and preferences, 4, 109ff., 139, 191
Phase change, 249, 286, 308
and friendship, 298
Physical accessibility of kin, 122–3, 126–8
Physical mobility, *see under* mobility
Politics in an African Urban Community, xiii
Port Moresby women, study of, 271
'Positional' technique, 325
Poverty, 68
Power,
concepts of, 60, 169
experience of, 163, 164, 165
and models of class, 175, 178
occupation as source of, 172
Prestige,
concepts of, 145, 146, 160, 169
experience of distinctions in, 163
and models of class, 175–8
in a small community, 162
Primitive communities, 9n., 99, 100, 116ff., 194
Professional families, 56, 73f., 84f., 108, 113, 122, 125
Professional upper-middle-class subculture, 263, 264
Project director, role of, 39
Projection,
in acquisition of norms, 200
in assimilation of norms, 166
in creation of class reference groups, 167
of faults on to kin, 150
of ideal norms, 211
Property, distribution of, 103, 118, 124
Psycho-analytical technique, 48
Psycho-analytic concepts, 7
Psycho-analytic theory, 31, 50

Psychoanalysis, 8, 36, 50
Psychological case studies, 8
Psychological mechanisms,
and attitudes to kin, 148–55
of norm acquisition, 214–5
Publication of research, *see under* research

'Quasi-groups', 322
Questionnaires, 30, 170, 203

Reciprocal role expectations, 3
Redfern, Mr., 42
Reference group, 165–8, 280, 309
and charge, 280, 291
concept of, 165–8
constructed, 167
use of by families in situations of change, 280, 291
as variable affecting network density and conjugal segregation, 309
Re-interpretation, in assimilating norms, 166
Relationship,
'autonomic', 112
brother-sister, 25
conjugal, *throughout*. See also conjugal role relationship
between conjugal segregation and network density, 251, 290ff., 301
external social, 74–9, 85–7, 94, 95, 100
extra-familial, 138, 149
family-friend, 25. *See also under* friends
family-parent, 107, 124, 129, 260
father-child, 80
field-worker-family, 2, 40–8, 170
field-worker-supervisor, 39
formal social, 23, 97, 102